ABORTION AND THE LAW IN AMERICA

With the Supreme Court likely to reverse *Roe v. Wade*, the landmark abortion decision, American debate appears fixated on clashing rights. The first comprehensive legal history of a vital period, *Abortion and the Law in America* illuminates an entirely different and unexpected shift in the terms of debate. Rather than simply championing rights, Mary Ziegler shows, those on opposing sides also battled about the policy costs and benefits of abortion and laws restricting it. This mostly unknown turn deepened polarization in ways many have missed. Never abandoning their constitutional demands, pro-choice and pro-life advocates increasingly disagreed about the basic facts. Drawing on unexplored records and interviews with key participants, Ziegler complicates the view that the Supreme Court is responsible for the escalation of the conflict. A gripping account of social-movement divides and crucial legal strategies, this book delivers a definitive recent history of an issue that transforms American law and politics to this day.

MARY ZIEGLER is one of the leading authorities on the legal history of abortion in America. She is the author of *Beyond Abortion* (2018) and the award-winning *After Roe* (2015).

Abortion and the Law in America

ROE V. WADE TO THE PRESENT

MARY ZIEGLER

Florida State University

CAMBRIDGE
UNIVERSITY PRESS

CAMBRIDGE
UNIVERSITY PRESS

University Printing House, Cambridge CB2 8BS, United Kingdom

One Liberty Plaza, 20th Floor, New York, NY 10006, USA

477 Williamstown Road, Port Melbourne, VIC 3207, Australia

314–321, 3rd Floor, Plot 3, Splendor Forum, Jasola District Centre, New Delhi – 110025, India

79 Anson Road, #06–04/06, Singapore 079906

Cambridge University Press is part of the University of Cambridge.

It furthers the University's mission by disseminating knowledge in the pursuit of education, learning, and research at the highest international levels of excellence.

www.cambridge.org
Information on this title: www.cambridge.org/9781108498289
DOI: 10.1017/9781108653138

First published 2020

A catalogue record for this publication is available from the British Library.

Library of Congress Cataloging-in-Publication Data
NAMES: Ziegler, Mary, 1982- author.
TITLE: Abortion in America : a legal history from Roe to the present / Mary Ziegler.
DESCRIPTION: New York : Cambridge University Press, 2020. | Includes index.
IDENTIFIERS: LCCN 2019038337 (print) | LCCN 2019038338 (ebook) |
ISBN 9781108498289 (hardback) | ISBN 9781108735599 (paperback) |
ISBN 9781108653138 (epub)
SUBJECTS: LCSH: Abortion–Law and legislation–United States–History. |
Roe, Jane, 1947-2017–Trials, litigation, etc. | Wade, Henry–Trials, litigation, etc. |
Trials (Abortion)–Washington (D.C.)
CLASSIFICATION: LCC KF3771 .Z54 2020 (print) | LCC KF3771 (ebook) | DDC 342.7308/4–dc23
LC record available at https://lccn.loc.gov/2019038337
LC ebook record available at https://lccn.loc.gov/2019038338

ISBN 978-1-108-49828-9 Hardback
ISBN 978-1-108-73559-9 Paperback

For my mom, who taught me how to fight

Contents

Acknowledgments

I could not have completed this book without the support of many people. I relied on the good offices of many librarians and archivists across the country. Thanks to the staff at libraries at Harvard University, Barnard College, the Catholic University of America, the College of the Holy Cross, Columbia University, Cornell University, Duke University, the State University of New York at Buffalo, the Wisconsin Historical Society, the Minnesota Historical Society, the University of Notre Dame, the Concordia Seminary of the Lutheran Church Missouri Synod, the George H. W. Bush Presidential Library and Museum, the William J. Clinton Presidential Library and Museum, the Gerald R. Ford Presidential Library and Museum, the Library of Congress, the University of California, Berkeley, Princeton University, the University of Arkansas, the Southern Baptist Historical Society, the University of Missouri–St. Louis, and the Wilcox Collection at the University of Kansas the Southern Baptist Historical Library and Archives, Mount Holyoke College, Smith College, Georgia State University, the University of Wyoming, the University of Michigan, and the Ronald Reagan Presidential Library.

Many wonderful people have shared comments on the ideas advanced in the book. Nancy Cott, Michael Dorf, Robert Gordon, Ken Mack, and Martha Minow offered invaluable help with the framing of the project. Others closely read parts of the manuscript, often more than once, including Deborah Dinner, Darren Dochuk, Marie-Amélie George, Leslie Griffin, Karissa Haugeberg, Amanda Hollis-Brusky, Kenneth Kersch, Felicia Kornbluh, Maya Manian, Serena Mayeri, Douglas NeJaime, Logan Sawyer, Chris Schmidt, Daniel Sharfstein, Ann Southworth, Ronit Stahl, Karen Tani, Katherine Turk, Anders Walker, John Witt, and Rebecca Zietlow.

I was particularly lucky to have the chance to share parts of the manuscript with those who have illuminated the history and politics of the abortion debate. David Garrow and Linda Gordon offered crucial comments in the early stages of the project. Jennifer Donnally, Gillian Frank, Rebecca Kluchin, and Daniel

K. Williams graciously read chapters and massively improved the manuscript. Leah Litman helped me sharpen the book's legal analysis. Andrew Lewis, Kristin Luker, and Joshua Wilson provided crucial context from the study of abortion in related disciplines.

I thank my editors at Cambridge University Press, John Berger and Jackie Grant, for improving the book immeasurably. Others at Cambridge University Press, including Danielle Menz, Joshua Penney, and Paris West have been unfailingly helpful. Katrina Miller, Margaret Clark, Kathryn Crandall, Elizabeth Farrell-Clifford, Kat Klepfer, Amy Lipford, Quinterrion Waits, and the library staff at Florida State have done more than I could have asked to keep the project on track. I also thank my tremendous research assistants, Matt Michaloski, Sahara Williams, and Bradyn Shock, for helping me sort through a ridiculous amount of archival material. The book is far richer because James Bopp Jr., Pam Lowry, and Karen Mulhauser shared papers from their personal collections.

This book would not be the same without those who agreed to share their stories of the abortion conflict. All of them entrusted their memories and experiences to a stranger. Many spent hours correcting my mistakes and recounting their own deeply personal experiences. Their voices reminded me of the complexity of the people who have defined American struggles over abortion.

Finally, I thank my husband, Dan, my daughter, Layla, and my mom and dad, all of whom made this book possible. My dad, Robert Ziegler, inspired me to become a professor and convinced me to go to law school. I will never write as well as he does or have his capacity for empathy, but this book is part of an ongoing effort to match either one. My mom has edited my writing since high school, weathering bad drafts and frustrations. During the completion of this book, she persevered in helping me while battling early-stage lung cancer. She is my hero.

As I completed this manuscript, Layla learned to run, love books, and tell me what to do. I hope that one day, she is as proud of me as I am of her. As for Dan, he forced me to confront the hardest questions about my project. When I had the least confidence in myself or my book, he cheered me on. He reminded me that history can help us understand ourselves better while reminding us of how different (and sometimes how much better) we could be. For all this, and for much more, this book is for him.

Timeline

1973 The Supreme Court decides *Roe v. Wade*. National Right to Life Committee (NRLC) is formally incorporated as an independent organization.

1975 Dr. Kenneth Edelin is convicted of manslaughter for performing an abortion.

1976 Congress passes the Hyde Amendment, a federal ban on Medicaid funding for abortion. The Supreme Court decides *Planned Parenthood of Central Missouri v. Danforth*, striking down several parts of a Missouri law but upholding an informed consent restriction.

1977 The Supreme Court rejects challenges to state and local laws prohibiting the use of public dollars or facilities in *Maher v. Roe* and its companion cases.

1980 Ronald Reagan, the first strongly antiabortion presidential candidate, wins the race for the White House. In *Harris v. McRae*, the Supreme Court upholds the Hyde Amendment.

1982 The Army of God, a pro-violence antiabortion group, kidnaps Dr. Hector Zevallos and his wife.

1983 In *City of Akron v. Akron Center for Reproductive Health (Akron I)*, the Court strikes down an Akron model law. Sandra Day O'Connor's dissent increases pro-life interest in the Supreme Court nomination process. The Hatch-Eagleton Amendment, which would have declared that the Constitution recognizes no abortion rights, fails in Senate vote.

1985 *The Silent Scream*, an antiabortion film, draws new attention to claims about fetal pain.

1986 By a 5–4 margin, in *Thornburgh v. American College of Obstetricians and Gynecologists*, the Supreme Court strikes down a Pennsylvania abortion regulation.

1987 Robert Bork's Supreme Court nomination fails in Congress.

1988 Anthony Kennedy, presumed to hold the vote that would overturn *Roe*, joins the Supreme Court.

1989   In *Webster v. Reproductive Health Services*, the Court upholds a Missouri law and criticizes *Roe*'s trimester framework. Operation Rescue announces itself on the national stage by holding major blockades in cities across the country.

1990   In *Hodgson v. Minnesota* and *Ohio v. Akron Center for Reproductive Health*, the Court upholds a pair of parental involvement laws.

1992   In *Planned Parenthood of Southeastern Pennsylvania v. Casey*, the Court retains the essential holding of *Roe* but rejects the trimester framework in favor of a new undue burden standard. Bill Clinton becomes the first strong supporter of abortion rights elected president since 1973.

1993   Debate begins about whether Clinton's proposed health care reform will include abortion coverage. In *Bray v. Alexandria Women's Health Clinic*, the Supreme Court holds that antiabortion blockades do not violate a federal civil rights statute or constitute a conspiracy against women. Dr. David Gunn becomes the first abortion provider murdered by antiabortion extremists.

1994   In *Madsen v. Women's Health Center, Inc.*, the Supreme Court rejects parts of a free-speech challenge to a court injunction limiting protest outside an abortion clinic. In the first round of litigation in *National Organization of Women v. Scheidler*, the Court allows a lawsuit against clinic blockaders to proceed. Republicans take control of the House of Representatives for the first time since 1952.

1995   Congress first debates a law outlawing dilation and extraction, a procedure that pro-lifers call partial-birth abortion.

1997   SisterSong Women of Color Reproductive Justice Collective forms. In *Schenck v. Pro-Choice Network of Western New York*, the Supreme Court strikes down parts of an injunction creating buffer zones around abortion clinics while upholding others.

1998   An effort to impeach President Bill Clinton for perjury and obstruction of justice falls short.

2000   In *Stenberg v. Carhart*, the Court strikes down a Nebraska law said to ban partial-birth abortion. In *Bush v. Gore*, the Court stops a manual recount in the deciding state of Florida, ensuring the victory of Republican George W. Bush. Norma McCorvey, the "Roe" in *Roe v. Wade*, and Sandra Cano, the "Doe" in *Doe v. Bolton*, file amicus curiae briefs in a wrongful death action filed by attorney Harold Cassidy based on the death of an unborn child.

2003   Congress passes the Partial-Birth Abortion Ban Act. NARAL renames itself NARAL Pro-choice America.

2006   In *Scheidler v. National Organization for Women*, the Court holds 8–0 that the Hobbs Act does not cover violence unrelated to robbery or extortion. The Court also holds that RICO did not apply to blockaders' actions.

2007   In *Gonzales v. Carhart*, the Court upholds the Partial-Birth Abortion Ban Act.

2008 The first of many state personhood amendments banning abortion appears on the ballot in Colorado. The proposal ultimately fails.

2009 Right-wing protestors identifying with the Tea Party hold rallies across the country. The circulation of the *Manhattan Declaration: A Call of Christian Conscience* increases the visibility of antiabortion arguments based on religious conscience.

2010 Nebraska becomes the first state to pass a fetal pain law, banning abortion at twenty weeks.

2011 States enact a record number of abortion restrictions.

2015 The Center for Medical Progress, an antiabortion group, releases videos that claim to show Planned Parenthood selling fetal tissue for a profit.

2016 In *Whole Woman's Health v. Hellerstedt*, the Court strikes down a Texas law, reasoning that *Casey*'s undue burden standard requires a balancing of the benefits and burdens of abortion regulations. Donald J. Trump becomes the forty-fifth president of the United States.

2019 After Trump nominates two justices to the Supreme Court, an unprecedented number of states pass "heartbeat bans," which outlaw abortion after the sixth week of pregnancy, often without exceptions for rape and incest. Georgia's law recognizes fetal personhood. Alabama passes a law criminalizing all abortions unless a woman's life is at risk. New York, Vermont, Illinois, and other pro-choice states liberalize their laws on abortion, anticipating the reversal of *Roe v. Wade*.

Abbreviations

ACCL	American Citizens Concerned for Life, Inc., Records, Gerald R. Ford Presidential Library and Museum, University of Michigan
ACLU	American Civil Liberties Union Records, Department of Rare Books and Special Collections, Seeley G. Mudd Manuscript Library, Princeton University
AUL	Americans United for Life Records, Executive File, Concordia Seminary, Lutheran Church-Missouri Synod
AUS	Americans United for the Separation of Church and State Subject Files, Rare Book and Manuscript Library, Columbia University
BAP	Bella Abzug Papers, Rare Book and Manuscript Library, Columbia University
BCP	William J. Clinton Presidential Library and Museum, Little Rock, Arkansas
BFP	Betty Friedan Papers, Schlesinger Library, Radcliffe Institute, Harvard University
BSP	Barbara Seaman Papers, Schlesinger Library, Radcliffe Institute, Harvard University
CKP	Claire Keyes Papers, David M. Rubenstein Rare Book and Manuscript Library, Duke University
DDP	Dexter Duggan Papers, on file with the author
DRP	David Reardon Papers, on file with the author
EGP	Edward J. Golden Collection, College of the Holy Cross Archives and Special Collections
FWHC	Feminist Women Health Center Records, David M. Rubenstein Rare Book and Manuscript Library, Duke University
GHW	George Huntston Williams Papers, Andover-Harvard Theological Library, Harvard Divinity School

GHWB   George Herbert Walker Bush Presidential Library and Museum, College Station, Texas
JBP   James Bopp Jr. Papers, Terre Haute, Indiana
JCK   John Cavanaugh-O'Keefe Papers, Wisconsin Historical Society, Library Archives Division
JHP   Jane Hodgson Papers, Minnesota Historical Society
JRS   Dr. Joseph R. Stanton Human Life Issues Library and Resource Center, Our Lady of New York Convent, Bronx, New York
KKP   Kathryn Kolbert *Planned Parenthood v. Casey* Records, Barnard Archives and Special Collections, Barnard College
LGP   Ella T. Grasso Papers, Mount Holyoke College Archives and Special Collections
MFJ   Mildred F. Jefferson Papers, Schlesinger Library, Radcliffe Institute, Harvard University
MHP   Merle Hoffman Papers, David M. Rubenstein Rare Book and Manuscript Library, Duke University
MRX   Meredith Tax Papers, David M. Rubenstein Rare Book and Manuscript Library, Duke University
NARAL   National Abortion Rights Action League Records, Schlesinger Library, Radcliffe Institute, Harvard University
NARALMA   NARAL Pro-choice Massachusetts Records, Schlesinger Library, Radcliffe Institute, Harvard University
NARALMO   NARAL of Missouri Records, University of Missouri–St. Louis
NCAP   National Coalition of Abortion Providers Records, David M. Rubenstein Rare Book and Manuscript Library, Duke University
NOW   National Organization for Women Records, Schlesinger Library, Radcliffe Institute, Harvard University
PAW   People for the American Way Collection of Conservative Political Ephemera, Bancroft Library, University of California, Berkeley
PCN   Pro-choice Network of Western New York Records, State University of New York at Buffalo University Archives
PJP   Margaret Peg Johnston Papers, David M. Rubenstein Rare Book and Manuscript Library, Duke University
PLL   Peg Johnston Lowry Papers, on file with the author
PLN   Pro-life Newsletters Collection, Schlesinger Library, Radcliffe Institute, Harvard University
PMP   Pauli Murray Papers, Schlesinger Library, Radcliffe Institute, Harvard University
PPFA   Planned Parenthood Federation of America Records, Sophia Smith Collection, Smith College
PPSE   Planned Parenthood Southeast Records, Special Collections and Archives, George State University Library

PWP	Paul Weyrich Papers, University of Wyoming, American Heritage Archive Center
R2N2	Reproductive Rights National Network Records, David M. Rubenstein Rare Book and Manuscript Library, Duke University
RCD	Robin Chandler Duke Papers, David M. Rubenstein Rare Book and Manuscript Library, Duke University
REC	Richard E. Coleson Papers, Terre Haute, Indiana
RHS	Reproductive Health Services Papers, University of Missouri–St. Louis
RJN	Richard John Neuhaus Papers, American Catholic History Research Center and University Archives, the Catholic University of America
RLM	Right to Life of Michigan Records, Bentley Historical Library, University of Michigan
RRP	Ronald Reagan Presidential Library, Simi Valley, California
SBL	Southern Baptists for Life Records, Southern Baptist Historical Library and Archives
TCP	Takey Crist Papers, David M. Rubenstein Rare Book and Manuscript Library, Duke University
WCX	Wilcox Collection of Contemporary Political Movements, Kenneth Spencer Research Library, University of Kansas
WSH	Wilma Scott Heide Papers, Schlesinger Library, Radcliffe Institute, Harvard University

Introduction

Something about the 2019 March for Life was different. Each year, the antiabortion event brought hundreds of thousands of protesters to Washington, DC. In 2019, busloads of high school and college students again joined grassroots activists, clergy members, and ordinary voters on the National Mall. The signs, speeches, and wintry temperatures were nothing new, but those present expressed a new sense of optimism. For the first time in decades, the pro-life movement stood on the cusp of seeing the Supreme Court overturn *Roe v. Wade*, the 1973 decision holding that the Constitution protects a woman's right to choose abortion. But although victory seemed within reach, speakers at the event did not focus on the Constitution. Instead, insisting that "pro-life is pro-science," marchers shared arguments about the costs of abortion for women and the communities in which they lived. Jeanne Mancini, the leader of March for Life, wrote that "the abortion debate isn't settled, but the underlying science certainly is." Months later, nine states banned abortion early in pregnancy. Lawmakers backing such laws in Alabama and Georgia claimed that "modern medical science" justified their sweeping legislation. Abortion-rights supporters hardly agreed that pro-lifers had a monopoly on scientific expertise. Sarah Horvath, a pro-choice fellow of the American College of Obstetricians and Gynecologists, labeled pro-life arguments about the costs of abortion for women "a misuse and manipulation of the facts."[1]

The arguments made during the 2019 March for Life offer just one example of how much the terms of the American abortion debate have changed. We often think that the claims made in the American abortion struggle reflect the clash of absolutes famously described by legal scholar Laurence Tribe. Supporters of legal abortion fight for a right to choose, and abortion foes defend a right to life for the unborn child. These arguments seem to reflect what legal theorist Ronald Dworkin called "rights as trumps" – constitutional protections that prevail over other policy considerations or even the preference of voters. The abortion debate seems to be at

1

an impasse because those on each side believe that they defend a right that outweighs any competing concern.[2]

To be sure, such rights-based arguments remain an important part of the discussion. But as this book shows, in recent decades, the core terms of the legal debate about abortion in America have changed in ways we have rarely appreciated. Between 1973 and 2019, the conflict has centered not so much on laws criminalizing abortion outright as on the quest for incremental restrictions designed to undermine *Roe v. Wade*. And with this change in emphasis, the struggle has increasingly turned not only on rights-based trumps but also on claims about the policy costs and benefits of abortion for women, families, and the larger society.[3]

This change was never straightforward or absolute. Indeed, before abortion was legal, those backing abortion rights often pointed to what they saw as the desirable consequences of legalization, such as fewer deaths from botched illegal abortions. *Roe v. Wade* itself spoke not only about a constitutional privacy right that encompassed a woman's abortion decision but also about the harms that could follow if women had to carry undesired pregnancies to term. Nor, in later decades, did those in opposing social movements uniformly stress claims about the costs and benefits of abortion. At times, groups instead played up contentions about constitutional rights or religious faith. Some activists, like clinic blockaders, consistently rejected claims about the costs and benefits of abortion.

And it is not always easy to draw a clear line between rights-based arguments and claims about the policy consequences of legal abortion. Legal philosophers such as T. M. Scanlon have argued that civil or human rights cannot be justified without reference to their consequences. Those who focus on costs and benefits have incorporated what appear to be trumps, like equality or liberty, into policy-driven calculations.[4]

Nevertheless, the distinction between rights- and policy- based arguments is conceptually valuable, especially when we seek to understand the modern American abortion conflict. When stressing constitutional rights, those on either side suggested that a particular right was priceless, grounded in the constitutional order, and deserving of protection irrespective of its costs and benefits. Abortion opponents often argued that the right to life protected a fetus or unborn child no matter how a woman came to be pregnant – and regardless of what would happen after a child was born. The idea of a right to choose suggested not only that women should have the liberty to decide for themselves when to have a child but also that women should get the final say about why a decision is the right one.

By contrast, when making arguments about the costs and benefits of abortion, activists on either side primarily discussed not what the Constitution allowed but whether legal abortion was socially, culturally, personally, and medically desirable or justified. Consequence-based arguments put greater emphasis on the reasons that individuals might choose or oppose abortion rather than on individual liberty from the state.

The Court did not drive many of the changes studied here. Between 1977 and the present, Supreme Court decisions did shape strategy in important and sometimes unpredictable ways. But many sincerely believed that the costs and benefits of abortion mattered as much as the rights at stake. Even when those on opposing sides made calculated strategic decisions, their arguments are worthy of study. By taking seriously claims about the consequences of abortion, we can gain perspective on how legal and political conversations have changed in the decades since 1973. We can better understand why clashing activists believe that women need (or should not have) a right to end a pregnancy. We can gain a fuller perspective on the state-by-state battles that would begin if the Court overturned *Roe* and the cases following it. And we can recognize that the abortion debate reflects a larger set of often unnoticed social and cultural transformations.

How and when did the terms of the abortion debate change, and what has it meant for the larger abortion conflict? As soon as the Court handed down its decision in *Roe*, American pro-lifers championed a constitutional amendment that would ban abortion outright. But when the campaign stalled in the mid-1970s, lawyers working with organizations like the National Right to Life Committee (NRLC) and Americans United for Life (AUL) proposed a temporary solution – incremental restrictions that made abortions harder to get. Lawyers like James Bopp Jr., a conservative Indiana attorney, and Victor Rosenblum, a liberal Jewish law profes-sor from Illinois, worked to draft model laws, statutes intended to serve as a blueprint for other states and cities. These regulations required a different defense than the absolute prohibitions pro-lifers had long defended. After all, many of these statutes, such as abortion-funding bans, did not clearly advance a right to life since they did not outlaw a single abortion. Instead, these laws created various obstacles that women had to overcome. Rather than invoking fetal rights, members of AUL and NRLC began justifying these laws by highlighting their supposed benefits for women, parents, taxpayers, and the country.

At first, in the late 1970s, despite the objections of some nonwhite and socialist feminists, the leaders of groups like the National Abortion Rights Action League (NARAL) and the Planned Parenthood Federation of America primarily argued that the new abortion restrictions violated the Constitution. Activists like Karen Mulhauser, a former biology teacher, believed that her movement needed to focus on making sure that women who wanted legal abortions could get them. By contrast, abortion-rights attorneys working with the recently founded American Civil Liberties Union Reproductive Freedom Project urged the Court to look below the surface of abortion regulations to identify their real-world costs – restrictions trau-matized women or forced them to put their health at risk.

When Ronald Reagan won the 1980 election and Republicans swept into power, antiabortion activists hoped that they could finally change the text of the Consti-tution. But the competing proposals available to Congress exposed fractures in the pro-life movement. While pragmatists like Bopp and Rosenblum warned their allies not to back a solution that the Supreme Court would strike down, absolutists like Judie Brown, a former NRLC executive director who denounced birth control, refused to endorse anything short of a national abortion ban. By 1983, these internal divisions forced pro-lifers to give up on a constitutional amendment.

The leaders of AUL and NRLC believed that they had already identified an alternative mission. Lawyers like Bopp and Rosenblum argued that abortion foes could pass and defend restrictions that chipped away at abortion rights, and by aligning with the GOP, could change the membership of the Supreme Court. AUL and NRLC leaders promised that in this way, abortion foes could ensure that the Court overturned *Roe v. Wade*. In defending incremental restrictions, pro-lifers often emphasized the costs of abortion – and the benefits of certain laws restricting it.

In the mid-1980s, groups like NARAL and Planned Parenthood responded by stressing claims about the benefits of legal abortion, especially for low-income, nonwhite, or disabled women. Later in the decade, abortion-rights groups rethought their strategies when new Supreme Court nominations – and adverse decisions – created an existential threat to *Roe*. The leaders of organizations like NARAL believed that voters would decide the fate of abortion rights. Convinced that many did not value the opportunities women might gain by virtue of legal abortion, groups like Planned Parenthood and NARAL instead emphasized rights-based claims thought to appeal to ambivalent voters. This strategy alienated some nonwhite feminists, like veteran activist Loretta Ross, who wanted the pro-choice movement to adopt an agenda that involved support for contraception, sex education, child-bearing, and childrearing – and who believed that their colleagues had not explained why women needed legal abortion in the first place. At the same time, newly mobilized clinic blockaders, many of them working with Operation Rescue, an antiabortion group committed to illegal protests, rejected a strategy based on claims about the costs of abortion. Stressing religious arguments, grassroots activists like Randall Terry, a veteran clinic protester and devout evangelical Protestant, believed that by breaking the law, they could clog the legal system and pressure godless judges and politicians to take action.

Despite a challenge from blockaders, attorneys in groups like NRLC and AUL still sometimes played up the costs of abortion, this time focusing on harms said to affect the family. When the opposition promoted laws mandating the involvement of parents or husbands, abortion-rights attorneys like Janet Benshoof, a Minnesota native deeply interested in human rights, countered that abortion restrictions took away emerging opportunities for women to pursue an education or a career.

In the early 1990s, after the Supreme Court agreed to hear its next abortion case, *Planned Parenthood of Southeastern Pennsylvania v. Casey*, ACLU attorneys made claims about the benefits of legal abortion for women a crucial part of the case for preserving legal abortion. These arguments spotlighted the relationship between abortion and equality between the sexes. This plan seemed to pay off in 1992 when the Court retained what it called the essential holding of *Roe*. The Court's decision in *Casey* increased the importance of arguments about the costs and benefits of both abortion and laws restricting it.

In the mid-1990s, with a sympathetic president, Bill Clinton, in office, groups like NARAL and Planned Parenthood finally took control of the agenda by emphasizing claims about the health benefits of abortion and lobbying for its inclusion in national health care reform. By spotlighting claims about the health benefits of legal abortion, abortion-rights supporters like Planned Parenthood leader Pam Maraldo, a former nurse with extensive health care experience, could better explain how even incremental restrictions affected women's interest in equal treatment. In the mid-1990s, some nonwhite feminists called for a different approach to the relationship between abortion and health care, demanding reproductive justice, rather than simply a right to choose, for all women. Rather than focusing on freedom from government interference, a reproductive-justice approach demanded for women the power and resources to have children, not have children, or to parent the children they already had.

A focus on health, however, ultimately helped groups like AUL and NRLC regain influence in the pro-life movement. In the mid-1990s, grassroots pro-lifers believed that neither courts nor legislatures would ever deliver meaningful change. Some instead worked in crisis pregnancy centers to prevent individual women from ending their pregnancies. Conservative Christian lawyers in organizations like Liberty Counsel and the American Center for Law and Justice invested more in cases involving the freedom of speech and religion than in any effort to convince the Court to overturn *Roe*. AUL and NRLC attorneys, however, used claims about the costs of abortion to outline a new plan of attack on *Roe*. Antiabortion attorneys insisted that far from preserving women's health, abortion caused psychological and physical damage.

As both sides disputed the costs and benefits of abortion, areas of disagreement multiplied. By the later 1990s, as part of a long struggle over a specific procedure, dilation and extraction, that pro-lifers called "partial-birth abortion," the two movements not only contested the effects of the procedure but also asked who had the authority to measure them. These disputes shaped *Gonzales v. Carhart*, the Court's 2007 decision to uphold a federal ban on partial-birth abortion. *Gonzales* reflected how the abortion divide continued to grow. Those on opposing sides could not agree even on the basic facts about abortion. *Gonzales* had given legislators more latitude to regulate when a scientific question appeared uncertain, and after the Court's 2007 decision, pro-lifers tried to generate scientific uncertainty. After Republicans' impressive results in the 2010 midterm election, state legislatures passed a stunning number of regulations. Both sides responded by increasingly questioning the integrity and motivations of those with whom they disagreed. By 2018, when Republican Donald Trump replaced the Court's longtime swing justice, Anthony Kennedy, it seemed inevitable that one of these restrictions would be the one the justices used to overturn *Roe*. For decades, the abortion debate had turned partly on the kind of policy-driven, cost-benefit analysis that *Roe* had supposedly put off limits. But focusing on claims about the costs and benefits of abortion had not tempered the conflict. The abortion divide was deeper than ever.

This history offers new perspective on the reasons for the polarization of the abortion conflict. Critics have long argued that by making abortion a constitutional issue, the Court made any common-sense compromise on abortion impossible. By extension, some scholars suggest that if the Court removed itself from the abortion wars, sensible, middle-ground solutions might come into view, and polarizing rights-based arguments would fade into the background. These arguments have high stakes at a time when the Court seems likely to reverse *Roe*. Indeed, some conservatives cite the dysfunction supposedly produced by *Roe* as a reason to overturn the 1973 decision.[5]

However, between 1973 and the present, those on both sides have often turned to questions about the policy costs and benefits of abortion that theoretically lent themselves to compromise. Battles about the costs and benefits of abortion were intense partly because these conflicts served as a proxy for ongoing disagreements about the right to life and the right to choose. And to be sure, any consensus on abortion seemed all but impossible, regardless of which arguments took center stage. But a focus on the real-world effects of abortion only intensified the conflict.

As early as the late 1970s, supporters and opponents of abortion rights disagreed about what counted as a cost or benefit. Activists' disagreements reached beyond abortion and even gender roles. Opposing movements sometimes held strikingly different views about everything from the welfare state to the nature of scientific authority. And in measuring the costs and benefits of abortion, those on opposing sides did not consult the same experts and evidence. Over time, pro-life and pro-choice activists gave radically different descriptions of the basic facts about the procedure. The conflict about abortion goes far deeper than the idea of two irreconcilable rights that became prominent in constitutional litigation.

The recent history of the abortion debate also shows that the struggle is far more unpredictable than many have concluded. By emphasizing the constitutional rights at stake in the conflict, we often see the abortion wars as a stalemate, marked by a familiar set of arguments and strategies. Commentators contend that both abortion opponents and abortion-rights supporters have a stable set of convictions about motherhood and gender. But the battle has reflected beliefs about much more. We can expect today's debate to move in equally unforeseen directions.

Ultimately, by grasping how much the abortion debate has changed, we can better understand the history of late twentieth-century America. The abortion debate touched on many of the questions that most deeply divided the country. Struggles over abortion funding mirrored shifting ideas about the role of the government and responsibility for the poor. Campaigns to require women to get the consent of their husbands or parents exposed disagreements about how the family should function or what defined maturity. The abortion struggle exposed disagreements about the need for health care reform and the dividing line between science and politics. The abortion fight both mirrored and changed larger arguments about the difference between fact and opinion, "fake news" and truth. The battle over abortion access reflected broader debates about the country's present and future.

Chapter 1 provides the background for the story told in the book. Arguments about the costs and benefits of abortion have a long history. In the nineteenth century, when mobilizing to ban abortion, physicians insisted that outlawing the procedure would strengthen the traditional family and improve the nation's genetic stock by forcing Anglo-Saxon women to have more children. While abortion was illegal for decades, physicians still performed the procedure, justifying it as necessary to save women's lives. But in the 1940s and 1950s, obstetric care improved, making it harder to invoke this justification. Doctors organized to change abortion laws, initially arguing that reform would improve women's mental and physical health. In the 1960s, however, when a major movement for reform got underway, grassroots activists emphasized several claims about the benefits of legalization. Reformers argued that legal abortion would prevent the birth of severely disabled children and preserve scarce environmental resources. In the 1960s, as groups formed to defend criminal abortion laws, pro-lifers stressed arguments about a constitutional right to life as a way to expand their movement beyond its existing Catholic membership. As more feminists joined the abortion-rights movement in the late 1960s and early 1970s, grassroots activists demanded the outright repeal of all abortion restrictions, and reformers highlighted rights-based claims of their own. *Roe v. Wade* made rights-based claims even more important to the discussion.

In studying the success of abortion-funding bans, Chapter 2 evaluates the rise of a strategy based on claims about the costs of abortion. In the mid-1970s, the antiabortion movement included self-described liberals and conservatives, absolutists and pragmatists, professionals and homemakers. All of these activists focused on a constitutional amendment that would have criminalized abortion, and groups like NRLC and AUL looked for laws that could reduce the abortion rate in the short term. In justifying laws like abortion-funding restrictions, pro-lifers highlighted what they described as the societal costs of paying for abortion. While groups like NARAL and Planned Parenthood reluctantly discussed the impact of abortion-funding bans on poor women, lawyers in the ACLU invited courts to look at the real-world effects of funding prohibitions on taxpayers and low-income women. Resulting in decisions like *Maher v. Roe* (1977) and *Harris v. McRae* (1980), this dialogue reflected broader changes in public attitudes about poverty and the social safety net.

Exploring the period between 1980 and 1986, Chapter 3 studies how groups like NRLC and AUL refocused on overturning *Roe*. After 1978, when Akron, Ohio, passed a law designed to serve as a model nationwide, NRLC and AUL lawyers contended that because abortion sometimes harmed women, incremental restrictions should be unconstitutional only if they unduly burdened women rather than helped them. The Supreme Court rejected abortion foes' arguments in *City of Akron v. Akron Center for Reproductive Health* (1983), but writing in dissent, Justice Sandra Day O'Connor adopted a version of the undue burden standard that pro-lifers championed. O'Connor's dissent solidified mainstream pro-life groups' commitment to a new strategy. Rather than prioritizing a constitutional amendment, abortion foes would gradually chip away at *Roe*, narrowing its protections and setting the stage for its overruling. By aligning with the GOP, pro-lifers would help to determine who sat on the Supreme Court. And in defending access restrictions, abortion foes would highlight their benefits – and what they saw as the costs of abortion.

Centered on the period between 1987 and 1992, Chapter 4 evaluates how the relationship between abortion and sex equality became central to both the fate of *Roe* and debate about the American family. As the Court's new majority appeared ready to overturn *Roe*, pro-lifers worried that GOP leaders feared a backlash on election day. To reassure Republican leaders that pro-life positions had a political payoff, abortion foes emphasized family involvement laws that seemed to enjoy popular support, including laws requiring women to notify their husbands or get their consent. In defending these laws, antiabortion activists insisted that abortion had serious costs for the family, disenfranchising men and dooming teenagers to a bleak and uncertain future.

Many on both sides resisted a focus on the costs and benefits of abortion. A new and predominantly evangelical clinic-blockade movement rejected consequence-based arguments in favor of religious ones. Believing that the Court would reverse *Roe*, larger abortion-rights groups like NARAL played up rights-based claims. In court, however, abortion-rights attorneys had to find a way to defend legal abortion and challenge family involvement laws. In the context of parental involvement, abortion-rights attorneys contended that if forced to carry their pregnancies to term, young women would lose out on emerging financial, political, or educational opportunities. Soon, these arguments played a key role in the discussion of *Roe's* fate. Lawyers highlighted the benefits of keeping abortion legal in arguments linking access to the procedure to equality for women. Shaping the Court's decision in *Planned Parenthood of Southeastern Pennsylvania v. Casey* (1992), this debate offered a window into how Americans understood the family.

Chronicling the mid-1990s, Chapter 5 traces a debate about the relationship between abortion and health care that evolved in the aftermath of *Casey*. After the election of Bill Clinton, the abortion-rights movement went on the offensive. In explaining how incremental restrictions affected women's equal citizenship, abortion-rights groups emphasized that regulations denied women crucial health benefits. In the political arena, abortion-rights advocates worked to guarantee coverage of the procedure in national health care reform, to repeal bans on Medicaid funding for abortion, to introduce legislation protecting access to clinic entrances, and to ensure access to medical abortion pills. In court, abortion-rights attorneys also described clinic blockaders – and all abortion foes – as sexists opposed to health care for women. This strategy played a part in the litigation of cases such as *Bray v. Alexandria Women's Health Clinic* (1993), *National Organization for Women v. Scheidler* (1994), and *Madsen v. Women's Health Center, Inc.* (1994). In the same period, building on the work of earlier activists, women of color offered a new framing of the relationship between health care and abortion, calling not for reproductive rights but for reproductive justice, shorthand for an agenda that addressed everything from abortion and contraception to adequate housing and quality childcare. Notwithstanding political and legal advances, however, abortion-rights supporters faced daunting new obstacles, including a shortage of abortion doctors and an effort to target abortion providers with medical malpractice lawsuits.

Although the abortion-rights movement had struggles of its own, *Casey* and the health-based offensive led by the abortion-rights movement caused some abortion opponents to lose faith in a strategy centered on the costs of abortion. To regain prominence in the movement, attorneys in groups like AUL and NRLC developed a new way of undermining *Roe*: If the Court saved abortion rights because women relied on it, the pro-life movement would demonstrate that the procedure damaged their health.

Examining the years from 1995 to 2007, Chapter 6 studies how those on opposing sides fought about ways to measure the costs and benefits of abortion when experts disagreed. In this period, larger pro-life groups sponsored a ban on the procedure they labeled partial-birth abortion. At the start, NRLC mostly urged voters to rely on their own moral compass to see that the procedure should be illegal. Drawing on support from medical experts, abortion-rights supporters responded that dilation and extraction sometimes best protected women's health. Abortion foes responded that both the mainstream media and organizations like the American College of Obstetricians and Gynecologists were biased. Since the debate turned partly on the costs of abortion (and abortion restrictions) for women, those on opposing sides increasingly fought about what should happen when experts disagreed. Should voters, experts, or individual patients have the final say when a scientific matter was in dispute? How should courts even define scientific uncertainty? Discussion of these questions reflected a larger national conversation about the line between politics and science.

Bringing the story up to the present, Chapter 7 considers how the breach between the two sides widened during battles about religious liberty and health care reform. In 2008, Barack Obama, the first pro-choice president since the 1990s, made the introduction of a federal health care bill his priority. In 2010, a backlash to Obama's Affordable Care Act (ACA), helped to give Republican lawmakers control of most state legislatures. These members of the so-called Tea Party passed an unprecedented number of abortion restrictions. Pro-lifers also joined an attack on the contraceptive mandate of the ACA, arguing that the government had denied believers their religious liberty. Working with new organizations, AUL and NRLC also sought to prove that Planned Parenthood, then the nation's largest abortion provider, harmed women by putting profit ahead of their health. While pro-lifers accused Planned Parenthood of illegal and immoral actions, abortion-rights supporters described pro-lifers as misogynist opponents of health care and birth control. Rather than just disagreeing about how to measure the costs and benefits of abortion, those in both movements more often questioned the integrity of their opponents.

The Court's most recent intervention also widened the gulf between the sides. In 2016, in *Whole Woman's Health v. Hellerstedt*, the Court made claims about the costs and benefits of abortion yet more central to constitutional doctrine. Striking down two parts of a Texas law, the Court held that courts had to consider both the benefits and burdens imposed by a statute. *Whole Woman's Health* intensified efforts to gather evidence about the effects of specific laws and of abortion itself.

When Anthony Kennedy announced his retirement, many expected the Court to overturn *Roe*. But rather than seeking to appeal to undecided justices or ambivalent voters, antiabortion absolutists pushed strict abortion bans. For their part, abortion-rights supporters tried to introduce state constitutional amendments and statutes that would protect abortion once *Roe* was gone. But these laws also struck some as extreme insofar as they extended protections for virtually all later abortions. Decades of debate about the policy costs and benefits of abortion had certainly not helped to repair the breach between those contesting the abortion wars; if anything, the two sides were even further apart.

The Conclusion considers what the book teaches us about the intractability of the abortion conflict and the predictability of future discussion of reproductive health. At the time of this writing, because of the possible overturning of *Roe*, those on both sides expect the arguments that define the abortion wars to evolve. But the terms of the debate have already changed in consequential ways. Lawyers, activists, politicians, and commentators all bemoan the never-ending polarization of the American abortion conflict. But the battle will never be any less intense if we do not understand how and why the two sides in the abortion wars have grown so distant. The idea of clashing rights has long defined the history of the American abortion debate. A parallel but profoundly important fight about the effects of legal abortion demands our attention now.

1

Roe v. Wade and the Rise of Rights Arguments

Arguments about the costs and benefits of legal abortion have always played a role in fights about the procedure. In the nineteenth century, when states began outlawing most abortions, the doctors leading the criminalization campaign claimed that legal abortion had done tremendous damage to the nation's future. Later, in the 1960s, after obstetric and gynecological care improved, doctors began demanding the reform of existing laws. At first, reformers defined a broader category of procedures needed to protect women's health. When the press reported on birth defects caused by the rubella virus and the medication thalidomide, abortion-rights advocates went beyond health justifications. Instead, reform-oriented physicians and their allies spotlighted claims about the benefits of legal abortion to prevent the birth of children with severe birth defects. Pro-lifers maintained that legal abortion would psychologically scar women and put disabled individuals at risk. For the most part, however, abortion foes primarily focused on what they described as a constitutional right for the unborn child. This argument allowed what had been a predominantly Catholic, faith-oriented movement to make a legal and moral argument to a broader audience.

By the late 1960s, both sides more often emphasized claims about constitutional rights that trumped any competing consideration. Abortion-rights supporters had grown frustrated with the reform laws already in place. Even in reform states, many physicians refused requests because of the specter of legal liability. Feminists increasingly endorsed the repeal of all abortion restrictions. The courts at times agreed that the Constitution protected a woman's decision about abortion. For many reasons, abortion-rights supporters more often asserted that women had a right to end their pregnancies regardless of their reasons for doing so or of the consequences of their decisions. As feminists reshaped the abortion-rights movement, pro-lifers elaborated on their own constitutional claims.

Roe ramped up interest in rights-based arguments. The Court held that the right to privacy was broad enough to encompass a woman's decision to end her pregnancy. Pro-lifers responded by championing a constitutional amendment that would criminalize virtually all abortions. Abortion-rights supporters, many of whom believed that the Court had resolved the issue in their favor, initially saw no reason to depart from rights arguments. Constitutional arguments seemed to define dialogue about legal abortion in America.

As the 1970s continued, however, abortion foes began pursuing a strategy that would reconfigure the abortion debate. While campaigning for a constitutional amendment, groups like Americans United for Life (AUL) and the National Right to Life Committee (NRLC) sought to reduce the abortion rate. But rights-based arguments seemed incongruous when used to defend incremental restrictions that did not prevent any procedures from taking place. Instead, antiabortion pragmatists stressed claims about the costs of abortion and the benefits of laws restricting it. At the time, these arguments seemed to be little more than the rationale for a temporary solution. But this antiabortion strategy eventually had much further-reaching effects. Over the course of several decades, the debate no longer turned so often on what the Constitution had to say. Instead, opposing movements clashed about whether abortion was good or bad for America.

THE REASONS FOR BANNING ABORTION

Arguments about the policy costs of abortion captured national attention during the fight to criminalize the procedure. Until the 1860s and 1870s, most states allowed abortion before quickening, the point at which fetal movement could be detected. To the extent that criminal laws addressed the subject, states tended to target abortifacient drugs as part of broader anti-poison regulations. Indeed, in the United States, abortion in the 1840s was arguably more commonplace than ever before, especially in larger cities. The practice had become commercialized. Newspapers hawked abortifacient drugs, and doctors and midwives performed surgical procedures. In that period, many of those seeking abortions were white, married, and middle class or wealthy. Given the commercial success of the business and the financial means of those terminating their pregnancies, it seemed likely that abortion would only spread. In response, between 1821 and 1841, states modestly revised their abortion laws, mostly tightening poison regulations and applying them to some abortifacient drugs. For the most part, states retained the quickening doctrine and did not authorize prosecutions earlier in abortion, and successful prosecutions were rare. Dr. Horatio Storer, a leading abortion opponent, noted that Massachusetts had not convicted a single defendant in an abortion case between 1849 and 1858.[1]

Under Storer's leadership, the American Medical Association (AMA) campaigned against abortion by highlighting claims about the harms done by the procedure. As historian James Mohr has argued, the "regular" physicians who belonged to the

AMA looked for an advantage over the midwives and homeopaths with whom they competed. Storer and his allies popularized the idea that only trained doctors understood the nature of fetal life. The AMA did not invoke constitutional rights, but "regular" physicians insisted that abortion was indistinguishable from infanticide.[2]

The AMA also justified an abortion ban by pointing to the societal costs of the procedure. Storer argued that unless states strengthened criminal abortion laws, the country would be swamped by inferior genetic stock. Immigration from Southern and Eastern Europe had spiked, and the birth rate among Anglo-Saxon women had fallen by half over the course of the nineteenth century – a result historians have attributed partly to women's use of abortion and birth control. Storer argued that criminalizing more abortions would reverse this trend. Who would populate the future United States? "This is a question our women must answer," Storer wrote.[3]

Between 1860 and 1880, many states answered Storer's call for strict new laws by outlawing abortions unless a woman's life was at risk. In 1873, Anthony Comstock, a United States Postal Inspector and anti–birth control crusader, lobbied for a federal obscenity law that covered abortion and contraception, and states and cities followed suit. The new law did not stamp out abortion. Notwithstanding periodic crackdowns, prosecutors most often brought charges after a woman died during a procedure. Abortion remained available in private homes and doctors' offices.[4]

The situation became much more unstable in the 1930s and 1940s when some obstetricians formally demanded legal changes. Again, those questioning the current legal regime did not invoke rights in defending or challenging existing abortion bans. Reform-minded physicians like obstetrician Frederick Taussig instead began popularizing arguments about the medical and social benefits of certain abortions. Pointing to the struggles many faced during the Depression, Taussig reasoned that women should be able to end a pregnancy to avoid dire poverty. Many physicians still supported abortion bans, but others began more openly performing the procedure, and some even specialized in the practice. As abortion moved into hospitals, physicians created committees to supervise and limit when the procedure could be performed. But the visibility of abortion spurred an increase in both raids on abortion clinics and criminal prosecutions. These changes encouraged some physicians to seek legal reform. When physicians could easily claim to have saved their patient's life by performing an abortion, few doctors saw any reason to demand a legal change. With better obstetric care, this justification lost credibility, and some physicians began lobbying for broader exceptions to abortion bans.[5]

ABORTION REFORM

Notwithstanding abortion opponents' emphasis on a right to life, some pro-legalization lawmakers and social-movement organizations initially avoided constitutional arguments. Instead, physicians, attorneys, and other reformers often played up the costs of denying certain women abortions. Often, reformers in organizations like the American Medical Association (AMA) – which endorsed legal abortion in 1967 – began by redefining the health benefits of legal abortion. Over time, reformers began justifying abortion without any mention of women's health, sometimes making claims about the burdens of bearing and raising children with severe disabilities. While seeking to refute these claims, abortion foes also began defending arguments about a constitutional right to life. By focusing on the Constitution, pro-lifers hoped to establish a secular movement that could draw supporters outside the Catholic Church.

In the late 1950s, some physicians began to question the adequacy of existing abortion laws. These doctors identified a mismatch between what current medical practice required and what the law allowed. By 1959, the American Law Institute (ALI), an expert organization that recommended legal reforms, proposed a model statute that permitted abortion in cases of rape or incest, severe fetal abnormality, or threats to a woman's health. Starting in the early 1960s, states began considering the ALI bill. Physicians often led the campaign for the proposal, championing its health benefits for women. Some of these arguments turned on the risks of illegal, black-market abortions. Ironically, concerns about abortion-related fatalities peaked when fewer women died as a result of illegal abortion. Because of widespread access to antibiotics, overall maternal mortality had declined significantly since World War II, and black-market abortions were no exception. Nevertheless, reformers viewed any loss of life due to abortion as tragic and unnecessary. Estimating that 10,000 women died annually as a result of illegal abortions in 1965, Larry Lader, a prominent reform proponent called abortion laws "an open scandal and a hidden crisis." Reformers like Lader emphasized that poor, often nonwhite women disproportionately relied on black-market abortions. Moreover, activists like the founders of the Association for the Study of Abortion, a group organized in 1964 to promote reform, insisted that even if abortion was illegal, it was not wrong. "[T]he morality of humane abortion," Lader wrote, "demands that we bring our laws up to date with medical progress."[6]

Lader, like his allies, also asserted that criminal abortion laws had produced a mental health crisis. In the 1960s, doctors had expanded the use of psychiatric indications for the procedure. Indeed, one study of abortions performed at major hospitals found that physicians justified nearly half on psychiatric grounds. As psychiatric justifications became more common, supporters of legal abortion argued that reform would benefit women by preventing the psychiatric trauma that accompanied unplanned pregnancies. The National Association for the Repeal of Abortion Laws (NARAL, later the National Abortion Rights Action League) issued a debate manual stressing: "While many women are known to be hospitalized with mental illness following childbirth, such severe psychosis following abortion is virtually unknown."[7]

Gradually, reformers moved beyond arguments about the health benefits of legal abortion, insisting that legalization would prevent the birth of severely disabled children, slash the cost of welfare programs, and conserve scarce ecological resources. Physicians first emphasized concerns about the mental health of pregnant women carrying children with severe disabilities.[8] In the 1960s, news broke that thalidomide, a sedative manufactured in Germany, had resulted in over 10,000 cases of major birth defects over the preceding several decades. Although regulators never licensed the drug in the United States, the 1962 case of Sherri Finkbine, a middle-class, white television presenter, gripped the nation. Finkbine had taken thalidomide during her pregnancy and became deeply concerned about the possibility of fetal defects. After a hospital refused Finkbine's request for an abortion, she filed a lawsuit, using the testimony of psychiatrists to establish that it would traumatize her to "have a deformed baby." A court dismissed Finkbine's suit, and Finkbine and her husband traveled to Sweden, a country that authorized abortions in cases of fetal defect. Finkbine's struggles sparked new arguments for abortion reform.[9]

In the wake of a rubella epidemic, advocates for legal abortion again pointed to the costs of forcing a woman to raise a child with severe birth defects. Rubella, a virus with relatively mild symptoms, caused birth defects in a substantial number of children exposed during the first trimester of pregnancy. In the winter of 1963, a rubella epidemic hit the East Coast of the United States. Massachusetts recorded five times the number of cases treated in the previous year, while New York City battled a sixteen-fold increase. By 1964, New York City reported more than 10,000 new cases.[10]

Pointing to the problems facing children born after exposure to thalidomide or rubella, some insisted on reform not as a way to protect a woman's mental health but as a way to eliminate the societal costs some associated with severely disabled children. In 1964, speakers at a convention hosted by the Planned Parenthood Federation of America justified legal abortion as a way to prevent the births of disabled children. "Our present law prohibits abortion with the result that many infants are forced to suffer through their blighted lives, a burden to themselves, their parents, and society," argued Robert Force, the author of a proposed abortion reform bill in Indiana. Dr. Ruth Lidz, another supporter of abortion reform, put the point bluntly: "As a physician, I believe that in [the case of a] proven abnormality of the fetus, it could be immoral and inhumane to subject the mother, her family, and perhaps even society to the burdens of bearing, nurturing, and rearing an abnormal child."[11]

In the early years of reform, Catholic activists and other abortion opponents sometimes responded that legal abortion itself would have powerful societal costs. Pro-life legal scholars and physicians first insisted that abortion had no health benefits. "[T]herapeutic abortion ... carries with it a degree of emotional trauma far exceeding that which would have been sustained by continuation of the pregnancy," wrote legal scholar Dennis Mahoney. Another antiabortion commentator concurred: "Social reasons can never be held sufficient to warrant the dangers of emotional trauma that . . . [women] will subsequently experience." By insisting that most therapeutic abortions had nothing to do with women's health, pro-life commentators hoped to prove that the opposition pursued something far more radical and more costly than reform.[12]

Later in the 1960s, when discussing thalidomide or rubella, abortion foes insisted that these abortions would lead down a slippery slope. Some warned that the law would soon devalue the lives of the disabled and the elderly. When speaking out against Illinois's proposed reform, Revd. Thomas McDonagh predicted that legal abortion would lead "to a general depression of respect for human life, legal sterilization, and legal euthanasia." Thomas Ford, a Catholic physician, echoed this argument in 1970: "If you want to relieve the population explosion, doesn't euthanasia logically come next?"[3]

During the 1960s, physicians led a movement to reform the law to reflect what some in the medical community already viewed as acceptable medical practice. At first, physicians, professionals, and community leaders defended reform by defining expansive health benefits that would accompany legalization, including the improvement of the mental health of women who no longer wanted to be pregnant and the prevention of deaths during illegal abortions. With thalidomide and rubella in the news, reform supporters insisted that legal abortion would have benefits beyond the context of women's health because it would prevent the births of children who would burden their parents and the larger society. Pro-life physicians and lawyers initially responded that abortion reform had nothing to do with better health outcomes. While questioning the accuracy of reported deaths from illegal abortion, pro-lifers contended that legal abortion would damage women's health and threaten disabled, elderly, and other vulnerable persons.

By the early 1970s, however, both sides dedicated more attention to claims about the Constitution. Abortion-rights supporters, frustrated by the limits of reform laws, began insisting that all women had a right to end their pregnancies, regardless of any benefit gained or lost as a result of that decision. Pro-life groups responded by elaborating on claims that the Constitution already protected a right to life for the unborn child. As abortion-rights groups began succeeding in the courts, rights-based arguments became even more central to the conflict. Before *Roe*, those on both sides expected that the future of the abortion wars would depend on how the courts interpreted the Constitution.

THE RISE OF CONSTITUTIONAL CLAIMS

As early as the 1960s, pro-life groups had emphasized constitutional claims in framing their cause. By 1967, three states had passed a version of the ALI bill, and reformers, for the most part, saw little reason to demand a sweeping right to abortion. Even sympathetic politicians and voters might balk at an argument that women should have a right to have an abortion for any reason. In 1967, when Colorado passed a version of the ALI bill, proponents emphasized the policy benefits of a limited reform. As one champion of the bill explained, its sole purpose was "to promote the well-being of the mother [and] to avoid impairment of her health."[14]

By contrast, abortion foes saw constitutional arguments as a way to avoid religious and even moral issues that might make their cause seem too sectarian. For example, when California considered a version of the ALI bill, the mostly Catholic opponents of the proposal responded by arguing that "[t]he unborn child is an individual person, endowed with a right to life."[15] Right-to-life arguments were not new in the late 1960s. For example, hospital manuals dating from the 1900s to the 1950s justified restrictive abortion policies by mentioning a right to life. The manuals reasoned that because the unborn child had not forfeited the right to life by committing a crime, abortion was impermissible.[16] Nevertheless, for decades, right-to-life arguments had often come second to faith-based contentions. But as public support for contraceptive access grew, Catholic antiabortion activists looked for secular arguments. In New York, Archbishop Bryan McEntegart wrote a 1968 pastoral letter asserting that "[e]ach individual has a right to life regardless of the state of his development or condition of his health." Archbishop Paul Hallinan, testifying against a proposed Georgia bill, simply stated: "Either the human fetus has a right to live or it does not."[17]

In the decade before *Roe*, as abortion foes distanced themselves from religious arguments, the new, constitutionally oriented movement captured the support of some non-Catholics. Over the course of the 1960s, pro-lifers elaborated on their constitutional logic by relying partly on the Fourteenth Amendment. That amendment, added to the text after the US Civil War, included two clauses to which the Court had often looked. The Due Process Clause prohibited the state from depriving persons of life, liberty, and property without due process of law. The Equal Protection Clause required equal treatment before the law. Pro-lifers looked to both clauses in advocating for fetal rights. First, insisting that the unborn child counted as a person for constitutional purposes, antiabortion scholars like Robert Byrn maintained that abortion denied fetuses equal protection of the laws by subjecting them to death or serious bodily harm because of mere age or residence in the womb. Second, pro-lifers asserted that if the unborn child was a person, reforming or repealing abortion laws would deny the fetus due process by allowing an execution without a hearing or other legal proceeding. These arguments assumed that undeniable biological evidence had established the personhood of the fetus.[18]

These constitutional arguments appealed to lay activists seeking to broaden their support and legitimize their cause. Consider the two women running California Right to Life in the mid-1960s. Elizabeth Goodwin, the wife of a doctor, was the president of the Council of Catholic Women of the Archdiocese of Los Angeles while Hermine Lees, a mother of five, edited Immaculate Heart College's alumni magazine. Without looking to the courts or to legal experts, both described their cause as a constitutional one. "[T]his is taking away the rights of another individual," Goodwin said of abortion. Lees agreed that after conception, "the child . . . has a right to life."[19] Predominantly (but never exclusively) white and Catholic, the new antiabortion activists included homemakers, physicians, lawyers, and blue-collar workers. The rallying cry of the movement involved the right to life mentioned in the Declaration of Independence.[20]

Abortion-rights supporters soon emphasized constitutional arguments of their own. In part, groups like the Association for the Study of Abortion (ASA) recognized the need for an effective counter to the opposition's constitutional claims. Writing in the early 1970s, Jimmye Kimmey of the ASA insisted on the "need to find a phrase to counter the Right to Life slogan." But the failure of reform itself inspired the repeal movement. Although some still preferred to retool existing laws, physicians and women resented the narrowness of those already in place. Others had noted that in reform states like Colorado, the number of illegal abortions had not declined. For proponents of legalization, it was not hard to spot the flaws of reform bills. Doctors worried about running afoul of the laws and resisted demands for abortion, even when women arguably could fit into one of the ALI categories. Poor women had a particularly hard time convincing a physician that they fell under one of the statutory exceptions. "The reformers no longer claim that the states, basically correct in regulating abortion, are simply too rigid in their application of that power," wrote journalist Linda Greenhouse. "Now, they are seeking to establish abortion as a positive legal right."[21]

As the repeal movement expanded, newly mobilized feminists, public health professionals, and population controllers asserted that abortion should be legal for all women. Some, like the members of Planned Parenthood Federation of America (then known as Planned Parenthood-World Population), had established political ties and defined themselves primarily as advocates of family planning. Founded in 1916, Planned Parenthood had opposed legal abortion for decades and in recent years had defined its cause partly as a fight to check out-of-control population growth at home and abroad. By the end of the 1960s, however, members of the group endorsed legal abortion. At a 1968 meeting, members of 650 Planned Parenthood affiliates voted for a resolution endorsing the repeal of all abortion regulations, describing abortion as a "medical procedure" that was "the right of every patient." While some Planned Parenthood affiliates would refuse for decades to perform abortions, the national organization took a prominent part in campaigning for legalization and contributing briefs in court cases. Planned Parenthood framed abortion as a constitutional right for patients, but in the political arena, members of the group often emphasized the benefits that would come with legalizing the procedure. For example, Planned Parenthood's Director of Information and Education suggested that in New York, a state with no abortion restrictions, legal abortion had decreased welfare costs and lowered rates of illegitimacy and child abuse.[22]

Feminist organizations, like the National Organization for Women (NOW) and the Women's National Abortion Action Coalition (WONAAC), argued that legal abortion would benefit women by allowing them to participate more equally in the life of the nation. Founded in 1966, NOW initially focused on issues like workplace sex discrimination and sex stereotypes in the media. Following an intense internal debate, NOW endorsed abortion repeal in 1967. Founded by socialist feminists, WONAAC organized in 1971 to campaign for abortion law repeal. Groups like NOW and WONAAC described abortion as a civil right for women. At the same time, NOW and WONAAC members emphasized the benefits women would gain if they chose when to carry a pregnancy to term. Other single-issue groups focused on the issue of abortion repeal. Organized in 1969, NARAL included population controllers, feminists, and physicians who prioritized repeal for different reasons. New members of the repeal movement often believed that women should have the ability to end their pregnancies without having to justify themselves to lawmakers or physicians.[23]

Legal changes strengthened the repeal movement. State and federal courts alike began recognizing constitutional abortion rights. In 1969, the California Supreme Court struck down a criminal abortion law by reasoning that "the fundamental right of the woman to choose whether to bear children follows from the Supreme Court's and this court's repeated acknowledgment of a 'right of privacy' or 'liberty' in matters related to marriage, family, and sex." In 1972, in *Abele v. Markle*, a federal district court in Connecticut reached a similar decision. Antiabortion attorneys also scored victories in state courts. Favorable judicial decisions increased the appeal of constitutional arguments for and against legal abortion.[24]

As the repeal cause defined itself by the pursuit of a constitutional right, pro-life groups intensified their own constitutional campaigning. Before *Roe*, national antiabortion organizations also took shape, some of them relying on strong state affiliates. In 1968, Father James T. McHugh, the director of the Family Life Bureau for the National Conference of Catholic Bishops (now called the United States Conference of Catholic Bishops), founded National Right to Life Committee (NRLC) as an umbrella for state groups.[25] Americans United for Life (AUL), another major antiabortion organization, brought together well-known academics, doctors, and lawyers. AUL initially prioritized public education about abortion over litigation and lobbying. Members also hoped to convince the public that the antiabortion movement included prestigious thinkers.[26]

When both sides framed their cause in constitutional terms, the fate of the conflict remained uncertain. In 1970, Hawaii and New York both passed broad repeal laws, but when a reform bill came up in Minnesota, abortion foes killed it in committee. The New York Right to Life Committee mounted a surprisingly successful attempt to restore earlier criminal prohibitions following repeal in 1970, failing only after Republican Governor Nelson Rockefeller vetoed the bill in 1972.[27] When the Supreme Court weighed in, it was much easier to identify winners and losers. Expanding on precedents involving privacy in the family, *Roe v. Wade* recognized a sweeping abortion right and invalidated most of the nation's abortion laws. In the short term, *Roe* made constitutional arguments more central to the struggle than ever.

THE CONSTITUTIONAL FOUNDATIONS OF AN ABORTION RIGHT

The constitutional case for legal abortion was complex. Most famously, attorneys relied on the right to privacy recognized in earlier Supreme Court cases, especially *Griswold v. Connecticut* (1965) and *Eisenstadt v. Baird* (1972). *Griswold* addressed a Connecticut law banning the use of contraception by married couples – the last such statute of its kind on the books. A previous challenge to the law had failed in 1961. Then, in *Poe v. Ullman*, the Court held that because Connecticut never enforced its law, no case or controversy existed to resolve.[28]

In *Griswold*, Justice William O. Douglas held that the Connecticut law violated the Constitution. *Griswold* suggested that the Constitution recognized a right to privacy broad enough to encompass married couples' use of birth control. Douglas reasoned that while this right did not appear in the constitutional text, the Bill of Rights implied the existence of other rights, among them, some kind of right to privacy. *Griswold* was far from a clear decision. Some read it as reflecting the constitutional importance of marriage. Others believed that *Griswold* implied the existence of a right to prevent pregnancy.[29]

In 1972, in *Eisenstadt v. Baird*, the Court shed some light on the meaning of *Griswold*. That case involved a Massachusetts law regulating contraceptive access. The law allowed single people to obtain birth control only to prevent sexually transmitted infections while permitting married people to purchase contraceptives for preventing pregnancy or disease. In an opinion by Justice William Brennan, the Court held that the measure violated the Equal Protection Clause by treating married couples and single people differently without adequate justification. While *Eisenstadt* did not turn on the right to privacy, the Court's decision suggested that right reached quite far. "If the right of privacy means anything, it is the right of the individual, married or single, to be free from unwarranted governmental intrusion into matters so fundamentally affecting a person as the decision whether to bear or beget a child," wrote Brennan.[30]

After *Griswold* and *Eisenstadt*, some proponents of legal abortion relied on a similar privacy argument in attacking criminal bans. After all, *Eisenstadt* suggested that the Constitution protected an individual's decision about when or whether to bear a child. Arguably, abortion was different since the procedure took place after conception rather than before. Nevertheless, if people had a right to make child-bearing decisions, the Constitution might protect the right to end a pregnancy as well as the right to prevent one. Abortion-rights supporters pointed not only to *Griswold* and *Eisenstadt* but also to decisions on parenting and marriage, reasoning that the Constitution protected a series of similarly crucial decisions about marriage and family.[31]

Abortion-rights attorneys stressed other constitutional rights implicated by criminal abortion laws. Some put more emphasis on equality between the sexes. Abortion-rights attorneys at times argued that abortion laws reflected outmoded stereotypes about women. Still others suggested that abortion laws violated everything from the Thirteenth Amendment's protection against involuntary servitude to the Eighth Amendment's prohibition of cruel and unusual punishment.[32]

But in the political arena, abortion-rights supporters always mentioned the benefits of legalizing abortion. Jane Hodgson, a physician and advocate who openly performed illegal abortions, claimed that repeal was desirable because patients would receive better health care. Feminist Betty Friedan joined other advocates of women's liberation in suggesting that abortion rights were justified because they would enhance women's social, political, and economic status.[33] Other supporters of abortion rights tied legalization to the then-popular population-control movement of the 1970s. Population controllers supporting legal abortion argued that it would curb growth rates, stabilize poorer communities, or prevent environmental degradation.[34]

Even lawyers invoking women's interests in privacy and equality pointed to the policy costs of denying women liberty. The lawyers litigating *Roe v. Wade* spotlighted the harm that an unplanned pregnancy could do, including the stigma of unwed motherhood, illegitimacy, poverty, and damage to women's physical and mental health. The costs of abortion bans made plain the importance of abortion rights and their connection to constitutional equality guarantees.[35]

Nevertheless, as the courts deepened their involvement, attorneys more often highlighted arguments about the rights at stake in the abortion decision. In 1973, a year after *Eisenstadt*, the Court issued its decision in *Roe v. Wade*. *Roe* addressed a Texas law banning all abortions that were not necessary to save a woman's life. *Doe v. Bolton*, *Roe*'s companion case, involved a Georgia law similar to the ALI model statute. In June 1970, a Texas federal district court had held that the Texas law violated a privacy right rooted in the Ninth Amendment of the Constitution. A month later, a Georgia federal court held unconstitutional much of that state's law.[36]

After the Supreme Court heard oral arguments in the case, Justice Harry Blackmun initially drafted the majority in *Roe*, the lead case, to strike down the Texas law as unconstitutionally vague. Vagueness doctrine derived from the Fifth and Fourteenth Amendments of the Constitution. The doctrine required criminal laws to give clear notice of what was punishable. Vagueness arguments had a history in abortion litigation. In *United States v. Vuitch* (1971), the Court had rejected a vagueness challenge to Washington, DC's ordinance outlawing abortions except in cases of a threat to the life or health of the mother, reasoning that the term "health" included a woman's physical and mental well-being. As Blackmun saw it, physicians would have no idea how to interpret the statutory exception. The open-ended definition raised due process concerns and subjected doctors to open-ended legal liability. However, Blackmun's colleagues in the Court's majority, who planned to vote that the law was unconstitutional, pressed for a broader opinion. The Court held the case over for reargument. When Blackmun issued a final opinion in January 1973, a 7–2 majority struck down both the Texas and Georgia laws. After *Roe* and its companion case, those on both sides of the abortion debate viewed rights-based arguments as more important than ever.[37]

THE *ROE* DECISION

Roe, the lead opinion, began by noting the controversy already surrounding the abortion issue, an explosive topic that touched on everything from race to population control and women's liberation. The Court then surveyed the history of abortion regulations. Blackmun noted that most such laws were of "relatively recent vintage." *Roe* then traced the history of abortion from the Hippocratic Oath to the recent support for legal abortion offered by the American Medical Association and the American Public Health Association.[38]

With this background in place, the Court turned to the justifications offered for the Texas law. *Roe* concluded that lawmakers could not have intended to deter fornication. A second possible rationale involved the protection of women against potentially dangerous abortifacient drugs and surgical procedures. The Court took note of evidence suggesting that abortion had become much safer, especially earlier in pregnancy. Nevertheless, *Roe* acknowledged that "the State retains a definite interest in protecting the woman's own health and safety when an abortion is proposed at a late stage of pregnancy." The Court would return to a third legislative interest, the protection of fetal life, later in the opinion.[39]

Without pinning down exactly where in the Constitution it was found, *Roe* held that the right to privacy was "broad enough to encompass a woman's decision whether or not to terminate her pregnancy." *Roe* identified ways in which the choice to terminate a pregnancy resembled other important decisions related to marriage, childbirth, parenting, and family. The Court framed the right to abortion as a natural extension of the Court's existing precedents. The Court further illuminated potential costs of unintended pregnancy, including "[p]sychological harm," "a distressful life and future," the burden of childcare, and the stigma of unwed motherhood.[40]

But the Court was quick to stress that the abortion right was not unlimited. To assess the government's power to regulate, *Roe* then turned to the state's interest in protecting fetal life. Texas had framed this argument in two ways. First, the state emphasized that the unborn child was a person within the meaning of the Fourteenth Amendment. The Court agreed that if the fetus was a constitutional person, the challenge to Texas's law would fail. But after surveying the use of the word "person" in the constitutional text, Blackmun concluded that it applied only after birth.[41]

Next, Texas argued that even if there was an abortion right, the government had a compelling interest in protecting life from the moment of conception. The Court emphasized disagreement on the subject in explaining why the state could not have a compelling interest in protecting fetal life. "When those trained in the respective disciplines of medicine, philosophy, and theology are unable to arrive at any consensus, the judiciary, at this point in the development of man's knowledge, is not in a position to speculate as to the answer [about when life begins]."[42]

Roe then set out a legal framework that would govern abortion rights. In the first trimester, states would have very little power to regulate abortion. In the second trimester, the government could restrict abortion only to protect women's health. It was not until fetal viability, the point at which survival was possible outside the womb, that the states could act to protect fetal life. *Doe v. Bolton*, *Roe*'s companion case, struck down Georgia's law, adopting a definition of "health" that included women's physical and mental well-being. Together, the two decisions meant that most abortion laws then on the books were unconstitutional.[43]

Abortion foes escalated the constitutional conflict surrounding abortion after *Roe*. Those on both sides had staked out opposing constitutional positions before 1973, and the organized antiabortion movement had already waged intense battles in several states to keep existing criminal abortion laws in place. But after *Roe*, the antiabortion movement organized at the national level, promoting a constitutional amendment banning the procedure coast to coast.

Immediately after *Roe*, it seemed that constitutional rights defined the terms of debate. Pro-lifers prioritized a constitutional amendment and emphasized fetal rights. Satisfied by their victory in Court, supporters of abortion rights battled against a constitutional amendment while seeking to ensure that more women had access to abortion services. But later in the decade, as the hope for a constitutional amendment gradually faded, the antiabortion movement focused more than ever before on limiting access. And instead of so heavily emphasizing the rights of the unborn child, pro-lifers often claimed that abortion had painful costs for women, families, and the larger society.

THE CONSTITUTIONAL AMENDMENT BATTLE

Before 1973, some pro-lifers had considered proposing a constitutional amendment spelling out rights for the unborn child, but the solution found little favor among organized antiabortion groups like NRLC and AUL. Asking for an amendment, it seemed, required the pro-life movement to admit that the Constitution did not already protect fetal rights.[44]

By contrast, after *Roe*, antiabortion organizations immediately rallied around the idea of an amendment. Less than a month after *Roe*, the leaders of most state antiabortion organizations gathered to discuss strategy. Abortion foes had already proposed laws restricting access, including measures requiring fathers or parents to consent before an abortion could take place. But those present mostly talked about the constitutional amendments already under consideration in Congress. As a resolution passed by the groups explained: "The State Right to Life groups and people pro-life everywhere unanimously support an effort ... that would guarantee the right to life for all humans." And in lobbying for a constitutional amendment, abortion foes continued stressing fetal-rights claims.[45]

The antiabortion movement's constitutional agenda involved far more than overruling *Roe*. Indeed, the movement opposed constitutional amendments that would have undone the 1973 decision if those proposals stopped short of recognizing fetal rights.[46] NRLC passed a resolution explaining: "a 'States Rights' amendment would not effectuate ... rejection [of *Roe*] but would rather reaffirm the Court's decision."[47]

For pro-life leaders, many of the years immediately after *Roe* were defined by intense debate about what the perfect constitutional amendment – one banning abortion rather than returning the question to the states – would require.[48] Anti-abortion attorneys worried about potential gaps in the protections offered by these amendments. Would the Supreme Court interpret these proposals to allow some abortions? How could abortion foes draft an amendment that stopped both private citizens and the government from performing abortions?[49]

Fights about which constitutional solution to back splintered an already fractious movement. In 1974, Nellie Gray, an attorney from Washington, DC, organized the first "March for Life" in the nation's capital. Excited by the success of the event, Gray founded an eponymous organization. Her members demanded that the Constitution ban all abortions, even if women would die if their pregnancies continued. In 1974, Marjory Mecklenburg, a member of the AUL board of directors and a leading NRLC member, also formed her own organization, American Citizens Concerned for Life (ACCL). ACCL prioritized measures believed to make abortion less common, including programs for unwed adolescent mothers and family planning initiatives. The period also saw the spread of crisis pregnancy centers (CPCs). Louise Summerhill founded Birthright, an organization that offered telephone counseling and material support for pregnant women. Birthright operated on the assumption that women had the right and desire to bring pregnancies to term and would do so if they received enough support. By 1973, there were Birthright affiliates in thirty-six states.[50]

Abortion foes were preoccupied with a constitutional amendment protecting a right to life. Pro-lifers took heart in 1974 when Senator Birch Bayh's (D–IN) Judiciary Committee began the first hearings on an antiabortion amendment to the Constitution. Antiabortion witnesses emphasized the religious diversity of their movement. Others highlighted what they saw as irrefutable biological evidence of fetal personhood.[51]

However, many antiabortion arguments were about a right to life that trumped other values, concerns, and even constitutional interests. Some pro-life witnesses, like Joseph Witherspoon, an NRLC member and professor at the University of Texas at Austin Law School, relied on the Thirteenth Amendment, a provision that had outlawed slavery. Witherspoon claimed that the framers of the amendment had recognized that slavery had denied men their rights as fathers. Witherspoon asserted that *Roe* similarly stripped fathers of protected rights. Others argued that the Declaration of Independence and Fourteenth Amendment implied the existence of a fundamental right to life for unborn children. While it did not explicitly create any rights, the Due Process Clause of the Fourteenth Amendment had been the source of several implied rights recognized by the Court, and pro-lifers looked to it in arguing that the Constitution also protected a right to life. As the Court had recognized an implied right for married couples to use contraceptives, the United States Catholic Conference argued in 1976, "the granting of legal personhood is ... properly the product of a constitutional analysis which recognizes the existence of rights which must be said to be implicit."[52]

Larger antiabortion groups would continue to prioritize a constitutional amendment until circumstances in the mid-1980s forced them to change course. But in the late 1970s, some pro-life attorneys and lobbyists already thought that more needed to be done in the short term. While fighting for a constitutional amendment, larger antiabortion groups tried to limit legal access to abortion.[53]

For example, antiabortion attorneys looked for alternative arguments when pursuing criminal convictions against doctors who performed later abortions. The 1975 manslaughter trial of Dr. Kenneth Edelin revealed intriguing possibilities for some antiabortion attorneys. Edelin, an obstetrician-gynecologist, served Boston's poorest women. His trial involved an abortion by hysterotomy, a relatively rare procedure that somewhat resembled a hysterectomy. Prosecutors alleged that Dr. Edelin had killed a child born alive after the abortion. Edelin responded that the child had not been born alive and that in any case, *Roe* protected him from prosecution. The *Edelin* prosecutors and their allies in the antiabortion movement did not say that *Roe* had been wrongly decided or that the Constitution protected a right to life. Instead, prosecutors insisted that *Roe* protected only a woman's right to end her pregnancy, not a physician's right to kill a child during or after an abortion. Antiabortion groups fielded witnesses and publicized trial proceedings. For some antiabortion attorneys, the *Edelin* trial suggested that abortion foes could gain more by claiming to comply with *Roe* than by championing fetal rights.[54]

Although a jury convicted Edelin, the Massachusetts Supreme Judicial Court reversed his conviction. In the short term, antiabortion organizations viewed the entire Edelin affair as an embarrassing loss. But over time, antiabortion attorneys saw the potential of similar arguments. Instead of repeating claims about the right to life, pro-life lawyers could try to reinterpret *Roe*. It might be possible to convince the courts that *Roe* allowed states to regulate abortion and undermine access to abortion.

If antiabortion lawyers could chip away at *Roe* in this way, the decision would appear less coherent. Then when the time came, abortion foes could persuade the Court to reverse the 1973 decision.[55]

Later in the 1970s, in seeking to gradually undermine *Roe*, antiabortion groups like AUL and NRLC defended new restrictions. These state and local laws required women to get the consent of their husbands or parents or to listen to information about the supposed risks of abortion. Other statutes limited the techniques that doctors could use, redefined fetal viability, or mandated that physicians perform later abortions in hospitals. Until the mid-1980s, pro-lifers simply hoped these statutes would lower abortion rates before a constitutional solution fell into place. But even in the short term, to justify new abortion restrictions, members of AUL and NRLC needed different arguments. Fetal-rights claims centered on the immorality of killing and the protection of fetal life. But at least on the surface, access restrictions merely required women to clear certain hurdles before receiving an abortion. Abortion opponents began justifying these laws not by invoking fetal rights but by explaining the benefits of individual restrictions – and the costs of abortion for women.[56]

Fights about access transformed and sometimes overshadowed the war about the right to choose and the right to life. At first, antiabortion groups primarily used incremental restrictions to hold down the abortion rate while Congress deliberated about a constitutional amendment. But these regulations, especially laws outlawing the public funding of abortion, had surprising success. Congress passed a funding ban, and the Supreme Court confirmed that it was constitutional. By the early 1980s, abortion regulations seemed to be much more than a short-term fix. As abortion foes aimed to overturn *Roe* rather than seeking to amend the Constitution, arguments about the costs and benefits of the procedure only became more central to the dialogue. As pro-lifers recognized, it would not much matter if women had a right to abortion if no one could exercise it.

2

The Hyde Amendment and Its Aftermath

Dexter Duggan and Karen Mulhauser recognized that the Hyde Amendment, a ban on Medicaid funding for abortion, might have changed the course of the entire struggle. Duggan was never sure if he qualified as a full-fledged activist, but he knew that he had fallen in love with journalism. After writing for his high school newspaper, he became the school correspondent for a weekly teen tabloid supplement. His passion for journalism grew so intense that after Americans first landed on the moon, he flew to Los Angeles and took a bus to Hollywood just to get a wider selection of newspapers covering the story. When Duggan attended college, one of the opinion editors of the *Arizona Republic* took him on as a member of the editorial staff. Once he caught the journalism bug, he never shook it.[1]

Duggan first gave serious thought to the abortion issue in 1972 after attending a packed pro-life presentation in downtown Phoenix. Soon, he learned that several female colleagues working on his paper's lifestyle section also served as volunteer counselors for women seeking abortions. Duggan was shocked that anyone he knew would do such a thing for money, much less for free. He began writing pro-life editorials, and a few months after the Supreme Court decided *Roe v. Wade*, a leader of the National Right to Life Committee (NRLC) asked him to become the executive director of the organization's Arizona affiliate.[2] Duggan's time as a movement leader was short-lived. The Arizona NRLC affiliate was so divided that he "could not even get the key to the office." But he never stopped writing about abortion, publishing in places like *The Wanderer*, the oldest national Catholic weekly newspaper in the United States, and *National Right to Life News*, the NRLC newsletter.[3]

In the 1970s, to his surprise, Duggan became part of one of the antiabortion movement's most important campaigns. He read a story in the *Washington Post* revealing that the federal government had paid "for hundreds of thousands of abortions." Duggan felt disgusted that his tax dollars could be used for something that he so strongly opposed. He wrote a letter, later republished in *National Right to*

Life News, to the Internal Revenue Service (IRS) outlining the reasons that he was refusing to pay part of his taxes. Throughout the 1970s, tax protesters like Duggan developed ideas about conscience and the role of government that would transform the abortion debate.[4]

Even more than Duggan, Karen Mulhauser found herself at the epicenter of conflict about abortion funding. In college, she had planned on going into medical research but decided that she would "rather work with people than with rats." After becoming a high school science teacher, she routinely found herself peppered with questions about reproduction and sexuality. She felt that she had no choice but to make reproductive health her cause, working in abortion counseling and then moving to Washington State to take a job at Planned Parenthood. After the Court decided *Roe*, Mulhauser opened the Washington, DC, office of the National Abortion Rights Action League (NARAL). By 1975, when the organization's national office moved to Washington, Mulhauser became its leader.[5]

After *Roe*, Mulhauser felt that her job would be easy. Because of the Supreme Court, Mulhauser and her allies "got what [they] asked for." Many Republicans and Democrats defended abortion rights. Mulhauser believed that "support for abortion rights and access was a bipartisan reality."[6] The passage of the Hyde Amendment was a rude awakening. She recognized that attitudes about poverty, race, and taxes were rapidly changing. In Mulhauser's view, it was hard to defend funding for anything when Americans believed that "poor people need[ed] to watch out for themselves."[7]

As Duggan and Mulhauser's experiences suggest, the Hyde Amendment was part of a larger story about the transformation of the abortion debate. Before and immediately after *Roe*, rights-based arguments often seemed to be center stage. Those defending legal abortion celebrated the liberty recognized in *Roe v. Wade*. Abortion opponents championed a constitutional amendment that would restore what they saw as a right to life.

Over the course of the 1970s, however, abortion foes realized that it would likely take a long time to change the Constitution. To keep down abortion rates in the meantime, pro-life lawyers promoted more modest laws, including bans on certain procedures and informed consent requirements. Over the course of the 1970s, pro-lifers hitched their star to laws prohibiting the public funding of abortion. While defending these statutes, antiabortion activists and politicians sometimes had to find a new justification. After all, funding bans did not treat abortion as murder or say anything about fetal rights. Often, abortion foes advocated for the new laws by emphasizing their desirable policy consequences. Larger pro-life groups elevated these claims largely for strategic reasons.[8]

However, arguments about the costs of abortion also often reflected a sharp turn in attitudes about the welfare state. In 1974, when Congress first began considering a ban on Medicaid funding for abortion, it still seemed possible that the nation would guarantee a minimum income.[9] By contrast, later in the decade, as the politics of welfare grew increasingly racialized, lawmakers in both parties embraced work requirements and decried welfare fraud. At the same time, political party polarization made Republicans increasingly hostile to both abortion and what party leaders described as government programs that increased dependence on the state. Both of these concerns weighed against government funding of abortion.[10]

Debate about the consequences of abortion funding reflected these changes. Early on, antiabortion activists in organizations like NRLC and Americans United for Life (AUL) contended that funding bans would help to decrease discrimination against the poor and people of color, arguing that the racist motives of providers and bureaucrats explained the fact that African-Americans had abortions at a higher rate than whites.[11] Later in the decade, AUL, NRLC, and allied groups mostly asserted that abortion funding would fuel welfare fraud and harm taxpayers. Rather than playing up the costs of unplanned children, organizations like NARAL and Planned Parenthood increasingly argued that abortion funding helped low-income women exercise more control over their lives. These arguments defined the debate about an amendment to an appropriations bill sponsored by Henry Hyde, a little known Republican congressman from an Illinois district near Chicago O'Hare International Airport. A veteran of bruising state battles, Hyde had been in Congress only a year when he proposed a rider to the bill funding the Department of Health, Education, and Welfare. The Hyde Amendment, as it became known, helped to change the course of political and constitutional dialogue about abortion.[12]

Funding bans like the Hyde Amendment encouraged abortion-rights attorneys to develop new arguments centered on the real-world effects of incremental restrictions. Starting in the mid-1970s, attorneys leading groups like the American Civil Liberties Union Reproductive Freedom Project (ACLU RFP) argued that to discover if a law violated the Constitution, courts should look beyond the text of a law to its real-world effects. Antiabortion lawyers, many of them just organizing their own groups, countered that poor women's inability to access abortion resulted not from funding bans but from their own unwise decisions and poverty.[13]

By the end of the 1970s, the leaders of groups like NRLC and AUL wanted to duplicate the success that their movement had experienced with funding bans. Access restrictions could lower abortion rates while pro-lifers fought for a constitutional amendment. And just as was the case with the Hyde Amendment, pro-lifers could defend individual restrictions by pointing to their benefits and the corresponding damage said to be done by abortion to women, taxpayers, or families.

The Hyde Amendment began a fight on each side about when a movement should prioritize winning in the short term, even if doing so required activists to set aside the constitutional arguments that had inspired them to mobilize. At the same time, the rise of arguments about the costs and benefits of abortion pushed clashing movements even further apart. Beyond core differences about constitutional values, those on either side disagreed more and more about how abortion had changed the nation.

GUARANTEEING ACCESS TO ABORTION

After *Roe*, abortion-rights supporters believed that they already had won. The Supreme Court had announced a sweeping privacy right that encompassed a woman's right to end her pregnancy. The Senate had a solid bipartisan majority that balked at any effort to curb abortion rights. As NARAL's outgoing executive director put it in February 1973: "The Court has spoken, and the case is closed."[14]

The challenge, as many saw it, was how to ensure that women who wanted abortions could get them. *Family Planning Perspectives*, a peer-reviewed journal put out by the Guttmacher Institute, the research arm of Planned Parenthood, suggested that access to abortion was still extremely uneven. According to *Family Planning Perspectives*, the number of abortions performed in the United States increased by 27 percent immediately after *Roe*, but in 1973, no doctor in Mississippi or Louisiana performed abortions. As late as 1975, only one in nine secular general hospitals offered the procedure. Access issues intersected with the racial politics of abortion. Nonwhite women remained more likely to have illegal abortions and to die as a result. Indeed, by 1974, nonwhite women made up 80 percent of deaths due to illegal abortion, up from 64 percent in 1972. Abortion-rights advocates believed that even if legal and political victories were secure, the movement needed to do more to ensure that women could exercise their rights.[15]

In 1973, Lee Gidding, then the organization's executive director, elaborated on what NARAL should prioritize now that the Court recognized abortion rights: expanding access and educating the public about "the Supreme Court decision and the rights and responsibility of those providing and receiving services." The group worked to persuade medical schools to train doctors in abortion care, to get the medical community to draw up regulations for second trimester abortions, and to "ensure the availability of abortion services in hospitals and high-quality, low-cost clinics."[16] The National Organization for Women (NOW), a major American liberal feminist organization, set out a similar agenda in the aftermath of *Roe*. Jan Liebman, the chair of the organization's Task Force on Reproduction and Population, identified two main objectives: that "[c]ontraception, sterilization, and abortion be made available at public hospitals for anyone who requests them" and that "[a] network of local public clinics be established to offer these services."[17]

In debating how best to deliver services, abortion-rights supporters struggled to balance access with the creation of high standards for care. As one movement sympathizer posed the question in 1977: "should those of us who support abortion support a doctor simply because he performs abortions regardless of the manner in which he does them?" In Tallahassee, Florida, for example, Planned Parenthood and NARAL got pulled into a fight between local obstetricians and the founders of a feminist women's health clinic. Physicians alleged that the feminist clinic had failed to meet the standard of care expected by the medical profession. The clinic responded with an antitrust suit, accusing the doctors of protecting a monopoly that allowed them to drive up prices. While NARAL stood by the feminist clinic, Planned Parenthood tried to mediate the dispute.[18]

A similar problem cropped up when abortion providers facing criminal charges or civil suits sought financial assistance from Planned Parenthood's Medical Rights Fund. Some of those overseeing the fund contended that antiabortion prosecutors simply targeted physicians to eliminate access. Other abortion-rights supporters worried that backing subpar doctors would expose women to unnecessary risks and fuel opposition arguments that providers were greedy or incompetent. Even in cases in which colleagues raised serious safety questions, Planned Parenthood sometimes helped to subsidize a physician's defense if he was the only one in a state performing abortions.[19]

On the political side, abortion-rights groups mobilized medical professionals, created model clinics, and helped to pay the legal fees of certain doctors facing criminal charges. The leaders of groups like NOW and Planned Parenthood shifted their focus to the medical side of the abortion issue, hoping to create a network of safe providers for women who wanted to end their pregnancies. But while founding new clinics, abortion-rights supporters brought suit against existing hospitals that refused to perform abortions. ACLU attorneys returned to court to argue that these medical providers violated the rights set out in *Roe*. Hospital cases, however, created new legal problems. ACLU attorneys had to explain why the Constitution required that abortion be not only legal but also accessible.

LITIGATING TO CHANGE HOSPITAL ABORTION POLICIES

Improbably enough, Nancy Gertner and John Reinstein's love story began with abortion litigation. Passionate about civil rights and equality for women, Gertner always wanted to use "her skills for social change." After she started practicing law, she met John Reinstein, an ACLU attorney, at one of the organization's functions. Their paths did not cross again until April 1973 when two physicians contacted Reinstein. A public hospital in Haverhill, Massachusetts, had stopped them from performing abortions. Reinstein planned to bring a constitutional challenge and called Gertner for assistance. In the next decade, the two would build a marriage and litigate "every abortion case in the Commonwealth of Massachusetts."[20]

It was no accident that Reinstein and Gertner worked with the ACLU. With the help of Planned Parenthood's Harriet Pilpel and veteran member Sylvia Law, an attorney who had previously focused on welfare-rights litigation, the ACLU Women's Rights Project spun off a Reproductive Freedom Project (RFP) in 1974. Judith Mears, the founding director of the RFP, developed a broad legal agenda that went beyond abortion rights. While groups like Planned Parenthood worried that a campaign against the sterilization abuse of nonwhite women would give the anti-abortion movement new arguments, Mears and the RFP made sterilization abuse a central issue, surveying hospitals and campaigning to ensure that informed consent protections were in place. When it came to abortion, RFP attorneys believed that under *Roe* and *Doe*, most hospitals had a constitutional obligation to perform abortions if women requested them. As early as 1974, Nadine Taub, an RFP attorney and law professor at the Rutgers School of Law–Newark, brought a class action suit against all nonsectarian, nonprofit private hospitals in New Jersey that refused to allow staff physicians to perform elective abortions.[21]

As attorneys like Gertner, Reinstein, and Taub recognized, poor women had abortion rights in theory more often than in reality. This was nothing new. Wealthier women had found ways to circumvent criminal laws against abortion for decades. After *Roe*, nothing seemed to have changed. Poor women might not live near a hospital that performed abortions. And if states restricted funding for abortions, the procedure might simply be too expensive for some patients. Less than a decade earlier, ACLU attorneys might have argued that the Constitution guaranteed actual access to services – and if poor women could not afford an abortion, the government would have to help them.[22]

The issue of welfare rights exploded onto the political scene in 1963 when poor, predominantly nonwhite mothers began organizing on the East and West Coasts. The welfare-rights movement also inspired legal theorists like Charles Reich and Edward Sparer. The Supreme Court initially seemed open to welfare-rights claims. In *King v. Smith* (1968), the Court invalidated Alabama's "substitute father" law, a measure that denied Aid to Families with Dependent Children (AFDC) funding to any woman who cohabited with an able-bodied man. A year later, in *Shapiro v. Thompson* (1969), the Supreme Court struck down a residency requirement written into Connecticut's welfare scheme. *Goldberg v. Kelly* (1970) held that some welfare recipients could demand a hearing before the government could take away their benefits. The idea of a guaranteed minimum income attracted support from both major political parties. In 1969, President Richard Nixon proposed the Family Assistance Plan (FAP), a law that would have provided a guaranteed income to all American families.[23]

But by 1974, when the ACLU RFP was mobilizing, support for the idea of welfare rights (or a guaranteed minimum income) collapsed. Although Nixon's FAP sailed through the House of Representatives, it stalled in the Senate, and by 1970, Nixon had lost interest. State legislatures and governors, including those who considered themselves to be relatively liberal, also opposed guaranteed-income proposals. The Supreme Court likewise dashed the hopes of welfare-rights attorneys. In the early 1970s, the Court held that wealth-based classifications were not constitutionally suspect. By mid-decade, the justices stated that there was no right to a guaranteed income or to decent, safe, and sanitary housing.[24]

Support for welfare rights vanished partly because so many families were struggling economically. In the 1970s, inflation averaged 8.8 percent, raising the price of housing and consumer goods. Because the nation's dependence on foreign oil made the American market vulnerable to price hikes, gas prices hit consumers particularly hard.[25] By 1975, the unemployment rate had reached nearly 9 percent – almost double what it had been only a year before. Widespread economic struggles did not translate into support for rights for the poor. Historians later observed that media coverage of welfare programs "was overwhelmingly negative in tone and dominated by pictures of African-Americans."[26]

Given the growing concern of working-class and middle-class whites about the welfare state, supporters of legal abortion did not assert that poor women had a right to abortion funding. The first step in finding a better way to talk about abortion access for poor women came in hospital cases. Here, the biggest legal hurdle for ACLU attorneys was the so-called state action doctrine. Under the doctrine, only the government and its agents could violate the Constitution. The difficulty came in defining who counted as a government agent. The Fourteenth Amendment clearly applied to laws passed by the federal, state, and local governments as well as to employees of those bodies. At times, however, the Court had treated private businesses and individuals as state actors: for example, when a private actor, such as a prison or military contractor, assumed a government power. The Court had also found state action when a private business got too entangled with the government. But predicting ahead of time how the Court would apply these precedents seemed impossible. Although commentators had questioned the coherence of the doctrine, it still often carried weight in court.[27]

In some instances, proving governmental interference was easy. Several states and cities passed laws forbidding any public hospital from performing abortions. Related statutes prohibited the use of public dollars, like those from the Title X family planning program or Medicaid, for abortion services. In other instances, government-run hospitals adopted their own bans or suspended the privileges of doctors who terminated pregnancies. In these cases, government involvement was obvious.[28]

But the ACLU did not stop with public hospitals, particularly since many small towns depended on one or two private facilities. In these cases, RFP attorneys developed creative theories about why a private hospital was a government actor in disguise. RFP lawyers invited the courts to look at the real-world consequences of a hospital's decision not to offer abortions. For example, Nadine Taub argued that private hospitals were unique because some patients had no real alternative for lifesaving care. Taub's arguments notwithstanding, the ACLU generally struggled in cases involving private facilities. The ACLU pointed to the entanglement of private hospitals with the state. These facilities accepted federal money, benefitted from state laws and contracts, and submitted to a variety of regulations. For many lower courts, however, there was no clear nexus between the state benefits hospitals received and the policies they adopted on abortion.[29]

ACLU and NARAL attorneys recognized that even laws banning public funding could trip them up. In these cases, there was obvious state action: a law outlawing Medicaid reimbursement or the use of public facilities for abortion. Nevertheless, the kind of obstacle faced by women in funding cases seemed significantly different from the ones the Court had identified in the past. *Roe* and its companion case, *Doe v. Bolton,* had invalidated laws that criminalized certain abortions. Funding laws were quite different. Rather than threatening to punish anyone, the government denied someone a benefit for which she might otherwise be eligible. The reasons that poor women could not access abortion were complex. Women's financial circumstances and the market for abortion services in a specific area might be obstacles as significant as a state law.

The ACLU set out to convince the Court that funding bans and similar laws deprived women of their rights as much as any criminal ban could. But the ACLU's mission had unintended consequences. Pro-lifers, most of whom had been preoccupied with an antiabortion constitutional amendment, feared that the ACLU would reverse their movement's single victory, protection for doctors and other health care providers with conscience-based objections to abortion. While reinvesting in litigation, abortion foes also put new energy into laws that outlawed taxpayer dollars for abortion. These funding bans – and arguments about the costs of abortion – became a model for pro-life activism in the years to come.

RACE, WELFARE, AND THE INTRODUCTION OF AN ABORTION-FUNDING BAN

The organized pro-life movement fiercely safeguarded its single post-*Roe* legal triumph: protection for physicians and medical professionals who objected to abortion. Of course, these conscience protections were not the antiabortion movement's main objective. Abortion foes primarily championed what they saw as constitutional rights of the unborn.[30] Post-*Roe* constitutional proposals defined unborn children as legal persons and banned most or all abortions. As one member put it, laws that would simply restrict abortion appeared to be "a back-pocket option."[31]

While prioritizing a constitutional amendment, groups like NRLC had the most success with conscience-based protections for some medical professionals. Passed in 1973, the federal Church Amendment allowed any medical facility or provider receiving federal funds to refuse for reasons of conscience to perform abortions or sterilizations. Part of a bill funding a dozen health programs, the Church Amendment reflected efforts by leaders of both parties to reach common ground on abortion. *Commonweal,* the largest national Catholic journal, explained the appeal of Senator Frank Church's (D–ID) proposal as follows: "Some are attracted by the basic anti-abortion features of the resolution, but some also see it safeguarding religious freedom and civil rights and perhaps heading off efforts in the direction of a Constitutional amendment, a move which many on both sides of the abortion issue fear would protract divisive-ness over abortion in state after state over many years." Abortion-rights supporters who ultimately voted for the bill, including Senator Jacob Javits (R–NY), expressed concern that the amendment applied to institutions as well as to individuals. Perhaps women in more rural communities would struggle to find a hospital willing to perform an abortion or sterilization. But the idea of a compromise bill that would defuse the abortion conflict appealed to most legislators. Congress approved of the Church Amendment by a margin of 92–1 in the Senate and 371–1 in the House.[32]

Any quest for compromise was short-lived. While pro-lifers hoped to pass an ever-growing number of abortion restrictions, ACLU attorneys took the position that private as well as public hospitals violated the Constitution by refusing to perform abortions as long as they took money from the government. As the group's Women's Rights Project explained in 1973: "Our position is that any institution which serves the public and receives public funds becomes, in effect, an arm of the state and therefore should be required to provide health services to everyone who needs them."[33]

But when the ACLU RFP began winning hospital cases, members of AUL and NRLC feared that the movement's victory on conscience had been hollow. As *National Right to Life News*, NRLC's flagship publication, explained: "Many observers feel that winning [these hospital cases] ... is of prime importance, not only on [their] own merits but also as a strong defense against expected efforts of the American Civil Liberties Union to force, through litigation, all hospitals, including denominational ones, to open their doors to abortionists."[34]

In trying to salvage conscience protections, abortion foes took fresh interest in incremental abortion restrictions. Rather than simply defending individual hospitals, abortion opponents could introduce laws that disallowed the use of government money or facilities for abortion. If more hospitals could turn women away, or if states could outlaw Medicaid funding for abortion, the abortion rate would inevitably decline. Indeed, the abortion rate among Medicaid-eligible women was disproportionately high. In 1976, the rate was 61.5 percent compared with only 20.7 percent of Medicaid-ineligible women. As early as 1974, Ray White, the new executive director of NRLC, insisted that cutting federal funding for abortion would stop 270,000 abortions a year.[35]

Abortion opponents in Congress quickly answered the call for laws restricting abortion funding. In the summer of 1974, Representative Angelo Roncallo (R–NJ) proposed a comprehensive Medicaid ban that covered all surgical abortion procedures and "abortifacient" drugs. To defend his idea, antiabortion lobbyists could not simply invoke a right to life. Roncallo's proposal would not prohibit any abortions. To justify his bill, NRLC and its allies initially insisted that abortion funding had destructive policy costs, especially for the poor and people of color. Some pointed to the connection between abortion-rights groups and certain population-control organizations like Zero Population Growth, Incorporated. The diverse population-control movement called for measures designed to curb demographic change at home and abroad. While many population-control groups disavowed racist aims, some population controllers believed that curbing demographic growth would have a eugenic effect. Pro-lifers spotlighted population controllers with questionable motives. These arguments oversimplified a complex web of relationships: Not all population controllers endorsed the legalization of abortion, and many of those who did were younger than the activists who still pursued a eugenic agenda. Nevertheless, abortion foes saw the connection between population control and abortion as a potent weapon. Abortion opponents, for example, emphasized that Margaret Sanger, the founder of Planned Parenthood, had sympathized with the eugenic legal reform movement. Sanger had died in 1966, and the organization's leadership had changed. Moreover, Sanger's views had not been unusual at the time. Nevertheless, her previous beliefs reinforced what pro-lifers saw as a connection between racism and support for abortion funding.[36]

Many people of color backed legal abortion, including nonwhite feminists who argued that women needed not just access to abortion but also protection from sterilization abuse. Florynce Kennedy, a black feminist, insisted that African-American women often lost out on valuable opportunities because of unplanned pregnancies. Puerto Rican feminists in the Young Lords, a Puerto Rican leftist group active in several major American cities, demanded reproductive rights. Nonwhite feminists also helped to found the Committee to End Sterilization Abuse (CESA), an organization that fought sterilization abuse while advocating for abortion rights.[37]

Nevertheless, after *Roe*, African-Americans remained divided about abortion. Jesse Jackson of Operation PUSH (People United to Serve Humanity) held a protest outside Chicago's Friendship Clinic, proclaiming that "[a]bortion [was] genocide" for people of color. Jackson believed that abortion would politically weaken African-Americans by reducing their numbers. Moreover, in Jackson's view, legalizing abortion allowed some politicians to prevent the births of poor, nonwhite residents rather than treating them with dignity and respect. An AUL member, Erma Craven, an African-American social worker who had once spoken before the Democratic National Convention, similarly suggested that many endorsed legal abortion as a way of eliminating anyone who was not white. Although some female members supported abortion services, the Black Panther Party circulated related arguments. In a 1973 edition of *Jet*, Father George Clements, the first black pastor of the Holy Angels Catholic Church in Chicago, summarized this perspective, stating: "I believe the whole question of abortions is part of a continuous series of events to eliminate the Black population." When defending funding bans, antiabortion lawmakers borrowed from these arguments.[38]

But in 1974, Roncallo's proposal failed not because of the racial politics of abortion but because of the congressman's strategic mistake. What counted as an abortifacient drug – the item that Roncallo proposed to defund? After all, some pro-lifers believed that a drug was an abortifacient if it blocked the implantation of a fertilized egg, a description that arguably fit leading forms of contraception. Members of Congress slammed Roncallo for trying to deny money for the birth control pill and intrauterine devices (IUDs). The argument worked, and the

Roncallo Amendment fell by a vote of 247 to 123, with more than fifty members of Congress abstaining.[39]

When Senator Dewey Bartlett (R–OK) introduced a similar funding ban that fall,[40] abortion opponents had good reason to shoot for bipartisan support. In the early 1970s, when the Bartlett Amendment came up for consideration, the differences in roll call voting between a typical Democratic and a typical Republican member of Congress were small. Highlighting the supposedly negative consequences of abortion funding seemed likely to attract a broader cross section of politicians, including those not interested in fetal rights.[41] The National Youth Pro-Life Coalition (NYPLC), a left-leaning antiabortion youth group, pursued this strategy by publishing an article emphasizing how often "the slaughtered unborn [child was] black." Groups like NYPLC began to reshape the conversation about abortion. In defending funding restrictions, these activists did not simply invoke a right to life. Instead, they illuminated what they described as the costs of abortion funding (and the benefits of laws restricting it). By the end of 1974, however, some pro-life letters to Congress began pointing out what they saw as the negative consequences of abortion funding for taxpayers.[42]

DEFENDING THE CONSCIENCE OF TAXPAYERS

As the funding battle consumed Congress, NRLC and AUL often played down claims about fetal rights. Of course, funding restrictions would make it impossible for some women to get abortions. Just the same, these laws did not criminalize any procedures and did nothing to discourage wealthier women from ending their pregnancies. At first, in justifying funding laws, NRLC and AUL denounced what they described as the discriminatory intentions of those who preferred that nonwhite children never be born. As the 1970s continued, hostility to the welfare state spread, and new Republican members of Congress, many of whom identified as pro-life, condemned lavish government spending. Along with their allies in Congress, AUL and NRLC gradually expanded on the idea of conscience-based objections developed during the fight for the Church Amendment. These pro-lifers stressed that funding bans protected taxpayers' wallets as well as their consciences. This strategic turn would lead to a broader change in the terms of the debate, sometimes obscuring the core principles that motivated those on either side.

In defending the conscience of taxpayers, abortion foes could draw on a recent tradition of tax protest. In 1966, for example, when President Lyndon Johnson asked for Congress to reinstate a 10 percent excise tax on phone calls to fund the deployment of additional troops in Vietnam, Karl Meyer, a Catholic activist, asked Americans to refuse to pay.[43] Conscientious objectors, draft card burners, and tax protesters to the Vietnam War set the stage for debate about the Church Amendment and for later conscience-based protections. Abortion foes could also look to the ideas of conscience developed during the debate about the Church Amendment itself. Proponents of the Church Amendment had maintained that conscience-based objections mattered to non-Catholics and even to those with moral, rather than religious, objections to abortion. Representative Ella Grasso (D–CT), for example, stressed in 1973 that "the protection from compulsion to perform abortions or sterilizations is just as necessary and desired by non-Catholic institutions and personnel as by Catholics." During the Church Amendment debate, pro-lifers had also finessed the question of what counted as direct involvement in a way that could help make a case for antiabortion taxpayers. Like Senator Church, a pamphlet put out by the Catholic Bishops of Connecticut differentiated between "primary involvement" in abortion, which the Church always condemned, and "secondary involvement," which might be defensible. The pamphlet authorized secondary involvement only when cooperation was not "an evil act in itself" or if the reason for cooperation was "sufficiently important." Although seemingly carving out a narrow category of conscientious objectors, the pamphlet also suggested that those who indirectly assisted with abortion should sometimes have a defensible moral and legal claim.[44]

By the mid-1970s, many grassroots abortion opponents sought to expand this idea of conscientious objection, describing the painful costs of funding what they saw as an abhorrent procedure. Florence and Mike Danninger paid their taxes in full but enclosed a note saying that they did so only because of the threat of criminal prosecution. Gert Houle told the IRS that she was withholding one dollar in protest, and Father Philip Reilly, a priest teaching at a Catholic preparatory school, did the same. Others took more drastic steps. Joseph Fahy, an elderly cabinet maker from New York, faced criminal charges for refusing to pay anything in either 1973 or 1974. Michael McKee, a father of three, took his case to court before the IRS had the chance to go after him, arguing that "[t]o force the conscientiously objecting taxpayers to contribute to the fund from which abortions are paid violates [the] right to privacy." Most pro-life tax protesters avoided any serious consequences, but the IRS had the power to pursue those who did not pay and sometimes used it, as in Fahy's case.[45]

For many abortion foes, Dexter Duggan's tax-protest letter to the IRS said it all. As early as 1973, Duggan had approached William F. Buckley Jr. of *National Review*, a conservative editorial magazine, asking him to adopt pro-life tax protest as his next cause. Duggan highlighted what he described as the cost of forcing pro-life taxpayers to violate their own deeply held principles. Buckley declined because of a general distaste for tax protest, but Duggan soldiered on.[46]

Duggan's request went well beyond the protections written into the Church Amendment. Conscience protections often covered the people most closely involved in abortions, including the doctors who offered reproductive health services. Taxpayers at most provided money to the government, a portion of which went into the Medicaid program. This distinction made no difference to Duggan. "Though citizen participation is sanitized through government taxing powers (the payment is indirect)," he wrote, "the bottom line is still that taxpayers pay the bill."[47]

Duggan reasoned that the Supreme Court saw abortion as a matter of individual privacy and personal responsibility. If poor women had a right to freedom from the government, why could hardworking taxpayers not expect the same? "We hear frequently about freedom of choice for abortion," Duggan explained. "So I conclude that there must be freedom of choice not to subsidize this abhorrent practice."[48]

Larger antiabortion groups did not rush to join Duggan's battle. Tax protest won a champion in Randy Engel, the leader of United States Coalition for Life, a group that openly opposed contraception. But because tax protesters were breaking the law, most abortion foes thought that Duggan's strategy was too risky. Indeed, when Duggan floated the idea to others in Arizona, the local NRLC affiliate turned him down flat.[49]

While distancing themselves from lawbreaking, antiabortion legislators had no problem presenting themselves as the American taxpayer's best friend. It made sense to emphasize claims about the benefits of funding bans (and the costs of abortion). Right-to-life arguments seemed out of place given that a funding ban allowed women to have abortions so long as they could pay for them. Senator Joe Biden (D–DE), a future supporter of abortion rights and vice president of the United States, joined many other Catholic Democrats in playing up claims about the benefits of funding bans. Biden urged his colleagues to respect taxpayers, "be consistent, and keep the federal government out of this issue." Senator John Pastore (D–RI) echoed Biden's reasoning: "There are many people in this country who pay money and pay taxes and have very strong feelings against this sort of thing. Why should their money be used and abused in this manner?" Pastore and Biden, like Duggan, began pitting hard-working taxpayers against poor women who were unwilling or unable to pay for their own abortions. "The question is whether taxpayer dollars, ... under the guise of health treatment, should be allocated to the purely arbitrary decision of the pregnant woman," Pastore stated. In the states, politicians similarly invoked taxpayers' conscientious objections. Roanne Shamsky, a leading Democrat in California, identified "extremely strong opposition expressed by citizens ... against the use of tax funds ... for a purpose they find morally repugnant."[50]

Although Bartlett had counted on his colleagues to push through his proposal, the Senate rejected it by a vote of 54 to 37. *National Right to Life News* predicted that Congress would pass a similar measure if it did not come as part of a broader appropriations bill. Leaders of groups like NARAL, NOW, and Planned Parenthood saw no reason to panic. Ann Liebman and Jan Scott, the NOW lobbyists charged with defending reproductive rights, simply instructed allies to emphasize that the Bartlett Amendment was unconstitutional.[51]

The strategy emerging around the Bartlett Amendment set traps for movements on both sides. Abortion-rights supporters too readily assumed that the Supreme Court would step in before any funding ban went into effect. Pro-lifers, by contrast, had found the seed of a powerful new strategy centered on arguments about the costs of abortion. But because leading antiabortion organizations still primarily favored the outright criminalization of abortion, pro-lifers had to strike a balance between tactical efficacy and the principles that had inspired people to mobilize. In the decades to come, larger antiabortion groups trying to strike this balance had reason to wonder if they had set themselves up to fail.

DOWNPLAYING THE THREAT OF FUNDING BANS

Even though the Bartlett Amendment seemed to have significant support in the Senate, leading abortion-rights groups were willing to take their chances if the Oklahoma senator tried again. Indeed, NARAL, like NOW, committed more resources to defeating the opposition's constitutional amendment. It was not lost on leaders of larger abortion-rights groups that incremental restrictions had spread rapidly. Moreover, the passage of a constitutional amendment seemed unlikely. Nevertheless, those leading organizations like NARAL thought that a fight against funding bans did nothing to motivate donors and voters. Believing that the courts were no longer in play, abortion-rights groups still invested more in rights-based arguments, seeing them as key to political success.

The funding-ban struggle came at a time of transition for NARAL. Before legalization, the organization relied on a small leadership group that could adapt quickly and resolve disagreements. After *Roe*, as new members joined, NARAL became a much larger and more unwieldy organization, and disputes over the group's future began almost immediately. Some feminists resented what they saw as control of the organization by a small group of New York men, including prominent activist Larry Lader. While trying to smooth over leadership struggles, NARAL also professionalized its operations, hiring direct-mail specialist Bea Blair to serve as executive director and coordinate the group's work in Congress.[52]

When crafting their fundraising, lobbying, and public relations campaigns, NARAL focused not on claims about the benefits of legal abortion but on the possibility that the states would once again criminalize the procedure. For example, NARAL's convention put out a message that "[a]s long as adequate contraceptive care is not available to all and not perfect, then legal abortion must be available as a backup." Karen Mulhauser, then the organization's executive director, told the organization's executive committee about a planned ad that would show "a grandmother describing her illegal abortion and her hope that abortion [would] remain legal."[53]

NOW's lobbying and public relations efforts also took aim primarily at attempts to ban abortion. In the mid-1970s, Wilma Scott Heide, a former nurse who had linked the organization's abortion-rights activism to population control, stepped down. Karen DeCrow, the group's new leader, was a feminist attorney who wanted NOW to vigorously defend constitutional abortion rights. NOW's focus on an antiabortion constitutional amendment reflected this strategy. "Do not argue the moral rights and wrongs of abortion," explained the organization's lobbying manual. "[I]nstead stress that everyone has the right to make their own moral decision for or against abortion, but not to force that decision on anyone else."[54]

Why did abortion-rights advocates spend so much time talking about a long-shot constitutional amendment? After the Court legalized abortion, groups like NOW and NARAL worried about complacency among both donors and grassroots recruits. The Supreme Court had legalized abortion across the land. Donors and voters could easily conclude that other causes needed more support. Those leading NARAL's first professional fundraising effort believed that Americans would give more generously if they worried about losing abortion rights. Focusing on incremental restrictions seemed less compelling to potential donors. Given the growing hostility to welfare and racialized anxiety about the poor, a fight for Medicaid funding might have been a particularly weak draw.[55] Second, abortion-rights leaders believed that courts would strike down any law like the Bartlett Amendment. "By and large, the courts ... have unanimously held that Medicaid must pay for elective abortions," argued a 1975 ACLU pamphlet. Just the same, abortion-rights groups badly misjudged the efficacy of both funding bans and arguments about the costs of abortion. These claims would alter constitutional doctrine as well as political dialogue.[56]

The trajectory of rights-based claims had much less to do with the Court than many would have expected. Indeed, abortion-rights supporters highlighted rights-based arguments as often in political debate as in court. In the political arena, activists asserted that voters and politicians cared far more about the criminalization of abortion than about restrictions or burdens on the poor. Invoking a right to choose energized the movement's supporters. By contrast, in court, abortion-rights lawyers sometimes had to explain why more modest-seeming laws harmed women as much as complete prohibitions. If the justices upheld some restrictions, then simply repeating claims about a right to choose would not be enough. The Court's intervention did not always put rights-based claims front and center. Arguments about constitutional absolutes often remained prominent because they delivered a political payoff.

PARTY POLARIZATION AND THE HYDE AMENDMENT

In 1976, few would have guessed that an appropriations amendment sponsored by Henry Hyde would bedevil the abortion-rights movement for decades. Hyde's amendment banned Medicaid reimbursement for abortion. In the years to come, to the surprise of many, the Hyde Amendment passed and survived a constitutional challenge in the courts. The congressman had stumbled onto a roadmap that larger antiabortion groups would use for years.

Hyde capitalized on the divisions that were just starting to emerge in Congress. At least on the abortion issue, the two candidates for president in 1976 held fairly similar positions. Jimmy Carter opposed a constitutional amendment but favored funding bans and promoted what he called alternatives to abortion, including expanded family planning programs. Following a difficult primary with Ronald Reagan, an openly antiabortion candidate, Gerald Ford had to declare his support for an antiabortion constitutional amendment. Just the same, Ford's wife, Betty, had already announced her support for abortion rights, and Ford, like Carter, tried to stake out a middle-ground position on the issue or avoid it altogether. The deeper partisan divide in Congress, however, was a sign of things to come. Starting in the mid-1970s, the ideological chasm between the Democratic and Republican Parties widened. Trends that were just becoming visible during Hyde's time would only accelerate later. Moderate Republicans began losing their seats. Over time, Southern Democrats started abandoning the New Deal coalition and joining the Republican Party.[57]

Although party polarization did not transform the Hyde Amendment debate overnight, freshmen GOP legislators eagerly endorsed funding bans. New members of Congress, like Representative Newt Gingrich (R–GA) and Senator Orrin Hatch (R–UT), were more socially and fiscally conservative than many veteran Republican members. As the Republican Party slowly tied itself both to pro-life politics and to fiscal conservatism, antiabortion leaders reframed their arguments for the Hyde Amendment.[58]

Those opposed to the amendment pressed Hyde and his allies on why the conscience-based beliefs of some taxpayers – or abortion opponents – deserved more sympathy than anyone else's. "Why should my tax dollars be used to dump napalm on defenseless civilians in Vietnam?" asked Senator Birch Bayh (D–IN). Senator Pastore and his allies fired back that unborn children were innocent in a way that enemy combatants were not. "We are talking here about the right of the people, because of their moral and religious views, not to support the taking of human life," explained one supportive lawmaker.[59]

When the amendment seemed to have a realistic chance of passing, NARAL's lead lobbyist, Carol Werner, urged her colleagues to step up their pleas to Congress. "I cannot even imagine how bad it would be to lose on this," she confided to her colleagues. But most supporters of abortion rights did not share Werner's fears. Many believed that the courts would bail the movement out if Congress took the Hyde Amendment too far.[60] NARAL circulated a strategy memo stressing that nine federal courts had struck down funding bans, and the Supreme Court had agreed to hear a challenge to similar laws. "The Hyde Amendment is clearly discriminatory and violates the Fifth and Fourteenth Amendments," the memo said.[61]

To the shock of many, Congress passed the rider, but shortly later, President Ford vetoed it, stating that Congress had spent too much in the rest of the appropriation bill. When Congress reconvened, Hyde's allies rallied to override the veto.

Supportive members pitched the Hyde Amendment as a way to shrink government. "Although the Supreme Court has ruled on the question of legality, the Court did not and could not mandate Congress to follow suit by spending taxpayer money on abortion," asserted Senator Bartlett. Senator Bob Dole (R–KS), one of the sponsors of an earlier version of the rider, simply explained that there had to be "some limit on the expenditure of government funds."[62]

Why was abortion that limit? Bartlett highlighted what he described as the unique costs of forcing taxpayers to support a procedure they opposed. The senator compared abortion funding to tobacco subsidies, describing both as harmful and morally objectionable. Hyde himself insisted that abortion was unique. If there was any limiting principle on the burdens faced by taxpayers, this had to be it. He urged his colleagues: "you cannot in logic and conscience fund the destruction of this innocent human life."[63]

ABORTION CONSEQUENCES COME TO COURT

Hyde had forged a new pro-life argument based on what the congressman claimed to be the societal costs of funding abortion. At first, the potential power of this argument was unclear. Justifications for the Hyde Amendment seemed to apply only to funding bans, and besides, a constitutional amendment, not incremental restrictions, still commanded the attention of most of those in the abortion wars. More than anything, it seemed that Hyde's schemes would not matter as soon as the Supreme Court stepped in.

The Court agreed to hear a trio of cases on abortion funding. *Maher v. Roe* involved a 1975 Connecticut welfare regulation that prohibited Medicaid reimbursement for any abortion that was not "medically necessary." In *Beal v. Doe*, abortion-rights attorneys contended that the federal Social Security Act preempted a Pennsylvania abortion restriction similar to the one in *Maher*. *Poelker v. Doe*, a third case, addressed a St. Louis, Missouri, policy prohibiting abortions in public hospitals. Abortion-rights supporters hoped that the Court would shut down efforts to restrict abortion. But the Court's decisions in *Maher* and its companion cases made the costs and benefits of abortion (and abortion restrictions) an important part of constitutional litigation.[64]

The antiabortion lawyers who litigated *Maher* had not yet given up on the courts. As early as 1973, Dennis Horan, one of the most influential members of AUL, had called for the creation of an antiabortion public interest law firm. Horan was a devout Catholic who often worked on cases with his wife, Dolores, another attorney. The Horans partnered with Victor Rosenblum, a liberal Jewish law professor who would eventually recruit several students to join the litigation effort. In 1975, when antiabortion lawmakers struggled to defend their laws in court, the time seemed right to shift AUL's focus from public education to litigation. NRLC, the largest national antiabortion organization, also invested more in the courts, hiring a general counsel and forming a Legal Action Project to bring test cases.[65]

Abortion foes hoped that it would be easier to defend funding bans than it had been to win in *Roe*. After all, funding prohibitions did not authorize criminal charges, much less prison time. Moreover, in 1976, the Court had proven willing to uphold some abortion restrictions. *Planned Parenthood of Central Missouri v. Danforth* had struck down most of a Missouri abortion law, but the Court upheld one provision and suggested others might have survived if they had been more narrowly drawn.[66]

For abortion-rights supporters, *Danforth* showed that invoking *Roe* would not be enough. In their brief in *Maher*, Lucy Katz and Catherine Roraback of the Planned Parenthood League of Connecticut relied partly on the so-called unconstitutional-conditions doctrine. Under the doctrine, there were constitutional limits on the government's ability to penalize the exercise of a fundamental right, especially if that involved the withdrawal of funding. By this logic, Connecticut unconstitutionally forced women to choose between exercising a fundamental right and receiving Medicaid benefits. Katz and Roraback further invoked the Equal Protection Clause. Their brief did not argue that Connecticut had impermissibly discriminated against the poor. Instead, they insisted that if states chose to fund any services related to reproduction, lawmakers could not leave out abortion, a procedure that women had a constitutional right to choose. Other abortion-rights attorneys stressed similar arguments. But abortion-rights attorneys knew the drawbacks of such arguments. In recent years, the Court had not always invalidated what appeared to be an unconstitutional condition, and the justices had generally rejected arguments based on wealth discrimination. Abortion-rights attorneys needed an alternative tactical plan.[67]

Katz and Roraback helped to develop a new approach. The two attorneys pointed to language in *Danforth* and a decision on minors' rights, *Bellotti v. Baird* (1976). According to Katz and Roraback, these cases showed that the Court struck down laws that "unduly burden ... the right to seek an abortion."[68] To identify such an undue burden, the Court had to look below the surface of a law to understand "the actual impact on the abortion decision." If Katz and Roraback succeeded, this approach promised to be revolutionary. Abortion-rights attorneys could smoke out the true purpose or effect of innocent-seeming laws. And since the Court no longer strictly applied the trimester framework (as evidenced by *Danforth*), Katz and Roraback hoped to offer a coherent framework for any abortion case.[69]

Antiabortion attorneys responded that poor women could hardly blame the government for their plight. AUL lawyers contended that if abortion was a privacy right, the Constitution at most protected women from government interference. But according to AUL, the obstacle facing low-income women came not from the government but from their own poverty.[70] "[T]his Court has never held that the indigent have an independent right to public welfare," AUL explained. Connecticut drew on the same strategy in *Maher*.[71]

The *Maher* litigation ushered in a new era in constitutional litigation over abortion. The Court set in motion an effort to prove how and why women were able to access abortion – and whether ending their pregnancies did women more harm than good. In the years to come, the Court routinely intervened in the abortion conflict. Nevertheless, the debate moved away from the two absolute constitutional rights many thought had defined the conflict. The Court pushed both sides to make arguments about the effects of abortion restrictions and even of the procedure itself. But focusing on the costs and benefits of abortion did nothing to create common ground. If anything, those on opposing sides increasingly disagreed about the basic facts about abortion.

MAHER, POELKER, AND BEAL

A few days after the House approved a version of the Hyde Amendment with narrow exceptions for rape and incest, the Supreme Court shocked abortion-rights supporters by upholding all three funding bans. *Maher*, the lead case, used the language of an unconstitutional undue burden, though hardly in the way abortion-rights attorneys had intended. "[W]e have held that a requirement for a lawful abortion is not unconstitutional unless it unduly burdens the right to seek an abortion," *Maher* stated. But a law could not be unduly burdensome if it "place[d] no obstacles— absolute or otherwise—in the pregnant woman's path to an abortion." As the Court saw it, the problem faced by women in Connecticut arose not because of the government but because of whatever made them poor. *Maher* entered into a broader conversation about why impoverished women could not afford to end their pregnancies. While abortion-rights lawyers pinned the blame on specific restrictions and on other structural barriers created by the government, antiabortion lawyers insisted that the true cause was a form of poverty that had nothing to do with the state. The Court agreed.[72]

Concluding that no fundamental right was at stake in the case, the Court next considered if there was a rational basis for the law. Rational basis described one of three levels of scrutiny the Court sometimes applied to constitutional challenges. Strict scrutiny, the most demanding, applied to laws that burdened a fundamental right or discriminated on the basis of race or (sometimes) national origin. The Court used intermediate scrutiny in cases involving gender or illegitimacy classifications, and rational basis applied to any other case where the parties could not point to a special constitutional interest. The Court had not applied the standard tiers of scrutiny in any abortion case before *Maher*. Nevertheless, the justices almost always found that a law had a rational basis, and *Maher* was no exception. The Court asserted that the government could permissibly encourage women to choose childbirth over abortion by covering the former and excluding the latter.[73] The Court's logic also echoed pro-lifers' arguments about conscience and spending cuts. "[W]hen an issue involves policy choices as sensitive as those implicated by public funding of nontherapeutic abortions," *Maher* explained, "the appropriate forum for their resolution in a democracy is the legislature." The Court also sided with the government in *Poelker* and *Beal*.[74]

Antiabortion groups saw these decisions as a potential turning point. According to some abortion foes, "[t]he U.S. Supreme Court . . . said that the government may be avowedly pro-life," allowing it to use a preference for childbirth as a reason to legislate. *Maher, Poelker,* and *Beal* further buoyed the confidence of activists who believed that they could introduce new limits on access to abortion by playing up claims about the procedure's costs. The fortunes of the Hyde Amendment looked particularly bright. "The high court's decision is also encouraging because it suggests that the Court must respect the authority of Congress to appropriate federal funds," explained a 1977 NRLC press release.[75]

PRIORITIZING POLITICAL SUCCESS AFTER *MAHER*

Maher sent a chilling message to larger abortion-rights groups: It had been a mistake to expect the Supreme Court to come to the rescue. If the Court would not strike down every abortion law, the leaders of groups like NARAL saw a straightforward solution. The abortion-rights movement had dedicated itself to changing the medical landscape for abortion care. But to the leaders of NARAL and Planned Parenthood, the Hyde Amendment proved that the opposition had a better understanding of the political game. To prevent the spread of funding bans, abortion-rights supporters would have to guarantee that Henry Hyde and those like him did not get elected in the first place.

Jean Weinberg and Pam Lowry helped to focus NARAL on political work. Lowry and Weinberg's paths to NARAL could not have been more different. Raised by old-fashioned parents, Lowry grew up in a "protective bubble." Her mother had a very strong view about "the path that proper young ladies should take" and encouraged Pam to join the Junior League, an organization that promoted volunteerism for wealthy young women. As part of her work there, Lowry became active at Planned Parenthood in Boston, and her ideas about what ladies did and should do "blew up." She abandoned the Junior League and became enraptured with her work at Planned Parenthood. There, she noticed how hard it was for poor women to decide when they had children. In 1970, she helped to found a NARAL affiliate in Massachusetts and to launch Pregnancy Counseling Services, a resource for women looking for information on how to terminate their pregnancies. By the late 1970s, Lowry had become the chair of the NARAL Executive Committee and a member of the organization's board of directors.[76]

While Lowry got her start in the most genteel form of abortion politics, Weinberg came up as a community organizer. In the fall of 1977, she was given a list of names and $2,000 to reactivate the NARAL affiliate in Massachusetts. She never turned back. When Weinberg joined the group's affiliations committee, she was struck by how much the organization – mistakenly, Weinberg thought – focused on education and advocacy. The turning point came in January 1978 when she and Lowry had been lobbying Senator Ted Kennedy (D–MA). Word came that an epic blizzard was about to hit New England. The two took the last airplane out but were stopped from landing in Boston. Stranded in Southport, Maine, for a week in a Holiday Inn, they had no choice but to pace the halls and talk. Weinberg took the chance to convince Lowry that America had a pro-choice voting majority that just needed to be woken up. NARAL had formed a political action committee in 1977, but Weinberg thought that NARAL had not done nearly enough. From that snowstorm was born "Impact '80," NARAL's first major political-organizing effort. The bottom line, as Weinberg still puts it, was the group's slogan: "I am pro-choice, and I vote."[77]

Battling the Hyde Amendment (or disproving claims about the costs of abortion) did not seem likely to capture the hearts of voters. Nor would some be moved by consequences of funding bans for the poor or people of color. Recognizing that Americans disapproved of the welfare state, a June 1977 NARAL model letter to members of the Senate instead emphasized that the Hyde Amendment "would directly contravene the intent of other government programs to help indigent women break the poverty cycle."[78]

Like NARAL, Planned Parenthood tried to remake itself into a fearsome political lobby. In 1978, Faye Wattleton, an African-American woman, became the organization's president. Shortly thereafter, she consulted with David Garth, a Democratic strategist with a record of winning elections, about how Planned Parenthood should advance its goals. Garth circulated a memo encouraging Planned Parenthood to become involved in national abortion politics – a move that offended many in the group's affiliates and national office. Some worried that Planned Parenthood would jeopardize its legitimacy as a health care provider. At the time, many affiliates did not even offer abortion services. Conflict about Planned Parenthood's political role would last for decades, but at the national office, Garth's view won out. He suggested that pro-lifers had already become "a national political force." Planned Parenthood had no choice but to do the same.[79]

In the late 1970s, NOW prioritized the Equal Rights Amendment (ERA), a constitutional proposal that would have written sex equality into the Constitution. But the organization's Reproductive Rights Committee tried to find new ways of discussing abortion, especially when it came to funding for the poor. Like Planned Parenthood, NOW opposed informed consent requirements for women before voluntary sterilizations. Both NOW and Planned Parenthood condemned forced sterilization but feared that if lawmakers could deny women access to sterilization, the government could do the same with abortion. This stance made it harder for either group to work with women of color concerned about sterilization abuse. To engage more nonwhite women in the campaign to win back abortion funding, NOW members hoped to talk more about the benefits of abortion for poor women, "encourag[ing them] to discuss their experiences and share them with others."[80]

While NOW and Planned Parenthood pursued political influence, the Hyde Amendment energized women of color and feminists aware that funding bans would disproportionately affect nonwhite women. In June 1977, representatives of NARAL, NOW-New York, the anti-sterilization-abuse group Committee to End Sterilization Abuse (CESA), and a variety of smaller feminist and socialist organizations formed the Committee for Abortion Rights and Against Sterilization Abuse (CARASA). CARASA operated primarily in New York but sought a model for other groups to use across the country. While CARASA included women from larger groups like attorney Rhonda Copelon of the Center for Constitutional Rights, the organization also attracted many skeptical of mainstream strategies. Some of these advocates, including Dr. Helen Rodríguez-Trías, a pediatrician and women's-rights activist, worked toward a new approach to reproductive health by demanding social justice for women, especially those who were not rich or white. Founded in 1975, the National Women's Health Network (NWHN) vowed to be a voice for feminist women's health activists in politics. NWHN sought support from women of color, had a diverse board of directors, and connected abortion to other issues, including sterilization abuse, that affected nonwhite women.[81]

Believing that the Hyde Amendment was racist in its aims and effects, groups like CARASA also emphasized different arguments about abortion funding, especially the costs of a funding ban for low-income women. As CARASA framed it, funding bans forced "poor, minority, and working women into unwanted childbirth, back-alley abortions, and unwanted sterilizations." Larger organizations like NARAL and NOW started to echo this logic. Rather than appealing to voters' desire to save money, abortion-rights supporters increasingly argued that funding bans unconscionably harmed nonwhite and poor women.[82]

Groups like NARAL and Planned Parenthood pursued what sometimes seemed to be contradictory aims. While courting undecided voters, larger abortion-rights groups also sought to mobilize women of color who felt uncomfortable with either an abortion-only focus or the rights-based rhetoric that some activists had favored. However, many white voters, indifferent to funding bans, gravitated to arguments about choice. Abortion-rights leaders wondered if their movement could be more politically effective or more diverse but not both.

ABORTION FUNDING AND THE EVILS OF BIG GOVERNMENT

Anyone who believed that congressional fights about abortion funding would simmer down after passage of the Hyde Amendment was sorely mistaken. Later in the 1970s, the fight still centered on arguments about the costs and benefits of abortion, this time reflecting rising anxieties about welfare fraud, an issue that potently mixed distrust of poor, often nonwhite women and anger about the welfare state. While opponents of the Hyde Amendment decried discrimination against poor women, pro-life members of Congress blamed welfare cheats for punishing innocent taxpayers. Senator Jesse Helms (R–NC), who cosponsored the amendment, argued that Congress should never "compel the taxpayer to finance a form of killing." Senator Bayh shot back that there was "a remarkable parallel between people who vote against financing for abortion and those who vote against funding for education, housing, and rat control." Senator Hatch quipped that the only parallel was between opponents of the Hyde Amendment and those who had committed to "spending us into oblivion."[83]

As the Hyde Amendment debate suggested, support for welfare programs continued to plummet.[84] The specter of welfare fraud loomed large. Reporters estimated that the bill for Medicare and Medicaid fraud ran as high as $3 billion per year. Ford Administration officials had estimated that the government wasted at least 40 percent of welfare funds because of clerical errors, fraud, overpayment, and eligibility errors. In the period, the racial politics of other policy issues also changed – a highly relevant factor given the proportion of Aid to Families with Dependent Children (AFDC) recipients who were women of color. Court-ordered desegregation created widespread opposition among whites; some polls showed that three-quarters of whites surveyed opposed busing throughout the decade. Allan Bakke, a white law school applicant rejected from the University of California, Berkeley, became the face of another controversy involving race-conscious affirmative-action admission policies.[85]

Some members of the Senate tried to broker a compromise by identifying specific medical conditions that could justify funding for abortion rather than relying on a broad definition of medical necessity. The American Medical Association (AMA) and the American College of Obstetricians and Gynecologists (ACOG) opposed the proposal, and the Senate ultimately pushed for a medical-necessity exception, along with others for rape and incest. At the end of November 1977, the House took a second vote on the Senate compromise and defeated it. In December, the Senate returned the favor.[86]

Antiabortion lobbyists insisted that if Congress made medical exceptions, women could simply lie about their health. Abortion funding, they suggested, meant painful costs for taxpayers and rampant fraud. Robert Krebsbach of NRLC insisted that fraud was almost inevitable when the "abortionist [got] to define the welfare of the mother." AUL lawyers claimed that the term "medical necessity" could become so all-encompassing that "in practice the state and federal government will have to fund *all* abortions performed by a physician."[87]

NRLC leaders similarly asserted that rape and incest exceptions all but invited welfare fraud. NRLC members argued that women would falsely claim to be victims of rape or incest to get their abortions paid for. Thea Rossi Barron of NRLC argued that rape victims should have to report to authorities within a week after a sexual assault took place. She told members of Congress that loose reporting requirements provided cover for welfare recipients using rape claims to hide "convenience abortions."[88]

Abortion-rights supporters insisted that funding bans, not legal abortion, imposed heavy costs on women and the larger society. "Without public funding for abortion, poor women face three tragic choices," argued a 1977 ACLU pamphlet. "They can get a legal abortion at a private clinic or a private hospital, . . . get an illegal abortion in a back alley, . . . [or] have a child they do not want. Each choice is unacceptable." Planned Parenthood materials contended that the Hyde Amendment had "the practical effect of preventing nearly all poor women from obtaining a safe and legal abortion."[89]

Second, supporters of abortion rights argued that funding bans cost women the religious freedom to make their own moral or spiritual choices about abortion. According to this claim, Congress intended the Hyde Amendment to impose abortion opponents' religious beliefs on women, health care providers, and taxpayers who believed that abortion was an ethical choice. The Religious Coalition for Abortion Rights (RCAR), an interfaith abortion-rights group founded in 1973, put out a pamphlet arguing that the Hyde Amendment violated the "right of religious freedom by limiting the right of poor women to follow their own consciences."[90]

The abortion-rights movement attacked the Hyde Amendment in court as well as in Congress. But as the case that would become *Harris v. McRae* made its way to the Supreme Court, hostility to the welfare state deepened. Resentment about public assistance programs had been visible for almost a decade, but in the late 1970s, a flurry of high-profile tax protests made the issue national news. It was no surprise that the most famous took aim at the housing market. As inflation drove up prices, steep property taxes caused some to lose their homes.[91]

In California, voters weighed a property tax cap of 1 percent of the fair market value of a home. Howard Jarvis, a wealthy former factory owner and devotee of Republican politics, had campaigned for property tax reform since 1966, but in 1978, his campaign gained unprecedented momentum. He joined forces with Paul Gann, a retired car and real estate salesman, to get enough signatures to put Proposition 13 on the ballot.[92] Jarvis argued that it was unfair that property taxes paid for "welfare, food stamps, and illegal aliens."[93]

When Proposition 13 passed by the stunning margin of two to one, similar efforts gathered steam in states from Massachusetts to Michigan. The Proposition 13 campaign did not directly alter the course of debate about the Hyde Amendment. But as tax protests spread across the country, anger about the welfare state colored fights about abortion funding. As politicians and voters cast blame on welfare recipients, it became harder for abortion-rights supporters to explain how the Hyde Amendment both contributed to poverty and shaped poor women's experiences. The Court's opinions reflected a wider belief that poor people, not the government, were responsible for their own plight.[94]

In 1980, the Supreme Court confronted the constitutionality of the Hyde Amendment itself. Abortion-rights attorneys had to explain how their constitutional claims differed from ones already rejected in *Maher*. The current version of the Hyde Amendment did ban funding for medically necessary procedures, while the law the Court upheld in *Maher* allowed for reimbursement in such cases. While attorneys could distinguish the Hyde Amendment and the Connecticut law that the Court upheld in *Maher*, abortion-rights attorneys had to reckon with how deeply attitudes about welfare had changed.

HARRIS V. MCRAE AND THE RIGHT TO BE LEFT ALONE

For the first time in decades, abortion-rights supporters dreaded a return to the Supreme Court. *Maher* seemed to spell trouble for those fighting the Hyde Amendment. There, the Court had said that some funding and facilities bans did not unduly burden women's rights. Abortion-rights attorneys had to find a way to distinguish the Hyde Amendment from the laws upheld in *Maher* and its companion cases. But there had not yet been full-scale retreat from *Roe*. *Colautti v. Franklin*, a 1979 case, struck down a provision requiring physicians to use abortion techniques most likely to result in a live birth in cases in which a child was or might be viable. The Court agreed with the challengers that the law was impermissibly vague and invalidated it.[95]

The Court's latest decision on parental involvement laws, *Bellotti v. Baird II* (1979), also suggested that *Maher* might not have started a broader trend. The case concerned a Massachusetts law requiring most minors to obtain the consent of both parents before getting an abortion. In 1976, the Court had asked the highest court in Massachusetts to clarify the meaning of the law. Three years later, when *Bellotti* returned to the Court, a majority struck it down, reasoning that the law "would impose an undue burden upon the exercise by minors of the right to seek an abortion." Although *Bellotti II* involved a very different kind of law, the Court's decision made it seem possible that the undue burden language in *Maher* might have some bite, even in contexts like parental involvement, in which abortion restrictions were popular.[96]

Colautti and *Bellotti* notwithstanding, it was still hard to explain away the Court's earlier decisions on abortion funding. That task fell to attorneys Rhonda Copelon and Sylvia Law. The two had been part of a circle of lawyers plotting an attack on the Hyde Amendment. Attorneys filed suit in states across the country, but it was Copelon and Law's New York case that ultimately went up to the Supreme Court. Both women took the issue of religion in the antiabortion movement head on. Not all of their colleagues agreed with this tactical approach. In Massachusetts, for example, Nancy Gertner and John Reinstein worried that religion-based arguments would anger Catholics who were undecided about the abortion issue. But Copelon and Law recognized that *Maher* and its companion cases had not left them too many choices.[97]

Copelon and Law reinvigorated the undue burden standard. Their brief reiterated that under *Maher*, courts had to weigh the burdens of a law against any results it delivered. Copelon and Law argued that while the amendment had no legitimate purpose, it created burdens far heavier than anything the Court considered in *Maher*. Because the Hyde Amendment made no exception for many medically necessary abortions, lawmakers "forced some women to carry health threatening pregnancies to term, with consequent aggravation of often precarious conditions."[98]

Copelon and Law also suggested that the Hyde Amendment impermissibly mixed the church in the business of the state. Under the Establishment Clause of the First Amendment, the government could not elevate one religion over another. Copelon and Law argued that the Hyde Amendment was unconstitutional partly because the Roman Catholic Church "played a significant part in bringing about Congressional legislation on [abortion funding]." While acknowledging the religious diversity of abortion foes, Copelon and Law nonetheless asserted that the movement as a whole – and the Hyde Amendment – enforced a form of "shared religious conviction."[99]

Copelon and Law further claimed that the Hyde Amendment violated the Free Exercise Clause of the First Amendment. That provision spoke to Americans' liberty to practice or believe in any religion or no religion at all. Copelon and Law reminded the Court that some women's faith led them to end their pregnancies. And yet the Hyde Amendment ignored these conscience-based objections while honoring others. They claimed that efforts to protect taxpayers' conscience sent a powerful message. "The statement," they wrote, "is not that some taxpayers believe that abortion is wrong, but rather that abortion is so clearly wrong that Congress can insist that poor women conform their conduct to these moral views by destroying existing Medicaid entitlement."[100]

NOW's amicus brief elaborated on this argument. According to NOW, the government had helped to make women poor by ignoring both the "sex bias that pervades educational institutions and job training programs" and the "occupational segregation and the wage gap between men and women." By refusing to help women and people of color who had been past victims of legal discrimination, the government rigged the game. "The pervasive sex discrimination in education and job training programs, particularly those specifically aimed at helping the poor achieve economic independence, serves to reinforce the indigent woman's poverty," NOW asserted.[101]

Those defending the Hyde Amendment saw *Maher*'s undue burden language quite differently. James Bopp Jr., NRLC's recently named general counsel, had embraced conservatism for as long as he could remember, cofounding a chapter of the Teen Republicans in Vigo County, Indiana. Bopp's father, a doctor, was very conservative and made politics a frequent topic of discussion at the dinner table. In high school, Bopp fell in love with the art of argument and dropped football to focus on the debate team. Returning to his home state after a stint in Florida for law school, Bopp began working as a prosecutor. He fell into an NRLC job almost by coincidence when a local activist recommended him for a job at one of the organization's affiliates, and he rose quickly through the ranks. *McRae* was in some ways a perfect case for Bopp, bringing together his suspicion of big government with his commitment to the pro-life cause.[102]

NRLC officials asked Bopp to explain the possible outcomes in *McRae*, and he suggested that the case turned almost entirely on how the Court defined an undue burden. Bopp made the same argument in an amicus curiae brief submitted to the Court. In a brief submitted on behalf of Representative Hyde and other pro-life legislators, AUL similarly contended that the Hyde Amendment created no burden heavy enough to violate the Constitution. The government did not make women poor, and poverty, not the Hyde Amendment, made it impossible for those women to get abortions. "The privacy right is a right to be free from unduly burdensome state interference in seeking an abortion," AUL asserted. "This right is not altered by the reason for which the abortion is sought, whether that reason is purely 'elective' or whether it is because the abortion is believed [to be] 'medically necessary.'"[103] According to AUL, a failure to fund a poor woman's decision was not a penalty. Nor could poor women blame the government for their inability to afford abortions. "The government has no obligation to fund even the most 'basic economic needs' in any case," AUL contended.[104]

In June 1980, when the Court issued a decision in *Harris v. McRae*, the attack on the welfare state seemed hard to stop. Ronald Reagan, the California governor who had long pledged to eliminate most of the social safety net, became the presumptive nominee of the Republican Party in the upcoming presidential election. Reagan's rise heralded the growing popularity of small-government politics.[105]

Voters certainly harbored doubts about the trustworthiness of government. Starting in the mid-1970s, polls established that government corruption consistently ranked toward the top of the list of public concerns. The reasons for the loss of faith in government were not hard to find. Media coverage of the Vietnam War convinced many voters that politicians had lied about the costs of war and the prospects of victory. In 1973, the press broke the news that members of President Nixon's reelection campaign had broken into the Democratic National Committee headquarters in Washington, DC, to steal documents and plant microphones. Top Nixon aides had also participated in a cover-up. The Watergate scandal, as it became known, contributed to declining belief in the government. In 1964, 77 percent of Americans agreed that they could trust the government most of the time. By the end of the 1970s, less than a quarter of respondents felt the same way.[106] As

Americans lost faith in the government, Reagan's proposals gained popularity. Neoliberalism did not begin with Reagan, but public support for free markets, low taxes, deregulation, and the withdrawal of government from many areas of public life grew exponentially in the 1970s.[107]

The Court seemed equally skeptical of the welfare state. The Court upheld both the federal law and, in *Williams v. Zbaraz*, a similar law from Illinois. In a five-to-four decision on the Hyde Amendment, the Court in *Harris v. McRae* rejected the argument that the Hyde Amendment violated the Establishment Clause because the law was "as much a reflection of traditionalist values, as an embodiment of the views of any particular religion." The Court found even less value in Copelon and Law's free-exercise claim, reasoning that those challenging the law did not have the standing to bring suit.[108]

The majority also expanded on the logic of *Maher*. The Court noted that the Hyde Amendment placed "no governmental obstacle in the path of a woman choosing to terminate her pregnancy but ... encourages an alternative." It was not important that the amendment restricted funding for medically necessary abortions. What mattered, as *McRae* explained, was that the poor had no right to financial support that they were unable or unwilling to secure for themselves.[109]

McRae made arguments about the costs of abortion restrictions an important part of constitutional doctrine. The Court insisted that there had been no retreat from *Roe*. But the existence of the abortion right had not resolved the issue in *McRae*. Instead, the majority asked why and to what extent poor women could actually obtain abortions. *McRae* suggested that clashing movements would have to make claims about the real-world effects of both abortion and laws regulating it.

IN THE AFTERMATH OF *MCRAE*

After *McRae*, abortion opponents hoped that they had finally found a tactical plan that would work while their movement sought to change the Constitution. In the short term, though, the fate of the Hyde Amendment reflected increasing disapproval of the welfare state. Following his election, Reagan took several major steps to shrink welfare programs, tightening AFDC eligibility requirements, cutting benefits, imposing work requirements, and defining a far narrower category of poor people deserving assistance.[110]

Abortion-rights supporters pleaded with donors to create an alternative to government funding. In 1981, only fourteen states continued funding abortions, a number that changed very little in the next several decades (in 2019, for example, fifteen states provided public funding for all or most medically necessary abortions). Even before *Roe*, in states where abortion was legal, Planned Parenthood offered abortion services for a sliding-scale fee based on need. More affiliates adopted this model after *McRae*. In the early 1980s, feminists also set up funds to help poor women pay for abortions. By 1987, two dozen such funds operated in cities across the country.

While getting help from small donors and foundations, fund operators often did not have enough money to help all the women who requested assistance.[111]

Meanwhile, as they solidified a partnership with the GOP, abortion foes more often denounced welfare programs. In the summer of 1980, James Bopp Jr. and Marlene Elwell of NRLC had successfully promoted strong antiabortion language in the Republican platform. The emerging Religious Right aided the two activists in their cause. Starting in the late 1970s, organizations like Christian Voice and the Moral Majority mobilized conservative evangelical Protestants. The Religious Right urged evangelicals, many of whom had been politically disengaged, to vote based on moral issues like opposition to abortion and gay rights. During the 1980 presidential race, conservative evangelicals joined Catholics in a new antiabortion coalition. For some abortion foes, the partnership with the GOP was never inevitable. Many pro-lifers, including Elwell herself, were registered Democrats, and some took liberal positions on important issues of the day. But as Republicans increasingly took a stand against abortion, the Democratic platform stated that "a woman has a right to choose when and whether to have a child." While parties' positions on abortion diverged, an alliance with the Republican Party seemed to be the only realistic choice for pro-lifers. From that standpoint, the 1980 election was a major triumph. The Republican Party gained thirty-four seats in the House and took control of the Senate. *National Right to Life News* crowed that "the pro-abortionists were left in shambles."[112]

Following the Republicans' electoral triumph, abortion foes planned to relaunch their constitutional campaign. But in the short term, some in the antiabortion movement believed that Henry Hyde had unknowingly forged a blueprint for some pro-life work. NRLC leaders initially promoted the Abortion Funding Proscription Act, a law that would have made permanent the funding ban created by the Hyde Amendment (because that provision was part of an appropriations bill, Congress had to renew it annually and could theoretically undo it). James Bopp Jr. acknowledged that the law did not outlaw any abortions. However, he still praised the act as "the most significant piece of legislation in Congress thus far suggested on abortion." Why were NRLC leaders so enthusiastic about a law that Dr. John C. Willke, then the president of NRLC, acknowledged would "have no effect on private killing"? Willke had a clear answer: The act was "as far as Congress can go ... through a statute that has a reasonable chance of being upheld by the Supreme Court." Moreover, as Willke and Bopp saw it, there was something to be said for winning soon. "A victory here will not only save countless babies' lives," Willke wrote. "It will gain us more support for our cause." Pro-lifers could promote incremental restrictions and emphasize arguments about the costs of legal abortion.[113]

Bopp and Willke began to articulate a new vision for the pro-life movement. Rather than a single-minded quest to change the Constitution, abortion foes would embrace realistic goals. By restricting abortion as much as the Supreme Court would allow, pro-lifers could prove their worth to new strategic partners in the

GOP. And by convincing the Court to uphold some restrictions, Bopp and Willke hoped to buy time for a constitutional amendment.

But the Abortion Funding Proscription Act went nowhere, and in the next several years, the strategy that Bopp and Willke described proved more controversial within the antiabortion movement than either could have anticipated. Pro-lifers clashed about whether restrictions would ever lead to a complete abortion ban – and even about whether bans should make exceptions for rape and incest, a threat to a woman's life or health, or fetal abnormality. Some ridiculed the idea that arguments about the policy costs of abortion would change anyone's mind about an unborn child's right to life. A strategy centered on the costs and benefits of abortion splintered the antiabortion movement.

For abortion-rights supporters, *Maher* and *McRae* provided just the first signal that the Court would no longer reliably protect abortion rights. Those who thought that *Roe* had put an end to the abortion conflict could not have been more wrong. Indeed, as incremental abortion restrictions proliferated, those in larger abortion-rights groups had a sense of déjà vu. Just as before *Roe*, poor, often nonwhite women often had trouble navigating restrictions and either delayed having abortions or brought pregnancies to term. To challenge the new status quo, the leaders of larger groups planned to explain not only why women had an abortion right but also why those rights had crucial benefits for women.

BEYOND THE WELFARE DEBATE

In the 1970s, many associated the abortion wars with two clashing constitutional rights: a woman's right to terminate her pregnancy and a fetus's right to life. After *Roe* came down, many in the abortion-rights movement believed that the political and legal struggle was safely in hand, but access to care was still an issue. Groups like the ACLU, NOW, and NARAL developed model plans for freestanding clinics and guidelines for doctors who wanted to perform abortions. To expand the availability of abortion services, abortion-rights lawyers in the ACLU RFP challenged the constitutionality of laws banning the use of public dollars for abortion and sued to force hospitals to allow abortions in their facilities. Antiabortion groups primarily pursued a constitutional amendment that would recognize fetal personhood and outlaw abortion nationwide.

The battle about abortion funding sent the debate in a different direction. While waiting for progress on a constitutional amendment, pro-lifers got behind a proposal to outlaw Medicaid reimbursement for abortion. Pro-lifers recognized that fetal-rights arguments did not work well for funding bans since these laws did not outlaw any abortions. To justify funding prohibitions, abortion opponents pointed to what abortion foes saw as their policy benefits (and the costs of legal abortion).

Over the course of the 1970s, the evolving abortion wars reflected a more general disillusionment with the welfare state. During the debate about the Hyde

Amendment, pro-lifers advocated for taxpayers with conscientious objections to abortion. As anger about the welfare state peaked, supporters of abortion rights suggested that the government stacked the deck against women, people of color, and the poor in a way that made poverty much harder to avoid.

In court, borrowing from undue burden language in the Court's opinions, abortion-rights attorneys explained that what mattered was how a law operated in the real world. These lawyers reasoned that if a law had the purpose or effect of punishing poor women, the law violated the Constitution. Pro-lifers successfully countered that poor women's struggle was a consequence of poverty, not of laws like the Hyde Amendment.

The Hyde Amendment struggle fundamentally reoriented the abortion wars. Limiting access to abortion allowed pro-lifers to flex their political muscle and prevent some women from ending their pregnancies. The Hyde Amendment campaign also convinced some pro-lifers of the potential of arguments about the policy costs of abortion. After pro-lifers gave up on a constitutional amendment, these claims took on even more importance. Rather than serving as a temporary solution, abortion restrictions became central to the campaign to overturn *Roe*.

As the battle focused more often on the policy costs and benefits of abortion, neither movement surrendered its commitment to a fundamental constitutional principle. But the course of the conflict proved far less predictable than many would have anticipated, reflecting differing beliefs about everything from the delivery of health care to the future of marriage. The decades after *Roe* revealed that those on opposing sides even disagreed about what counted as a cost or a benefit, either for women or for the country as a whole.

3

Launching a Quest to Reverse *Roe*

In the first part of the 1980s, Paige Comstock Cunningham and Judy Goldsmith saw the abortion debate become a battle about the fate of *Roe v. Wade*. Cunningham joined a new generation of antiabortion lawyers convinced that they had found a better way to advance their cause. Both her parents were Republican, conservative, and involved in missionary work. As Cunningham still puts it, in her mother's Iowa farm town, "Democrat was a dirty word." As a young woman, however, she did not think much about abortion. In college, if anyone asked her, Cunningham would have said that she would never have an abortion herself but that the decision might be right for some people. But at law school at Northwestern, she took constitutional law from Victor Rosenblum, a leading member of Americans United for Life (AUL). Rosenblum's class changed her mind, and she became a lifelong opponent of abortion. By June 1983, she became AUL's executive director and general counsel.[1]

Cunningham considered herself a feminist and thought that society failed its obligations to mothers. In her view, as long as the "responsibilities of pregnancy and childbirth and childbearing fell only on women," there would be no real equality between the sexes. Later, she would favor federal legislation protecting women from domestic violence, and she worked at AUL even after the birth of her three children. But Cunningham, like many pro-lifers, believed that moving beyond single-issue politics was dangerous for a diverse movement. And she thought that the attack on *Roe* in the courts, not the fight for a constitutional amendment, was the antiabortion movement's future. In chipping away at *Roe*, Cunningham and her allies publicized a film, *The Silent Scream*, that pro-lifers claimed depicted a real abortion.[2]

In the early 1980s, Judy Goldsmith, a veteran member of the National Organization for Women (NOW), found herself caught up in the maelstrom created by *The Silent Scream*. Goldsmith's interest in women's issues stemmed from the challenges of her childhood. She was born poor in Sheboygan Falls, Wisconsin, and things got harder after her mother and father separated. At one point, Goldsmith's family had to live in a converted chicken coop with no running water or indoor plumbing.[3]

Even though her mother eventually got a factory job and joined a union, Goldsmith's family still struggled financially. Her mother once had so little money that she could not afford to buy her children shoes for the new school year. She took a bus to the town where her estranged husband worked and asked the factory manager for a portion of his paycheck. The manager told Goldsmith's mother to ask her husband directly. When she did, he told her that shoes or not, the money was his, and none of the children would see a penny of it. Goldsmith would never forget this experience, and she spent much of her career trying to help women like her mother.[4]

Goldsmith got involved with NOW after completing her master's degree. After holding local- and state-level jobs, she took on positions in NOW's national leadership in Washington. She became the organization's leader in 1982.[5] After taking the helm at NOW, Goldsmith and her organization focused more often on the abortion issue, especially after *The Silent Scream* made headlines. Goldsmith insisted that if *The Silent Scream* asked what abortion really involved, viewers should ask the women who had benefitted from the procedure.[6]

Cunningham and Goldsmith witnessed a fundamental change in the focus of the abortion wars. Rather than fighting about a constitutional antiabortion amendment, both sides sought to determine the fate of *Roe v. Wade*. At first, following the Republican victory in the 1980 election, pro-lifers relished the chance to change the text of the Constitution. But even after an impressive electoral win, abortion opponents lacked the votes in Congress to push through an absolute ban. Republicans proposed several alternatives, including a statute defining the fetus as a rights-holding person and a constitutional amendment allowing (but not requiring) the states to outlaw abortion. The fight about which of these options deserved support ripped the antiabortion movement apart. Absolutists, many of them Catholic grass-roots activists, contended that Americans would never vote to ban abortion unless pro-lifers defended fetal rights. As absolutists saw it, arguments about the policy costs of abortion were a damaging distraction. Pragmatists insisted that access limits deserved support because they would withstand constitutional challenge, lower abortion rates, and set the stage for a challenge to *Roe v. Wade*. And pragmatists saw value in spotlighting the negative policy consequences of abortion. After all, fetal-rights arguments had not worked with voters, Congress, or the Court. If Americans believed that the costs of abortion were too high, new political and constitutional opportunities might still open up.[7]

Because of internal divisions, neither major antiabortion proposal passed, and by 1983, pro-lifers were at a crossroads. In the mid-1980s, as many evangelical Protestants mobilized, some favored protest over litigation and lobbying. Antiabortion extremists, some of them connected to anti-government militias, gave up on ending abortion through the law and launched violent attacks on abortion clinics. But larger organizations like NRLC and AUL remained dominant in antiabortion circles, and many newly mobilized evangelicals joined them. These pro-lifers changed their movement's near-term goal. Instead of amending the Constitution, abortion foes would ensure that the Court overturned *Roe*. To achieve this objective, groups like NRLC and AUL fought to influence presidential elections and Supreme Court selections. And to create a perfect test case, these activists promoted incremental restrictions designed to lower abortion rates, often emphasizing claims about the toll abortion took on the country.[8]

Abortion-rights groups no longer simply invoked the virtues of choice, no matter how little such arguments might speak to donors or ambivalent voters. In the media and in lobbying, larger groups more often detailed what they described as the benefits of abortion for women. Before *Roe*, women had sometimes shared their stories, but in the mid-1980s, groups such as NARAL, Planned Parenthood, and NOW collected and shared the testimony of women willing to explain how abortion had improved their lives.[9]

In court, abortion foes tried to whittle away at abortion rights by making claims about the procedure's medical, economic, and social effects. In defending a model ordinance from Akron, Ohio, abortion foes contended that restrictions were constitutional if they helped women rather than hurting them. Some abortion-rights attorneys urged the Court to apply the strictest form of judicial scrutiny to any abortion regulation. But recognizing the Court's willingness to uphold some abortion laws, other supporters of reproductive rights proposed a far more exacting interpretation of an undue burden, arguing for the invalidation of most laws that meaningfully limited abortion access.

Over the course of the next several decades, larger antiabortion groups made the future of *Roe* the defining issue in the conflict. Strangely, although both sides became preoccupied by a single Supreme Court decision, rights-based arguments sometimes faded into the background. The prominence of rights-based claims often depended less on the Court than on what larger organizations thought would work on election day or during discussions with prospective donors.

Nor did the conflict deescalate at times when the parties put less emphasis on rights-based claims. As those on opposing sides fought about the costs and benefits of abortion, it became clear that disagreements in the abortion conflict reached beyond questions about reproduction and even gender. Clashing activists held different views about everything from the future of the medical profession to the role of government. Rather than illuminating possible common ground, arguments about the policy costs and benefits of abortion made compromise even more unimaginable.

THE AKRON ALTERNATIVE

Even while holding out hope for a constitutional amendment, antiabortion lawyers were already on the hunt for laws that would limit abortion rights. Attorneys like James Bopp Jr. of NRLC and Dennis Horan of AUL took special interest in an ordinance introduced several years earlier in Akron, Ohio. As early as 1973, pro-life lawyers had developed similar model laws, including a Missouri law partly struck down by the Supreme Court in *Planned Parenthood of Central Missouri v. Danforth* (1976). There, the Court upheld a law requiring a woman to sign a consent form before a physician could perform an abortion. Describing women's abortion decision as "stressful," Justice Harry Blackmun, the author of *Roe*, concluded that it would be "desirable and imperative that [the choice] be made with full knowledge of its nature and consequences."[10]

It was significant that the Court had upheld any abortion regulation, but this one captivated abortion foes. In using informed consent laws, pro-lifers hoped to convince women not to choose abortion by detailing what abortion opponents described as the physical and psychological costs of the procedure. And by presenting judges with the same information, pro-lifers could erode support for abortion rights while biding their time for a constitutional amendment. The Akron ordinance served as a model for similar restrictions nationwide. The rise of these model laws crystallized the importance of arguments about the costs of abortion.

After the Akron city council approved a second trimester hospitalization requirement but voted down other proposed abortion restrictions in 1976, pro-lifers proposed a more comprehensive ordinance. Akron activists tapped into a strategy developed by national organizations like NRLC. By convincing legislators and judges that abortion was harmful, pro-lifers hoped to justify broad restrictions even if the Court still theoretically protected fundamental rights. Jane Hubbard, the President of the Greater Akron Right to Life Society, insisted that the law's aim was "to ensure that a woman who decides to abort her child will have ... scientifically and medically accurate information: that the child she aborts is alive and growing, and the procedure may cause her physical or psychological harm." Marvin Weinberger, one of the leaders of Citizens for Informed Consent, reinforced this point. "We are not trying to cause guilt feelings," he told the *New York Times*. "All we are giving [women] are the biological facts." The mandatory counseling provision provided a perfect vehicle for claims about the costs of abortion.[11]

The Akron model ordinance also had the potential to stop most abortions after the first trimester of pregnancy. The law required that after that point, all abortions be performed in a hospital. The regulation fit well in a strategy based on claims about the costs of abortion. Pro-lifers stressed the relative dangers of later abortions and what they described as the lower quality of care available in freestanding clinics. In practice, however, the regulation could eliminate access for many women seeking later abortions. In 1973, more than half of all abortions took place in hospitals. By 1980, that number had dropped to 22 percent, and the decline showed no sign of stopping. Roy Lucas, one of the attorneys who had argued for abortion rights in *Roe*, wrote his colleagues that "[t]he worst outcome in 1983 could be a decision allowing extensive overregulation of abortion clinics and banning second trimester abortions except in a few hospitals."[12]

In 1978, James Bopp Jr. of NRLC got involved with the Akron case notwith-standing the financial turmoil engulfing his organization. The fight for the Hyde Amendment had been more expensive than many anticipated, and NRLC members believed that the spending habits of Mildred Jefferson, the organization's charis-matic president, had put the organization in a bigger hole. During NRLC's 1978 internal election, Jefferson lost both her seat on the board of directors and the presidency. Her divorce from NRLC was messy. After quitting, she founded her own organization, Right to Life Crusade (RLC), and retained NRLC's former fundraiser, James Bothell, Inc. Bothell, in turn, claimed that NRLC had breached its contract with the fundraiser and got a court order preventing NRLC from using its donor list. The Bothell litigation posed an almost existential threat to the nation's largest pro-life organization. Without access to its donor list, NRLC would have struggled to continue functioning. A sympathetic attorney managed to get a copy of the list to NRLC, and NRLC President, John Willke, paid out of pocket for a fundraising campaign. Just the same, the financial picture for NRLC was bleak.[13]

Even if resources were scarce, Bopp felt obligated to defend the Akron law. Leading antiabortion academics had helped to write the ordinance, and pro-life attorneys advocating for it highlighted new claims about the costs of abortion. "This case will probably prove to be the most significant case involving abortion regulation this year," Bopp wrote to the group's Legal Liaison Committee. "This is true not only because of the extensive publicity that the passage of this ordinance has engendered, but also because [m]any states and localities are considering the adoption of this ordinance."[14]

Why did Bopp put so much on the line for an ordinance that affected only one town in northeast Ohio? For several years, attorneys working with AUL and NRLC had envisioned a sneak attack on *Roe*. The Akron ordinance offered a glimpse of how this strategy could work outside the context of abortion funding. Instead of talking so much about the right to life, pro-lifers hoped to create more uncertainty about what abortion was really like – and how much women really knew about it. By arguing about the costs of abortion, pro-lifers planned to whittle away at abortion rights while the fight for a constitutional amendment continued.

Abortion-rights supporters recognized that a different kind of strategy would be needed to defuse the threat posed by the ordinance. Cheryl Swain, a feminist from Akron, began by disputing the factual claims by local antiabortion activists.[15] She had communicated with state and national abortion-rights organizations to coordin-ate opposition to the ordinance. The ordinance had become a national news sensation. Sit-ins, film screenings, and demonstrations rocked Swain's town. The passions on both sides reflected the importance of the ordinance to the national debate. Recognizing that pro-lifers planned to use the statute as a "national precedent," Swain told Jane Hodgson, a Minnesota obstetrician-gynecologist and leading figure in the abortion-rights movement, that the ordinance would "severely limit the availability of abortion as well as psychologically intimidate women."[16]

In her testimony before the Akron city council, Hodgson tried to pick apart the claims made by the informed consent regulation. "Psychological studies have failed to show any more effects from abortion such as depression and suicide than would occur from compulsory child bearing," she asserted. Hodgson also offered advice to lawmakers on how to separate real from phony evidence. She pleaded with council members to rely on organizations of experts, like the American Public Health Association, in knowing where the truth lay.[17]

Hodgson and her colleagues faced a new challenge: how to get everyone to agree on the same facts. In defending a woman's right to choose, abortion-rights supporters had stressed that there was no universal truth when it came to the rights and wrongs of abortion. While pro-lifers defended what they described as moral absolutes, larger abortion-rights groups contended that there was more than one legitimate way to understand the ethics of ending a pregnancy. But as pro-lifers highlighted claims about the costs of the procedure, abortion-rights supporters like Hodgson rejected relativistic arguments. But how would abortion-rights advocates establish consensus about the facts about abortion? This challenge would both define the Akron struggle and continue well after that battle had ended.

THE AKRON LITIGATION BEGINS

At the end of February 1978, when the city council passed the Akron ordinance, other states and cities rushed to do the same. By 1979, eleven states had introduced similar legislation.[18] The ACLU Reproductive Freedom Project (RFP) challenged the Akron ordinance, and James Bopp Jr. represented antiabortion intervenors.[19]

In court, pro-life attorneys moved away from claims about fundamental rights, insisting that reasonable people disagreed about the basic facts of abortion. As early as the 1960s, abortion foes had put on slideshows showing viewers images of aborted fetuses. But the Akron litigation encouraged abortion opponents both to put new emphasis on claims about the costs of abortion and to explain their constitutional relevance. Lawyers defending the Akron law planned to prove "[t]he development of the fetus as human life" and the "trauma" women suffered when "they [found] out they had killed a human." While ACLU attorneys argued that the law would cost women much needed pay, put jobs at risk, and make an already stressful experience more painful, Bopp and his colleagues emphasized that current statistics on post-abortion complications were unreliable. ACLU witnesses reasoned that the law traumatized women, while pro-life lawyers put on testimony suggesting that abortion itself was to blame for any trauma. The ordinance presented a woman "with facts pertinent to the momentous decision she is about to make, facts she should have so that she can deal with them before she acts," wrote one supporter. "Should she find them out only after acting, then truly she may be burdened by guilt, since she can never undo what she has already done."[20]

Following the trial, Judge Leroy Contie Jr. struck down some parts of the Akron ordinance and upheld several others, including the second trimester requirement. In 1979, the Sixth Circuit Court of Appeals concluded that the entire ordinance was unconstitutional. Lawyers for the city initially seemed inclined to give up, but to the surprise of many, asked the Supreme Court to hear the case in the fall of 1981.[21]

By that time, the Court's composition had changed. In July 1981, Potter Stewart announced his retirement from the Court. While Stewart had written the majority in *Maher*, an abortion-funding case, he had also joined the Court's opinion in *Roe*. Abortion foes did not know what to expect from Reagan's Supreme Court nominee, Sandra Day O'Connor. Indeed, after news broke about her nomination, rumors ran rampant that she had supported abortion rights during her time in the Arizona legislature and would do the same on the Court. Some pro-lifers vigorously protested her nomination before the president reassured them. Nevertheless, for abortion opponents, O'Connor's elevation at least made progress seem possible in the Court as well as in Congress.[22]

In the short term, the Court seemed unlikely to turn its back on *Roe*. But even if the courts defended abortion rights in the early 1980s, abortion foes could still dispute the facts about how regulations worked and whether they helped women. Perhaps pro-lifers could persuade justices supportive of abortion rights to sign off on regulations said to make women safer or more informed. Such laws could lower the abortion rate, demonstrate the savvy of antiabortion lawyers, and sow confusion in abortion jurisprudence. While this strategy certainly had untapped potential, pro-lifers had yet to encounter its downsides. If abortion foes still believed that the right to life was a constitutional and moral absolute, contesting the costs and benefits of abortion did only so much. While abortion restrictions multiplied, pro-lifers still searched for a way to convince Americans to endorse a right to life. Claims about the costs of abortion, it seemed, might not do the job.

A RENEWED PUSH FOR A CONSTITUTIONAL AMENDMENT

As the Akron case made its way through the courts, pro-lifers gradually gave up on their dream of amending the Constitution. Ironically, the prospects for an antiabortion amendment faded in the early 1980s not because pro-lifers had lost control of the government but because they could not agree on which law Congress should pass. On the surface, the fight pitted pragmatism against principle. Pragmatists generally preferred the Hatch Amendment, a constitutional proposal that would undo *Roe* and allow individual states to make their own decisions about abortion. Absolutists more often supported the Human Life Bill, a federal statute declaring that personhood began at fertilization.

The debate about the Hatch Amendment and Human Life Bill revealed a profound fracture in the antiabortion movement. Those in groups like NRLC and AUL contended that abortion foes should promote only laws, like the Hatch

Amendment, that would aid political allies and survive in the courts. Pragmatists also planned to stress arguments, like those involving the costs of abortion, calculated to appeal to ambivalent politicians, voters, and justices, even if those claims did not involve the right to life. Absolutists like Judie Brown of American Life League (ALL) countered that claims about the costs of abortion would never convince Americans to endorse an outright abortion ban. Absolutists opposed most exceptions to abortion bans and urged abortion foes to settle for nothing less than the complete criminalization of abortion, even at the expense of immediate progress.

These disagreements were not apparent immediately after the 1980 election. NRLC leaders recognized that they did not have enough votes in Congress for an outright abortion ban, but some antiabortion attorneys believed that lawmakers might adopt something almost as good. Stephen Galebach, a young lawyer at the Christian Legal Society, drafted an article in the *Human Life Review*, a pro-life journal, arguing that Congress had the authority to pass a federal statute banning abortion. Galebach's proposal caught the attention of Senator Jesse Helms (R–NC), who introduced what he called the Human Life Bill in January 1981. By treating unborn children as legal persons from the moment of conception, the bill functionally outlawed abortion. Skeptics argued that Congress did not have the constitutional authority to pass the bill. Helms relied on Section Five of the Fourteenth Amendment, which gave Congress some power to enforce the amendment. Galebach argued that under Section Five, Congress could recognize fetal rights even if the Supreme Court had never done so. Many, including critics of *Roe*, disagreed, suggesting that Congress could at most remedy violations of rights clearly established by the Court.[23]

David N. O'Steen, a leading NRLC member, offered his own view about what should be done immediately. Although O'Steen was not a lawyer, he insisted that the Human Life Bill was "ultimately doomed to fail before the Supreme Court." He advised pro-lifers to back a two-step strategy. First, abortion opponents would pass a constitutional amendment allowing (but not requiring) Congress and the states to ban abortions. Pro-lifers could then campaign in the states to ban abortion. As public attitudes shifted, the argument went, it would be much easier to introduce a constitutional abortion ban. In October 1981, Senator Orrin Hatch (R–UT) introduced an amendment patterned on O'Steen's proposal.[24]

The debate about the Hatch Amendment exposed deep fissures in the antiabortion movement. Some cracks had been visible since the later 1970s. Judie Brown, the former executive director of NRLC, quit and formed American Life League (ALL) in 1979 with seed money from New Right leader Richard Viguerie. Unlike larger pro-life groups, ALL presented itself as a faith-based, Catholic organization and openly opposed birth control, sex-education programs, and homosexuality. Joseph Scheidler, a former member of Illinois Right to Life, formed the Pro-Life Action League, a group committed to more confrontational tactics and arguments. While absolutists like Brown and Scheidler questioned the strategies pursued by groups like NRLC, antiabortion extremists insisted that legal and legislative strategies would never be enough. These militants captured the nation's attention in 1982 when three "men identified with a group called the Army of God" kidnapped an abortion provider, Hector Zevallos, and his wife, Rosalie Jean, and held them prisoner for eight days. Although the Army of God would not make headlines again for several years, the rise of violent extremists further highlighted tensions within the antiabortion movement.[25]

Debate about the Hatch Amendment would open a far deeper wound in the antiabortion movement. For almost a decade, NRLC and AUL had promoted incremental restrictions with little criticism, even from absolutist groups. As pragmatists rallied around the Hatch Amendment, however, absolutists expressed grave concern about the priorities that their movement had embraced for years. Absolutists concluded that by focusing so much on what courts and voters would tolerate, groups like NRLC had set themselves up to fail.

THE HATCH AMENDMENT CONTROVERSY

During the Hatch Amendment debate, absolutists began to second-guess a strategy based on claims about the costs of abortion. As absolutists realized, if the Hatch Amendment became part of the Constitution, most states would not quickly criminalize all or most abortions. More likely would be the kind of access restrictions that groups like NRLC and AUL had refined. And absolutists increasingly believed that these incremental laws would never lead to an abortion ban. Hoping to make headway inside and outside of court, those arguing for the Hatch Amendment (and for access limits) did not always discuss fetal rights. Absolutists increasingly saw this argumentative plan as cowardly and counterproductive. Brown and her allies asserted that any abortion was unacceptable, and the antiabortion movement still had to prioritize arguments about the right to life.[26]

Even within NRLC, roughly half of the organization's board denounced the Hatch Amendment. By December 1981, when a divided NRLC endorsed it, ALL came out in favor of the Human Life Bill. Brown and her followers maintained that arguments about the costs of abortion would not change American attitudes about fetal rights. "We cannot join any group of individuals who believe that regulation of abortion is an acceptable path for the pro-life movement to follow," she explained.[27] Brown spoke for pro-lifers who believed that talking about the policy costs of abortion was simply not enough. If pro-lifers did not emphasize arguments about a right to life, how did they expect anyone to care about it? "If we educate enough people on the issue of abortion, then they will become as inflamed over the wholesale murder of millions of innocent children as we are," she wrote. Some NRLC leaders agreed with Brown, demanding that John Willke, the organization's president, step down because of his support for the Hatch Amendment.[28]

Willke and other defenders of Hatch's proposal replied that access restrictions were the best the antiabortion movement could do in the foreseeable future. The Hatch Amendment would allow for more regulation, and arguments about the costs of abortion were effective. "Authentic pro-life principles in no way prevent us from doing as much as we can, when we can, to curb abortion," NRLC argued in a brochure on the Hatch Amendment.[29]

In December 1981, a Senate subcommittee voted to advance the Hatch Amendment by a vote of ten to seven, but the divisions within the pro-life movement guaranteed that it would not get much further. Pro-lifers failed to secure the votes to overcome a filibuster by Senator Robert Packwood (R–OR), and Hatch temporarily withdrew his amendment.[30] In 1982, Willke and his allies made a last-ditch attempt to pass Hatch's proposal. The Senate Judiciary Committee agreed to put Hatch's proposal before the full Senate, but Jesse Helms publicly derided the bill as "ineffective and half-baked." Even within the Reagan White House and Congress, no one could stop the infighting. When Stephen Galebach took a position at the White House that year, Senator Hatch complained that Galebach had talked the president out of supporting the senator's proposal. Although Galebach refuted the charges, the two sides seemed impossibly far apart. At the end of 1982, Hatch announced that he would postpone debate until after the midterm election in the hope of winning more votes.[31]

Despite the nasty struggle over the Hatch Amendment, pragmatists found themselves in an unexpectedly strong position. In ruling on the Akron case, Sandra Day O'Connor, Reagan's nominee, wrote a dissent rejecting *Roe's* trimester framework as unsound. O'Connor's dissent convinced some in the antiabortion movement that the Supreme Court might deliver the change that Congress could not. Larger pro-life groups successfully urged their colleagues to refocus on the overturning of *Roe* – and to emphasize arguments about the policy costs of abortion. Nevertheless, the Hatch Amendment debacle exposed contradictions in the strategy that would define future pro-life work. Often, pro-lifers stressed these arguments because they expected a strategic payoff. But as absolutists recognized, the debate over the costs of abortion increasingly obscured the rights that still motivated those on both sides to stay in the fight.

DODGING THE ISSUE OF ABORTION ACCESS

The Hatch Amendment disaster proved to be a blessing in disguise for larger groups like NARAL and Planned Parenthood. Abortion-rights donors and voters believed that the recriminalization of abortion was unacceptable. As long as debate focused on a possible constitutional amendment, then NARAL and Planned Parenthood could expect donations to keep coming in. Access restrictions, by contrast, did not get anyone excited. The threat of a constitutional amendment galvanized support for abortion rights, regardless of how badly the Hatch Amendment seemed likely to flame out.

NARAL invested heavily in defeating a constitutional amendment. The organization sent activists to states that seemed especially likely to ratify an antiabortion
constitutional amendment and encouraged members to become involved in local
elections. NARAL leaders also met with Roger Craver, a direct-mail fundraising
guru, to find ways to raise more money. In 1982, Craver insisted that NARAL would
have trouble in the long term unless the group began "to build a sense that access
issues are critical." After all, if the Hatch Amendment did not pass, restrictions on
abortion would continue to pass. But what Craver described was easier said than
done. For some donors and voters, it was hard to see the threat posed by incremental
restrictions. Laws requiring informed consent or limiting abortion funding did not,
on the surface, stop anyone from doing anything. Moreover, many prospective
donors would have the resources to circumvent incremental abortion restrictions
even if poorer women did not. When NARAL tried to follow Craver's advice, the
results were not heartening. The group struggled to raise money that year, running a
budget deficit by the start of 1983.[32]

Partly because of fundraising and political concerns, Planned Parenthood leaders
also gravitated to rights-based arguments. For much of the 1970s, various affiliates
had refused to perform abortions or participate in the political struggle around
abortion. But by 1980, Planned Parenthood leaders recognized that battles in
Congress had just begun. In the early 1980s, Faye Wattleton, the head of the
organization, tried to bring reluctant affiliates like the one in Santa Ana, California,
into the political conversation. "We must assure that abortion is ... an issue for
which legislators are held accountable," Wattleton announced.[33]

It certainly had not grown any easier to convince affiliates to speak out about
abortion. After a major increase in the 1970s, only two or three new affiliates began
performing the procedure in the early 1980s. Planned Parenthood members had
reason to view the abortion issue as politically toxic. In addition to proposed cuts to
Title X family planning funding, a major source of financial support for Planned
Parenthood, Congress launched a federal investigation into whether the organization illegally misused federal funds for performing abortions. Moreover, even the
most committed supporters of abortion rights recognized that access issues did not
motivate voters or donors in the same way that a constitutional prohibition could.[34]

Some groups had tried to make access for more women a focal point of abortion-
rights organizing. For the Committee for Abortion Rights and Against Sterilization
Abuse (CARASA) and the Reproductive Rights National Network (R2N2), a group
cofounded by CARASA in 1979, access to abortion was one of several social justice
concerns that mattered, especially for poor and nonwhite women. Like CARASA,
R2N2 tried to create a broader agenda, but the group was divided about how much
to prioritize the fight against racism. In 1981, the organization ultimately dissolved
because of disagreements about the issue. Other groups continued to take seriously
the perspectives of women of color. For example, the National Women's Health
Network addressed a variety of reproductive health issues, and individual women of

color both highlighted the importance of abortion access and called for a more comprehensive agenda.[35]

For their part, in the early 1980s, mainstream abortion-rights organizations like Planned Parenthood and NARAL often downplayed access issues, seeing them as less politically compelling than the Hatch Amendment. In a memo to other abortion-rights leaders, Jeannie Rosoff of Planned Parenthood recognized that incremental restrictions could devastate low-income women, women of color, rural women, and teenagers. Rosoff acknowledged that despite their practical effect, access issues might not be a winning political issue. "To be fair," she wrote, "the rights of poor women involved are viewed as secondary (very secondary) to the principle of legality." Rosoff was right. Despite her call to action, her allies emphasized the threat posed by an antiabortion constitutional amendment as soon as Hatch reintroduced one.[36]

ABORTION FOES' NEW DOCTRINAL APPROACH

Although opposing movements often focused on a potential constitutional amendment, the Supreme Court would soon move to the center of debate. In litigating the constitutionality of the Akron ordinance, pro-lifers had to push beyond the claims that had worked for funding bans. To do so, antiabortion lawyers pulled language from the Court's opinions to formulate a new doctrinal approach to abortion. These attorneys insisted that restrictions were constitutional if they benefitted women rather than harming them. As the Court considered the fate of the Akron ordinance, lawyers on both sides increasingly clashed about whether women suffered because of legal restrictions or because of the abortion procedure itself.

In 1983, while the Akron litigation was pending, the Court considered two more abortion cases. *Planned Parenthood Association of Kansas City, Missouri, Inc. v. Ashcroft* addressed a multipart Missouri law requiring a pathology report be completed after each abortion, mandating that two physicians be present if a child might be viable, and directing that all abortions be performed in a hospital after the twelfth week of pregnancy. *Simopoulos v. Virginia* focused on a law requiring that second trimester abortions be performed in "hospitals," a term that the law defined to include licensed clinics performing surgical procedures.[37]

Sylvia Law, one of the lawyers who had been involved in challenging the Hyde Amendment, came to see *Akron I* as a turning point in abortion litigation. Before 1973, she had worked as a welfare-rights attorney, but after *Roe*, she could not deny the importance of reproductive rights. After the Ford Foundation funded a Women's Rights Project within the ACLU, Law was upset that the money could not be used for reproductive-rights litigation. Working with Harriet Pilpel of Planned Parenthood, she helped to launch the ACLU's Reproductive Freedom Project and later had a hand in many major abortion cases.[38] Sandra Day O'Connor's dissent in the Akron case shook Law to the core. Under O'Connor's proposed rule, abortion laws would be unconstitutional only if they created a severe or absolute obstacle to women seeking abortion. For Law, it was frightening to think about what the law would look like if O'Connor's undue burden test became the governing law.[39]

Those defending the Akron ordinance, by contrast, desperately hoped that O'Connor would listen to what abortion foes described as the costs of abortion. Alan Segedy, an Akron abortion opponent who had coauthored the ordinance, and his brother-in-law, Robert Destro, defended the ordinance all the way to the Supreme Court. Segedy and Destro also worked with James Bopp Jr. of NRLC in shaping their strategy. Segedy, a partner in a local law firm, had specialized in estate planning and real estate law, but he and his wife, Ann Marie, were active in local pro-life groups. After a stint practicing law in Cleveland, Destro had become the general counsel for the pro-life Catholic League for Religious and Civil Rights in 1977. Segedy, Destro, and antiabortion amici tried to show that some abortion regulations were constitutional under *Roe* because they helped women.[40]

James Bopp went a step further, arguing that the Court had already adopted a new approach to abortion laws. It was true that the Court had used the language of an "undue burden" in earlier opinions. *Bellotti v. Baird I* and *II* had tackled the abortion rights of minors. *Maher v. Roe* and *Harris v. McRae* involved abortion funding. But none of these decisions rejected *Roe*'s trimester framework or proposed a rule that would obviously apply to all abortion cases. Nor had the Court's undue burden language always signaled a retreat from abortion rights. For Bopp, however, undue burden language could be the start of a full-blown alternative to *Roe*'s trimester framework. "[T]o determine if an abortion regulation is unconstitutional, the court must find as a matter of fact that: (1) the regulation affects the woman's abortion decision, (2) the regulation unduly burdens the decision or its effectuation, and (3) the regulation is not supported by a compelling state interest," he wrote. The undue burden test he described would mean that most abortion restrictions were constitutional. "[T]here are no hard-and-fast rules for determining the limit of the regulation power," Bopp argued. "The facts in every case are crucial."[41]

In its Supreme Court brief, the City of Akron similarly argued that the Constitution allowed for abortion restrictions that helped women. "The initial question posed on review before this Court," they wrote, "is whether the state's interest in maternal health and well-being is such that it may regulate abortion in a reasonable manner which is not unduly burdensome."[42]

Amicus curiae briefs submitted by AUL and the Reagan Administration repeated this point. "In *Roe v. Wade* and *Doe v. Bolton*, the Court prohibited the state from regulating doctors only in ways which burden the woman's fundamental right to decide," explained AUL attorney Dolores Horan in a brief for Feminists for Life. "It is impossible for the state to burden the woman's right to decide by requiring that she be given factual information which ... enhances her ability to decide."[43]

As Horan's argument suggested, AUL, Destro, and Segedy insisted that the Court could identify an undue burden only if a restriction hurt women. It is worth considering how this proposal differed from *Roe*. Under *Roe*'s trimester framework, the states could theoretically not regulate abortion at all in the first trimester. In the second trimester, the government could regulate solely to protect women's health. Only after a child became viable outside the womb could the states promote an interest in fetal life. Using the undue burden standard, AUL invited the Court to draw a line between costly and beneficial restrictions, even in the first trimester. AUL suggested that the justices could do so by considering whether abortion helped or hurt women.

Some abortion-rights attorneys thought that any undue burden test did too little to protect abortion rights. But most attorneys recognized that the Court had already upheld restrictions, including funding bans, that applied throughout pregnancy. These lawyers hoped to rework the idea of an undue burden to help women seeking abortions. To distinguish the Akron ordinance, some abortion-rights attorneys asserted that its purpose and effect much more closely resembled those of an outright ban. A brief submitted by NOW and NARAL contended that while "benign sounding on its face, the requirement that a second trimester abortion be performed in a hospital effectively eliminate[d], for many women, the ability to exercise their fundamental right to reproductive choice." Planned Parenthood focused on some parts of the Akron law, including the mandatory counseling provision, the waiting period, and the hospitalization requirement, asserting that all three "unduly burden[ed] a woman's right of choice regarding abortion." This idea of an undue burden differed from the one articulated by pro-lifers. Rather than urging the Court to uphold laws that supposedly helped women, abortion-rights supporters focused on how neutral-seeming laws cost women as much as complete prohibitions.[44]

THE *AKRON I* DECISION

Abortion-rights supporters could focus more on the Court after the threat of a constitutional amendment fizzled. In 1983, Hatch joined Senator Thomas Eagleton (D–MO) in proposing a modified version of his amendment, and lawmakers slated the bill for a full Senate vote in June. Behind the scenes, almost everyone had given up. Willke privately informed NRLC affiliates that no antiabortion amendment had the votes to pass. His prediction was right: In June 1983, the Senate defeated the Hatch-Eagleton Amendment by a vote of 49–50.[45]

The same month, the Supreme Court issued an opinion on the Akron, Virginia, and Missouri cases. In a six-to-three decision, the Court struck down the entire Akron ordinance. The *Akron I* majority did mention the idea of an undue burden on abortion but ignored the version of the standard proposed by pro-lifers. Rather than looking only at legal formalities, the Court emphasized the real-world consequences of the Akron law. Citing the findings of the American College of

Obstetricians and Gynecologists and the American Public Health Association, the Court concluded that the second trimester hospitalization requirement created "a significant obstacle in the path of women seeking an abortion." The majority also waded into the conflict about the costs and benefits of abortion. *Akron I* described much of the information laid out in the informed consent measure as "dubious." By leaving physicians no discretion, the ordinance "unreasonably ... placed obstacles in the path of the doctor upon whom [the woman was] entitled to rely for advice in connection with her decision." The Court struck down restrictions involving parental consultation, the disposal of fetal remains, and a mandatory waiting period.[46]

Sandra Day O'Connor's dissent garnered more attention than the outcome in *Akron I*. Whereas pro-lifers had contended that abortion restrictions benefitted women, O'Connor primarily meant something else when she described an undue burden. In her view, *Roe* had struck the wrong balance between women's rights and the government's interest in fetal life. As an alternative, she proposed her own version of the undue burden test. Under this approach, abortion regulations were constitutional unless a law created an "absolute obstacle ... or severe limitation ... on the abortion decision." Many more abortion laws would survive if O'Connor's proposed test applied.[47]

O'Connor's dissent sent shockwaves through the abortion conflict, particularly when pro-lifers read it together with the Court's other decisions. While striking down a hospital requirement like the one in *Akron I*, *Ashcroft* upheld measures requiring that more than one doctor be present at a post-viability abortion and mandating that a pathologist examine any tissue resulting from an abortion. *Simopoulos* sustained a hospitalization requirement after interpreting it to allow abortions in state-licensed clinics. Nevertheless, O'Connor's dissent in *Akron I* received the most attention from those in opposing movements.[48]

In the aftermath of *Akron I*, abortion-rights supporters debated whether the Supreme Court would safeguard legal abortion for much longer. While maintaining that courts should apply strict judicial scrutiny to all abortion regulations, some leaders of the ACLU Reproductive Freedom Project thought that the Court's undue burden language could shield women's reproductive rights. Janet Benshoof, a leading RFP attorney, expressed this view. She had grown up in Minnesota and counted Jane Hodgson as a hero. After deciding to become a lawyer, she paid her way through Harvard Law School using money from her job at an A&W Root Beer stand. Benshoof began working at the ACLU in 1977 and steered RFP for the next fifteen years. In 1983, she argued that the majority in *Akron I* had articulated an undue burden standard that could strongly protect abortion rights. She wrote that the Court was willing to tolerate only laws that had "no significant impact," even if they served "important health objectives."[49]

For Benshoof, the bottom line was that the meaning of an undue burden remained in dispute. Some form of an undue burden test – although certainly not the one O'Connor described – might help abortion-rights supporters defeat new abortion restrictions. As Benshoof explained: "Any first trimester regulation which can be shown to impose a burden on the exercise of the abortion right [should be] invalid."[50]

Akron I only reinforced NARAL's political focus,[51] inspiring a campaign called "40 More Years?" Lawyers for the group circulated a memo contending that *Roe* had required strict judicial scrutiny for abortion regulations, whereas the undue burden standard that O'Connor proposed allowed states to pass laws that would create "substantial delay, cost, and/or emotional suffering." To fight back, NARAL leaders planned to take their case to voters. As NARAL explained: "The next President of the United States could likely decide whether abortion will be legal or whether it will be outlawed."[52]

Together with the fall of the Hatch-Eagleton Amendment, *Akron I* sent a confusing message about the constitutional future of abortion rights. On the one hand, the Court had seemingly adopted a constitutional approach advocated by abortion-rights supporters since the late 1970s, asking whether innocuous-seeming laws functionally eliminated abortion access. On the other hand, O'Connor and two other justices apparently no longer believed in the basic tenets of *Roe*. Although O'Connor's dissent was good news for abortion foes, their way forward was not clear. For a decade, the pro-life movement had embraced a single mission – changing the text of the Constitution to recognize a right to life. If a constitutional amendment was dead, then what made it worthwhile for abortion foes to remain active?

AUL AND THE QUEST TO REVERSE *ROE*

In 1983, AUL attorneys, recently dependent on the charity of other pro-life groups, took on the role of master strategists. These lawyers asked their colleagues to find another way to get rid of abortion rights. AUL attorneys suggested that if a constitutional amendment would not work, the pro-life movement should take aim at *Roe v. Wade*. AUL lawyers met with other antiabortion attorneys to develop a litigation strategy that would end legal abortion. AUL insisted that the selection of test cases and the crafting of model laws were only part of the puzzle. As AUL lawyers saw it, their movement also needed fresh evidence that abortion had real costs for society.

A *Roe*-centered strategy emerged out of the desperation that followed the defeat of the Hatch-Eagleton Amendment and a spike in antiabortion violence. Between 1982 and 1985, the press covered thirty incidents of bombing or arson, the majority of them taking place in 1984 alone. With his friend and sometime employer Thomas Spinks, Michael Bray, a former youth pastor in Bowie, Maryland, concluded that any true Christian would have to do more to stop abortion than wait for politicians or the courts. Starting in January 1984, Bray, Spinks, and an accomplice bombed clinics in Delaware, Virginia, and Maryland. Abortion-rights activists presented these attacks as proof of the real motives of people who claimed to be pro-life. For example, at a

1985 conference for the National Abortion Federation (NAF), an organization of abortion providers, provider Peg Johnston claimed that the bombings proved that "pro-life is anti-life because they use terrorism." Mainstream pro-life activists denounced the violence, but the bombings showed the ugliest side of antiabortion activism, making it even harder for abortion foes to find a future political path.[53]

At the NRLC convention in August 1983, James Bopp Jr. of NRLC and Maura Quinlan of AUL held a closed-door meeting with state lawmakers to discuss the possibilities that remained open after *Akron I*. The options that were suggested showed how many abortion foes despaired of any meaningful progress. Larger antiabortion groups focused on laws that did not directly address abortion, including statutes involving the disposal of fetal remains, the wrongful death of unborn children, and criminal laws against fetal homicide (but not abortion). Even AUL attorneys, many of whom wanted to pursue a more aggressive strategy, admitted that state lawmakers might balk when confronted with a more ambitious plan.[54]

For abortion foes, the reasons for despair were self-evident. Since 1973, abortion opponents had treated the battle for a constitutional amendment as a matter of life and death for their movement. Pro-lifers, many of whom had long voted for the Democratic Party, switched their allegiance to push for constitutional change. A decade later, it seemed quite possible that a constitutional amendment would never pass – and certainly not in the foreseeable future. What should pro-lifers seek to do if their constitutional objective was politically impossible? AUL attorneys reasoned that the answer had stared abortion foes in the face since O'Connor's dissent became public. Instead of amending the Constitution to undo *Roe*, pro-lifers could seek to change the Court and ultimately reverse *Roe*.

AUL's tactical plan helped the group establish its relevance. Trouble for the organization had started when AUL lawyers had stepped in to defend a 1979 Illinois antiabortion law. After the district court blocked enforcement of the law, Illinois gave up on it. AUL lawyers took over the defense of the statute but continued to lose. In 1984, in *Diamond v. Charles*, the district court entered a judgment requiring payment of more than $200,000 in attorneys' fees, at the time, a crushing penalty for the organization. To protect Dr. Eugene Diamond, the named plaintiff, from having to pay the judgment himself, AUL had to get a loan from NRLC. The organization's financial struggles made it harder for AUL to attract talent. Thomas Marzen, one of the group's most distinguished lawyers, was hired away by James Bopp Jr. of NRLC to work at the National Legal Center for the Medically Dependent and Disabled, a group that worked on issues of euthanasia, infanticide, and assisted suicide.[55]

After *Akron I*, what had been a financially struggling, small-time upstart was reborn as the logical home for the movement's legal elites. The organization hosted a conference "to unite the movement around the relatively uncontroversial proposition ... that the Court should reverse itself." A new generation of young attorneys helped to develop the attack on *Roe*. The organization had been religiously diverse from the beginning. Victor Rosenblum was a Reform Jew; Dennis Horan was a Catholic, and the organization's first president was a Unitarian minister. But in the early 1980s, a newly mobilized generation of Catholic, Lutheran, and evangelical attorneys helped to refashion the pro-life cause, making it a quest to overturn *Roe* rather than a fight to change the text of the Constitution.[56]

Those assembled at AUL's conference saw the most immediate promise in redefining fetal viability. *Roe* allowed the state to protect fetal life after the point at which a child could survive outside of a woman's body. O'Connor's dissent had flagged the changing age of viability as one of the weaknesses of *Roe*, and those at the AUL conference hoped to capitalize on that. O'Connor reasoned that the date of viability changed as technology improved, and abortion became safe later in pregnancy. These shifts, O'Connor argued, made *Roe's* trimester framework unworkable, encouraging courts to pretend to act as science review boards.[57]

But AUL attorneys believed that O'Connor's dissent hinted at a more complete roadmap for antiabortion litigation. Victor Rosenblum and Thomas Marzen believed that their movement could rack up more wins if pro-lifers identified enough "[f]avorable statistical data" showing the costs of abortion and the benefits of laws regulating it. As the two explained:

> "Accepted medical practices" must change before barriers to reversal can be broken down; whether or not abortion is "acceptable" is determined by the view and customary practices of the very people who perform abortions. They are unwilling to increase the state's authority to regulate abortion. A possible long-term approach to meeting this dilemma is the development of new sources for abortion data.[58]

As Rosenblum and Marzen saw it, the members of the Supreme Court would not give a fair chance to arguments about the constitutional rights of the unborn child. What the justices did instead was to fall back on the opinions of the American Medical Association and the American College of Obstetricians and Gynecologists, members of which often saw abortion as safe and normal.

Rosenblum and Marzen insisted that their colleagues had to fight fire with fire. Inside of court, the movement could push O'Connor's undue burden standard as a true alternative to *Roe's* trimester framework. Outside of court, abortion foes could produce data that would undercut support for legal abortion and establish the societal costs of the procedure.[59] Rosenblum and Marzen further encouraged their colleagues to use the claims about the costs of abortion in service of laws that would demonstrate "just how radical *Roe v. Wade* is." Other pro-lifers approved of this approach. If the Supreme Court defined abortion as a legitimate choice for women and a safe medical procedure, pro-lifers would have to prove both wrong.[60]

The litigation strategy that AUL helped to shape would transform the terms of the abortion war. Rather than criticizing the *Roe* Court for failing to recognize a right to life, abortion foes would sing the praises of individual restrictions. And in explaining the need for tough abortion regulations, AUL would develop arguments about the costs of abortion for the country. But this strategy had its pitfalls. Incremental restrictions fell far short of what pro-lifers wanted. And rather than lowering the temperature of the conflict, focusing on the costs of abortion only multiplied the areas on which opposing activists disagreed.

REVERSING *ROE* BY SHAPING ELECTIONS

The political wing of the antiabortion movement also settled on a strategy to overturn *Roe*. For several years, NRLC had defined itself as the political power in the pro-life movement, and NRLC leaders could boast inside connections with the Reagan White House. But pro-lifers had prioritized an alliance with the GOP as a way to improve the odds of passing a constitutional amendment. By 1984, that campaign had indefinitely been postponed. What use was an alliance with the GOP if the text of the Constitution stayed the same?

A February 1984 fundraising letter offered one explanation of the continuing importance of the NRLC's alliance with the Republican Party. "The stakes [of the 1984 election] are tremendous," the fundraising letter stated. "If President Reagan wins reelection, he will appoint at least two and maybe even three new Supreme Court justices." More justices like O'Connor could make the difference. And the Court's membership could change soon. "The five oldest Supreme Court justices all voted in favor of the fatal 1973 *Roe v. Wade* decision," the letter noted.[61]

That year, NRLC leaders dug out of a year of infighting. Internecine struggles between the organization's president and executive committee had grown increasingly personal, and in 1984, to reestablish peace, Dr. John Willke, a veteran leader, returned to serve as president. In an election year, the group's top priority remained the reelection of Ronald Reagan, a leader who, as NRLC predicted, would "replace up to 5 pro-abortion justices." But NRLC hoped to use television, print media, and radio to persuade more people to reject abortion independently of what the Court did. While abortion foes had used fetal images since the 1960s, NRLC planned a more sophisticated national campaign in the mid-1980s. The group spearheaded a $3 to $5 million-dollar media campaign "to tell Americans the truth about abortion."[62]

The media campaign came as part of the professionalization of NRLC. In 1984, the group renovated its office, installed a computer system, and took out its first full-page advertisement in *Time* magazine. NRLC leaders claimed that the ad inspired hundreds of recruits to sign up. Profiting from the new attention, NRLC launched "To Change the Nation," a media campaign including radio and television spots and "newscasts" aired on over 300 religious radio stations. The group also planned to spend at least $1.6 million on television spots in eight states.[63]

"Telling the truth" about abortion through the media made sense partly because the media campaign turned out to be a fund-raising bonanza. Mary Reilly Hunt, then the group's chief fundraiser, wrote that donors, particularly foundations and wealthy individuals who had not previously contributed, responded to the idea of a media campaign. But as importantly, the media initiative spread a message about abortion that might shift the debate in a way that fetal-rights claims had not. NRLC hoped that broader use of television, radio, and other media would not only demonstrate "the grace and beauty of the unborn child" but also present "hard-hitting facts about abortion that [would] be hard to ignore."[64]

NRLC also hoped to repair their movement's relationship with the Republican Party. Some pro-lifers had grown disenchanted with the Reagan Administration because of a lack of progress made during Reagan's first four years in office. However, for groups like NRLC and AUL, success depended on an alliance with the GOP – one that could remake the Supreme Court and eventually allow for the overruling of *Roe*. Although the clinic attacks of 1984 did not visibly damage the relationship between Reagan and larger antiabortion groups, the specter of violence motivated larger groups to change the subject, condemn the violence, and redefine themselves in the process. To do so, the leaders of groups like NRLC tried to direct attention back to what members described as the costs of abortion, especially fetal pain.

THE SILENT SCREAM AND THE COSTS OF FETAL PAIN

In decrying the pain caused by abortion, pro-lifers sent a different message about abortion. Regardless of what the Constitution said, larger antiabortion groups insisted that no woman should knowingly inflict unnecessary pain on an unborn child. NRLC's early claims about fetal pain peaked with the organization's distribution of *The Silent Scream*, a twenty-eight-minute movie. The film showed ultrasound images of the abortion of a twelve-week old fetus, complete with voiceover narration by Dr. Bernard Nathanson, then one of the most controversial figures in the abortion debate. Formerly a prominent NARAL member, Nathanson claimed to have performed roughly 5,000 procedures. But after viewing an ultrasound, he became pro-life. While serving as the obstetric chief at New York's St. Luke's Hospital in the late 1970s, he stopped performing the procedure and became an outspoken opponent of legal abortion. When Nathanson presented an excerpt of *The Silent Scream* at the 1984 NRLC Convention, the organization immediately saw its potential as a mobilizing tool. By the winter of 1985, NRLC had mailed the film to members of the Supreme Court and Congress, and portions of it aired on most major networks.[65]

Apart from its slick packaging, *The Silent Scream* struck a nerve partly because of the claims it made about fetal pain.[66] Jerry Falwell, the leader of the Moral Majority, asked viewers to trust the accuracy of *The Silent Scream* because Nathanson, the force behind the film, was a "scientist and a doctor." In defending *The Silent Scream*, abortion foes pointed to Nathanson's education and medical expertise.

The film's champions also presented Nathanson's former support of abortion rights as a sign of his credibility.[67]

The Silent Scream effectively drew on public uncertainty about both the medical profession and fetal life. For over a decade, pro-lifers had insisted that the moral and constitutional stakes of abortion were black and white. Abortion, as they saw it, both violated fundamental constitutional rights and basic moral norms. But by focusing on claims about the costs of abortion, pro-lifers sometimes took a different approach, insisting that the facts about abortion were far from settled. For example, groups like NRLC contended that voters should seriously question the trustworthiness of abortion doctors. By the 1980s, moreover, the prestige of the medical profession had eroded significantly. The public's loss of confidence in the medical profession partly reflected changes to the way care was delivered. Urgent-care clinics, once a rarity, became a common feature of American strip malls. For-profit hospitals and business-run medical facilities seemed to be everywhere, and some patients lost faith in the system. At the same time, because life expectancy had climbed over the course of several decades, more Americans experienced painful interventions that did not always seem justified. Unhappy consumers often turned to medical-malpractice litigation, and as many as one in ten physicians found themselves the target of a suit in the mid-1980s. These trends empowered abortion opponents, many of whom played on new public suspicions of the medical system.[68]

Fetal images had a longer history, and starting in the 1960s, abortion opponents had encouraged Americans to visualize fetal life when making up their minds about abortion. In the mid-1980s, technological developments made it easier for some to identify with the fetus. Surgical advances allowed more physicians to treat fetuses directly. Increasing use of ultrasound imagery made unborn children more visible both to medical professionals and potential parents. In-the-womb surgery and advanced neonatal intensive care units that spread in the mid-1980s encouraged physicians and women to view the unborn child as a patient.[69]

Technological advances also motivated abortion opponents to refocus on later abortions. The likely age of viability had already moved two weeks earlier than the *Roe* Court had estimated, and abortion foes insisted that fetal survival would soon be possible even earlier in pregnancy. Pro-life groups responded by promoting fetal anesthesia laws that supposedly prevented the pain described in *The Silent Scream*. Other proposed restrictions focused on fetal viability. The Pennsylvania Abortion Control Act and laws modeled on it set standards of care and reporting requirements for physicians dealing with later abortions. Such laws called into question the credibility of many viability determinations. As importantly, pro-lifers hoped that viability regulations would intensify public discomfort with later abortions.[70]

Worried that the tide seemed to be turning against them, abortion-rights organizations in the mid-1980s insisted that lawmakers and judges had all but ignored the ways that legal abortion benefitted women. At first, the leaders of groups like NARAL and NOW primarily disputed the accuracy of pro-life claims about fetal development and abortion techniques.[71] Over time, however, abortion-rights activists insisted that Americans interested in what abortion really involved had been asking the wrong questions. Instead of zeroing in so much on claims about the costs of abortion, the real issue was the way that women benefitted from abortion access.

SILENT NO MORE

By the mid-1980s, major abortion-rights organizations realized that arguments about a right to choose alone would not solve their movement's problems. The makers of *The Silent Scream* seemed to understand that rights-based arguments left open a strategic weakness that pro-lifers could exploit. Yes, women had a right to abortion, but should they exercise it? In the mid-1980s, abortion-rights supporters answered this question by telling the stories of women who felt that abortion had changed their lives for the better.

By the time that clips of *The Silent Scream* aired on the national news, larger abortion-rights organizations had more time to dedicate to the fight to shape public attitudes about abortion. In the early 1980s, NOW had mounted a last-ditch attempt to pass the Equal Rights Amendment (ERA), a constitutional provision guaranteeing equality on the basis of sex. In 1979, NOW convinced Congress to extend the deadline to 1982, but the organization failed to get three additional states to ratify. In the meantime, reproductive issues took up more of NOW's resources. Judy Goldsmith, NOW's leader since October 1982, organized a picket at the Reagan White House following the firebombing of abortion clinics. NOW also led thirty around-the-clock vigils to prevent further clinic attacks. But in 1985, Goldsmith lost a heated reelection battle to Eleanor Smeal, a former NOW president who returned to lead the organization. In part, Goldsmith's defeat stemmed from the results of the 1984 election. During the campaign, Goldsmith and other NOW leaders had heralded an apparent gender gap in party affiliation that would hurt the GOP. But Reagan coasted to victory in 1984, and Republicans defended their Senate majority while picking up seats in the House.[72]

Smeal and her allies interpreted the 1984 election as evidence that NOW needed to invest more in grassroots activism than in party politics. Kim Gandy, a future leader of NOW, remembered this moment in the abortion debate. In 1973, she first became involved in abortion politics in New Orleans when she helped women dodge the protesters at a clinic, the local Delta Women's Clinic. As she took on more work for the women's movement, abortion remained center stage. Gandy played a part in organizing bicoastal events for the 1986 March for Women's Equality/Women's Lives, a major abortion-rights event. When Smeal organized the march, skeptics worried that no one would show up, but the numbers were a pleasant surprise. For activists like Gandy, the 1986 march reflected a new feminist energy around abortion – and a commitment to talking about the real-world benefits of keeping it legal.[73]

Although Planned Parenthood affiliates remained divided about how much to dive into abortion politics, the organization's leaders worried that *The Silent Scream* would demonize abortion providers. As it was, Planned Parenthood had all the controversy it could handle. The organization had to deal with a regulation mandating that family planning advocates inform the parents of teenagers seeking birth control and grapple with the aftermath of the Mexico City policy, a rule that banned federal aid to organizations, such as Planned Parenthood's international arm, that performed abortions abroad. Clinic bombings further alarmed those who wanted to stay away from the abortion issue. Other local and state affiliates stepped up their involvement in the abortion issue, however, and members of national Planned Parenthood took part in the effort to counter *The Silent Scream.*[74]

Planned Parenthood initially put together a panel of medical experts who described the film as manipulative and misleading, particularly when it came to fetal pain. But Dr. Louise Tyrer, the organization's vice president of medical affairs, thought that it did no good to talk so much about specific abortion techniques. "[R]ather than permitting the debate to center around the fetus," she wrote, "it is up to us to direct attention to the woman and her problem."[75]

The leaders of NARAL and NOW came to share Tyrer's view. Nanette Falkenberg of NARAL worried that her colleagues struggled with a "sense of powerlessness and frustration." She proposed a strategy intended to "recapture the emotional side of the issue." If pro-lifers discussed the costs of abortion for the unborn child, supporters of abortion rights directed attention to its benefits for real women.[76]

As important, invoking a right to choose could make a mockery of the struggles of poor women of color who had no real options in the first place. As an alternative, larger groups joined women of color in discussing the benefits of abortion access for women. The first women-of-color organization focused on reproductive health, the National Black Women's Health Project, organized in 1984 to advance a more comprehensive agenda. The National Latina Health Organization, founded in 1986, similarly fought not only for legal abortion but also for "access to quality education [and] the right to jobs that are environmentally safe and afford us the economic means for good, safe housing." Individual women of color also worked within larger abortion-rights organizations. These activists helped convince bigger groups to reexamine their rhetorical strategy. As the organizers of the symposium explained: "The definition and singular goal of this symposium [are] specifically based on the belief that to protect the right to choose for all women, we must create a construct for that right beyond the framework of *Roe v. Wade.*"[77]

Many of those present believed that the abortion-rights movement should tackle more policy issues, such as "prenatal care, childcare, supportive services for the disabled, [and] education." Symposium attendees wanted to share the benefits of legal abortion for women of "different classes, races, or disabled women."[78] Based on feedback from the symposium, NARAL launched *Silent No More*, a program supported by other major pro-choice organizations designed to center political conversation on the benefits of abortion. Falkenberg explained its purpose as follows: "The current challenge is to ensure that as the issue is discussed in increasingly emotional and medical/technological terms, the emotion and reality of the abortion experience in the lives of women and men is not lost."[79]

NARAL set about collecting letters from women and men describing their personal experiences of abortion. Falkenberg insisted that the movement should share a broad range of these letters with the public and the media. "We must *not* focus only on the hardship cases," she contended, referring to abortions in cases of rape, incest, or a serious health condition. The letters solicited by NARAL and other abortion-rights groups differed considerably from one another, but most shared "positive feelings about abortion" and other "positive things [that could] result [from it]." Many of the women of color who wrote in explained that it was "very hard to talk about 'choice' when there isn't money, . . . when racism pervades every aspect of life."[80]

By describing abortion as one of a series of painful choices forced on families by a difficult economy, *Silent No More* presented an idea about what abortion involved that differed considerably from what pro-lifers described in *The Silent Scream*. High rates of unemployment and inflation, competition from Japan and Europe, higher energy prices, and a wave of mergers and consolidations prompted companies – and particularly manufacturers – to lay off a significant number of workers.[81] Describing the benefits of abortion for individual women made perfect sense when many families struggled to make ends meet. These stories would also personalize, rather than medicalize, abortion by reminding everyone of the benefits experienced by the "1.5 million women who [had] abortions each year." As NARAL explained, *Silent No More* would inform the "American people that every woman who chooses to have an abortion does so for reasons that are compelling."[82]

While *Silent No More* presented the perspectives of nonwhite women, some organizations, like NOW and the Religious Coalition for Abortion Rights (RCAR), created outreach programs for women of color. In 1984, Judy Logan-White, a black feminist, cofounded the Women of Color Partnership Project within RCAR, working with churches to organize pro-choice women of color. The following year, Loretta Ross, a black feminist and veteran civil rights activist, became the first director of NOW's Women of Color Programs. Both initiatives reflected concern that the mainstream women's movement – and the larger abortion-rights organizations – did too little to attract and retain the support of women of color.[83]

Abortion foes had a similar problem diversifying their movement. Catherine Davis, a pro-life woman of color, understood some of the reasons why her movement struggled. Raised in a conservative black family in Stamford, Connecticut, Davis described herself as a child of the 1970s, open to the new sexual freedom offered to women of her generation. As an undergraduate at Tufts, Davis learned she was pregnant and flew to New York to have an abortion. Although she found the entire experience disturbing, she pushed it to the back of her mind. The next year, she spoke to her mother about *Roe v. Wade.* She still recalls her mother saying that no black woman would abort a child. Abortion, as she put it, was "white woman nonsense."[84]

Years later, as an unemployed mother of one, Davis again decided to end a pregnancy. She felt that she could not support another child without jeopardizing her graduate studies and her ability to support her son, but the abortion procedure again troubled her. She recalls a doctor counting to make sure he had not left any fetal parts in her uterus.[85]

She did not think much about abortion until 1987 when she started attending lunchtime Bible study. One day, the session touched on abortion. Davis found herself overwhelmed with guilt. The pastor present prayed until he felt that Davis knew she was forgiven. He then charged her to do more about her experience. After volunteering for a Virginia NRLC affiliate, she remained in pro-life work for years. Davis later went on to cofound the National Black Pro-Life Coalition and create the Restoration Project, a pro-life group designed to speak to black Americans. As she saw it, larger pro-life organizations almost inevitably misunderstood what her community needed to hear.[86]

Davis's concerns reflected the pro-life movement's struggles to diversify. NRLC had a black woman serve as president for years but looked to recruit more rank-and-file members of color. Kay James, a black woman who had served as NRLC's communications director, founded Black Americans for Life (BAL) in 1985 as an outreach program. By 1987, James claimed that the program had 3,000 members nationwide. In 1985, William Keyes, the founder of the conservative Black Political Action Committee, ran for a spot on NRLC's board of directors. But NRLC remained a mostly white organization. Relatively few African-Americans joined BAL, and it would not be until 1991 that NRLC created a Latino outreach program through the work of newly elected board member Raimundo Rojas.[87]

By foregrounding the benefits of legal abortion, abortion-rights activists forged claims that appealed to a more diverse group of prospective recruits. Moreover, such contentions confronted the stigma that pro-lifers tried to create. Nevertheless, campaigns like *Silent No More* suggested that the benefits of abortion were deeply personal. In this way, abortion-rights proponents inadvertently suggested that there was not one truth about the procedure but many – a problematic claim when both sides contested the scientific facts surrounding abortion. Moreover, after Reagan's election, abortion-rights groups desperately needed an effective argument for preserving *Roe.* If Reagan further changed the Supreme Court, then abortion rights would be in jeopardy. Abortion-rights groups would have to both appeal to voters and sway the Court.

An imminent threat to *Roe* came much sooner than many expected. When the Supreme Court agreed to hear *Thornburgh v. American College of Obstetricians and*

Gynecologists, Charles Fried, the solicitor general, penned a brief that asked for *Roe* to be overruled. Given the result in *Akron I*, Fried's approach was obviously risky, but when the Court decided the case, four justices seemed to share the solicitor general's concerns. *Thornburgh* marked the start of a new era in the abortion wars – one in which it was all too easy to imagine a world in which states outlawed abortion once again.

THE *THORNBURGH* CASE

When the Supreme Court agreed to hear *Thornburgh*, some antiabortion lawyers felt uneasy. The case involved the Pennsylvania Abortion Control Act, a 1982 statute partly based on an AUL model. However, impatient lawmakers tweaked the model to make it more aggressive. Although the Court had recently struck down a carefully crafted model law, state legislators still wanted to forge ahead. AUL attorneys worried that the legislature had practically invited the justices to overturn the statute.[88]

While the Women's Law Project, a Philadelphia-based feminist public interest litigation firm, challenged the law almost as soon as it passed, there was no decision on the merits of the case until the Third Circuit Court of Appeals ruled in May 1984. That court upheld parts of the law, including several viability-based regulations, but struck down the rest. The Supreme Court heard oral arguments in the case in November 1985.[89]

Abortion-rights attorneys relied on *Roe* and *Akron I*. After all, the Court had recently struck down almost any abortion restriction it encountered. According to the ACLU's brief, the Court made clear that any law that "substantially burden[s] access to abortion absent a compelling state interest will not withstand judicial scrutiny." In her brief for the appellee, Kathryn Kolbert suggested that no one could distinguish the Pennsylvania law from the one already struck down in *Akron I*.[90]

Some abortion-rights briefs highlighted arguments about the benefits of abortion. In its amicus brief, NARAL relied on the testimonies of a diverse group of women gathered during the *Silent No More* campaign. One mother of three, happy with her "booming" business, terminated her pregnancy after her contraceptive routine let her down. Another woman reasoned that if she "had had the baby [she] would have had to quit [her] job and go on welfare." Terminating the pregnancy allowed her "to make ends meet and get the kids thr[ough] school."[91]

In the context of constitutional law, NARAL argued that these stories had special significance. "With the right to choose abortion," NARAL contended, "women are able to enjoy, like men, the right to fully use the powers of their minds and bodies." The right to choose abortion mattered because of its benefits: It allowed women to pursue a career, marry for the right reasons, make wise parenting decisions, or get an education. NARAL suggested that if the Court wanted to know the truth about abortion in America, the justices simply needed to ask women.[92]

Other briefs gave a more focused analysis of the reasons that women chose abortion later in pregnancy. For example, the Center for Constitutional Rights and other pro-choice organizations described the crises that women would face if all later abortions were out of reach. The Center reminded the Court that many who chose abortion after the first trimester had planned their pregnancies but later discovered a serious fetal condition or a threat to their own health.[93]

Most antiabortion lawyers in *Thornburgh* realized that a majority still supported an abortion right for women. However, doctors were a different story.[94] NRLC attorneys justified Pennsylvania's informed consent law as a reasonable response to the commercialization of abortion.[95] Here, NRLC addressed the Free Speech Clause of the First Amendment, which protected the freedom of expression. American courts protected certain categories of speech less vigorously, including so-called commercial speech, statements, and other forms of communication designed to make money. NRLC lawyers recognized that physicians had once seemed entirely different from car dealers, shopkeepers, and others hawking their wares. But NRLC reasoned that as abortion practice became a big business, these doctors could no longer be trusted. "Because of the contractual, consumer-oriented nature of medical practice in general and abortion practice in particular," the brief argued, "the information supplied by a physician to his patient is a form of 'commercial speech' subject to reasonable regulation by the state pursuant to its interest in protecting consumers from deception."[96]

While larger antiabortion groups had plotted a slow attack on *Roe*, the Reagan Administration wanted to move faster. The amicus brief for the United States described both lower court decisions in the case as sloppy and impossible to justify. However, for the administration, the blame fell on the Court. United States Solicitor General Charles Fried wrote that *Roe* was "so far flawed and ... such a source of instability in the law" that the Court had no real choice but to abandon it.[97]

Only the most optimistic antiabortion advocates believed that the Court would take Fried up on the invitation to overrule *Roe*. Indeed, when the Court issued a decision in July 1986, *Thornburgh* struck down six provisions addressed in the Third Circuit's opinion. But the news for the pro-life movement was not all bad. The majority supporting *Roe* had shrunk to five votes, and one of those who had joined the original opinion in *Roe*, Chief Justice Warren Burger, dissented.[98]

Based on their movement's reaction, it was hard to tell that pro-lifers had lost in *Thornburgh*. Doug Johnson of NRLC told the media that the country was "just one vote away from a Court which may be willing to overrule *Roe v. Wade*." On the eve of the organization's national conference, NRLC President John Willke presented *Thornburgh* as a vindication of his organization's focus on overturning *Roe*. However morbid it seemed, Willke made clear that pro-lifers would not have to wait long for a new opening on the Court if they held on to the White House. "The votes to maintain abortion are those five old men," he observed.[99]

Nevertheless, the expected payoff from *Thornburgh* was not immediately evident. Pro-lifers suffered a setback during the 1986 midterm election when pro-choice members of Congress won several contested seats and voters rejected several ballot measures proposed by AUL and its allies. In November, the Court delivered another disappointment by holding that states could not deny family planning funding to organizations because they used private donations to perform or advocate for abortions.[100]

But for abortion opponents, the heady environment created by *Thornburgh* would soon return. In June 1986, Chief Justice Warren Burger retired, and Reagan asked Associate Justice William Rehnquist, a consistent critic of *Roe*, to take Burger's place as chief justice. To fill Rehnquist's spot, Reagan nominated Antonin Scalia, a judge on the DC Court of Appeals known for his intellect and his conservative record. Congress confirmed Scalia by a unanimous vote. In June 1987, Justice Lewis Powell announced his retirement. Reagan waited less than a week to announce his replacement, Judge Robert Bork of the DC Circuit. While Powell had carved out a role as a swing vote in abortion cases, Bork was an outspoken critic of *Roe*.[101]

Over the course of 1987, Bork's nomination quickly became extremely divisive, and by that October, his bid for the Court failed in committee. Although many expected the nominee to concede defeat, Reagan called for a full Senate debate. Given that Democrats controlled the Senate, the outcome of the final vote did not come as a surprise: Bork's nomination fell by a vote of 42–58. Pro-lifers clearly saw a silver lining in the result. Even abortion-rights advocates agreed that one more vote on the Court would spell the end for *Roe*. The Court's most recent abortion case, a parental involvement matter, sent a similar message. There, the Court deadlocked four-to-four, ensuring that Illinois could not reimpose a 1983 parental notification law. If Reagan put a new justice on the Court, the outcome would be very different.[102]

Weeks after Bork conceded defeat, Reagan nominated Anthony Kennedy, a judge from the Ninth Circuit Court of Appeals, to take Powell's seat on the Court. By February 1988, the Senate had voted unanimously to confirm him. NRLC leaders obviously saw Kennedy and other Supreme Court nominees as the linchpin of a bold attack on *Roe*. "Justices Antonin Scalia and Anthony Kennedy have not yet voted directly on a law restricting abortion, ... but [i]t is hoped that [they] will vote to overrule *Roe v. Wade* if and when the time comes," Willke explained. Although AUL leaders often took a more cautious approach, AUL President Guy Condon similarly predicted that "[t]he additions of Justice Antonin Scalia and Justice Anthony Kennedy [would] upset the balance historically tilted in favor of abortion on demand."[103]

In 1988, George H. W. Bush, Reagan's vice president, won the presidential race. The Democratic Party slightly increased the majorities it held in both houses of Congress, and some movement members harbored doubts about Bush himself, given his past reluctance to endorse a fetal-protective amendment. Nevertheless, for many in NRLC, the reasons to move aggressively were obvious.[104] With so many pro-lifers preparing for a final attack on legal abortion, AUL leaders, particularly Ed Grant, the organization's executive director, sounded a note of caution. He insisted that the "[t]he strategy to reverse *Roe* requires a momentum that can be provided only by a series of court victories." Whatever opportunities *Thornburgh* might hold out, Grant believed that the time had not yet come to abandon O'Connor's undue burden test.[105]

In antiabortion circles, disagreements ran deeper than Grant might have believed. Randall Terry, an activist inspired by Joseph Scheidler's clinic protests, launched a movement to blockade abortion clinics. Terry and his allies made a play for the leadership of the pro-life movement in the process. Terry's organization, Operation Rescue, further insisted that pro-lifers needed to say that abortion was murder and act like it by breaking laws that allowed abortion clinics to function.[106]

In the aftermath of *Thornburgh*, abortion-rights organizations changed as well. Developed in 1986, NARAL's three-year strategic plan assumed that Congress and the states would lean further left in the years to come as the Religious Right lost influence. The group further reasoned that the courts would no longer reliably defend abortion. In response, NARAL demanded a political show of force. Kate Michelman, NARAL's new leader, explained: "We intend to leave no doubt that a court action that would restrict or end a woman's right to choose will create immediate social and political upheaval." Michelman advocated for rights-based arguments that seemed to resonate most with voters who felt ambivalent about abortion, but NARAL's new approach worried pro-choice activists who thought that their movement would lose sight of the benefits of abortion for women once again.[107]

ABORTION'S EFFECTS

Abortion opponents never wavered in their commitment to an outright ban on abortion. But by 1983, pro-lifers had given up on changing the text of the Constitution. Because a constitutional amendment was out of reach, larger antiabortion groups set out to undo *Roe v. Wade*. As part of this mission, pro-lifers hoped to solidify their partnership with the Republican Party and reshape the Supreme Court. Abortion foes also emphasized laws limiting abortion access.

In championing these statutes, the antiabortion movement often relied on a different message, one centered not on the rights of the unborn child but on the costs of legal abortion for women and for the entire country. This strategy did not command universal support in the 1980s, and absolutists and recently mobilized evangelicals sometimes worried that an incremental campaign would never pay off. Nevertheless, larger antiabortion groups insisted that the Court, like politicians, might pay attention to arguments about the consequences of abortion.

In *Akron I*, pro-lifers claimed that abortion regulations did not violate the Consti-tution unless they unduly burdened women. And since many laws aided women, as abortion foes reasoned, the Court should permit some statutes to stand. Abortion-rights groups responded by trying to debunk the factual claims offered by the opposition and by rejecting the proposed antiabortion undue burden standard out of hand.

By often focusing on claims about the costs and benefits of abortion, those on opposing sides in theory might have been more willing to compromise. There are degrees of access that the state could permit. In practice, however, neither side changed its fundamental constitutional values, only temporarily pushing them aside for strategic reasons. Moreover, in focusing on the policy consequences of abortion, opposing movements only found more sources of division.

When the Supreme Court decided *Thornburgh*, the stakes of this debate got higher. Four justices seemed prepared to overrule *Roe*. Once Kennedy took his seat on the Court, many predicted that the justices would overrule *Roe* in short order. Abortion foes started a different discussion about the costs of abortion for the nation. Had abortion undermined the already fragile American family or allowed women to flourish within it?

4

Planned Parenthood v. Casey, the Family, and Equal Citizenship

At a time when many expected the Court to overturn *Roe*, Rachael Pine and Ed Grant saw how important the fortunes of the American family had become to abortion law. As a law student, Pine was passionate about civil liberties but did not begin with a singular interest in reproductive rights. After she completed a federal clerkship, however, a special fellowship at the American Civil Liberties Union Reproductive Freedom Project (ACLU RFP) led to a full-time position. During that fellowship year, Pine spent three frigid winter months building the factual record in a federal trial, *Hodgson v. Minnesota*, a landmark challenge to a law restricting minors' access to abortion.[1]

Pine felt that prior to *Hodgson*, courts had upheld similar statutes based on assumptions about how restrictions that were not yet in force would affect families. Pine coined the term "operational challenge" to describe litigation that would reveal how parental involvement laws actually affected minors. As she saw it, judges seemed not to understand "what lies behind the closed family homestead door." Like many of her colleagues, Pine would remain involved in the fight to preserve minors' rights for years. Many of the cases on which she worked addressed the real impact of abortion restrictions on the all too common challenges of American family life.[2]

Edward Grant of Americans United for Life (AUL) agreed with Pine on the importance of arguments about abortion and the family. Growing up Catholic in northern New Jersey, Grant tended toward the Republican side of a family with parents who voted for different political parties. A runner and self-proclaimed nerd in high school, he paid little attention to the abortion issue before *Roe v. Wade* came down.[3] While he instinctually found the decision to be disturbing, Grant did not become deeply involved in the pro-life movement until the fall of 1979 when he arrived in Chicago to attend law school at Northwestern. A classmate told him about an internship at AUL, and Grant soon took a position with the organization. In 1984, after a stint working in Philadelphia, Grant agreed to return to AUL, loaded up his Ford Fiesta, and drove west to become the organization's executive director.[4]

Grant sat in the Court the day the justices announced their decision in *Planned Parenthood of Southeastern Pennsylvania v. Casey* (1992), preserving the right to choose abortion.[5] While *Casey* devastated his colleagues, Grant began to see that the battle was no longer about the rights of the unborn or even about whether *Roe* should be overruled. The debate would turn on what it meant that "an entire culture ha[d] grown up dependent on *Roe*."[6]

As Grant and Pine's experiences suggest, in the late 1980s and early 1990s, the fate of the American family and women's place in it cast a long shadow over abortion law. Earlier in the 1980s, pro-lifers had given up on a constitutional abortion ban, instead prioritizing a campaign to overturn *Roe v. Wade*. As part of this effort, the movement spotlighted what pro-lifers described as the costs of abortion. Later in the 1980s, pro-lifers homed in on one particular set of harms: those involving damage to family relationships.

Some abortion opponents resented what they felt were dizzying changes to the family. But in the mid-1980s, larger antiabortion groups like National Right to Life Committee (NRLC) and Americans United for Life (AUL) also had strategic reasons for stressing family involvement laws, statutes requiring a woman to consult with her parents or spouse. Antiabortion leaders relied on an alliance with the Republican Party. However, the election of George H. W. Bush, a candidate lacking strong pro-life credentials, raised concern that the GOP would abandon the anti-abortion movement. To strengthen their partnership with Republicans, pro-life lawyers prioritized laws that they believed would not only survive constitutional challenge but would also help conservative candidates on election day. For pro-life lobbyists and lawyers, family involvement mandates seemed to be a perfect choice.

By the later 1980s, however, those steering political discussion sometimes down-played claims about the policy consequences of abortion. As the Court seemed ready to reverse *Roe*, NARAL leaders stressed rights-based arguments, believing that even voters who did not care about feminism generally opposed government interference. In the late 1980s, a new clinic-blockade movement emphasized reli-gious arguments. Blockaders, many of them evangelical, saw claims about abortion's costs as cowardly or even complicit.

But contentions about the costs and benefits of abortion still played a defining role in the battle about family involvement requirements. Abortion-rights attorneys challenging family involvement laws invoked the importance of equality for women. These lawyers contended that without access to legal abortion, women might lose newly available economic, social, and political opportunities. When the Supreme Court declined an invitation to overturn *Roe*, the justices' decision reflected more than a decade of debate about the costs and benefits of abortion for the family. While not adopting Justice Sandra Day O'Connor's earlier version, the Court made the undue burden test the controlling doctrinal approach for all abortion regula-tions. The Court's formal adoption of the undue burden test encouraged both sides to focus even more on both the effects of abortion and abortion restrictions. At the same time, *Casey* identified new opportunities available to women in explaining why reversing *Roe* would devastate so many.

Constitutional theorists wondered if *Casey* offered a better foundation for abortion rights, one centered on women's interest in equal opportunity as well as autonomy. But *Casey* very much reflected the abortion debate leading up to it, grounding much of its analysis in claims about whether and how abortion helped women. Instead of simply turning attention to equality arguments, *Casey* firmly tied constitutional law, like politics, to arguments about the costs and benefits of abortion.

EARLY DEBATE ABOUT ABORTION AND THE FAMILY

Almost before the ink had dried on the *Roe* decision, pro-lifers proposed laws mandating the involvement of husbands and parents. Indeed, between 1973 and 1982, not a year went by without states passing another such statute.[7] For pro-lifers, family involvement laws seemed to be a winning issue. The Supreme Court had never ruled on the constitutionality of mandated family involvement, and polls showed that otherwise ambivalent Americans endorsed such statutes. The relative popularity of family involvement laws did not shock abortion opponents, many of whom shared anxieties about how the family was changing. Prior to 1969, no state authorized a divorce unless one spouse could prove her innocence and the guilt of the other spouse. By 1973, following the advent of no-fault laws, the divorce rate climbed dramatically, and the nation appeared ready to break the divorce record each year. By the mid-1970s, national opinion surveys documented a decline in opposition to premarital sex, and prominent gay and lesbian rights groups put the issue of sexual orientation front and center. The 1950s ideal of a woman's home-making role also seemed increasingly untenable. Between 1950 and 1974, women's rate of workforce participation increased by roughly 35 percent, with nearly half of all women over 16 working by the mid-1970s.[8]

But abortion-rights supporters contested the constitutionality of family involvement laws. The first major abortion case after *Roe*, *Planned Parenthood of Central Missouri v. Danforth* (1976), struck down a spousal consent provision, concluding that when spouses disagreed, women should have the final say because pregnancy burdened them the most heavily. *Danforth* also invalidated a parental consent requirement because it awarded parents a veto regardless of a minor's best interests. But *Bellotti v. Baird II* (1979), a Massachusetts parental involvement case, showed that the fight over parental consultation was far from over. There, the Court held that "[i]f a state required a minor to obtain her parents' consent," the law had to provide her with a judicial bypass. By using such a procedure, a minor could prevail by convincing a judge "that she [was] mature enough and well enough informed" to make a decision or that "the desired abortion would be in her best interests."[9]

The issue of parental consultation returned to the Court not long after *Bellotti II*. In a six-to-three decision, *H. L. v. Matheson* (1981), the Court upheld a Utah parental notification law after concluding that the minor did not even have the standing to challenge the law.[10] In 1983, by contrast, *Akron I* struck down a parental consultation law. The Court interpreted an ambiguous Akron ordinance as "a blanket determination that all minors under the age of 15 are too immature to make this decision or that an abortion never may be in the minor's best interest without parental approval."[11] Later in the 1980s, *Danforth* and *Akron I* notwithstanding, abortion foes had specific reasons for stressing what they saw as the costs of abortion for families.

CEMENTING A PARTNERSHIP WITH THE REPUBLICAN PARTY

Larger antiabortion groups turned to claims about the benefits of parental involvement laws partly to mend their relationship with the GOP. Ronald Reagan appeared to have nominated enough justices to guarantee that *Roe* would be overruled. By the late 1980s, however, Republican leaders worried that the reversal of *Roe* would trigger painful electoral defeats. Polls consistently showed that most Americans did not wish *Roe* to be overturned and wanted abortion to be legal in some or all circumstances. Antiabortion groups wanted to show their political allies that pro-life laws still enjoyed popular support. Parental involvement laws seemed to be just the ticket. Indeed, abortion foes successfully promoted twenty-three such laws between 1974 and 1985 – one of the most successful antiabortion efforts in what had otherwise been a disappointing period.[12]

A new generation of antiabortion attorneys helped to handle the push for parental involvement laws. A graduate of Valparaiso University School of Law, Clarke Forsythe saw so much importance in AUL's work that he worked for free for several years after being turned down for a paid internship. He had voted for left-leaning candidates like Senator Eugene McCarthy (D–MN), but in 1980, when taking constitutional law, Forsythe grew frustrated with the direction of American jurisprudence. Only conservative candidates, it seemed, shared his views about the courts.[13]

In the late 1980s, when some GOP leaders seemed ready to sever ties with abortion foes, the push for parental involvement laws took on new urgency. During the 1988 presidential primary, strong pro-life candidates like Representative Jack Kemp (R–NY) and televangelist Pat Robertson had faded in the primaries, and Vice President George H. W. Bush, a leader with a questionable antiabortion commitment, took the nomination. As a member of Congress, Bush had been an outspoken proponent of family planning legislation, and he had opposed an antiabortion constitutional amendment until 1980. Abortion-rights supporters hoped that Bush's rise augured a broader shift in the GOP's stand on abortion. The Republican National Committee's platform committee allowed NOW and NARAL to campaign for an abortion-rights plank. Although he was ultimately unsuccessful, Senator

Lowell Weicker Jr. (R–CT) also made a push to soften the GOP platform's anti-abortion language.[14]

To some in NRLC and AUL, the platform fight showed that Republicans had grown gun-shy about working so closely with pro-lifers. The reasons for hesitation were not hard to find. Polls suggested that a majority of Americans wanted abortion to remain legal, if heavily regulated and rare. The Supreme Court might soon overturn *Roe* and enable states to criminalize abortion. Perhaps voters would punish the GOP at the polls if the justices changed abortion law too radically. In 1988, NRLC heavily lobbied the platform committee, and NRLC leader Jack Willke insisted that "past elections [had] shown a position against abortion can prove to be a 'margin of victory' for the pro-life candidate." When Republicans seemingly wavered in their commitment to the pro-life movement, it made sense to find laws and arguments with the broadest appeal.[15]

A focus on family involvement laws also fortified AUL's new ties with evangelical pro-life organizations. Guy Condon, a young graduate of Wheaton College, the so-called Harvard for evangelicals, had successfully professionalized the organization's fundraising operation. After becoming the organization's president, Condon pursued financial support and closer relationships with pro-life evangelical organizations such as the Arthur S. DeMoss Foundation, a family foundation started in 1955. Since the late 1970s, conservative evangelicals like those aligned with the DeMoss Foundation had defended what they saw as an embattled traditional family. In championing family involvement laws, antiabortion lawyers further asserted that abortion would decimate the authority of husbands and parents.[16]

Many grassroots pro-lifers also genuinely worried that legal abortion put unbearable pressure on already crumbling families. Sexually active teenagers seemed to pose a particularly acute threat. As one veteran NRLC board member explained, pro-lifers believed that "abortion facilities [particularly] promoted themselves and made themselves available to teenagers and young women." NRLC members argued that without parental support, teenagers could make an abortion decision that would derail their lives. By highlighting claims about the costs of abortion for the family, larger pro-life groups hoped to lower the abortion rate and solidify their political alliances.[17]

The prominence of these claims was evident at a 1987 AUL conference centered on ways to reverse *Roe* in the Court. Even before pro-lifers believed they had the votes to dismantle the 1973 decision, AUL lawyers still thought that they could shape public opinion – and eventually chip away at the Court's pro-*Roe* majority. "The legal strategy to reverse *Roe* depends on documenting the decision's devastating impact on the whole of society," explained Laurie Ann Ramsey in detailing the conference's conclusions. Laws about the effect of abortion on the family would play a central role in the mission to overturn *Roe*, albeit much sooner than Ramsey might have expected. After Anthony Kennedy and Antonin Scalia joined the Court,

AUL continued emphasizing parental consent laws, this time, hoping to set the stage for a decision reversing *Roe*.[18]

CHALLENGING PARENTAL INVOLVEMENT LAWS

Abortion-rights attorneys challenged parental involvement laws as soon as they passed, but the task was not easy. The laws enjoyed popular support, and abortion-rights attorneys had to tread carefully to avoid damaging their movement's cause politically. Moreover, the Supreme Court had struck down only certain laws requiring parental consent to an abortion. States experimented with laws simply requiring minors to notify one or both parents. How did such laws burden anyone, and why were they a bad idea?

In answering these questions, lawyers for groups like Planned Parenthood and the ACLU Reproductive Freedom Project (RFP) focused on claims about the costs of parental involvement laws. Abortion-rights litigators asserted that for many minors, parental involvement laws took away the chance for a career or education. These claims often invoked the idea of equality between the sexes, a concept anchored in the Equal Protection Clause of the Fourteenth Amendment.

This strategy came to the forefront in *Hodgson v. Minnesota*, the next parental consultation case to reach the Supreme Court. *Hodgson* involved a Minnesota law requiring most minors to notify both parents before getting an abortion. Minors could avoid the requirement if only one parent could be located, if their lives would be at risk if a pregnancy were carried to term, or if the authorities knew that the minor would be a victim of physical or sexual abuse if she told her parents about a pregnancy.[19]

RFP attorneys first contended that the costs of family involvement laws were too high for women from abusive families. While expert witnesses testified that information about a minor's pregnancy could trigger abuse, abortion clinic staff told stories about "violence in the family, a mentally or terminally ill parent, incest, fear of being thrown out of the home, vehement antiabortion beliefs of the parents, no relationship with the non-custodial parent, and the like."[20]

The ACLU RFP also asserted that many minors had the maturity to benefit from making a difficult abortion decision for themselves. This claim captured shifting views of the nation's youth. In 1985, the *New York Times* reported the widely held view that "today's [college] students are significantly less mature than their parents and grandparents were at the same age." Commentators blamed children's failure to grow up on everything from women's higher rates of workforce participation to Americans' longer life expectancy.[21]

Nor did as many young Americans get married or start a career – steps that had conventionally defined maturity. Women in their mid-20s were increasingly likely to remain single. It could not be taken for granted that younger Americans would establish their own homes. In the mid-1980s, more young adults lived with their parents, a phenomenon that researchers attributed to everything from an economic slowdown to Americans' willingness to delay marriage. Experts debated whether the definition of maturity had changed or whether young people had simply failed to achieve it. Whereas adulthood had once arrived predictably, maturity now seemed like a prize that no one could easily define or attain.[22]

ACLU RFP attorneys repeated that it had grown much harder to determine who was mature – and that a woman's decisions and experiences counted far more than her age. Moreover, Janet Benshoof and her colleagues at ACLU RFP presented evidence that forcing minors to depend on their parents stunted personal growth. Maturity came through making smart, if difficult, decisions. One expert witness explained that "separation from parents and developing a sense of personal privacy are critical to adolescent development."[23]

Finally, ACLU attorneys asserted that parental involvement laws could rob women of opportunities that were just becoming available. An unplanned pregnancy could disrupt a woman's plans for college, career, and financial independence. These advocates contended that far from causing psychological distress, abortion alleviated the struggles of minors overwhelmed by the consequences of an unintended pregnancy.[24]

Abortion opponents relied much more on parents to decide what was good for their children. Vincent Rue, a veteran pro-life witness, suggested that parents, if informed, would be the only ones able to provide crucial medical information. Mark Lally, an attorney working with an NRLC affiliate, made similar arguments in defense of Ohio's parental involvement law. "Since even mature adults are susceptible to the problems of unrecognized denial and repression of abortion trauma," he wrote, "a mature minor can benefit from a notified parent who can remain observant for symptoms of problems."[25]

For ACLU RFP attorneys, *Hodgson* was about more than the fate of a single statute. Would the courts recognize that the family was changing – and that incremental abortion restrictions could have the same effect on women as an outright ban on the procedure? As Benshoof explained in an internal memo, "[a] 'win' which would render the *Hodgson* case a landmark ... would require [the court] to find that the parental notification statute is premised on ... antiquated notions about teenagers and family which are wholly unsupported by empirical evidence."[26]

The trial court gave Benshoof what she wanted, and the Sixth Circuit also held that the Ohio statute was unconstitutional. While abortion-rights lawyers might have had reason to celebrate, the victory seemed anything but secure. After Anthony Kennedy took a seat on the Court, it seemed that the justices would overrule *Roe*. Family involvement laws no longer seemed to be just a way to shape public opinion or limit abortion access. Instead, by playing up the costs of abortion for the family, antiabortion attorneys hoped to offer the Supreme Court the chance to overrule *Roe*.[27]

FATHERS' RIGHTS

After Anthony Kennedy's arrival, antiabortion attorneys hoped that fathers' rights cases would sound the death knell for abortion-rights. Spousal involvement laws, like parental consultation laws, had long been a standard part of the antiabortion arsenal. In advocating for these laws, pro-lifers played up claims about the costs of abortion for the family. But for a variety of reasons, the fathers' rights litigation of the late 1980s was more ambitious. In parental involvement litigation, abortion foes often presented both parents and minors as the victims of scheming abortion doctors. In fathers' rights cases, by contrast, pro-life lawyers increasingly argued that some women did not benefit from abortions that cost men their emotional well-being. Indeed, some antiabortion attorneys suggested that women had abortions for trivial, wholly unjustifiable reasons. The new fathers' rights litigation also had a far more ambitious aim. Whereas some parental notification laws arguably could pass muster under *Akron I* or *Thornburgh*, fathers' rights cases mounted a more direct challenge to *Roe*. For James Bopp Jr. and his colleague Richard Coleson, that was hardly a problem. The time had come, they believed, for *Roe* to go.

The first fathers' rights case began after John Smith (a pseudonym), a 24-year-old delivery truck driver from Vigo County, Indiana, asked if there was a way to stop his 18-year-old ex-girlfriend from terminating her pregnancy. It was no accident that antiabortion attorneys represented men like John Smith. Rather than just defending the interests of the married or wealthy, Bopp and Coleson often took on the cases of young, blue-collar, unmarried men who articulated complex ideas about fatherhood.[28]

After going to juvenile court to establish Smith's paternity over the fetus his girlfriend was carrying, the two attorneys used a balancing approach that recalibrated arguments about the costs and benefits of abortion. Under *Roe*, any first-trimester regulation was constitutionally suspect. Although the Court had upheld several abortion restrictions since 1973, the justices still closely scrutinized any abortion law. Bopp and Coleson proposed a very different approach, arguing that the Court should consider whether the reasons a woman wanted an abortion outweighed a man's interests in forcing a pregnancy to continue. Bopp and Coleson insisted that abortion had no real benefits for women who chose the procedure for frivolous reasons. "I believe the key is to show that *Roe* did not settle the matter, nor did *Danforth*, and then to go through the elements mentioned in *Roe* and *Doe v. Bolton* (education, stigma, employment, other children, poverty, etc.) and show that they are not present or do not outweigh the father's interest in his child," Coleson asserted. And Bopp and Coleson hoped that arguments about the costs of abortion could justify not only incremental restrictions but also the immediate overruling of *Roe*.[29]

After Jane Doe refused to testify, viewing the entire hearing as a privacy violation, Judge Robert Howard Brown of the Vigo Circuit Court sided with Bopp and

Coleson. The court further reasoned that John Smith would suffer considerable emotional harm if his child died. As Judge Brown saw it, the only trauma Jane Doe faced if the pregnancy came to term involved her "desire to look nice in a bathing suit this summer, her desire to not be pregnant this summer, and her desire not to share the petitioner with the baby."[30]

While seeking expedited review from the Indiana Supreme Court, Jane Doe ignored the judge's order and terminated her pregnancy. Bopp and Coleson still asked the United States Supreme Court to review the case after losing in the Indiana Supreme Court. Both parties' filings revealed deeply different views about what the Constitution had to say about the costs and benefits of abortion. Jane Doe argued that the trial court's decision ignored the costs of forcing her to continue a pregnancy, especially the opportunities she would have to give up and the loss of her dignity and privacy.[31]

When Bopp and Coleson asked the Supreme Court to hear their appeal, their petition highlighted claims about the benefits of forcing certain women to continue their pregnancies. The two insisted that Indiana had a compelling interest in protecting fathers' relationships with their unborn children. "[W]hen fathers seek to protect their children from peril, whether the children are born or unborn, and to provide for them, society — and the courts — should encourage such attitudes," Coleson and Bopp wrote. Bopp and Coleson maintained that at a minimum, under some circumstances, fathers' interests would outweigh women's liberty, and John Smith's was one such case.[32]

Although Bopp and Coleson intended their arguments for the courts, cases like John Smith's rallied grassroots activists who saw benefits in restoring some men to a more traditional role in the family. At the time, a broader fathers' rights movement, first formed in the 1960s, continued pursuing reforms of laws governing alimony and child custody after divorce. Biological fathers had asserted rights in other contexts, especially when seeking to block adoption by third parties.[33]

Antiabortion lawyers decried what they saw as similar discrimination against potential fathers. Following the publication of a 1988 *Wall Street Journal* article on Bopp and Coleson's fathers' rights litigation, dozens of pro-lifers wrote in with their support. "It is logically absurd and intolerable that one party, the mother, may exercise a judicially permitted right to abort the baby and the other party, the father, has no legal right in preserving the living, unborn baby that the parties jointly generated," wrote one correspondent from Highland, Indiana.[34]

These cases put on display clashing ideas about the costs of abortion for the family. Bopp and Coleson interacted with many men who felt devastated by what they experienced as the loss of a child with whom they already felt bonded – and perhaps the loss of a family life they had once imagined. One pro-life activist from South Carolina reported on an unsuccessful case, stating: "The young man and his parents are grieving and yet willing to do anything to prevent this from happening to other fathers and grandparents." The women involved in fathers' rights cases described the costs of litigating their rights to end a pregnancy. ACLU attorneys explained that women forced into court often had to delay abortion until later in pregnancy when the procedure carried greater risks. Worse, trials forced women to disclose the most intimate details of their lives in open court. Women like Jane Doe saw fathers' rights cases as a way to deny them control over their own relationships and futures.[35]

In litigating father's rights cases, antiabortion attorneys put on trial women who did not want to bring their pregnancies to term. Bopp and Coleson lauded the intentions of John Smith, a man who wanted to marry his sweetheart and provide for his baby. By contrast, the two questioned Jane Doe's motives, presenting her as shallow and immature. This case fit into a broader strategy. Bopp and Coleson suggested that only certain women should have the right to choose abortion. If abortion-rights were so narrow, the argument went, there would be less reason to retain *Roe v. Wade*.

Cases like John Smith's sparked a larger conversation about pregnant women's behavior – one tied up in the war on drugs of the late 1980s. In the mid-1980s, crack cocaine, a smokable and relatively inexpensive form of the drug, became widely available. Crack use in poor, predominantly nonwhite, inner-city communities became a media preoccupation, especially following publication of research suggesting that cocaine use during pregnancy could cause miscarriages, low birth weight, and birth defects. Some prosecutors pursued charges against pregnant crack users. AUL proposed model legislation explicitly allowing states to prosecute pregnant women for illegal drug use. "A clear, high standard should be placed on the prosecutor to determine willful, malicious child abuse before any woman is charged," explained Clarke Forsythe. "That would exclude misconduct like smoking and nutrition, which [are] not willful and malicious misconduct."[36]

AUL recognized the tactical advantages of highlighting drug abuse by pregnant women. AUL's newsletter reported that such prosecutions created "yet another opportunity for AUL to defend the state's compelling interest to protect viable fetal life, a critical element in the strategy to reverse *Roe*." AUL leaders also wanted to draw attention to what they saw as the unwise or even criminal decisions some women made about reproduction. These claims would highlight the costs of allowing certain women to make decisions about abortion. Larger antiabortion groups further hoped that if voters disapproved of a woman's reasons for choosing to end a pregnancy, they would approve of laws banning the procedure under some circumstances.[37]

As was the case with prosecutions of pregnant drug users, fathers' rights litigation suggested that the Constitution did not protect all women who wanted to end their pregnancies. Increasingly, however, Bopp and Coleson reasoned that men's fundamental parental rights always trumped whatever was left of *Roe*. The two advanced this argument in the summer of 1988 on behalf of Erin Conn, a military veteran who worked as a toy store manager to put himself through school. Conn and his wife,

Jennifer, had a five-month-old daughter, but their marriage was failing. Nineteen-year-old Jennifer told Erin that she was filing for divorce and ending her latest pregnancy. Bopp and Coleson stepped back from criticizing Jennifer's reasons for wanting an abortion. Instead, the two attorneys argued that all men had fundamental rights that deserved consideration before a woman ended her pregnancy,[38] including the right to procreate, the "right to care, custody, control, and management" of his child, and a right "inherent in his status as a husband in a family unit." Those representing Jennifer Conn responded that *Roe* and *Danforth* meant that no man had "an affirmative constitutional right to use the power of the government to interfere with a woman's private and constitutionally protected right to choose." Although the Supreme Court refused to hear *Conn* in November 1988, Bopp and Coleson were simply biding their time. With Anthony Kennedy on the bench, the two lawyers soon hoped for a different outcome.[39]

Bopp and Coleson recognized that arguments about the costs and benefits of abortion could lay the foundation for a decision overturning *Roe*. In the mid-1980s, abortion-rights attorneys had defended reproductive freedom by telling the stories of women who needed or benefitted from the procedure. Bopp and Coleson turned this argument on its head. The two insisted that the Constitution should honor the wishes of men with compelling justifications for wanting a pregnancy continued. While this argument failed in Court, the antiabortion movement understood its power. NRLC and other larger groups concluded that abortion-rights were not just personal but also conditional on a woman's reasons for ending a pregnancy.

For much of the 1980s, larger antiabortion groups had prioritized arguments about the costs of abortion, tying those claims to incremental restrictions. Some abortion foes, however, argued that lawyers like Bopp and Coleson had made fools of themselves by waiting for the Supreme Court to save them. A predominantly (but not exclusively) evangelical Protestant clinic-blockade movement urged abortion foes to stop waiting on the Court. Break the law, blockaders promised, and you can stop abortions immediately. Blockaders had no time for arguments about the costs of abortion. Instead, they talked about their faith and denounced abortion as murder. While the fate of a right to abortion hung in the balance, pro-lifers seemed increasingly divided about a strategy centered on the costs of abortion.

THE RISE OF OPERATION RESCUE

For Randall Terry and other members of an emerging clinic-blockade movement, antiabortion arguments about the policy consequences of abortion must have seemed to be a sick joke. Terry and his supporters thought that abortion was murder, plain and simple. Talking so much about the policy costs of abortion seemed counterproductive, if not a touch unhinged.

For the leaders of larger antiabortion groups, Operation Rescue's explosive growth likely came as a surprise. The organization's rapid ascent reflected a surge in evangelical pro-life involvement – one that manifested, in part, in blockades that started erupting across the country. Although antiabortion pickets began before 1973, organizations like Joseph Scheidler's Pro-Life Action League pioneered more ambitious efforts to close clinics altogether. Scheidler was Catholic, as were many who joined early pickets. In 1986, Terry, a devout evangelical, founded his own organization, Operation Rescue. Terry took inspiration from Scheidler's protests, and within a few years, Operation Rescue had upended the antiabortion movement. Leading major blockades in Atlanta, Los Angeles, and Cherry Hill, New Jersey, Terry's organization routinely made front-page news.[40]

Although Catholics participated in early blockades, Operation Rescue attracted attention from evangelical Protestants who had not participated in groups like NRLC or AUL. For example, Judy and Bob Tunkel, a couple who had traveled to an Atlanta blockade, explained that Operation Rescue had developed tactics and scriptural arguments that spoke to their religious convictions. "[Before], we felt we had done nothing to come between a baby and a killer," Judy told a reporter. Operation Rescue invited blockaders to ignore trespassing laws and face arrest, but the relationship between blockades and the antiabortion violence of the 1980s was complex. Operation Rescue asked participants to sign a nonviolence pledge and sometimes explicitly linked blockades to the nonviolent civil disobedience of the civil rights movement. To be sure, many blockaders, including some in the organization's leadership, opposed violence. However, prominent leaders of Operation Rescue had ties to the pro-violence Army of God. Jayne Bray, a board member of the organization, was the wife of convicted clinic bomber Michael Bray, a prominent defender of killing abortion doctors. Jayne Bray and some leaders of the group seemed open to some justifications for violence and even murder.[41]

The debate about violence aside, Operation Rescue tapped into some pro-lifers' frustration with an incremental plan of attack. Terry and his followers thought that no one was listening to claims about the costs of abortion. "Over fourteen years of mostly education and political lobbying has got us virtually nowhere," Terry wrote. Operation Rescue leaders concluded lawbreaking and mass protests would make everyone uncomfortable enough to face the need for change, as would arguments equating abortion and murder. "Politicians see the light when they feel the heat," Terry explained.[42]

Operation Rescue sought to assert leadership in the antiabortion movement. In 1988 and 1989, blockaders reported impressive numbers of participants willing to risk jail time. For example, the organization spearheaded blockades at three Atlanta clinics in the summer of 1988, and over 1,200 faced arrest. Judie Brown's American Life League endorsed Operation Rescue and encouraged abortion foes to participate. Jerry Falwell, the founder of the Moral Majority, described nonviolent civil disobedience as the antiabortion movement's only real chance. Dr. James Dobson, the founder of Focus on the Family and a conservative evangelical media icon, embraced Operation Rescue. So did Beverly LaHaye's organization for conservative evangelical Protestant women, Concerned Women for America. Established antiabortion groups viewed clinic blockades with ambivalence. NRLC issued a policy prohibiting employees, directors, and state affiliates from engaging in any illegal activity, including trespassing. AUL leaders believed that litigation and lobbying would work better than lawbreaking. Nonetheless, larger antiabortion groups seemed to be fighting a losing battle. As evangelical participation in the pro-life movement intensified, it seemed that Operation Rescue and its religious arguments might represent the movement's future.[43]

Operation Rescue exposed a tension in the strategy pursued by larger antiabortion groups. Pro-lifers still fiercely believed in a fundamental right to life. But those prioritizing arguments about the costs of abortion sometimes said little about fetal rights. Operation Rescue became only the latest antiabortion group that bridled at a strategy based on the costs of abortion. An impending decision on *Roe's* fate did nothing to heal this breach.

PEOPLE OF COLOR ON THE SIDELINES

Operation Rescue won over some conservative evangelicals by making a claim on the legacy of the civil rights movement. The reality was that Operation Rescue overwhelmingly (but never exclusively) attracted white protesters. Some black pastors and evangelical Protestants, such as Rev. Johnny Hunter of the Western New York Pro-life Rescue Movement, joined in rescues and framed them as part of an effort to follow God's will and protect people of color from extermination. But Hunter was an exception in a movement that primarily attracted white protesters. Larger antiabortion groups fared no better, although not for lack of trying. In the late 1980s, Black Americans for Life continued its outreach efforts. Other prominent pro-life activists, like Mildred Jefferson and Erma Craven, spoke out against legal abortion, and in earlier years, Jefferson had served as president of NRLC. Prior to his death in 1985, Dr. Jasper Williams, the former head of the National Medical Association, had been an outspoken abortion foe and frequently served as an expert witness in abortion cases. But groups like BAL struggled to grow.[44]

Similarly, larger abortion-rights groups also remained far more racially homogenous than their leaders would have liked. In the spring of 1989, the National Organization for Women (NOW) called a march in Washington, DC, to protest the Court's likely retreat on abortion-rights. The march attracted roughly 300,000 participants, but only 5 percent of attendees were women of color. Loretta Ross of NOW and Melanie Tervalon of NARAL, both women of color, held leadership positions in major abortion-rights organizations. Groups like the National Black Women's Health Project and the National Latina Health Organization identified new recruits, as did outreach projects launched by NOW and the Religious Coalition for Abortion-Rights. But these efforts only brought into relief how much larger groups struggled to recruit and retain nonwhite women.[45]

Why did both movements remain predominantly white? The civil rights movement mostly stayed on the sidelines of the abortion conflict, not steering black Americans into either the pro-choice or pro-life camp. Polls indicated that nonwhite Americans were often divided about abortion. Evangelical and Catholic churches stoked opposition to abortion for some African-American, Asian, and Latino Christians. At the same time, the abortion rate among women of color, particularly African-Americans, was disproportionately high, and limits on access seemed likely to have a particularly powerful impact on women of color.[46]

Divided communities explained only part of the struggles of the two movements to diversify. Abortion foes' single-issue focus alienated some nonwhite women, as did the movement's burgeoning partnership with the Republican Party. In earlier years, prominent black Republicans like Audrey Rowe Colom, the head of the National Women's Political Caucus, and Senator Ed Brooke (R–MA) supported legal abortion. Nonetheless, the GOP denounced affirmative action and vowed to shrink the welfare state. Some people of color felt out of place with a pro-life movement that had become part of the political right.[47]

The story on the abortion-rights side was complicated. In 1988, people of color voted overwhelmingly for the Democratic nominee, Michael Dukakis, and the Democrats willingly proclaimed their support for abortion-rights. Although some people of color opposed abortion, those who favored a right to choose often felt marginalized by larger organizations. Younger activists, like the founders of Students Organizing Students (SOS), tried to develop a broader agenda designed to empower women of color, as did local organizers focused on defending clinics. But for the most part, as legal abortion seemed to be at risk, larger abortion-rights organizations prioritized political success even if that came at the cost of greater racial diversity. If, as many predicted, the Court overturned *Roe*, only legislators could protect abortion. Groups like NARAL recognized that more voters favored legal abortion than backed a more comprehensive reproductive health program. And public support for arguments about the evils of government meddling ran higher than it did for claims about the economic, social, or political opportunities gained by women who could decide when to have a child. Rather than highlighting the benefits of abortion for women, NARAL and its allies retooled rights-based arguments, asking Americans to act on their distaste for big government.[48]

BUILDING A POLITICAL MAJORITY FOR THE RIGHT TO CHOOSE

In the late 1980s, larger abortion-rights groups like NARAL, NOW, and Planned Parenthood formed a tightly knit coalition that coordinated everything from messaging to tactics. Despite internal disagreements, most coalition members argued that the Supreme Court would overturn *Roe*. The only way forward, it seemed, was to ask voters to restore reproductive rights. Ironically, when larger abortion-rights groups assumed that the courts would no longer protect abortion, rights-based arguments took on more importance. Such claims, as leading abortion-rights groups saw it, would play better with both politicians and the voters who elected them than would arguments about the benefits of abortion.

Starting in the late 1980s, NARAL and its allies developed claims intended to provide "evidence of numbers and [a] potential pro-choice majority." Hickman-Maslin Research, a political polling firm working with NARAL, urged the group to "[a]void belligerent feminist rhetoric" in favor of the argument that the "Constitution ... protect[s] every woman's right to make her own decision, ... free from the dictates of government." In the early 1980s, conservatives had popularized certain related arguments about the problems with government. Speaking to concerns sparked by the Vietnam War, a sputtering economy, and the Watergate scandal, Ronald Reagan made the fight against "big government" a central message of his two terms in the White House. NARAL developed a different way to address anxieties about state interference. Of course, all rights-based arguments for abortion, including those made in earlier years, involved a demand for liberty from government. In the late 1980s, however, NARAL altered these claims. Rather than emphasizing women's interests, NARAL played up public disapproval of government meddling.[49]

Tamar Abrams, one of the women who helped to shape this message, grew up in an Air Force family. She never stayed in one country for long, living in Japan, Germany, and Canada before going to college in St. Louis, Missouri. Finding herself in a political "twilight zone," Abrams immediately got involved in women's issues. In her second year of college, she unexpectedly found out that she was pregnant. When she had an abortion, she told only the roommate who drove her home. It struck her at the time as "something that was very shameful and very private and very sad."[50]

After graduation, Abrams moved to Washington, DC, and began working in the nonprofit sector, but her abortion experience was never far from her thoughts. In 1987, she saw that NARAL hoped to hire a communications professional and got the job. During her time there, the organization played down claims about the benefits of abortion. Like her colleagues, Abrams felt that NARAL had to change its message "to go after those people for whom abortion was kind of muddy."[51]

By stressing the kind of argument that Abrams described, NARAL and its coalition partners planned to "create a political climate in which it is unacceptable to erode or overrule *Roe*." The organization's advisors worried that most voters did not care about whether legal abortion benefitted women. Hickman-Maslin Research explained: "Remember, there are millions of people who agree with us about the basic issue of CHOICE who may not agree on any other issue, including those we may assume are interrelated, i.e., civil rights, feminism, labor issues, etc."[52]

In championing a small-government message, NARAL increasingly coordinated with other abortion-rights groups. The threat posed by Operation Rescue encouraged coalition building. As early as May 1989, the leaders of many abortion-rights groups gathered to discuss what to do about blockades. Those present at one such strategy summit explained the importance of taping protests, identifying participants, and working with local prosecutors to enforce injunctions and criminal laws. In fighting Operation Rescue, groups like Planned Parenthood, NARAL, and NOW did not emphasize the benefits of abortion care. Instead, pro-choice representatives framed blockades as a waste of time (and described blockaders as bumbling misogynists). Planned Parenthood planned to portray protesters – and all abortion opponents – as anti-woman extremists. Attendees explained that "[s]ince the majority of the Operation Rescue leadership [were] men," those present would "project the image of men trying to prevent women from exercising their rights."[53]

NARAL and its allies expected the Supreme Court to forsake their movement. But rather than downplaying rights-based arguments, groups like NARAL and Planned Parenthood saw abstract constitutional rhetoric as more politically valuable than ever. Americans did not agree about whether abortion had benefits or even about what counted as a benefit in the first place. Indeed, many seemed to support specific restrictions on abortion. By contrast, many thought that the government should stay out of everyone's business. The likely dismantling of *Roe v. Wade* did not dampen enthusiasm for rights-based arguments. Nor did the prospect of the Court overturning *Roe* lead anyone to look harder for middle-ground solutions. Instead, groups like NARAL spent even more time talking about why the government should not interfere with women's constitutional rights.

WEBSTER AND THE BEGINNING OF THE END

In 1987, when Richard Coleson graduated from law school, it was hard to picture a more exciting time to be an antiabortion attorney. He grew up in the Wesleyan Church, founded in 1843 when abolitionists left what was then called the Methodist Episcopal Church because of a dispute over slavery. Wesleyan values defined Coleson's early life. In his law office, he kept a brick from a building that served as a station on the Underground Railroad. His parents schooled him in the importance of equality between men and women at work, and his grandmother and mother were both Wesleyan ministers. Coleson was born during a mission in India, and after a spell in the United States, he moved with his parents to Sierra Leone for a second mission. His father's health troubles finally sent the family back to the United States for good. Coleson spent the rest of his childhood in Indiana, deciding to major in theology at Indiana Wesleyan University. He spent his junior year as a student in Jerusalem, where his Middle Eastern studies included the history of anti-Semitism, and he was deeply affected and motivated by visiting Yad Vashem – The World Holocaust Remembrance Center.[54]

Coleson became an ordained minister and taught at Oklahoma Wesleyan University where he served as a school chaplain. He was a natural academic, but he had always had an interest in the intersection of "faith and public policy," and he felt especially compelled, when teaching the Hebrew prophets, by Isaiah's command to "seek justice" by "defending the oppressed." Coleson went to law school and began working under James Bopp Jr. of NRLC. Bopp, as Coleson put it, was "the big picture guy," while Coleson focused on the details. Coleson seemed to have found an ideal time to become a pro-life lawyer. The two had high hopes that *Roe* would be overruled very soon.[55]

Roger Evans experienced the end of the 1980s quite differently. Evans grew up in Cleveland, Ohio, before attending law school in New York and working as an attorney for poor clients. He landed at Planned Parenthood almost by accident. Looking for the logical next step in his career, Evans applied when the organization was looking for an in-house lawyer to spearhead litigation. A relationship that began because of "good fortune" would define the rest of Evans' career. He worked on abortion laws from start to finish, overseeing legislative strategies, writing and giving testimony, offering comments on regulations, and bringing challenges in court.[56]

For Evans, the late 1980s brought a "dwindling majority on the Supreme Court." When lawyers like Coleson eagerly anticipated the Court's next move, Evans lived through a "whack-a-mole situation," waiting for the next restriction to pop up. He challenged the family involvement laws increasingly championed by lawyers like Bopp and Coleson. The job required him to "count heads" and see who remained committed to the principles that *Roe* had announced. Increasingly, it seemed, the number was distressingly low.[57]

In the late 1980s and early 1990s, both Coleson and Evans expected that the Court would soon overturn *Roe*. The justices had the chance to do so in *Webster v. Reproductive Health Services*, a case addressing the constitutionality of a multipart Missouri statute passed in 1986. The Court also took two parental involvement cases, *Hodgson* and *Ohio v. Akron Center for Reproductive Health* (*Akron II*). *Webster*, however, was the case everyone was watching. Three parts of the law came before the Supreme Court: a preamble stating that life began at conception, a prohibition on the use of public funding, counseling, or facilities for abortion, and a statutory definition of viability. Insiders believed that *Webster* gave the Court a perfect chance to overturn *Roe*.[58]

A gathering of antiabortion attorneys submitting briefs in that case buzzed with excitement. Clarke Forsythe of AUL speculated that the Court was considering "at least altering the standard of review [for abortion regulations]."[59] James Bopp Jr. and Burke Balch of NRLC dismissed the possibility that the Court would strongly reaffirm *Roe*. When summarizing possible outcomes in *Webster*, the two explained: "The Court could effectively overturn *Roe v. Wade* either by saying there is no constitutionally protected right to abortion and saying that laws banning or restricting abortion will be upheld as long as they are rational, or perhaps by saying that the state has a compelling interest in the unborn child from conception."[60]

New lawyers joined antiabortion litigation efforts, many of them headed by evangelicals. One of these groups, Focus on the Family, began with a radio program hosted by televangelist and psychologist James Dobson in 1977. By the late 1980s, the group joined the abortion battle, submitting a brief in *Webster* with an aligned lobbying organization, the Family Research Council. Other groups had formed to defend what they saw as faith-based interests distinct from those highlighted by NRLC and AUL. In 1988, Jay Sekulow, a lawyer who would go on to become President Donald Trump's personal attorney, founded Christian Advocates Serving Evangelism (CASE) to litigate religious-liberty cases and defend clinic blockaders. Working with veteran pro-life attorneys, new antiabortion lawyers argued that *Roe* had no justification in the text or history of the Constitution. Amicus briefs in *Webster* suggested that *Roe* had hopelessly distorted not only abortion law but also other rules governing everything from wrongful death lawsuits to the meaning of a constitutional right to privacy.[61]

Bush Administration officials also believed that the Court might overrule *Roe* but showed considerably less enthusiasm about the prospect. "The Administration's position on this case has been extremely important to a significant part of your constituency," aides C. Boyden Gray and William Roper wrote of *Webster*. "For that reason, enough people could read sinister motives into the lack of an immediate response ... Were we to [say something] on the spot, however, these issues are emotionally charged enough that any misstep could be disastrous."[62]

Even after the Court decided *Webster*, abortion opponents disagreed about precisely what the Court had said. A majority voted to uphold the Missouri law. The viability provision required that if any woman was twenty or more weeks pregnant, physicians had to perform tests to determine a fetus' ability to survive outside the womb. The plurality acknowledged that under *Roe* and the cases following it, the Missouri law might be unconstitutional because it "superimposed state regulation on the medical determination of whether a particular fetus is viable." But the plurality thought that the law exposed problems with *Roe* itself, not with the Missouri law. *Webster* suggested that contrary to what *Roe* reasoned, the state's interest in protecting fetal life existed throughout pregnancy. Nor, the plurality concluded, was there any constitutional foundation for "the key elements of the *Roe* framework – trimesters and viability." The plurality still stopped short of saying that *Roe* should be overturned, insisting that it was "distinguishable on its facts." Justice Antonin Scalia went a step further, calling on the Court to immediately overturn *Roe*. But Sandra Day O'Connor did not join parts of the plurality criticizing *Roe*'s trimester framework. As she interpreted the viability-testing requirements, there was no conflict with *Roe* or any of the abortion decisions following it. Nevertheless, *Webster* implied that five justices were highly skeptical of *Roe*, if not ready to undo abortion-rights altogether.[63]

Webster did not settle pro-life conflicts about a strategy centered on claims about the costs of abortion. Indeed, abortion foes could not agree on what *Webster* meant for the future of the abortion conflict. While some dedicated themselves to an incremental approach, others thought that the time had come for a more aggressive attack. Even blockaders believed that *Webster* signaled that *Roe* was not long for this world. For pro-lifers, the question was whether claims about the costs of abortion could convince the Court to overturn *Roe* immediately.

OVERTURNING *ROE* AS QUICKLY AS POSSIBLE

Because *Webster* was a fractured opinion, abortion foes disagreed about what exactly the Court had said and what should be done about it. While Operation Rescue framed *Webster* as a sign that lawbreaking had worked, larger groups wagered that the Court would soon validate a strategy centered on the costs of abortion. The race was on to set up the perfect test case to end legal abortion.[64]

Webster jump-started fundraising efforts for larger antiabortion groups. NRLC affiliates requested model legislation to pass in their states, and both AUL and NRLC's legislative-drafting efforts went into overdrive. In 1990, NRLC had a budget of $12 million, twenty-four times larger than a decade before. In the mid-1980s, AUL had struggled to lift itself out of desperate financial circumstances. Between 1988 and 1991, the organization doubled in size. In 1990, AUL leaders projected nearly $3 million in income, and the following year alone, the group reported an additional 32 percent increase in fundraising, opened an office in Washington, DC, and created programs to train both clergy and grassroots activists.[65]

New conservative Christian litigation groups also opened shop after *Webster*. Many became active because of the work of prominent evangelical theologian Francis Schaeffer. In 1981, Schaeffer published the deeply influential *A Christian Manifesto*, urging Christian lawyers to do more to shape the law. *How Should We Then Live? The Rise and Decline of Western Thought and Culture*, a film series narrated by Schaeffer and Dr. C. Everett Koop, brought these arguments to a larger audience. After *Webster*, conservative Christian lawyers increasingly answered Schaeffer's call to action. In 1989, Anita Staver and her husband, Mathew, a recent graduate of the University of Kentucky College of Law, cofounded Liberty Counsel, a group dedicated to free speech and religious liberty for conservative Christians, including clinic blockaders. At first, Staver's operation was small, mostly focused on the Southeast, and largely funded by Staver's Orlando law firm. Other Christian lawyering organizations were better funded from the outset. Following his failed 1988 presidential bid, televangelist Pat Robertson founded the American Center for Law and Justice (ACLJ), a group that would litigate on behalf of conservative evangelicals, and hired Jay Sekulow to head it. With an initial budget of $6 million, ACLJ also benefitted from ties to Robertson's Regent University School of Law.[66]

Other antiabortion lawyers thought that larger groups simply rehashed arguments that had already failed. Harold J. Cassidy, a New Jersey attorney, believed that other pro-life attorneys had ignored one particular cost of the procedure: the loss of a pregnant mother's right to retain her constitutionally protected relationship with her child. In 1981, he began taking the cases of birth mothers who suffered from separation from their children after losing them in adoption. He attended counseling sessions with some of his clients and was impressed by the trauma experienced by birth mothers who acutely felt the loss of their children. He became a volunteer lawyer for Concerned United Birthparents, an advocacy group for mothers and other parents who lost children through adoption. This work, in turn, brought him to the attention of surrogate mothers who wanted to keep the children they had carried. Cassidy ultimately represented Mary Beth Whitehead, the surrogate in the best known such case, *In re Baby M.*[67]

In 1990, a couple asked him to bring a wrongful birth lawsuit against a doctor who had not performed an amniocentesis that would have detected that the child had Down Syndrome (given that the mother was over 35 years of age, the doctor would have had to perform the amniocentesis to comply with the standard of care at the time). The couple would have ended the pregnancy if they had known about the disability. Although he declined the case, the couple's request haunted him. He became convinced that after abortion, women would suffer the same trauma experienced by birth mothers in the context of adoption and surrogacy. When he read *Roe v. Wade*, the Court's description of motherhood stuck out. While *Roe* had presented motherhood as "eternally distressing," Cassidy believed that the justices had all but ignored how abortion cost a pregnant woman the constitutional and even intrinsic right to maintain her relationship with her unborn child.[68]

Cassidy got involved with attorneys who had broken with the litigation strategy of larger antiabortion groups. Cassidy's first appeal involved Alex Loce, a young man who had tried to stop his fiancé from getting an abortion. Loce and fourteen others chained themselves together in the doctor's office and remained there for eight hours.[69] Loce planned to use a necessity defense, arguing that he broke the law to prevent the greater harm of abortion. The necessity defense almost never worked, and Cassidy did not feel that *Loce* was the ideal case in which to raise what he saw as the crucial issue of a pregnant woman's right to preserve her relationship with her unborn child. But he hoped that *Loce* would give him the opportunity to establish the "science of whether abortion takes the life of a whole, separate human being." Working with expert witnesses like Drs. Jérôme Lejeune, a prominent researcher and outspoken abortion opponent, and Bernard Nathanson, Cassidy saw *Loce* as a potential starting point for efforts to prove scientifically that the unborn child was a human being.[70]

Pro-lifers like Cassidy stood to gain the influence that Operation Rescue had started to lose. A jury had convicted Randall Terry of criminal trespass charges resulting from his conduct during a 1989 blockade. Federal courts imposed heavy fines on Operation Rescue and its members for violating court orders and injunctions. NOW brought lawsuits maintaining that blockaders violated laws on racketeering and civil rights. Despite these legal struggles, Operation Rescue still maintained a mailing list of over 35,000 and a $900,000 budget. While Terry called blockaders to more actively support political reform, he pressed his allies to continue the lawbreaking that made Operation Rescue a household name. "We've got to keep rescuing children more than ever," Terry wrote.[71]

While Operation Rescue tried to steal headlines from the mainstream antiabortion movement, AUL lawyers generally took a quite cautious approach. "While certainly opening the door to restrictions, . . . *Webster* also indicates that it is not certain that there is a majority to overturn *Roe*," Clarke Forsythe wrote in a confidential 1989 memo to pro-life state legislators. Forsythe expressed special concern about Sandra Day O'Connor, who had not joined the parts of *Webster* that most directly attacked *Roe*. Forsythe worried that if O'Connor, the only woman on the Court, joined an opinion preserving *Roe*, that decision would devastate the pro-life movement. AUL counseled against "direct assault" legislation that would require the Court to reconsider *Roe*.[72]

NRLC leaders, by contrast, were far more confident that arguments about the costs of abortion might soon persuade the Supreme Court to overrule *Roe*. In proposing aggressive model legislation, NRLC lawyers built on arguments made about the costs of legal abortion for the family. As part of father's rights cases, antiabortion lawyers asserted that women sometimes had abortions for frivolous reasons. After *Webster*, antiabortion attorneys elaborated on this claim. In Idaho, NRLC proposed the first model law outlawing abortion "as a method of birth control." Like similar statutes rejected in Minnesota and Utah, the law allowed for legal abortion only in cases of rape, incest, fetal abnormality, and threats of "severe and long-lasting health damage" to a woman. Pro-lifers argued that beyond these narrow exceptions, women did not benefit enough from abortion to justify the decision to end a pregnancy.[73]

NRLC lawyers bet that five Supreme Court justices would uphold the proposed statute, even if they were not willing to go any further.[74] "[T]he proper way to interpret the effect of *Webster* is by a predictive approach, i.e., what the judges are likely to decide," Coleson wrote. "From such an analysis, we argue that *Roe* is de facto largely overruled."[75] Coleson and Bopp predicted that O'Connor, who had not wanted to confront the overruling of *Roe* in *Webster*, would be the Court's new swing vote. Since O'Connor had already urged her colleagues to adopt the undue burden standard in place of the more protective trimester framework, Bopp and Coleson saw no way that the Court would enforce abortion-rights for long. Some absolutists found even NRLC's approach unnecessarily apologetic. As Richard John Neuhaus, an AUL board member and the editor of *First Things*, an ecumenical religious journal, explained: "The fear that many have is that the incrementalist [strategy] is too clever by half, resulting in our settling for far less than was available."[76]

Despite deep strategic disagreements, many pro-lifers saw considerable value in arguments that abortion damaged the family, and the next cases that came to the Court more directly involved that issue. As the justices upheld new parental involvement laws, the future of *Roe* seemed bleak. Abortion-rights attorneys responded by reinventing arguments about the benefits of legal abortion, tying them to women's interest in equal citizenship.

HODGSON, *AKRON II*, AND PARENTAL INVOLVEMENT

By 1990, the fate of abortion-rights was hopelessly tangled up with litigation about parental involvement. Abortion foes used parental involvement cases to establish that the Court had already silently overturned *Roe*. In the same cases, abortion-rights attorneys experimented with claims about how abortion-rights related to equal treatment, explaining how legal abortion allowed women to pursue new opportunities.

Pro-lifers still promoted parental involvement laws partly because teenagers' futures seemed to be so seriously in flux. In 1990, roughly 70 percent of teenagers lived with two parents, down from almost 90 percent in the 1960s. The 1990 census showed that women had surpassed men in choosing to enter college and had achieved parity with men in completing four years of study. At the start of the 1990s, increasing average educational attainment carried more weight. The earnings of men and women with college degrees rose significantly, while those of men without a high school diploma began a steady decline. The wages of college-educated women even began to catch up to men's. Inequality of both wealth and income began a steady increase that would last for decades.[77]

During the litigation of *Hodgson* and *Akron II*, opposing attorneys debated in the media what these changes meant for teenagers.[78] Benshoof, Pine, and the ACLU argued on behalf of the petitioners that minors who chose not to tell their parents had good reasons to do so: "the psychiatric or physical illness of a parent; chemical abuse and dependency on the part of a parent; the antiabortion stance of a parent; the likelihood of a verbally, physically, or sexually abusive response by a parent, or the fact that the minor was not in contact with the parent." Nor did forcing minors to tell their parents strengthen the family, the petitioners contended. When parents had a track record of abuse, the news of an unplanned pregnancy was no different from "showing a red cape to a bull."[79]

The State of Minnesota insisted that minors in "good, functional families" did not tell their parents because they harbored a "general fear of ruining [their] relationship with [their] parents."[80] Antiabortion organizations maintained that minors who terminated their pregnancies did so not because they stood to lose a chance at a college education or a career but because profit-seeking abortion providers manipulated them into a decision. The Elliot Institute for Social Sciences Research, an antiabortion research organization, contended: "[P]resent law acts as a one way funnel which allows parents to pressure their daughters into abortions, yet prevents those parents who would support childbirth from helping their daughters avoid unwanted abortions." "The bottom line is that vulnerable adolescents are exploited," asserted Focus on the Family and the Family Research Council.[81]

Both sides also fought about whether the definition of maturity should change. Antiabortion briefs suggested that teenagers rarely made good decisions, especially when facing pressure from an abortion counselor. By contrast, a brief submitted on behalf of the American Psychological Association and other professional groups emphasized that maturity no longer happened automatically when a woman reached a certain age. The brief stressed that "the assumption that adolescents as a group are less able than adults to understand, reason and make decisions about intellectual and social dilemmas is not supported by ... research."[82]

But lawyers on both sides fully understood that *Hodgson* and *Akron II* might dismantle the right to choose abortion. Focus on the Family and the Family Research Council suggested that *Webster* had already put in place the most deferential standard of review for any abortion law. The Solicitor General explained that the Bush Administration and abortion opponents took issue with the undue burden test because it "*presuppose[d]* that there is a fundamental right [to abortion]." According to pro-lifers, after *Webster*, the Constitution did no such thing.[83]

ACLU attorneys hardly wanted the Court to rethink *Roe*. Just the same, in *Hodgson*, RFP attorneys transformed claims about the benefits of abortion. RFP attorneys focused partly on the relationship between abortion and sex equality. These arguments primarily drew on the Equal Protection Clause of the Fourteenth Amendment. The Court had held that under that clause, certain legal classifications were inherently suspect, among them, classifications on the basis of sex. Building on these rulings, feminist attorneys experimented with a variety of claims about the relationship between abortion and sex discrimination. Some scholars and lawyers reasoned that antiabortion lawmakers sought to enforce outmoded sexual stereotypes about women's role as mothers. Others insisted that abortion regulations singled out women for a uniquely invasive form of public regulation.[84]

One powerful form of the equality argument suggested that abortion regulations denied women the benefit of controlling their own futures. The ACLU updated this claim by emphasizing that abortion regulations prevented young women from taking advantage of the new opportunities available in the 1990s. "Pregnancy continuation poses not only greater physical risks for teenagers, but greater psychological, economic and educational consequences as well," argued the ACLU in *Hodgson*. "Teenage motherhood eliminates life choices, not only for the teenage mother, but for her children."[85]

Without addressing the future of the *Roe* decision, *Hodgson* and *Akron II* delivered mixed results for supporters of abortion-rights. *Hodgson* had two primary holdings, with Justice O'Connor casting the decisive vote for each one. First, O'Connor joined the more liberal justices in holding that the two-parent notice requirement on its own violated the Constitution. Second, O'Connor voted with the conservative justices in concluding that if the law provided a bypass procedure – an opportunity for a minor to prove to a judge that she was mature or that abortion would be in her best interest, then the law would be constitutional. Abortion-rights supporters rightly felt conflicted about the *Hodgson* opinion. On the one hand, *Hodgson* suggested that Minnesota's two-parent notification requirement would be unconstitutional without a bypass provision. Writing for the Court, Justice John Paul Stevens further recognized that minors forced to tell their parents about an abortion decision sometimes found themselves in homes affected by divorce, parental illness, desertion, and abuse. While upholding the Minnesota law, the Court seemed convinced that abortion doctrine had to grapple with the reality of the American family, not the ideal. Justice O'Connor, who for the first time voted that any abortion regulation was unconstitutional, also emphasized the real-world effects of a notification requirement on minors who "who live[d] in fear of physical, psychological, or sexual abuse."[86]

On the other hand, both *Akron II* and *Hodgson* rejected arguments that judicial-bypass procedures themselves had become part of the problem. Planned Parenthood's case in *Akron II* centered on the burdens imposed by Ohio's complex procedural rules. First, Ohio created an arcane pleading process seemingly calculated to trip up minors already scared of going to court. Judges could intimidate minors or deem virtually anyone to be immature. Planned Parenthood and other abortion-rights groups argued that minors would be frightened by the idea of having to make their case to a judge – or might believe that going to court would effectively notify their parents of their desire to have an abortion. Judicial-bypass procedures themselves, abortion-rights attorneys suggested, could unduly burden women's abortion-rights.[87]

While notification laws might discourage young women from terminating their pregnancies, a majority in both *Hodgson* and *Akron II* agreed that a conventional bypass option did enough to safeguard minors' interests. Because Minnesota's law offered a bypass option similar to ones the Court had already upheld, the justices declined to invalidate the state's notification law. *Akron II* reached a similar conclusion.[88]

More noteworthy was the language the Court used in analyzing the Minnesota and Ohio laws. Even Justice Stevens, who saw constitutional problems with the Minnesota statute, asked whether the law "reasonably further[ed] any legitimate state interest." The Court seemed to apply rational basis, the least demanding form of judicial review, to the challenged laws. When applying rational basis review, the Court almost always upheld a challenged law. Significantly, rational basis review also differed a great deal from *Roe's* trimester framework, which seemed to forbid any regulation of abortion in the first trimester. If the justices asked so little of states regulating abortion, it seemed unimaginable that *Roe* would remain good law for long.[89]

Between 1990 and 1991, every month seemed to bring word of new cases that could spell the end for legal abortion. Guam passed a near-total ban on abortion in March 1990. Pennsylvania soon introduced a multi-restriction law that included parental and spousal involvement provisions. In May, the Supreme Court agreed to hear *Rust v. Sullivan*, a case on Reagan-era regulations prohibiting any entity receiving Title X family planning funding from doing abortion-related counseling or referrals. Bopp and Coleson hoped that *Rust* would reverse *Roe* but continued looking for other cases. After Idaho Republican Governor Cecil Andrus vetoed a version of the NRLC model law, Louisiana considered a similar proposal in July. NRLC lawyers argued that even under O'Connor's undue burden standard, such sweeping laws were constitutional. "Because the statute allows for abortions in what are generally assumed to be the 'hard' cases—risk to the life of the mother, rape, and incest—there is no 'severe limitation' imposed on abortion," Bopp and Coleson wrote.[90]

Although Louisiana Republican Governor Buddy Roemer vetoed the Louisiana statute in July (the state would later pass a similar law), pro-lifers celebrated when William Brennan, a consistent vote for abortion-rights, announced his retirement the same month. George H. W. Bush chose David Souter, a New Hampshire Supreme Court judge, to replace Brennan. Hoping that Souter and Kennedy would vote to overturn *Roe*, NRLC attorneys continued pressing bans like the failed effort in Idaho. In January 1991, the effort paid off when Utah passed the strictest antiabortion law in the nation, outlawing abortion except in cases of rape, incest, "grave" fetal defect, or certain limited threats to a woman's health. In advocating for the Utah law, NRLC reiterated that many women did not have a good enough reason to end a pregnancy and could constitutionally be prevented from doing so. NRLC attorneys insisted that at a minimum, states could outlaw abortions under such circumstances.[91]

Although *Rust* stopped well short of overturning *Roe*, the Court further stoked the fears of those who believed that abortion-rights would soon be lost. In May 1991, the Court upheld Title X family-funding regulations preventing any recipient from making a referral for counseling about abortion. Those challenging the regulations had argued that they violated women's abortion-rights and physicians' right to freedom of speech. The Court disagreed with both arguments. On the question of freedom of speech, the Court held that the government had not impermissibly discriminated on the basis of speakers' viewpoint about abortion but had instead expressed its own preference for childbirth over abortion. When it came to abortion-rights, the Court relied on its decisions about Medicaid funding. The obstacle a woman faced, *Rust* reasoned, depended not on the government but on a woman's economic circumstances. "The difficulty that a woman encounters when a Title X project does not provide abortion counseling or referral leaves her in no different position than she would have been if the Government had not enacted Title X," *Rust* held. NRLC lawyers were only a little disappointed. As many believed, it was not a matter of whether the Court would overturn *Roe*, but when.[92]

PARENTAL INVOLVEMENT IN THE SHADOW OF *ROE*

While antiabortion lawyers searched for an ideal test case, claims about the costs of abortion to the family reassured politicians worried about a pro-choice backlash. In

1990, Lee Atwater, one of Bush's closest advisors and the chair of the Republican National Committee (RNC), gave a speech to the RNC urging his colleagues "to support Republican candidates regardless of their position on abortion." As Atwater feared, public opinion seemed to be shifting. Gallup polls found that the number of respondents who opposed abortion under all circumstances hit a record low that year. Republicans in local and national elections faced abortion-rights challengers in primaries. The political party alignment that had defined abortion discussions for almost two decades suddenly seemed to be up in the air. Pro-lifers hoped that claims about the costs of abortion for the family would appeal to politicians otherwise questioning their commitment to the antiabortion movement.[93]

Operation Rescue's troubles also encouraged larger pro-life groups to reestablish their place in the political mainstream. Randall Terry had been in prison for refusing to pay a fine levied against him. Following his 1990 release, Terry announced that Operation Rescue was badly in debt and closing shop. A new organization, Operation Rescue National, took its place. The organization continued mounting high-profile blockades, including the 1991 "Summer of Mercy" in Wichita, Kansas. Operation Rescue's strategies had always been divisive. But under the leadership of Keith Tucci, Operation Rescue National emphasized more controversial tactics, including efforts to surveil and intimidate abortion providers. One protest, as Tucci explained, sent "another group ... to the residential area where the abortionist lives." As Operation Rescue National abandoned the blockades that had attracted a broader audience, pro-lifers had to fend off accusations that they had extended "a license for mayhem."[94]

Together with the decline of Operation Rescue, changes to the composition of the Supreme Court increased the power of establishment antiabortion groups like AUL and NRLC. In July 1991, Thurgood Marshall retired, and as his replacement, George H. W. Bush nominated Clarence Thomas, a judge on the DC Circuit Court of Appeals. Since Thomas was expected to vote to overrule *Roe*, it seemed to be only a matter of time before the Court held that *Roe* was no longer good law.[95]

While legal abortion hung in the balance, those on both sides still emphasized opposing claims about the costs and benefits of abortion for families.[96] While abortion foes used parental involvement laws to beat back accusations of extremism, larger abortion-rights groups struggled to convince voters that parental consultation restrictions did more harm than good. Harrison Hickman, a pollster for NARAL, explained the political problem that his colleagues faced:

> Simply stated, when left to their own devices, voters do not think of these attempts to mandate parental involvement in a minor's abortion decision as "abortion issues" in the strictest sense ... In part, the fact of a teenager facing an unwanted pregnancy is taken as evidence of parents' having lost control of their daughter's life or having been bad parents.[97]

To counter the persistent idea that parental involvement always helped teenagers, abortion-rights leaders borrowed arguments made in court about the price young women paid when they could not choose to end their pregnancies. The National Women's Law Center stressed that "[t]eenage mothers [were] less likely to complete school" and "earn[ed] less than half the lifetime income" of a woman who postponed childbearing. While repeating concerns about the loss of an education or career, NARAL insisted that it was disingenuous to treat minors' abortion-rights differently. "This issue is just a smokescreen," NARAL leaders argued. "Those raising it want to prohibit all abortions."[98]

Pro-lifers contended that pregnant young women facing a difficult decision needed their parents' help. In response, abortion-rights activists attacked parental consultation laws by showing how much the loss of abortion-rights would cost teenagers. Pointing to the new options available to young women, abortion-rights leaders insisted on a connection between abortion and equal citizenship. After the Court agreed to hear a Pennsylvania abortion case, abortion-rights attorneys expanded on this logic. Reproductive-rights supporters hoped to find a sounder foundation for abortion-rights. After all, *Roe* had attracted criticism from academics across the ideological spectrum. An equality rationale for abortion-rights might win over more jurists and scholars. However, in connecting abortion access to newly available opportunities for women, abortion-rights supporters unknowingly reinforced the importance of claims about the costs and benefits of abortion.[99]

ARGUMENTS IN *CASEY*

After the Supreme Court agreed to hear *Planned Parenthood of Southeastern Pennsylvania v. Casey*, abortion-rights attorneys wanted the justices to think carefully about the ways that legal abortion benefitted women. In highlighting claims about the benefits of the right to choose, pro-choice attorneys asked the Court to reevaluate the relationship between abortion and constitutional equality. Abortion-rights lawyers tapped into a decade-long debate about the costs and benefits of abortion for the American family. These lawyers contended that as the understanding of maturity changed, and as new economic and educational options became available, women forced to continue a pregnancy had everything to lose.

Kathryn Kolbert of the ACLU and her co-counsel, Linda Wharton, found themselves at the center of litigation in *Casey*. The day Kolbert started work at the Women's Law Project, a Pennsylvania public interest law center committed to women's rights, her superiors asked her to testify against an Akron-style antiabortion bill. Although she landed in reproductive-rights work almost by chance, Kolbert liked the combination of politics and litigation that the work involved, believing that the two could not be understood as separate endeavors. She had argued *Thornburgh* before the Supreme Court and watched as the majority strongly protecting abortion-rights slipped away.[100]

Wharton had taken an interest in women's issues for as long as she could remember. As a girl, she was struck by how her mother shouldered much more of the responsibility than her father both at work and at home. A series of female mentors strengthened Wharton's commitment to women's rights, and after law school, she aspired to do public interest work.

While working at a major firm in Philadelphia, Wharton continued to pursue her passion through the pro bono work authorized by the firm and later litigated to prevent Operation Rescue from blockading clinics in Philadelphia. Eventually, she joined the staff of the Women's Law Project and worked alongside Kolbert in a case that would reshape abortion law.[101]

A trial in *Casey* began in July 1990, and the district court invalidated most of the multi-restriction Pennsylvania statute at issue in the case. The results were very different on appeal. After applying Justice O'Connor's undue burden test, the Third Circuit upheld every part of the law but a spousal notification measure. Most observers expected *Casey* to be the decision that overturned *Roe*. Abortion-rights leaders still planned to continue litigating in a post-*Roe* world. Indeed, to pursue this goal, the ACLU Reproductive Freedom Project broke away from its parent organization in April 1992. Janet Benshoof and her colleagues relaunched an independent group, then called the Center for Reproductive Law and Policy, hoping an independent outfit would be particularly effective and nimble.[102]

In the meantime, Wharton, Kolbert, and their colleagues hoped to profit from what seemed to be certain defeat. *Casey* seemed likely to come down months before the 1992 election. A devastating decision might bring voters who supported legal abortion to the polls in unprecedented numbers. Winning the White House and Congress would make the loss of *Roe* sting less. With a solid majority in Congress, abortion-rights supporters could pass a federal law protecting abortion-rights or even restoring funding for abortion. Seeking to energize potential voters, NOW planned a major march for April 1992.[103]

For attorneys, the trick was to make sure that everyone knew that *Roe* was gone. After all, the Court could issue a vague decision that voters would not understand, much less condemn. For example, relatively few Americans knew about the trimester framework. A decision jettisoning it might not upset voters unless they realized that the Court no longer recognized a right to choose abortion. Kolbert, Wharton, and their colleagues strategized about how best to force the justices to show their hand. At a December 1991 meeting of attorneys and amici, Kolbert and Wharton proposed stressing that changing *Roe* at all was the same as getting rid of it. The two explained that "[b]y adopting the undue burden test, the Court [will have] overruled *Roe v. Wade*."[104]

While expecting the justices to overturn *Roe*, Kolbert, Wharton, and their colleagues still made the case that women had benefitted profoundly from having a right to choose. The two attorneys further described the costs of Pennsylvania's restrictions. For example, their brief contended that Pennsylvania's spousal notification law victimized women already confronting domestic violence. "The dangerous and potentially deadly consequences of forced notification cannot be overstated," the brief reasoned.[105]

Their brief also explained that *Roe* fit well in the Court's jurisprudence. The Court had relied on the Due Process Clause of the Fourteenth Amendment to recognize rights to marry, to procreate, to use contraception, and to direct the upbringing of one's children. Kolbert and Wharton reasoned that *Roe* also addressed the importance of allowing individuals to make deeply personal and important decisions about reproduction and family life. But rather than simply explaining *Roe*'s place in the constitutional order, they insisted that women would miss out if they could no longer decide when to carry a pregnancy to term. Kolbert and Wharton explicitly relied on the Equal Protection Clause in challenging Pennsylvania's husband-notification provision. The brief argued that the provision imposed "duties on women alone" and did so on the basis of outmoded stereotypes about "sex differentiated roles in marriage." But sex-equality arguments played a far greater role in the case for saving abortion-rights. The brief argued that as more women launched careers, started businesses, or pursued an education, the right to abortion delivered benefits that were more important than ever. "The option of safe, legal abortion has enabled great numbers of women to control the timing and size of their families and thus continue their education, enter the workforce, and otherwise make meaningful decisions consistent with their own moral choices," the brief argued. Amicus briefs similarly described the life-changing opportunities women had gained as a result of legal abortion. One, coauthored by Sarah Weddington, an attorney who had helped to litigate *Roe*, explained: "*Roe* enabled millions of American women to enter the work force, continue their education, fulfill their responsibilities to their families, and escape the devastating consequences of illegal abortions."[106]

Regardless of what anyone said, the Court seemed ready to overturn *Roe*. In January 1992, James Bopp Jr. of NRLC and Clarke Forsythe of AUL hosted a conference for antiabortion lawyers submitting amicus briefs in *Casey*. Those present did not bother to hide their confidence. The agenda focused partly on the myriad ways the Court could reverse *Roe*. Some wondered if the Court would announce that abortion was not a fundamental right or that the state had a compelling interest in protecting fetal life. A few hoped that the Court would formally recognize fetal personhood. Amici planned on explaining how the undue burden test applied while criticizing it and "offering a better standard."[107]

For the most part, antiabortion attorneys asked the Court to focus on what they saw as the benefits of overturning *Roe* for constitutional jurisprudence and American politics. NRLC blamed *Roe* for the culture wars and suggested that overturning *Roe* would make for a saner political dialogue. "Because of its weak foundation, *Roe* exacerbated the abortion controversy," the organization argued. NRLC and other antiabortion groups also insisted that reversing *Roe* would allow the Court to create a more coherent approach to the status of unborn children and the scope of privacy rights.[108]

Some antiabortion briefs, especially those written by newly active evangelical attorneys, did discuss what Focus on the Family and the Family Research Council called "the traumatic effects of abortion on many American families." ACLJ attorneys representing Feminists for Life lingered over claims about the psychological and physical wounds produced by abortion. For the most part, however, antiabortion briefs invited the Court to focus on the consequences that overturning *Roe* would have for constitutional jurisprudence, not for women and families. Antiabortion lawyers repeated that the reasoning of *Roe* was utterly unpersuasive. Pro-life briefs further argued that the Court had perverted other areas of the law, including privacy jurisprudence, to conform to *Roe*.[109]

Antiabortion lobbyists and media specialists eagerly anticipated the outcome in *Casey*.[110] Within the White House, the mood was much more somber. The 1992 election season had painted George H. W. Bush into a corner. Bush's opponents, Bill Clinton and Ross Perot, an independent candidate, both identified as pro-choice, and the tide seemed to be shifting in their direction. Nevertheless, Bush feared that he would lose existing support if he watered down his opposition to abortion.[111]

"The worst of all possible worlds," staffers suggested, would be a decision that upheld most or all of the statute without overturning *Roe*. One staffer wrote that following such a decision, "[t]he President would be buffeted from the left and the right, and there would be an increasing likelihood that the rad-fems [radical feminists] would be legitimized on this issue." For Bush, as his staffers reasoned, an ambiguous decision would be "[v]ery dangerous."[112]

THE *CASEY* DECISION

When the Court handed down its decision in *Casey* in June of 1992, it turned out to be just the thing that almost no one had wanted. In a fractured plurality opinion, the Court concluded that the undue burden test represented the most "appropriate means of reconciling the State's interest with the woman's constitutionally protected liberty." But *Casey*'s undue burden standard differed from the one O'Connor had previously laid out. Rather than striking down statutes that created a severe or absolute obstacle, *Casey* invalidated those laws that had the "purpose or effect of placing a substantial obstacle in the path of a woman seeking an abortion of a nonviable fetus." The plurality discarded *Roe*'s trimester framework, reasoning that states had an important interest in protecting fetal life throughout pregnancy. However, *Casey* retained viability as the point at which states could ban abortion and declined an invitation to overrule *Roe*.[113]

While the meaning of the undue burden standard was not clear, it seemed less demanding than O'Connor's version. The rule asked litigants to prove the costs and benefits of specific regulations. At least implicitly, the standard also invited attorneys to weigh in on the value of certain abortions. For example, in upholding an informed consent restriction, the Court stressed that women suffered crippling regret because they had not understood what an abortion involved before terminating their pregnancy. *Casey* suggested that lawmakers could regulate abortion when the procedure would cost women too much.[114]

The Court also weighed arguments about the costs imposed by the Pennsylvania statute. Although the Court upheld almost every disputed provision, the plurality highlighted arguments about domestic violence in striking down the state's spousal notification law. After canvassing record evidence of domestic violence, the Court insisted: "we must not blind ourselves to the fact that the significant number of women who fear for their safety and the safety of their children are likely to be deterred from procuring an abortion as surely as if the Commonwealth had outlawed abortion in all cases." The Court also rejected the picture of marriage written into the spousal involvement law. Pennsylvania's law reflected "a view of marriage ... repugnant to our present understanding of marriage and of the nature of the rights secured by the Constitution."[115]

The Court highlighted the benefits of legal abortion in explaining why *stare decisis*, a doctrine encouraging courts to abide by earlier decisions on the same subject, militated in favor of preserving *Roe*. To be sure, *Casey* made a broader case for preserving abortion-rights. The plurality reasoned that *Roe* fit well in a larger body of law identifying rights tied to procreation, marriage, and parenting. The Court further addressed antiabortion arguments that *Roe* had deepened cultural conflict. However, for *Casey*, political disputes weighed in favor of retaining *Roe*. "[T]o overrule under fire in the absence of the most compelling reason to reexamine a watershed decision would subvert the Court's legitimacy beyond any serious question," the Court explained.[116]

But in addressing *stare decisis*, the Court primarily focused on how abortion access had benefited women. As a general matter, in weighing whether to overturn a precedent, the Court considered whether a decision was unworkable, whether changed circumstances or fresh doctrinal developments undermined a rule, and whether anyone relying on a right would suffer if the rules suddenly changed. When it came to reliance, the Court usually hesitated before retooling the rules governing contracts or other commercial transactions, where the parties planned in advance. In abortion, by contrast, women often did not plan to become pregnant. Nevertheless, the Court found that many women relied on legal abortion. Here, the Court echoed claims made during decades of conflict about parental involvement laws: women could pursue new avenues when they had more control over childbearing. The rationale for saving *Roe*, the Court explained, depended on "the fact that, for two decades of economic and social developments, people have organized intimate relationships and made choices that define their views of themselves and their places in society, in reliance on the availability of abortion."[117]

Casey still presented abortion as a matter of autonomy for women. But *Casey* also connected abortion to interests in equal treatment. Although the plurality repudiated sex stereotypes in striking down Pennsylvania's spousal notification law, the Court mainly focused on why abortion benefitted women in a rapidly changing society. Highlighting "decades of economic and social developments," *Casey* reasoned that abortion allowed women to seize new opportunities. The plurality concluded that abortion gave women the ability "to participate equally in the economic and social life of the Nation" because the country itself had changed so much.

Casey put the costs and benefits of both abortion and laws regulating it at the center of constitutional discourse. The Court had relied on arguments about legal abortion's effects on the lives of American women in preserving abortion-rights. And after *Casey*, those challenging abortion laws had to gather evidence of how restrictions actually affected women. The Court's willingness to preserve abortion-rights, it seemed, depended on evidence that abortion helped women achieve more equal citizenship.

CASEY AND THE FORTUNES OF FAMILY

When the Court decided *Casey*, it had been less than a decade since pro-lifers had reluctantly turned their back on a constitutional amendment. Recognizing that they could not change the text of the Constitution, pro-lifers eventually vowed to undo *Roe* instead. To chip away at the decision, larger pro-life groups defended incremental restrictions, stressing claims about the costs of abortion and the benefits of restricting it.

By the late 1980s, larger antiabortion groups often focused on what they described as the havoc wreaked on the family. Antiabortion lawyers spoke up for fathers and insisted that some women did not deserve abortion-rights. And larger pro-life groups sponsored laws requiring young women to notify their parents or obtain their consent. Abortion-rights activists fired back that parental consultation laws cost women the chance to pursue an education or career.

Casey picked up on arguments that both movements had made about the costs and benefits of abortion for the family. For over a decade, abortion-rights attorneys had argued that parental consultation laws deprived young women of important new career or educational options. In *Casey*, abortion-rights attorneys reworked this claim into a justification for saving *Roe*. These lawyers explained that women relied on the availability of abortion to achieve equal citizenship, and the Court agreed.

But *Casey* also reflected the collapse of any consensus about the facts about abortion. In rejecting the trimester framework, the Court adopted the undue burden standard. That rule, in turn, encouraged opposing sides to focus on the effects of both abortion and abortion restrictions. Disagreements about those effects would only intensify after *Casey*.

On the day the Court decided *Casey*, Kathryn Kolbert navigated a maze of reporters and television trucks. "It was," as she put it years later, "a zoo." While she initially read the decision as a major defeat, she changed her mind the same day. Kolbert later recognized that "sav[ing] *Roe* in any form" was "huge," a transformational change for women who relied on the ability to control when (or if) they had children.[118]

In the short term, she saw some hope in the Court's adoption of an undue burden test, but over time, she took a much darker view, seeing the standard as often little more than a way for courts to rubber stamp abortion regulations. Kolbert nevertheless remained proud of how her arguments about the family had contributed to *Roe*'s fate. She still believes that she gave a more equal voice to "the women who have enjoyed legal abortion [ever] since."[119]

Ed Grant's experience of *Casey* was almost the reverse. In the days after the Court's decision, Grant largely shared his colleagues' despair about *Casey*. Over time, though, Grant began to see potential in the undue burden test. After all, the Court had hardly spelled out exactly what an undue burden was.[120]

Later, Grant would help to emphasize antiabortion arguments about abortion's effects on women. At the time, he remembered the slogan sometimes used by the other side: keeping abortion safe, legal, and rare. Why, Grant wondered, would you want abortion to be rare? In the mid-1990s, despite constitutional and political setbacks, mainstream antiabortion groups reestablished their influence by taking up the challenge that Grant laid out. Rather than explaining how legal abortion afforded women an equal opportunity to pursue a career or education, pro-lifers wanted the nation to believe that abortion had "adverse consequences for women's health."[121]

5

Contesting the Relationship between Abortion and Health Care

David Reardon and Pam Maraldo believed that health care should be at the center of the abortion debate. Reardon was raised in a Catholic family in small-town Illinois. A high school student when *Roe v. Wade* legalized abortion, Reardon always had pro-life sentiments but did not become active until he read an article about Nancy Jo Mann's Women Exploited by Abortion (WEBA), a peer support group for women seeking emotional healing after abortion. The article made Reardon think that everyone in the abortion wars had forgotten about "the practical question of what women go through."[1]

At the time he read the WEBA article, Reardon was working on a novel. But he set it aside for what he thought would be a short-term project to help WEBA members tell their stories. With Mann's help, Reardon developed a survey, sent it to WEBA members, gathered their testimonies, and began researching the existing medical literature on the physical and psychological effects of abortion. After the 1987 publication of his first book, *Aborted Women, Silent No More*, he planned to complete more formal studies. Reardon founded the Elliot Institute for Social Sciences Research, a nonprofit group, and gave it "as neutral sounding a name as possible."[2]

Under his direction, the Elliot Institute studied what Reardon described as abortion's negative health effects and the frequency with which women felt pressured into abortion. Reardon believed that he had found a way for the pro-life movement to make real progress. He reasoned that the overwhelming majority of people could agree on a "pro-woman agenda" designed to prevent unsafe, unnecessary, or coerced abortions.[3]

Pam Maraldo also argued that the abortion debate should focus more on women's health. Like Reardon, she grew up in a Catholic family, but Maraldo ardently supported abortion-rights, as did her parents. When she was a teenager, her father sat her down and told her that if he was a woman, no one would tell him what to do with his body. She became a nurse and saw firsthand the devastating health consequences of illegal abortions. As a nurse, she primarily treated cancer and heart disease patients before joining the National League for Nursing, an organization focused on nursing education. By 1985, she had become that organization's chief executive officer.[4]

Following the retirement of Faye Wattleton, Maraldo became the head of Planned Parenthood. As health care reform rose to the top of the nation's agenda, she asserted that rather than identifying as an abortion-rights organization, Planned Parenthood should emphasize a more comprehensive health care delivery system for women and their families.[5] But her proposals met with far more resistance than she could have imagined. While Maraldo concluded that Planned Parenthood would be left behind if the organization did not emphasize comprehensive health care, some affiliates believed that a health-based strategy would dilute the organization's focus on abortion.[6]

As Reardon and Maraldo's experiences suggest, arguments about the costs and benefits of abortion became part of a larger discussion about what defined health care in America. Since the early 1980s, pro-lifers had dictated the terms of the abortion debate. Abortion foes had promoted incremental restrictions and often defended them by emphasizing claims about the costs of abortion. Following the election of Bill Clinton and the decision of *Casey*, abortion-rights activists, lobbyists, and attorneys went on the offensive for the first time in decades. *Casey* had preserved abortion-rights partly because the justices concluded that abortion benefitted women by helping them participate more equally in the life of the nation. However, abortion-rights activists still had to explain how incremental restrictions affected women's interests in equal treatment, especially when some regulations at most seemed to increase the costs of abortion or force delays. To do so, abortion-rights advocates emphasized the health benefits of abortion. Activists argued that delaying an abortion could have damaging health consequences and that abortion writ large was an important public health issue.

In the political arena, abortion-rights supporters used these arguments to demand the inclusion of abortion in national health care reform, the restoration of Medicaid funding for abortion, and legislation protecting access to abortion clinics. In court, lawyers affiliated with the National Organization for Women Legal Defense and Education Fund (LDEF) and the Feminist Majority Foundation accused antiabortion blockaders of violating civil rights and racketeering laws and defended new clinic-protection rules.

In the mid-1990s, in the aftermath of the United Nations International Conference on Population and Development, women of color developed a more expansive approach to reproductive health. These activists coined the term reproductive justice to frame their demands, fusing the ideas of reproductive rights and social justice. In addition to legal abortion, these grassroots activists demanded health care, jobs, and the ability to parent in safe conditions. Throughout the 1990s, as the rise of reproductive justice arguments suggests, abortion-rights supporters disagreed about what it meant to emphasize the health benefits of abortion.[7]

Nevertheless, many abortion-rights activists and lawyers sincerely believed that women's health would suffer if they lacked access to safe, low-cost abortion, especially when many often struggled to find a willing abortion doctor. Medical malpractice lawsuits led by antiabortion activists, an extremely challenging insurance market, and a shortage of abortion providers threatened to make a mockery of any protected right.[8]

Abortion foes thought they fared far worse. The election of a hostile president, the disappointment of *Casey,* and the flurry of negative coverage surrounding the murder of abortion providers by antiabortion extremists forced larger pro-life groups to reconsider their strategies. Some redirected their resources to crisis pregnancy centers (CPCs). At times, mainstream antiabortion groups like AUL or NRLC did not even define their movement's litigation agenda. In 1994, when a group of conservative evangelical leaders formed the Alliance Defense Fund (ADF, later the Alliance Defending Freedom) to fund socially conservative litigation, ADF focused primarily on the free speech of conservative Christians, not on an attack on *Roe* or *Casey.*[9]

The leaders of larger antiabortion groups like NRLC and AUL regained influence by returning to claims about the costs of abortion, this time arguing that abortion was a threat to women's health. As NRLC and AUL attorneys saw it, *Casey* had preserved abortion-rights partly because the Court believed that abortion benefitted women by helping them to participate more equally in the life of the country. By contending that abortion cost women their health, antiabortion attorneys hoped to take away the rationale for a right to choose.[10]

The abortion fight formed part of a larger dialogue about what should define health care in modern America. Bill Clinton made health care one of the signature issues of his campaign, but no politician lost sight of the number of Americans who lacked coverage.[11] The issue took on significance partly because the medical system had changed so much. Health maintenance organizations (HMOs) and related plans multiplied and increasingly adopted a for-profit model. Patients faced sometimes painful trade-offs between lower prices and expanded choices.[12]

By mid-decade, the campaign for health care reform had failed, and the Democratic Party had suffered stunning losses in the House of Representatives. The dream of universal insurance for abortion was over. The abortion-rights movement had nevertheless gained some ground. Congress passed federal legislation protecting access to the entrances of abortion clinics. Women of color supportive of abortion-rights launched a more concerted campaign for reproductive justice. Just the same, supporters of legal abortion soon found themselves on the defensive again. Abortion foes revived claims about the costs of abortion, insisting that the procedure damaged women's health.[13]

Casey made equality-based arguments more central to constitutional conflict about abortion. Abortion-rights groups contended that abortion access allowed women to achieve better health outcomes. But a focus on equality did not lower the temperature of the abortion conflict. Nor did the emphasis on equality mean that arguments about the costs and benefits of abortion became less important. Instead, abortion foes started a new fight about whether the access to the procedure actually made women more healthy, independent, or equal.

DOWNPLAYING HEALTH-BASED ARGUMENTS

Arguments about the health costs and benefits of abortion stretched back decades. Well before *Roe*, those on both sides debated whether abortion saved women from mental illness or made them sick. Nevertheless, health-based arguments did not become especially prominent until the 1990s. A minority on either side resented the marginalization of health-based claims. Among pro-lifers, self-identified feminists emphasized claims about the health risks of abortion, as did those leading support groups for women who regretted ending their pregnancies. While Nancy Jo Mann's WEBA (founded in 1982) worked primarily with evangelical Protestants,[14] Project Rachel, a group started two years later, mainly served Catholic women.[15]

NRLC and AUL leaders happily included Project Rachel and WEBA in their national conventions and sometimes cited their work. Wanda Franz, the head of a West Virginia NRLC affiliate, launched the Association for Interdisciplinary Research in Values and Social Change, a "professional organization for pro-life researchers and educators." While touching on a variety of topics, as NRLC explained, the association focused on "psychological problems suffered by some women after abortion." By 1991, Franz had become NRLC's president.[16] Starting in 1985, NRLC's National Right to Life Educational Trust Fund also provided financial and logistical support for American Victims of Abortion (AVA), another outreach group for women who experienced post-abortion regret. Leaders hoped that the group would refute arguments that pro-lifers were indifferent to women.[17]

Furthermore, some AUL leaders worried that existing messaging strategies painted pro-lifers as anti-woman. For example, in 1990, Guy Condon, the president of AUL, expressed this concern after that organization asked Gallup to conduct a study on public attitudes about abortion. Summarizing the results of the study, Condon wrote that without a change in rhetoric, Americans would continue to believe that pro-lifers were "against women, against the democratic process . . ., and even against one another."[18] A study conducted for the National Conference for Catholic Bishops' Secretariat of Pro-life Activities reached a similar conclusion.[19] Along with some other AUL members, Condon urged his colleagues to adopt a different tactical plan. In 1991, he circulated a strategy paper to other AUL members that called for arguments that not only "personalize[d] the unborn" but also "personalize[d] women as victims."[20] Nevertheless, before *Casey*, even AUL stressed arguments that could alienate women by painting them as shallow or amoral. Condon, like other AUL members, wished to stress "the extent of abortion license [and] the rampancy of the practice" to show that women had abortions for what pro-lifers viewed as trivial reasons.[21] Describing their organization's argumentative strategy, the National Right to Life Educational Trust Fund similarly focused on "the early development of the unborn child, ... the numerous deficiencies in the *Roe v. Wade* decision, and ... the intricacies of public opinion polling."[22]

Between 1987 and 1989, the Reagan White House gave Reardon and his allies hope that arguments about the health costs of abortion would finally command more attention. At the prompting of Dinesh D'Souza and other staffers, President Reagan instructed Surgeon General C. Everett Koop to study the health effects of abortion on women. Koop, an antiabortion activist, had penned a 1976 pro-life book and had long served on AUL's board of directors. Both sides of the abortion issue began to lobby Koop's office. Reardon, for example, wrote to Koop: "I pray that your report will launch this nation into a new era of debate about abortion, one based not on fetus versus women rhetoric, but rather on the facts of what abortion does to women alone."[23]

But in January 1989, a letter written by Koop to Reagan had leaked to the media. The surgeon general refused to declare that post-abortion trauma had created a national health crisis. "The available scientific evidence about the psychological sequelae of abortion simply cannot support the preconceived beliefs of those of the pro-life or of the pro-choice [movements]," Koop concluded. In response, NRLC again downplayed claims about women's health.[24]

AUL leaders also flirted with a more woman-protective strategy in the late 1980s after the *Chicago Sun Times* ran a series on substandard care in some area abortion clinics. Illinois lawmakers responded with a statute that regulated abortions performed outside of ambulatory surgical centers, medical facilities that specialized in elective, outpatient surgeries. The regulations addressed everything from the maintenance of clinic records to the construction of new facilities.[25]

Richard Ragsdale, a doctor from Rockford, Illinois, challenged the constitutionality of the statute after he had trouble finding a site for his new clinic.[26] Ragsdale and other Illinois doctors argued that the law violated women's right to choose by making abortion more expensive and far less available. In 1985, a district court enjoined enforcement of the law. In 1988, the Seventh Circuit Court of Appeals affirmed most of the district court's decision, and the Supreme Court agreed to hear the case. In July 1989, when the Supreme Court agreed to hear *Turnock v. Ragsdale*, AUL attorneys celebrated.[27] But by the end of 1989, Illinois Attorney General Neil Hartigan faced increasing pressure to drop the case. Hartigan planned to seek the Democratic nomination for governor of Illinois and worried that *Ragsdale* would alienate left-leaning voters. A few days before oral argument at the Supreme Court, the two sides reached a settlement agreement. Under the terms of the settlement, Illinois agreed to regulate abortion very little before the eighteenth week of pregnancy. In return, those challenging the law accepted stricter regulations for later abortions and a requirement that physicians performing abortions have admitting privileges at a licensed Illinois hospital. Ann-Louise Lohr of AUL complained that because of the settlement, no one would "protect women nationwide from unscrupulous abortion providers."[28]

But for the most part, NRLC and AUL continued to emphasize claims about the costs of abortion for unborn children and the medical profession. The reasons that Reardon and his allies encountered resistance were complex. First, some antiabortion absolutists, especially those aligned with Operation Rescue, rejected the idea that women were victims rather than perpetrators. And as Republicans reshaped the Supreme Court, it also seemed realistic that abortion foes could soon pass the kind of complete ban that all pro-lifers favored.[29]

Similarly, in the late 1980s and early 1990s, the abortion-rights movement did not primarily emphasize the health benefits of abortion. Before 1973, proponents of legalization asserted that criminal abortion laws cost some women their lives. Later in the 1970s, feminist health care providers and their allies called for a more comprehensive approach to reproductive politics, one that would include contraception, childcare, a living wage, and protection from sterilization abuse. Organizations like the Reproductive Rights National Network found the mainstream abortion-rights movement alienating because of its single-issue focus and demanded a more comprehensive (and health-centered) approach.[30]

By the late 1980s, however, larger abortion-rights groups began to think that most voters would not warm to arguments about the health benefits of abortion. As Kate Michelman of NARAL explained in December 1988: "Our public education effort will be built upon three major themes: the absolutely compelling need to keep reproductive rights free from government intrusion; the dangers women will face if safe, legal abortion is not available; and the urgency with which our side must respond to what is truly a serious threat."[31] While some feminists resisted the direction chosen by NARAL, prominent abortion-rights organizations generally followed Michelman's lead.[32]

For several years before Clinton made health care reform a hot-button issue, however, NARAL and Planned Parenthood experimented more often with health-based arguments. For example, when debuting "Real Choices," a campaign intended to broaden the group's agenda,[33] Kate Michelman of NARAL told her colleagues to use the health benefits of abortion to help the public better "understand [t]hat pro-choice means ... we work toward a whole range of options."[34]

By the early 1990s, with members of both political parties addressing a perceived health-care crisis, antiabortion and abortion-rights activists turned more attention to claims about the health benefits of abortion. In the opening years of the decade, the idea of health care reform enjoyed bipartisan support. On the campaign trail in 1992, George H. W. Bush and Bill Clinton offered competing reform plans. It seemed to be only a matter of time before the nation's leaders worked out how to fix an ailing system.[35]

When Clinton won, speculation began almost immediately about what his reform plan would include. The media aired suggestions that the government would overhaul Medicare, a federal health insurance program for people over 65. The administration reportedly considered imposing cost controls for vital drugs or experimenting with new taxes on tobacco, alcohol, and guns. In the spring of 1993, staffers revealed that health care reform would include abortion coverage. Clashes about the proposal began immediately.[36]

Casey had made it more urgent to explain how abortion helped women achieve equal citizenship. Abortion-rights supporters had convinced the Court that criminalizing abortion might prevent women from taking advantage of new career and educational opportunities. But what about regulations that only made abortion harder to get? Health-based arguments helped to answer this question by explaining how delays and other obstacles harmed women. Without their health, women could never achieve equal citizenship.

A few years earlier, abortion-rights supporters had not wavered from a different priority: passage of the Freedom of Choice Act (FOCA), a federal statute that would protect abortion-rights. However, by 1993, the campaign had largely fallen apart because of conflict about whether to back a bill with exceptions for abortion-funding bans and parental involvement restrictions.[37] In moving past FOCA, those in larger abortion-rights groups developed a new platform that included national health care reform, the legalization of medical abortion, the restoration of Medicaid funding for abortion, and legislation protecting access to clinic entrances. In court, abortion-rights attorneys working with the Feminist Majority Foundation and NOW LDEF, NOW's litigation arm, similarly stressed the health benefits of access to abortion.

But for some members of the abortion-rights movement, emphasizing the medical benefits of abortion care created hazards of its own. Some grassroots activists and abortion providers worried that their colleagues would not spend enough time defending a fundamental right or explaining what made abortion unique. Others argued that voters would lose sight of the constitutional significance of abortion. For this reason, throughout the health care debate, abortion-rights supporters debated the pros and cons of framing abortion as a medical matter, a moral dilemma, or something in between.

THE REASONS FOR REPOSITIONING ABORTION AS A VITAL HEALTH SERVICE

With Clinton's win and the decision of *Casey*, abortion-rights leaders confronted a novel problem. For almost two decades, antiabortion groups had largely dictated the debate, first pushing a constitutional amendment, then crafting a gradual attack on *Roe. Casey*, together with the election of a pro-choice president and Congress, changed all that. Finally, rather than simply reacting to the opposition, abortion-rights supporters had control of the agenda. The question was what they would do with it. As important, leaders of groups like NARAL and Planned Parenthood had to decide how to talk about abortion when there seemed to be no imminent threat to the right to choose. Complacency could easily set in. For a variety of reasons, larger abortion-rights groups emphasized the health benefits of abortion access.

Casey encouraged NARAL and Planned Parenthood to rely more often on health-based arguments. Publicly, Planned Parenthood described *Casey* as a devastating loss. The group took out full-page ads in the *New York Times* and *Washington Post* claiming that the undue burden standard meant that most "state laws that restrict abortion can be upheld by federal courts." Internally, reaction to the decision was more complex. In July 1992, Planned Parenthood's legal department put out a confidential analysis of *Casey*, celebrating the fact that the "Court ... endorsed the principles of liberty and personal autonomy that animated the *Roe* decision." Nevertheless, lawyers for the group recognized that "[t]he undue burden/substantial obstacle test allows many more restrictions to be passed than was formerly the case." Planned Parenthood predicted that the movement could make the most progress after *Casey* by taking advantage of "the opportunity to show more facts." Discussing the health benefits of abortion access made sense when even constitutional doctrine required proof of how the law affected women. Abortion-rights attorneys could show how restrictions made abortion inaccessible – and how women's health suffered as a result.[38]

As more affiliates performed abortions, Planned Parenthood had another reason to define abortion as a beneficial medical procedure. In 1982, only forty affiliates offered the procedure. Over the course of the year, Planned Parenthood clinics performed roughly 83,000 abortions. By 1991, sixty-two affiliates provided abortion services, and the number of procedures performed at Planned Parenthood facilities had climbed to more than 132,000. Offering abortion as one of several services, Planned Parenthood organizers had more reason to describe its health benefits for some women.[39] The organization put out briefings and brochures describing itself as "the most trusted provider of health care to women and adolescents."[40]

NARAL unveiled a related message in a 1992 internal strategy document. The group's leaders made clear that health care reform provided NARAL with a chance to "change direction." By advocating for access to a variety of reproductive services, the group hoped both to appeal to a broader audience and to establish the health benefits of abortion access. NARAL urged members to contend that "[o]nly a comprehensive approach to reproductive health can effectively reduce the rates of unintended and teen pregnancy, abortion, sexually transmitted disease, and infant death."[41]

The group refined this plan during a 1993 tactical session. At the end of the summit, attendees agreed to stress that "[r]eproductive health care is an essential component of primary care for women and must be included in a comprehensive benefits package." Many of the other goals outlined in the strategic plan – the renewal of public funding for abortion, access to clinics, and efforts to address a shortage of abortion providers – reframed abortion as one of several services that delivered important medical benefits for women.[42]

Why did the abortion-rights movement focus on claims about the health benefits of abortion access? First, such a strategy could energize the movement's supporters when it seemed that *Casey* had made abortion-rights safe.[43] At the same time, the decline of Operation Rescue made it much harder for NARAL and Planned Parenthood to raise money. Because Operation Rescue was the perfect villain, clinic blockades had been a boon for abortion-rights groups' fundraising efforts. But by 1993, Operation Rescue National was in freefall. That spring, Michael Griffin, an antiabortion protester murdered Dr. David Gunn outside of his Pensacola, Florida, clinic. Although the leaders of Operation Rescue National condemned the murder, the issue of violence against abortion doctors divided the organization. Operation Rescue National further faced a damaged reputation and overwhelming financial penalties. As Operation Rescue National lost influence, it was harder for abortion-rights groups to raise money.[44]

A better political environment also made it more difficult for abortion-rights supporters to thrive financially. Clinton went out of his way to reassure the abortion-rights movement. On his very first day in office, he invited members of prominent pro-choice groups to the White House to watch as he nullified the gag rule, a regulation preventing family planning providers from counseling about or advocating for abortion. Clinton's support made abortion-rights seem secure, and it was harder to convince donors to loosen their purse strings when there was no immediate danger to abortion-rights.[45]

Roger Craver, the mastermind behind much of the movement's fundraising strategy, had long recognized that donors responded when they were afraid that *Roe* would soon be overturned. Unsurprisingly, for this reason, NARAL had flourished financially during the Reagan and Bush Administrations. Membership of the organization grew from 250,000 in 1989 to 750,000 in 1992. Relative political security brought this growth to a crashing halt. After the election, NARAL's direct-mail receipts dropped so dramatically that the organization had to cut its staff by one-fourth. Planned Parenthood's budget fell from $90 million in 1990 to only $44 million in the fall of 1992. The attack on Dr. Gunn energized the abortion-rights movement and dramatically improved fundraising prospects. Nevertheless, it seemed important to convince donors of the need for their ongoing support. Arguments about the health benefits of abortion seemed to motivate supporters to open their checkbooks. Advocates could argue that even if abortion was legal, women's health would suffer if the procedure was inaccessible. And because Clinton had made reform a signature issue in his campaign, connecting abortion to other medical services made larger abortion-rights groups seem relevant and responsive to voters.[46]

Abortion-rights advocates also hoped that a health care framework would help to retain nonwhite members.[47] Women of color had long pushed for a comprehensive approach that underlined the health benefits of abortion and demanded protection for related services, like prenatal care.[48] In 1994, following the United Nations International Conference on Population and Development, the Illinois Pro-choice

Coalition hosted a gathering for abortion-rights supporters. Eleven women of color present at the event worried that their movement mostly neglected issues that mattered to nonwhite women, such as immunizations for their children. These activists described their cause as a fight for both reproductive rights and social justice. In 1997, Luz Rodríguez, a member of Latina Roundtable on Health and Reproductive Health, expanded on the idea. A Ford Foundation officer contacted Rodríguez and asked for her help in reaching grassroots women of color organizations that would not ordinarily receive the foundation's support. The effort led to the founding of SisterSong Women of Color Reproductive Justice Collective. At its inception, SisterSong included sixteen diverse groups committed to exploring how "human rights are intertwined with reproductive health and sexual rights of women of color."[49]

Established groups like the National Black Women's Health Project joined SisterSong. So did more recently formed organizations such as the National Asian Women's Health Organization (founded in 1993). A health-based argument promised to allow larger abortion-rights organizations to build credibility with women of color like those who had joined SisterSong.[50]

At the same time, arguments about the health benefits of abortion reflected sincere worry about a growing shortage of abortion doctors. Low pay, antiabortion violence, and political stigma had discouraged new physicians from providing abortion services. A contemporaneous study conducted by Columbia University found that only 20 percent of medical students had spent time, as part of their training, in an abortion clinic or service, and 47 percent had never performed a first-trimester procedure. *Family Planning Perspectives* found that between 1992 and 1996 alone, the number of providers declined by 14 percent.[51]

The price of malpractice insurance created a new crisis. Mark Crutcher's Life Dynamics, Inc. a well-funded litigation-sponsorship organization based outside of Dallas, sent attorneys across the country a seventy-nine-page manual on how to sue abortion providers for medical malpractice. Life Dynamics also created an information service, "Spies for Life," that fielded undercover researchers to gather damning evidence against abortion providers. "Right now," Crutcher wrote, "the future of abortion in America is in serious jeopardy simply because access to abortion is evaporating." Crutcher's focus on insurance was smart. Faced with the prospect of extensive litigation in the early 1990s, insurers significantly raised rates for malpractice policies for clinics. Very few insurers participated in the malpractice market, making providers dependent on suppliers with little incentive to lower prices. The head of the National Coalition of Abortion Providers estimated that 20 percent of independent clinics were completely unable to find coverage.[52]

Abortion-rights supporters looked for new ways to encourage doctors to provide abortion services. The National Abortion Federation (NAF) launched the Access Initiative Project, an effort to encourage medical schools to train doctors in abortion.

Planned Parenthood of New York offered its own training program, and some facilities, including the Atlanta-based Feminist Women's Health Center, allowed physician assistants to perform abortions, an option restricted by law in many states. Given the shortage of abortion providers, it seemed important to reestablish that abortion care delivered important health benefits for women. Such claims might convince medical schools, doctors, and even insurance companies that a lack of access to abortion could have consequences for women's health.[53]

Between 1993 and 1995, arguments about the health benefits of abortion also made a difference in court. *Casey* increased the importance of both autonomy and equality arguments for abortion-rights. But the equality arguments in *Casey* explained the need to keep abortion legal. Pro-choice attorneys had to work out how to tie equality interests to abortion access. Abortion foes insisted that incremental restrictions at most delayed abortion or made it more expensive. Were such limits mere inconveniences, or did they actually affect women's equal citizenship? Health-based arguments helped to answer these questions. Groups such as the NOW LDEF and the Feminist Majority Foundation tried to brand all pro-lifers as sexists dedicated to depriving women of beneficial health care.

EQUATING OPPOSITION TO ABORTION WITH HOSTILITY TO HEALTH CARE

When abortion-rights attorneys returned to the Court, they tried to expand on the connection between the benefits of abortion and constitutional equality at which *Casey* hinted. Focusing on clinic blockades seemed to be a perfect way of doing so. While implying that protesters tried to enforce sex stereotypes, abortion-rights attorneys also asserted that blockades denied women valuable health benefits tied to abortion. For the most part, antiabortion attorneys responded that the First Amendment's Free Speech Clause protected blockaders. Pro-life lawyers also began arguing that abortion actually cost women their health. Blockaders could not discriminate against women if they sought to protect them from a harmful procedure.

At first glance, abortion-rights litigation in the mid-1990s offered little in the way of surprises. While Kathryn Kolbert and Linda Wharton tried to get the lower court to reopen the record and consider new factual evidence about the effects of the Pennsylvania law challenged in *Casey*, the effort failed. For the most part, courts upheld laws modeled on the one considered in *Casey* or struck down statutes that went further. The most intense action involved a concerted attack on the clinic-blockade movement.[54]

Rather than just attacking Operation Rescue, abortion-rights attorneys cast doubt on the motives of the entire antiabortion movement. Did pro-lifers oppose health care for women or discriminate on the basis of sex? These questions shaped the Court's decision in *Bray*.[55] The case began when Washington, DC, area abortion clinics sought to prevent a planned blockade. NOW LDEF contended that blockaders had conspired to deprive women of protected rights under the Civil Rights Act of 1871, a landmark law passed after the US Civil War. Organized in 1970, NOW LDEF had litigated sex-discrimination and sexual-harassment cases in addition to helping with *Thornburgh* and *Webster.* To make a case under the Civil Rights Act, NOW LDEF had to prove that blockaders had an animus against an identifiable, protected group. The organization argued that blockaders discriminated against women, especially those who flouted traditional roles. "The animus driving petitioners' conspiracy was to deprive women of their constitutional right to elect abortion," NOW attorneys wrote. Jay Sekulow's organization, Christian Advocates Serving Evangelism (CASE), worked with veteran pro-life attorney T. Patrick Monaghan's Free Speech Advocates in defending clinic blockaders. In 1989, a district court permanently enjoined blockaders from trespassing or obstructing the entrance of the nine plaintiff clinics, and in September 1990, the Fourth Circuit Court of Appeals affirmed.[56]

Sekulow and Monaghan appealed in 1991, but following oral argument, a short-handed Supreme Court deadlocked four-to-four and set a date for reargument.[57] When *Bray* returned to the Supreme Court, Sekulow and Monaghan insisted that the last thing blockaders wanted to do was deprive women of beneficial health care. "In essence, respondents ... mischaracterize petitioners' undisputed actual motive —sincere opposition to the practice of abortion—as discrimination against a class," the two attorneys explained. But how could Sekulow and Monaghan distinguish opposition to abortion from sex discrimination? The two tried reminding the Court that women numbered among the blockaders. As importantly, Sekulow and Monaghan asserted that protesters launched blockades "to save babies and mothers from abortion." As Sekulow and Monaghan framed it, blockaders wanted to protect women's health, not deny women medical care.[58]

NOW LDEF replied that denying access to abortion care necessarily affected women as a class. "[T]he capacity to bear children and the ability to undergo abortion, and the capacity to make decisions in respect thereto, link all the women who are the objects of the conspiracy," NOW LDF reasoned. In NOW's view, only women lost crucial health benefits because of the blockades. As the organization's brief explained: Only women "suffer[ed] the potentially serious health consequences of delayed or prevented abortion."[59]

When the Supreme Court issued a decision in January 1993, a 5–4 majority rejected the equation of pro-life sentiment and hostility to health care for women. Writing for the majority, Justice Antonin Scalia concluded that blockaders had not deprived women of any right under the Civil Rights Act of 1871. In deciding that the blockades did not target a class protected by the statute, Scalia also suggested that blockaders did not discriminate against women. "Whatever one thinks of abortion, it cannot be denied that there are common and respectable reasons for opposing it, other than hatred of, or condescension toward (or indeed any view at all concerning), women as a class," Scalia wrote.[60]

Abortion-rights groups returned to the Court a year later, again highlighting the health benefits of abortion. First came the January 1994 decision of *National Organization for Women v. Scheidler*. *Scheidler* began in the summer of 1986 when NOW and several local clinics filed suit. NOW argued that clinic pickets and blockades violated the Sherman Antitrust Act, the Racketeer Influenced and Corrupt Organizations Act (RICO), and the Hobbs Act, an anti-extortion law. By 1988, NOW had expanded the suit to include Operation Rescue. In 1991, a trial judge dismissed NOW's suit because the defendants lacked an economic motive for their actions – an element that the district court believed was required by the federal RICO law. The following year, the Seventh Circuit Court of Appeals affirmed, and the Supreme Court agreed to hear the case. In its complaint, NOW LDEF contended that blockaders "used threatened or actual force, violence, or fear to induce clinic employees, doctors, and patients to give up their jobs, give up their economic right to practice medicine, and give up their right to obtain medical services at the clinics." RICO prosecutions brought to mind mafia bosses in major urban centers, but NOW lawyers saw a parallel to those leading blockades. NOW reasoned that just as crime family bosses conspired to fix races, run brothels, and start protection rackets, blockaders plotted to deny women the benefits of legal abortion and other health services. The 1994 Supreme Court appeal involved only one element of the RICO case: whether that law covered actions taken with an economic motive, as the Seventh Circuit Court of Appeals had held earlier in the litigation. NOW took the position that RICO did not require such a motive. As important, NOW insisted that denying women health care counted as an injury under RICO. "When a clinic is under siege, women are denied access not only to abortion services but also to routine gynecological health care," NOW LDEF explained.[61]

In the trial court and on appeal before the Seventh Circuit, a number of antiabortion attorneys accused NOW of sacrificing free speech principles for a cheap political payoff. On appeal to the Supreme Court, Paul Benjamin Linton, an attorney working with AUL, argued that applying RICO to blockaders would require "a radical change in First Amendment theory." Jay Sekulow and other attorneys from the American Center for Law and Justice (ACLJ) representing Operation Rescue and Randall Terry agreed that blockaders did not extort women or use force or threats to deprive them of health care. Instead, blockaders engaged in "[c]ivil disobedience and social or political pressure," tactics "as American as apple pie." Tom Brejcha, an attorney at a Chicago-based law firm, worked with Clarke Forsythe of AUL on Joseph Scheidler's brief. Brejcha asserted that NOW's demands ran "[c]ontrary to our nation's fundamental commitment to the freedoms protected by the First Amendment."[62]

In *Scheidler I*, the Supreme Court held that RICO did not require an economic motive. As a result, NOW's suit against blockaders continued, and the two sides clashed for years after the Supreme Court first weighed in. But later in 1994, abortion-rights attorneys had more luck in *Madsen*. That case began with a single clinic in Melbourne, Florida. Pro-life activists routinely protested near the entrance of Melbourne's Women's Health Center, singing, chanting, speaking with patients, and even using bullhorns. In September 1992, a state judge enjoined protesters from blocking access to the clinic or abusing those who tried to go inside. Six months later, the clinic was back in court, arguing that the original injunction had done nothing to protect patients from the protesters. The judge issued a broader injunction that set noise limits, blocked certain visible signs, and created "buffer zones," areas in which protesters could not enter or approach patients, including a 300-foot zone around people entering the clinic and a 36-foot zone around the clinic entrance. Working with Mathew and Anita Staver's Liberty Counsel, picketers sued.[63]

According to Liberty Counsel, the injunction violated the First Amendment because the court had discriminated on the basis of the picketers' viewpoint. "After singling out abortion related speech, the Injunction allows pro-choice speech but prohibits pro-life expression," Liberty Counsel argued. Working with the Feminist Majority Foundation, attorneys for the clinics responded that picketers really cared about depriving women of health care, not expressing themselves. "Activities such as inhibiting access to medical facilities, blocking roadways, threatening Clinic workers, and intentionally frightening Clinic patients before and during surgery do not constitute expression protected by the First Amendment," their brief argued.[64]

Madsen upheld parts of the injunction (including the buffer zone around the clinic entrance and the noise limits) but struck down others (including the 300-foot buffer zone around people entering the clinic and the signage limitations). The Court first held that the injunction did not regulate speech on the basis of a speaker's viewpoint or the content of her message – something strictly forbidden by the Free Speech Clause of the First Amendment. *Madsen* acknowledged that the injunction allowed patients and staff, but not pro-life protesters, within buffer zones. However, *Madsen* reasoned that the difference depended on protesters' conduct, not their speech. The Court then addressed whether each part of the injunction burdened more speech than was necessary to achieve the government's goal. In upholding parts of the injunction, the Court emphasized the importance of the government's interest in protecting women's access to health care. *Madsen* emphasized that the injunction advanced "a strong interest in protecting a woman's freedom to seek lawful medical or counseling services in connection with her pregnancy."[65]

Clinic access cases continued to move through the courts after *Madsen*. For example, in 1997, the Supreme Court issued an opinion in *Schenck v. Pro-choice Network of Western New York*. In that case, abortion-rights supporters filed a lawsuit to stop clinic blockades in parts of Western New York. After Project Rescue, an antiabortion group, repeatedly violated a temporary restraining order, the district court created two kinds of buffer zones that protesters could not enter: fixed buffer zones that prohibited protests within fifteen feet of a clinic entrance and "floating" buffer zones that prevented anyone from coming within fifteen feet of people or vehicles seeking to enter a clinic. Project Rescue argued that the buffer zones violated the Free Speech Clause of the First Amendment. A district court disagreed, as did the circuit court of appeals. Citing *Madsen*, abortion-rights groups again argued that the injunction was constitutional – a necessary step to restrict conduct that "harms patients and impedes the provision of safe and effective medical care." Representing Project Rescue, Jay Sekulow argued that the fixed and floating buffer zones differed from the provisions upheld in *Madsen*: In particular, there were not many past incidents of lawlessness to justify sweeping restrictions on speech. In 1997, a divided Supreme Court struck down the floating buffer zone and upheld the fixed buffer zone.[66]

Notwithstanding mixed results in cases like *Bray*, *Scheidler*, *Madsen*, and *Schenck*, the abortion-rights movement emphasized health-based arguments in the political arena as well as in court. While defending free speech sometimes worked in court, abortion-rights attorneys felt that their opponents did not have an effective political answer to arguments about the health benefits of abortion. By treating abortion as a public health issue, larger abortion-rights groups could explain how restrictions forced women to delay abortions, undergo riskier procedures, or carry pregnancies to term. Abortion, in this analysis, was a matter of equal health care for women.[67]

The period immediately after *Casey* offered a fresh start to abortion-rights activists. Scholars across the ideological spectrum had criticized the *Roe* decision. The *Roe* Court identified a right to privacy that many commentators believed had no clear foundation in constitutional text, history, or precedent. Feminists criticized the Court for focusing on doctors rather than on women. Tying abortion to equal citizenship – and linking both to health care benefits – seemed to create a sounder foundation for the right to choose. Health-based claims also reflected abortion-rights supporters' deeply held convictions about the benefits of safe abortion. But before long, abortion-rights supporters realized that post-*Casey* debate had come to bear a striking resemblance to the one that came before. Pro-lifers still focused on what they described as the costs of abortion, now claiming that abortion shattered women's physical and mental well-being.

A PROACTIVE POLITICAL AGENDA

With Clinton in office, abortion-rights supporters stood to make legislative gains for the first time in years. NARAL, NOW, and Planned Parenthood hoped to legalize new abortion methods, restore Medicaid funding for abortion, ensure access to abortion clinics, and legitimize the procedure by ensuring its inclusion in the Clinton health care bill. By playing up claims about the health benefits of the procedure, abortion-rights supporters hoped to undercut the stigma surrounding abortion and frame abortion as a normal medical service.

The Clinton Administration was far less sanguine about an abortion-focused dialogue, fearing that controversy about the procedure would overtake the health care debate. Leaders of Clinton's health care team called abortion "one of our most problematic issues." Indeed, the administration used talking points emphasizing that the reform would do little to change abortion coverage. The talking points reiterated that "[m]ost private health plans [already] cover[ed] the full range of reproductive services."[68] Fearing that President Clinton would sacrifice abortion to ensure the success of the bill, NARAL, Planned Parenthood, NOW, and ACLU created a coalition called Health Care for All to push for the coverage of all reproductive health services. NARAL organized a call-in day to show that "[u]niversal health care is not universal if it does not include women's health." NRLC responded with a pamphlet claiming that Clinton's plan ignored people's moral positions and required "mandatory payments for abortion on demand."[69]

The debate over the Freedom of Access to Clinic Entrances Act (FACE) also turned partly on whether abortion clinics delivered necessary health services. Introduced in March 1993 by Senator Ted Kennedy (D–MA), FACE attracted attention because of the recent murders and attempted murders of abortion doctors. Earlier that month, Michael Griffin, an antiabortion protesters, murdered Dr. David Gunn outside of his Pensacola, Florida, clinic. The same year, Shelley Shannon, an Army of God member, tried to kill abortion provider Dr. George Tiller in Wichita (Tiller would later die at the hands of another extremist). Pointing to the attacks on Gunn and Tiller, Senator Kennedy and FACE supporters insisted that without the law, the violence would escalate, and women would lose out on crucial health benefits tied to abortion and other reproductive health services. NRLC and AUL denounced the killings. Groups like ACLJ nonetheless insisted that the law should not treat abortion clinics like health care facilities. "[T]he law governing public protest of abortions must be the same as the law which governs public protest of blockbusting realtors, officers of major corporate polluters, slumlords, [and] pornographers," contended Walter Weber of ACLJ.[70]

Abortion providers and clinic staff further praised the health benefits of abortion. "Because thousands of you mobilized each day to ensure women's access to health care, no women were denied that right," argued one feminist group that helped women pass through blockades. Planned Parenthood wrote to New York clinic defenders that their shared mission was simple: to "portray ... clients as patients seeking medical care" and "plac[e] abortion in a broader health care context."[71]

At the time, NARAL's debate manual offered any number of claims about the health benefits of abortion. One emphasized: "Doctors earn less from abortion than they do from prenatal or childbirth services; yet RTL [Right to Life] uses the word 'industry' to make this part of the medical profession seem dirty." Without challenging the idea that abortions mostly took place in stand-alone facilities, NARAL also told activists to contend that "[o]nly a small percentage of doctors perform abortions; yet most support legal abortion in the interest of good medical care."[72]

NARAL made similar claims to take down the most visible pro-life success of previous decades, the Hyde Amendment, a ban on the use of federal Medicaid dollars for abortion. Because the ban was an amendment to an annual appropriations bill, Congress could theoretically remove it the next time a budget came up for consideration. Clinton had publicly opposed the Hyde Amendment during the 1992 campaign, and some members of both major parties shied away from any strong antiabortion position.[73]

Clinton's support aside, NARAL members understood that it would not be easy to repeal the Hyde Amendment, particularly when voters worried so much about government spending. In the 1992 election, Ross Perot, a billionaire who ran as an independent, won 18.9 percent of the popular vote, the highest total for a third-party candidate since 1912. Perot had drawn support from liberal and conservative voters because of his outsider image. But Perot's specific policy proposals also drew in voters. Perot took aim at what he described as a dangerous federal deficit. Even after Clinton prevailed at the polls, voters did not let go of their fears about government spending and the national debt.[74]

NARAL leaders had to refute claims that the "government [could] not afford to fund abortion on demand." If abortion was a valuable health service, then funding it made sense, even at a time when lawmakers had to cut spending. The debate manual argued: "Abortion is not a luxury item; it is a necessary component of women's health care."[75]

Larger abortion-rights groups hailed the health benefits of legal abortion in advocating for access to medical (as opposed to surgical) abortion. Medical abortion involved two pills, mifepristone, or RU 486, and misoprostol. In Europe, physicians commonly used the combination to terminate early pregnancies, but for years, no United States drug company had been willing to manufacture RU 486. The George H. W. Bush Administration prohibited personal importation of the pill, and NRLC and its allies vowed to organize a boycott of any company that sold RU 486 in the United States. On the campaign trail, however, Bill Clinton pledged to reverse Bush's policy.[76]

In 1992, when the Food and Drug Administration (FDA) considered an application for approval of the drug, the stakes of the decision to legalize RU 486 seemed difficult to overstate, particularly at a time when many women could not find a doctor to perform an abortion. Rosemary Dempsey of NOW suggested that if women could get abortion pills on their own, then RU 486 might help "remov[e] the debate from the public forum." NRLC emphasized what abortion foes saw as the potential safety risks of the drug. The organization put out a press release stating that "RU 486 is deadly to unborn babies and dangerous to women."[77]

The relationship between abortion and health care also defined discussion of the so-called morning-after pill. In 1973, Canadian physician Albert Yuzpe discovered that a combined estrogen-progestin regimen taken within seventy-two hours of intercourse could prevent ovulation, fertilization, or the implantation of a fertilized egg. Although the FDA had approved the pills Yuzpe had in mind, the agency had not signed off on the four-pill protocol as a form of emergency contraception. Nevertheless, in the mid-1990s, private physicians and Planned Parenthood clinics made the morning-after pill available. The FDA eventually approved the emergency contraceptive Plan B as a prescription drug in 1999. Nevertheless, for some time before, debate about what the morning-after pill did – and whether it was safe for women – required those on both sides to analyze whether abortion was a valuable medical service.[78]

In the mid-1990s, abortion-rights supporters counted down the days until some form of health care reform passed. If lawmakers would treat abortion just like any other vital service, then Congress might normalize the procedure. But Clinton's proposal would flop much faster than even its most vocal critics might have guessed.

THE FORCES AGAINST REFORM

Health-based arguments allowed abortion-rights supporters to better explain how the procedure helped women achieve equal citizenship. *Casey* had reasoned that eliminating legal abortion would make it harder for women to take advantage of economic, political, and social opportunities. But most post-*Casey* regulations at first seemed innocuous. In practice, the restrictions introduced in the 1990s primarily forced women to delay abortions or dramatically increased the cost of the procedure. By highlighting the health benefits of abortion, groups like NARAL could explain what women lost when they had to wait until later in pregnancy when abortion was more dangerous. And by emphasizing the health benefits of abortion, pro-choice groups insisted that women should have the same access to vital care that men enjoyed. Limiting access to abortion, the argument went, made the American health care system anything but equal. First, by emphasizing the health benefits of the procedure, larger abortion-rights groups presented themselves as champions of comprehensive health care for women. Health-based arguments, as NARAL explained, proved that abortion-rights supporters "believe[d] in giving women a broad range of reproductive options, including comprehensive family planning." NARAL could criticize pro-lifers for burdening women's access to abortion and other forms of care that "improve[d] [their] health and lives."[79]

It made sense to focus so much on the political arena when the Supreme Court seemed to have a solid majority on abortion. When Justice Byron White retired in 1993, Clinton nominated Ruth Bader Ginsburg to replace him. During her time on the DC Court of Appeals, Ginsburg had earned a reputation as a moderate, and conservative Senator Orrin Hatch (R–UT) had recommended her. However, Ginsburg's published work made clear that she believed that the Constitution recognized a right to choose abortion.[80] In the political arena, by contrast, the opposition often thwarted NARAL and its allies. The House voted to keep the Hyde Amendment by a vote of 255–178, and in the fall of 1993, the Senate voted 59–40 to preserve the same restrictions. Although Congress passed FACE, the consensus on health care reform seemed to have collapsed.[81] By January, Congress had as many as six alternative plans under consideration. Ross Perot, apparently toying with the idea of another run for the White House, mocked Clinton's plan as "an airplane with no wings."[82]

The possible inclusion of abortion coverage only added to the divisions holding up health care reform. Planned Parenthood leaders emphasized that most health insurance plans already covered abortions. Members of the group suggested that by including abortion as a "medically necessary service," Clinton's reform simply ratified what patients and doctors already expected. Pro-lifers opposing the bill still searched for an effective response to equality-based claims for abortion. For the most part, abortion foes focused on the freedom of speech or religion of those who opposed abortion. "In effect," wrote Doug Johnson of NRLC, "the President—at the behest of groups such as the National Abortion-Rights Action League (NARAL)—is seeking to enlist the power of the federal government to compel all employers and all citizens to collaborate in providing abortion as a method of birth control."[83]

Over the course of 1993, however, NRLC leaders benefited from the discomfort of different constituencies with emerging details of Clinton's plan. Several governors complained that a national reform would preempt promising state experiments. The American Medical Association argued that cost controls would make it hard for doctors to recoup the costs of valuable (but expensive) training. Insurers, the heads of health maintenance organizations, and the chief executive officers of major businesses claimed that cost controls would come at the expense of patient choice. NRLC addressed these fears, hosting seminars for lobbyists and activists opposing the bill. One of the central messages pushed by the group involved anxiety about cost containment and managed care: a claim that "[h]-ealth insurance companies [would] have to ration lifesaving medical treatment."[84]

NRLC appealed to those worried about how HMOs were changing the health-care system. HMOs were not new in the 1990s; indeed, in the 1920s and 1930s, reformers and unions had discussed the merits of prepaid group plans, a forerunner of the managed-care model. When Congress passed the Health Maintenance Organization Act of 1973, the legislation created a grant and loan program that would eventually provide assistance to over 40 percent of HMOs.[85] The direct-grant program ended under the Reagan Administration, and for-profit businesses began to play a more significant role in the HMO market. After 1990, the number of employees enrolled in HMOs exploded. A slow economy and escalating health care costs helped the industry to expand. Nearly 80 percent of employees with insurance plans belonged to an HMO by the late 1990s.[86]

By the 1990s, however, a backlash against HMOs was underway. For many, managed care became synonymous with shorter visits, longer wait times, and overwhelmed physicians. Studies suggested that HMOs made it impossible to get certain expensive services or restricted patients' choice of a primary care physician.[87] Some doctors attacked the HMO model because it undermined the autonomy and professional standards of doctors who became part of a profit-making operation.[88]

Uncertainty about the meaning of health care in the HMO era shaped the abortion conflict. Abortion opponents claimed that the reform law rationed care for most Americans while forcing them to pay for abortions. Providers and abortion-rights supporters invested more in establishing that both HMOs and the reform bill should cover abortion.

The relationship between abortion and health care also still set the terms of struggles over Medicaid funding for abortion. Congress refused to eliminate the Hyde Amendment. Ambiguous language in the bill that lawmakers ultimately passed fueled additional controversy. In the most recent version of the Hyde Amendment, Congress authorized Medicaid reimbursement "when it is made known to the Federal entity or official to which funds are appropriated under this Act that such procedure is ... the result of an act of rape or incest." Clinton interpreted this language as requiring funding in cases of rape or incest, but some state directors disagreed.[89] In the spring of 1994, Sally Richardson, the director of the federal Medicaid program, ordered state directors to reimburse in cases of rape or incest, and some states sued rather than complying with her order.[90]

The arrival of the issue in the courts seemed to harden positions on whether abortion was a beneficial medical service. So, too, did party polarization in the aftermath of revelations about the Clintons' involvement in the Whitewater scandal. When Clinton served as governor, he and his wife had invested in a plan to build a retirement community in the Ozarks. A jury had convicted James McDougal, Clinton's partner in the Whitewater venture, of charges related to a series of fraudulent loans. Some accused the president of pressuring people into giving the McDougals loans and destroying documents concerning his involvement in the venture. The media seized on the story following the summer 1993 suicide of Deputy White House Counsel Vince Foster. When files on the Whitewater affair went missing from Foster's office, Republicans insisted that a cover-up was in the works.[91]

Whitewater stiffened the resolve of conservatives committed to defeating Clinton's plan. For Clinton, in turn, Whitewater made it more tempting to sacrifice abortion coverage to save an already controversial reform bill. In the summer of 1994, seventy Democratic members of the House of Representatives sent a letter to their leadership explaining that they would support a reform bill only if it included contraceptive and abortion services. But antiabortion violence again stole headlines from health care reform. In late July, Paul Hill, a member of the pro-violence Army of God, murdered Dr. John Britton and his bodyguard outside of a Pensacola, Florida, abortion clinic. Chillingly, Hill admitted that he had aimed for Britton's head, believing that the doctor was wearing a bulletproof vest. Britton's murder convinced the leaders of groups like the Fund for a Feminist Majority, Planned Parenthood, and NARAL that unless abortion was included in a basic benefits package, providers and women would continue to be "marginaliz[ed], picked off, terrorized, and tortured."[92]

Hill's crime met with almost universal condemnation, but it soon became clear that bipartisan support for health care reform had broken down completely. Led by Senator Bob Dole (R–KS), Republicans denied the existence of a health care crisis. Positioning himself for a presidential run, Dole insisted that Clinton should not prescribe a "massive overdose of government control."[93]

Concern about welfare costs also undermined support for health care reform. Many of the arguments about welfare reform centered on Aid to Families with Dependent Children (AFDC), a program that disproportionately served women of color. In 1994, Clinton vowed to end "welfare as we know it." His proposal would have introduced work requirements and time limits for AFDC and other welfare programs. Republicans tried to beat Clinton at his own game by proposing hard caps on how much (and for how long) a recipient could get from AFDC. It was harder for some politicians to square demands for health care expansion with an apparently bipartisan consensus that the welfare state otherwise invited laziness or abuse.[94]

By the middle of 1994, no one thought that Clinton would be able to pass a bill requiring universal coverage, much less a plan that covered abortion. The prediction was prescient. After the 1994 midterm election, for the first time since 1952, Republicans took control of the House of Representatives. By the following year, the GOP had majorities in both houses. The Republicans matched these successes in state legislatures and gubernatorial races. New Republican members of Congress were far more conservative than their GOP predecessors. The new GOP leaders, Dole among them, framed the election around Clinton's health care reform and broader platform. Dole described the election as a "vote of no confidence in the Clinton agenda" – proof that Republicans needed "to develop a new one."[95]

Although Clinton's reform proposal fizzled, antiabortion groups did not have much to celebrate. Since 1973, larger pro-life groups had promoted restrictions that limited access to abortion by emphasizing claims about the costs of the procedure. But after *Casey*, it seemed that decades of careful legal work had backfired. Notwithstanding widely held expectations, the Supreme Court, carefully shaped by Republican presidents, had decided to preserve the essential holding of *Roe*. *Casey* created an identity crisis for the antiabortion movement. For over a decade, overturning *Roe* had become synonymous with the antiabortion cause. Had that time come and gone?

EMPHASIZING WOMAN-PROTECTIVE ARGUMENTS

In 1993, Guy Condon, the leader of AUL, came to regret his faith in arguments about the costs of abortion. Condon's change of heart was striking. After all, for some time, he had helmed the organization best known for leading pro-life litigation efforts – and was a champion of claims about the costs of abortion. Yet by the mid-1990s, Condon vowed not to make the same mistake twice. The evangelical Christian Action Council (CAC) hired him to spearhead a new tactical plan. Whereas CAC once lobbied and litigated, Condon directed the group, renamed Care Net, to focus exclusively on crisis pregnancy center (CPC) work. "I believe that we can no longer hope that the courts and legislatures will protect women from the abortion system," Condon explained. Care Net offered a different vision of anti-abortion advocacy – one often centered on religious and moral arguments. As a Care Net brochure explained, a CPC should work with "the Christian Church [to] be father to the fatherless and husband to the widow."[96]

Abortion Alternatives International (AAI), another umbrella organization of CPCs founded in 1971, also stepped up its work after *Casey*. AAI's early leaders, like many abortion foes at the time, strongly opposed the use of religious arguments at affiliated CPCs. By contrast, in 1992, when AAI leaders began calling the organization Heartbeat International, the group proudly proclaimed itself to be a Christian organization. Similarly, Birthright USA, the stateside affiliate of Birthright International, continued expanding following litigation about which of two competing camps could use the Birthright name. Thomas Glessner, the former executive director of the Christian Action Council, also founded a new organization, the National Institute of Family and Life Advocates (NIFLA), to offer legal support for CPCs. CPCs, like picketing, appealed to a relatively small group of black evangelical Protestants who remained in the movement, many of them former participants in clinic blockades. For example, Rev. Johnny Hunter, a former blockader, founded the Life Education and Resource Network (LEARN), a Christian group that attracted some black evangelical Protestants.[97]

The CPC movement spread at a time when donors directed resources away from mainstream antiabortion litigation groups like AUL and NRLC. Some looked for new ways to influence elections. Rachel MacNair, a member of Feminists for Life, read glowing headlines about female candidates who had shattered the glass ceiling during the 1992 election. For MacNair, these stories made it even more painful that most pro-life candidates were male. By the mid-1990s, EMILY's List, a pro-choice political action committee that worked to elect women supportive of abortion-rights, had become a formidable opponent. MacNair founded an organization, the Susan B. Anthony List (SBAL), to help elect pro-life women. Although SBAL remained small for some time, the organization represented another option for activists and donors disenchanted with the strategies pursued before *Casey*.[98]

Even those interested in the courts doubted the wisdom of a strategy based on the costs of abortion. In 1994, a group of prominent evangelical leaders that included Bill Bright of Campus Crusade for Christ, James Dobson of Focus on the Family, D. James Kennedy of Coral Ridge Ministries, Larry Burkett of Christian Financial Concepts, Marlin Maddoux of Point of View Radio Program, and Don Wildmon of the American Family Association, launched the Alliance Defense Fund (ADF) to fund lawsuits, coordinate litigation strategies, and train attorneys advocating for a variety of conservative causes. From the beginning, ADF founders prioritized cases involving the speech and religious freedom of conservative Christians, not an attack on *Roe*. ADF founders saw the group as a conservative Christian equal of the ACLU. "These battles will be waged in the courts whether or not Christians show up to fight," explained ADF cofounder and president Alan Sears. ADF both participated in and facilitated a broader expansion of Christian lawyering in the mid-1990s, building up a $4.7 million budget by 1997.[99]

Early on, ADF did not back a campaign based on claims about the costs of abortion. Indeed, the common denominator in ADF-funded suits often proved to be freedom of expression or religion for conservative Christians, not a campaign to end *Roe*. In addition to *Madsen*, the group supported cases involving religious speech on college campuses and waged a war against possible state recognition of same-sex marriage. Liberty Counsel and ACLJ continued working on cases involving religious liberty for students and defending clinic picketers.[100]

As ADF's funding decisions reflected, many antiabortion lawyers questioned whether arguments about the costs of abortion would ever work. Even those most dedicated to undoing *Roe* believed that AUL and NRLC's strategy would continue to fail. In the fall of 1992, one movement attorney wrote to James Bopp that antiabortion attorneys should abandon claims about the costs of abortion. "It should be clear, in analyzing *Casey* and the individual legal philosophies of the seven Judges of the Dissent and joint opinion, that there is only one issue on which all of them could be brought together to reverse *Roe*: that a child, in fact, exists prior to birth and enjoys protectable rights," the attorney wrote.[101]

AUL and NRLC attorneys thought that *Casey* sent the opposite message: abortion would never become illegal unless pro-lifers proved that it had powerful costs for women. In a July 1992 strategy memo, AUL attorneys seized on what they saw as the most transformational part of *Casey* – the Court's idea that women relied on legal abortion. In considering whether to overturn a precedent, the Court typically considered whether reversing a decision would disturb settled expectations. As *Casey* framed it, women stood to lose out on valuable life opportunities if they counted on the availability of abortion and lost access to it. For AUL attorneys, the connection between abortion and equal treatment, central to *Casey*, was laughably wrong. Nonetheless, AUL leaders believed that abortion opponents would never get anywhere unless they could show that women did not, and *should* not, rely on legal abortion. "The irony in the Court's position," the memo explained, "is that *Roe v. Wade* introduced a nationwide social policy ... which has undermined secure, independent, and healthy lives for American women."[102]

AUL attorneys planned to use *Casey*'s undue burden test to show that women could not rely on legal abortion because of its health risks. AUL lawyers promoted informed consent laws like the one that the Court upheld, eventually expanding on the model used in Pennsylvania. "By guaranteeing that women are informed about fetal development, the risks of abortion, and the availability of compassionate alternatives," AUL argued, "such laws could help bring about the societal change that has eluded the pro-life movement." As important, over a longer stretch, AUL could chip away at *Casey* (and *Roe*). If the Court acknowledged that women could and should not rely on legal abortion, there would be no more reason to preserve legal abortion.[103]

NRLC leaders zeroed in on a different dimension of the *Casey* decision. James Bopp Jr., Burke Balch, and other leading strategists sent a flurry of faxes to one another in the aftermath of the decision. Bopp reasoned that because the group had focused on presidential elections and Supreme Court slots, NRLC had missed the reasons that even a Court stocked with GOP nominees might hesitate to overturn *Roe*. "The most pressing need, in my view, is to recapture public opinion on this issue," Bopp explained. As Bopp and his colleagues saw it, *Casey* had stopped short of overruling *Roe* because the justices feared that such a decision would undermine the legitimacy of the Court. Legitimacy, in turn, depended on the likely popular reaction to the Court's decisions.[104]

The question was how to convince the Court that NRLC's position was in line with public attitudes. Balch did not see a reason to stray from the laws promoted before *Casey* came down. "Mandating abortion on demand, effectively throughout pregnancy, is emphatically neither moderate nor in step with public opinion," he reasoned. "One way of demonstrating this would be to pass, for example, legislation preventing the performance of abortion for sex selection." Bopp, by contrast, argued that abortion foes had to refute sex-equality arguments for abortion. He urged his colleagues to advocate for woman-protective laws, such as "health and safety regulations of clinics" and "laws that regulate physician conduct.[105]

Within a short time, those who wanted to stress claims about abortion's costs regained power. Antiabortion attorneys certainly faced less competition from Operation Rescue. The blockade movement shrank because some of its members embraced violence. The horrific murders of Dr. Gunn and Dr. Britton followed a series of bombings, acid attacks, and death threats.[106] Woman-protective arguments seemed to be the perfect response to accusations that anyone in the pro-life movement could be a murderer. By stressing arguments about the damage that abortion did to women, pro-lifers hoped to convince voters that most movement members were more compassionate, honest, and reasonable than their opponents.[107]

Larger antiabortion groups overhauled their message by emphasizing the costs of abortion for women's health. At an April 1993 board meeting, Paige Comstock Cunningham, the organization's new leader, announced "a major shift in the rhetoric of AUL." "We must help people understand that abortion hurts women too," she told her colleagues.[108] Clarke Forsythe explained that the organization had already begun working with state legislators to introduce informed consent laws. Myrna Gutíerrez, the organization's director of public affairs, agreed that only by focusing on "the harm abortion does to the woman" could activists "start changing hearts and minds."[109] NRLC affiliates also asserted that abortion damaged women's health. Massachusetts Citizens for Life (MCFL), a NRLC affiliate, argued that informed consent restrictions benefitted women by giving them "nonjudgmental, scientifically accurate medical facts." But NRLC had already expanded on the model law upheld in *Casey*. Rather than sticking to undisputed statements, MCFL defended a bill connecting abortion to suicidal ideation, psychological trauma, and infertility.[110]

Feeling vindicated, David Reardon argued that by claiming that abortion damaged women's health, pro-lifers could finally outmaneuver the opposition.[111] In court, pro-lifers could argue that regulations helped women rather than unduly burdening them. And in politics, pro-lifers could try to take away their opponents' best argument. "By demanding legal protection," he wrote, "we force our opponents to either side with us in defending women's rights or be exposed as defending the abortion industry at the expense of women's rights."[112]

Many pro-lifers sincerely believed that abortion harmed women. These included activists like Olivia Gans, the founder of American Victims of Abortion, who had regretted their own abortions. Other abortion opponents knew women with similar experiences or simply believed that abortion inevitably hurt women. But woman-protective arguments had obvious strategic advantages. These claims appealed to the evangelicals, Catholics, and other activists working primarily in CPCs, giving them a way to talk women out of abortion. Arguments about the harm caused by abortion also motivated donors, politicians, and attorneys who had come close to giving up on an incremental attack on *Roe*. In the short term, groups like NRLC and AUL could draft and promote mandatory counseling laws. These statutes spread arguments about the damage abortion did to women's health and perhaps discouraged some women from terminating their pregnancies. In the longer term, attorneys could build a case that women could not and should not rely on legal abortion, *Casey* notwithstanding.[113]

In the years to come, the idea of protecting women's health ran through a comprehensive attack on legal abortion. The antiabortion movement had not been on the defensive for long. Less than a decade after *Casey*, abortion foes launched a fresh war against legal abortion by presenting themselves as the true protectors of women's health. *Casey* had drawn attention to arguments linking abortion and equal citizenship. But the Court had only made arguments about the costs and benefits of abortion more important. Rather than rejecting an equality framing of the issue, abortion foes claimed to have concrete evidence that women were worse off because of legal abortion. Larger pro-life groups contended that women would never achieve equal citizenship by a having a procedure that made them sick.

SECOND-GUESSING A HEALTH-BASED APPROACH

The spread of pro-life woman-protective arguments created a crisis of confidence for some abortion-rights supporters, many of whom questioned the value of arguments about the health benefits of abortion access. Providers agreed that abortion was an important health service. However, some worried that by presenting abortion as one more medical service, political organizations and lawyers ignored the experiences of real patients, who understood their choices to be both more important and more morally complex than many other health care decisions. Planned Parenthood activists also worried about a plan for affiliates to perform abortions alongside primary care services. While leaders pitched the plan as a way to ensure financial stability and normalize abortion, some Planned Parenthood activists felt that by blurring the distinctions between abortion and other health services, their organization failed to address moral and constitutional claims made by the opposition and neglected what made abortion unique.[114]

The National Coalition of Abortion Providers (NCAP), an organization formed in 1990 to meet the needs of independent clinics, highlighted some of these concerns. NCAP members believed that their side had not done enough to explain how providers worked. In the aftermath of *Casey*, Planned Parenthood and NARAL had condemned all the abortion restrictions introduced by the states. The problem, as NCAP members saw it, was that these broadsides created "the impression that supporters of choice, including providers, don't believe in any kind of regulation."[115]

The broader movement also felt the reverberations of a rebellion within Planned Parenthood against a strategy centered on health-based arguments. First disseminated at the 1994 annual meeting, the organization's reinvention plan would have changed Planned Parenthood's organizational structure, created incentives for affiliates to band together, awarded board seats based on the number of patients served, and tied affiliates more closely to the national office. The plan further urged all affiliates to offer comprehensive primary care for women and their families, not just reproductive health services. Pam Maraldo and other backers of the reinvention plan responded partly to a changing health care environment. Planned Parenthood faced new competition from HMOs offering similar services and struggled to secure desirable contracts with managed-care networks. A Republican-controlled Congress debated whether to eliminate $193 million in family planning funding on which Planned Parenthood relied.[116] To the backers of the reinvention plan, the message that would help Planned Parenthood thrive in this difficult environment was simple: "[r]eproductive health care is basic health care." Pam Maraldo, the group's leader, and her supporters believed that abortion-rights would be more secure if Planned Parenthood included them as part of comprehensive primary care for women and families.[117]

To some, the plan and the arguments for it ignored Planned Parenthood's mission and values, particularly the right to abortion. To these affiliate leaders, abortion was about more than just beneficial medical care. Fundamental values, like equality and dignity for women, came into play. Some leaders of the organization circulated a confidential letter complaining that abortion had been mentioned only eight times in the sixty-eight-page document laying out the plan. "[N]ever has a document been so out of touch with our basic mission," complained the letter's authors.[118]

Maraldo's plan particularly angered Gloria Feldt, the leader of an Arizona affiliate, and Alex Sanger, the head of an affiliate in New York City. Feldt had grown up in a small Texas town, got pregnant young, married, and had three children before she was twenty. Then, as Feldt still puts it, she "woke up" and realized that she could "do more than be behind the picket fence." She began college and got involved in the civil rights movement. At this point, she realized that "if there were civil rights, then women must have them too." She took on a role in a local Planned Parenthood affiliate and quickly moved up through the organization. From 1996 to 2005, she served as Planned Parenthood's national president, securing contraceptive coverage in most major insurance plans and rewriting the Freedom of Choice Act as a civil rights bill.[119] Feldt remembers the years between 1992 and 1996 as being particularly dark for her organization. Why would anyone care about Planned Parenthood, Feldt wondered, if the organization did not explain how abortion restrictions stopped women from participating fully in the life of the nation?[120]

Alex Sanger shared Feldt's concerns about the reinvention plan. As a college student at Princeton, Sanger first took an interest in the abortion issue when he wrote his senior history thesis on the work of his grandmother, Margaret Sanger, the founder of Planned Parenthood. He did not become deeply involved until 1984 when he accepted an invitation to join the board of directors of Planned Parenthood of New York City (PPNYC). He chose to leave his law firm to become president and CEO of that organization in 1990.[121]

Sanger's experience with abortion was also personal. When he was in college, a friend called and asked for his help in dealing with an unplanned pregnancy. Her boyfriend had split, and she did not have any idea how to get an abortion. He asked upperclassmen and learned about a willing abortion provider in Washington, DC. He managed to raise the $300 fee by collecting $5 to $20 from different classmates, but there was not enough for Sanger to accompany his friend. Even though the procedure went well, Sanger could not shake the feeling that his friend had been made to "feel dirty and shameful" when she had done nothing wrong. He would carry her experience with him when he began working with Planned Parenthood.[122]

Sanger had always been on the side of expanding services. Nevertheless, he thought that the reinvention plan raised crucial "questions of identity" about how Planned Parenthood would define itself in a changing health care environment. As he still puts it: "We're here because women need us, and that has to come first."[123]

The reinvention plan divided both affiliates and the board of directors. Some affiliate directors believed that the reinvention plan ignored what made reproductive rights unique. Other Planned Parenthood members held fast to concerns about equality for women that they thought the reinvention plan swept under the rug. "The goal is not to make sure we stay in business but to make sure that every woman has access to reproductive health care," argued Alex Sanger.[124]

By April 1995, Planned Parenthood had given up on the idea that every affiliate should go into primary health care. Although affiliates voted to expand the services offered at each clinic, there was no longer a one-size-fits-all plan nationwide. While Maraldo had been hired partly because of her vision for a national network of primary care centers for women and their families, affiliate pressure gave the board second thoughts. By that July, Maraldo had tendered her resignation.[125]

Later in the 1990s, Planned Parenthood leaders, like those in other large abortion-rights organizations, had their hands full putting a stop to the latest antiabortion initiative, one focused on later abortions. Pro-lifers strived to make the health benefits seem like a distraction from the morality of a procedure claimed to resemble infanticide. But as important, major antiabortion groups insisted that the health benefits of abortion – like the idea that abortion helped women become equal citizens – were a myth. Indeed, those on both sides increasingly fought not only about the costs and benefits of abortion but also about who had the expertise to measure either one. Those in clashing movements more often claimed that that the opposition refused to disclose accurate information about the procedure.[126]

HEALTH, COSTS, AND BENEFITS

Starting in the early 1980s, abortion opponents prioritized the overturning of *Roe v. Wade*. Even though pro-lifers had to give up on a constitutional amendment, refocusing on control of the Court – and on the reversal of *Roe* – seemed to put the antiabortion movement in a position of strength. By drafting state legislation and defending it in court, pro-lifers wrongfooted their opposition. Abortion-rights supporters struggled to keep up with the endless restrictions. As states promoted incremental regulations, debate turned on the costs and benefits of abortion.

However, after *Casey*, for the first time in decades, abortion-rights supporters took the initiative. *Casey* had reasoned that women relied on abortion access to take advantage of crucial opportunities. Building on this conclusion, abortion-rights supporters emphasized the benefits of abortion access for women seeking better health care. Groups like NARAL and Planned Parenthood called for the repeal of abortion-funding bans, the legalization of medical abortion, coverage of abortion in universal health care legislation, and laws guaranteeing access to abortion clinics. In court, NOW LDF and the Feminist Majority Foundation accused clinic blockaders of discriminating against women in ways that denied them access to health care.

Casey, it seemed, sent the antiabortion movement into a downward spiral. A growing number of activists lost faith in a legal strategy. At first, ADF and conservative Christian lawyers did not support a renewed attack on *Roe*. But AUL and NRLC attorneys thought that *Casey* only reinforced the importance of arguments about the costs of abortion. In claiming that abortion damaged women's health, pro-life activists could more effectively work in CPCs. Mandatory counseling laws patterned on the one upheld in *Casey* could reduce the abortion rate by informing women of what pro-lifers saw to be the risks of abortion. And antiabortion lobbyists and attorneys could build a case that contrary to what *Casey* suggested, abortion wounded women rather than freeing them to pursue new opportunities.

As pro-lifers increasingly highlighted claims involving health damage done by abortion, the abortion-rights movement accused them of lying to the public and fabricating facts. Abortion foes responded that their opposition relied on a politically correct media and medical establishment to hide the truth about abortion. In the later 1990s and early 2000s, supporters and opponents of legal abortion addressing these questions fought about a proposed ban on dilation and extraction, a procedure popularly known as partial-birth abortion. The debate turned not only on the costs and benefits of abortion but also on who had the authority to measure both.

6

Partial-Birth Abortion and Who Decides the Costs and Benefits

Donna Harrison and Nancy Yanofsky knew that the politics of science had remade the abortion debate. Harrison grew up very poor in a "culturally Catholic but functionally atheistic family," one of nine raised by a struggling insurance agent. A self-identified liberal teenager, Harrison had a high school teacher ask her to write on abortion from a pro-life standpoint. She refused. Harrison thought that anyone who knew that "women were just as good as men" would share her support for legal abortion. Everything changed after she attended a slide show by Dr. John C. Willke of NRLC. She could not shake the images of aborted fetuses in the presentation, and in college, while studying biology, she concluded that human life really did begin at fertilization. She later joined the American Association of Pro-life Obstetricians and Gynecologists (AAPLOG), a group founded in 1973 shortly after *Roe* came down. She eventually became a board member of both that organization and Americans United for Life (AUL). Harrison, like many her of colleagues, argued that abortion-rights supporters had taken over the American College of Obstetricians and Gynecologists (ACOG) and had made it their mouthpiece.[1]

During the mid-1990s, Harrison helped a new group, Physicians Ad Hoc Coalition for Truth about Partial-Birth Abortion (PHACT), to direct the campaign to ban dilation and extraction (D&X), a procedure that pro-lifers dubbed "partial-birth abortion." Whereas providers described dilation and extraction as a surgical procedure in which a provider removed a fetus intact from the uterus, National Right to Life Committee (NRLC) framed partial-birth abortion as a "procedure in which the abortionist removes all but the head of the living baby from the mother's womb . . . the baby's head is stabbed with a pair of scissors . . . [and] the brains are suctioned out to collapse the head to make it easier to remove the dead baby from its mother's womb.'" Harrison urged listeners to decide for themselves about the morality and safety of the procedure rather than placing their faith in biased doctors and reporters.[2]

Nancy Yanofsky fought to establish that only her side provided accurate information about the procedure she called dilation and extraction (D&X). A linguist by training, she had been involved in education her entire life. Married in 1962, she had three "very planned children" and was always able to continue working. She wanted all women to have the same control over their futures. Yanofsky jumped at the opportunity to change the way people talked about abortion. She served as the head of the Pro-choice Resource Center from 1991 to 2001.[3]

Her organization trained affiliates of groups like Planned Parenthood and NARAL (later NARAL Pro-choice America) in how to deliver the pro-choice message to more Americans. Yanofsky transformed the Pro-choice Resource Center into a $2 million organization. But in the late 1990s, she struggled, as did many of her colleagues, when discussion centered on the D&X procedure. Yanofsky and her colleagues asserted that D&X was sometimes the safest procedure for women, but abortion foes fired back that both leading medical organizations and the media distorted the truth. As Yanofsky recognized, the abortion debate reflected a larger discussion about where the public could turn for valid information about the science of abortion.[4]

In the late 1990s and early 2000s, as the experiences of Harrison and Yanofsky suggest, the American abortion fight forced those on both sides to explain how anyone could reliably measure the costs and benefits of abortion, especially when medical details were in dispute. After Republicans gained a majority in the House in 1994, antiabortion lobbyists promoted a ban on D&X. Pro-lifers in groups like NRLC initially framed the fight as a moral crusade. NRLC further contended that much more than other abortion procedures, partial-birth abortion had grave costs, damaging the reputation of doctors and coarsening attitudes toward human life.

Relying on support from leading medical organizations, including ACOG, abortion-rights supporters contended that D&X was sometimes the safest procedure for women. Pro-lifers responded that both the media and groups like ACOG could not be trusted to tell the truth about D&X because they openly endorsed abortion or espoused politically correct positions on reproductive rights. Those on opposing sides debated not only what counted as a cost or benefit of abortion but also who had the skill, honesty, and evidence to measure either one. The abortion fight centered on debates over the facts about the procedure and the trustworthiness of the medical establishment, the media, and politicians. This discussion paralleled struggles over the science of climate change, vaccine safety, and breast cancer.

Soon, the courts took up questions about the line between science and politics. Abortion-rights attorneys challenged the constitutionality of state partial-birth abortion bans, and in 2000, in *Stenberg v. Carhart*, the Supreme Court struck down one of the state statutes that closely tracked legislation proposed in Congress.[5] However, the ongoing fight about D&X illuminated strategic disagreements in both movements. On the abortion-rights side, women of color, reproductive justice proponents, and certain abortion providers neither challenged the stigma surrounding abortion nor expanded on a single-issue agenda. While some antiabortion attorneys thought that the partial-birth abortion campaign simply recycled failed arguments, other grassroots activists saw that campaign as morally bankrupt.

For leading antiabortion groups, however, the D&X campaign still seemed to be a political godsend. Congress passed a federal D&X ban in 2003, and the Supreme Court rejected a constitutional challenge to the law in *Gonzales v. Carhart* (2007). In a 5–4 opinion authored by Justice Anthony Kennedy, *Gonzales* treated women who claimed to regret their abortions as experts on the subject. *Gonzales* also concluded that the safety and health benefits of D&X were unclear. The Court reasoned that when medical evidence was contested, elected officials, not judges or doctors, had the authority to break the tie.[6]

After *Gonzales*, compromise on the abortion issue seemed further away than ever. Pro-choice and pro-life activists fought about what counted as a cost or benefit and how anyone could reliably measure either one. Those on both sides still passionately believed in clashing visions of the Constitution. But as the D&X fight showed, opposing movements also drew on different sources of evidence and proposed alternative experts. Pro-choice and pro-life activists more often saw one another as deluded or manipulative, not just as wrong on questions of principle. Finding common ground seemed even more unlikely when no one could agree on common facts about abortion.

INTRODUCING A PARTIAL-BIRTH ABORTION BAN

In 1992, Dr. Martin Haskell, an Ohio-based abortion provider, delivered a paper at the annual conference of the National Abortion Federation (NAF), an organization of abortion providers, on a relatively unknown abortion technique, dilation and extraction (D&X). The most common second trimester procedure, dilation and evacuation (D&E), removed a fetus in parts and required a physician to make multiple passes with a sharp instrument. Because Haskell's technique, D&X, removed the fetus in one piece, he believed that the procedure would be safer for certain women. At the time, Haskell's paper might not have seemed extraordinarily important. The doctor had not even invented D&X. NAF conferences routinely featured similar discussions of strategies for maximizing patient comfort or minimizing surgical risk. But within a few weeks, Haskell's paper had inspired a political campaign that would last more than a decade. Even if D&X was not new, the uproar surrounding it was unparalleled.[7]

The partial-birth abortion campaign began less than a month after Haskell's presentation when an anonymous source sent a copy of the doctor's paper to NRLC leaders. By June 1993, Minnesota Citizens Concerned for Life (MCCL), an NRLC affiliate, ran an ad in the *Minneapolis Star Tribune*, complete with line drawings of D&X. The ad urged readers to write members of Congress and called on them to oppose the federal Freedom of Choice Act (FOCA), a federal statute that would have protected abortion-rights.[8]

Pro-choice divisions doomed FOCA,[9] but the 1994 election promised to transform partial-birth abortion bans into a potent political strategy. Pointing to a favorable electoral map, Carol Long (later, Carol Long Tobias), then the head of NRLC's political action committee, predicted that Republicans would regain control of the Senate. When the polls closed in November, the result exceeded Long's expectations. Republicans had picked up fifty-four seats in the House and eight in the Senate. The GOP controlled state legislatures in seven of the eight largest states. Gains in the American South were especially striking. For the first time in decades, Republicans, once irrelevant below the Mason-Dixon Line, achieved parity with their Democratic colleagues. Abortion opponents no longer had to be on the defensive.[10]

The question was what groups like NRLC or AUL should prioritize, especially with a pro-choice president still in office. AUL continued stressing informed consent laws, but as Doug Johnson, the NRLC's legislative director, contended that promoting a partial-birth abortion ban made sense for several reasons. First, NRLC attorneys thought that Supreme Court justices responded to what they saw as shifts in public attitudes. Johnson explained that to "shape public opinion," NRLC sought to force "the opposition to defend extreme and unpopular positions." In Johnson's view, partial-birth abortion bans enjoyed support partly because they focused attention on late-term procedures, a strong subject for pro-lifers. And descriptions of partial-birth abortion could convince even ambivalent voters that the procedure was closer to infanticide than to an early abortion. Johnson argued that these laws put Clinton in a difficult position, giving him a choice of "vetoing popular legislation . . . or else alienating his pro-abortion voting block by allowing some abortion-regulating legislation to become law."[11]

Early on, however, abortion-rights supporters asserted that D&X was sometimes the safest procedure for women. Since the two sides disagreed about the need for and even safety of D&X, how could courts, politicians, or voters get a fair answer about the costs and benefits of the procedure? NRLC and AUL activists initially insisted that no one needed scientific experts to understand the moral costs of keeping D&X legal. Americans could simply look at the line drawings of partial-birth abortion and make up their own minds.

In 1995, with help from NRLC, Representatives Charles T. Canady (R–FL) and Barbara Vucanovich (R–NV) sponsored a bill banning the procedure. Antiabortion witnesses emphasized that common sense should dictate the availability of D&X. Brenda Pratt Shafer, a nurse who had worked briefly in Dr. Haskell's clinic, asked voters to look at sketches of partial-birth abortion. "I think every member [of Congress] should be marched into an operating room and actually made to watch an actual abortion, and then you make your own decisions," she said. Helen Alvaré, an attorney for the National Conference of Catholic Bishops (now the United States

Conference of Catholic Bishops), made the same point. "A description of partial-birth abortion is the best argument against its continued existence," she testified."[12]

While agreeing that scientific expertise should not dictate the course of the struggle, organizations like Planned Parenthood and NARAL asked the public to focus on the way that the procedure benefitted some women. Colleen Costello, a conservative Christian woman, testified about her decision to undergo the procedure after learning that her unborn daughter had a fatal neurological disease. Costello believed that D&X would have the least severe impact on her future fertility. As groups like Planned Parenthood and NARAL framed it, women like Costello should be the ones who decided about D&X because they were the ones who had benefitted from it firsthand. "We are the ones who know," Costello testified. "We are the families who will forever have a hole in our hearts."[13]

While framing the question as a matter of morality or common sense, both sides also fought about who had the expertise to decide on the costs and benefits of the procedure. Dr. Nancy Romer suggested that D&X might damage women's health. Abortion-rights activists responded that Congress tried to place decisions about D&X in the hands of politicians who did not understand the first thing about the medical costs and benefits of any procedure. "With all due respect, the Congress of the United States is not qualified to stand over my shoulder in the operating room and tell me how to treat my patients," testified Dr. J. Courtland Robinson.[14]

Congress passed the ban in December 1995, but the following April, Clinton vetoed the bill because it lacked a health exception.[15] In a major drive to override the veto, NRLC insisted that Clinton falsely claimed that D&X was safe and rarely used. According to NRLC, the health exception promoted by so-called experts boiled down "to partial-birth abortion on demand." Any health exception would swallow the broader ban, NRLC argued, because the Court "defined 'health' abortions to include those requested on the basis of 'all factors—physical, emotional, psychological, familial and the woman's age.'"[16]

Because opposing movements disagreed on the need for a health exception to bans on partial-birth abortion, the debate touched on both the costs and benefits of the procedure and on who could competently evaluate them. Pro-lifers formed new medical organizations and argued that established groups placed political correctness before the facts. Abortion-rights supporters sometimes defended the authority of the American College of Obstetricians and Gynecologists, but at other moments, pro-choice leaders suggested that women's personal moral compass, not scientific facts, should decide the availability of D&X. As the debate unfolded, agreement about the facts became harder and harder to find.

REDEFINING MEDICAL EXPERTS

If abortion-rights supporters argued that only experts could measure the costs of abortion, pro-lifers would need more of their own scientists and medical professionals. Antiabortion physicians had already formed their own groups, including American Association of Pro-life Obstetricians and Gynecologists (1973) and Physicians for Life (1986). But by the mid-1990s, with what pro-lifers viewed as a takeover of the American College of Obstetricians and Gynecologists (ACOG) by abortion-rights supporters, abortion foes decided to form more organizations of their own. In the summer of 1996, a group of pro-life physicians founded Physicians Ad Hoc Coalition for Truth (PHACT). "We, as physicians, can no longer stand by while abortion advocates, the President of the United States, and newspapers and television shows continue to repeat false medical claims to members of Congress and to the public," PHACT proclaimed in a letter announcing its founding. PHACT suggested that groups like ACOG and the American Public Health Association concealed the truth because it was politically inconvenient. As the group argued: "Congress, the public, but most importantly women need to know that partial-birth abortion is never necessary to protect their future health or fertility."[17]

NRLC also argued that Americans could not trust the media to fairly cover the medical costs and benefits of partial-birth abortion. Doug Johnson frequently wrote the editors of magazines, newspapers, and television programs about bias in coverage of partial-birth abortion. In one criticism of an episode of the news program *60 Minutes*, Johnson accused the media of offering "one-sided medical information."[18]

Although the Senate failed to override Clinton's veto in the fall of 1996, pro-lifers renewed the push to ban partial-birth abortion not long after the new year.[19] Polls showed consistent public support for the proposal. Worried that opposing a D&X ban outright would damage their political chances, Democrats rallied behind an alternative sponsored by Senator Tom Daschle (D–SD). Daschle pledged to outlaw all post-viability abortions but did not prohibit any technique earlier in pregnancy and created an exception for women's health. While abortion-rights activists viewed Daschle's bill with ambivalence, NRLC leaders pointed to the Daschle bill (and coverage of it) as further evidence that Americans could trust neither the media nor politicians to describe the true costs and benefits of abortion. As Doug Johnson saw it, Daschle's bill seemed to limit later abortions but really allowed for abortion whenever a woman claimed her health was at risk. NRLC accused the media of whitewashing Daschle's bill. Abortion foes contended that pro-choice members of Congress lied, and the media made it all too easy for them to get away with it.[20]

The Daschle bill did nothing to dash pro-lifers' enthusiasm for a ban on partial-birth abortion. Nor did Clinton's defeat of Bob Dole, the Republican nominee, in the 1996 presidential election. Even before Dole's disappointing performance, pro-lifers at the Life Forum, a strategy summit, resented what they felt was the GOP's shabby treatment of their movement.

Life Forum gatherings began in 1989. As Connie Marshner, a social conservative activist, explained, its founders intended Life Forum to be a "peacemaker" for the warring factions of the antiabortion movement. Over time, Life Forum meetings came to mean much more. A wide variety of pro-life groups came to Washington,

DC, to debate strategy and trade information. For this reason, attendees kept strictly secret anything said at the meeting – and indeed the existence of Life Forum itself. Although Life Forum attendees relied on Republicans to pass D&X laws, many of those present in 1996 believed that GOP leaders took pro-lifers for granted – and would never actually introduce an outright abortion ban. "We are trotted out at the last minute [by Republicans] to cause [pro-lifers] to vote, and then put in the closet," one attendee objected in the fall of 1996. Not long thereafter, Paul Weyrich, one of the architects of the relationship between the Republican Party and the pro-life movement, complained that Representative Newt Gingrich (R–GA), the target of an attempted GOP coup in the House, was no longer a reliable ally. By the fall of 1997, Weyrich and other Life Forum participants had grown disgusted with the Republican leadership after Governor Christine Todd Whitman (R–NJ) vetoed a ban on partial-birth abortion without losing the support of her party. Weyrich went so far as to say that "it was a mistake to facilitate the marriage of the Republican Party and the pro-life movement." Despite certain pro-lifers' frustrations with the GOP, the fight for a partial-birth abortion ban generally enjoyed strong support within the movement. Even if the path to criminalizing all abortions seemed far from clear, the short-term payoff from a D&X ban was obvious. Gallup found that starting in the mid-1990s, the number of Americans who supported legal abortion under all circumstances dropped from roughly 34 percent to approximately 22 percent. The pollster attributed the decline to public debate about partial-birth abortion, which a majority wished to ban.[21]

As the D&X battle escalated, both sides fought over the need for a health exception, debating how to fairly assess the costs and benefits of abortion. At times appealing to common sense, pro-lifers also asserted that the scientific conclusions drawn by groups like ACOG were either biased or inconclusive. The abortion conflict reflected broader questions about the line between politics and science in fights about everything from global warming to breast cancer.

ACTION IN THE FACE OF SCIENTIFIC UNCERTAINTY

Fights about D&X put center stage a debate about who had the credibility, honesty, and expertise to measure the costs and benefits of abortion. In the later 1990s, similar questions about the line between politics and science erupted in a variety of contexts. After Americans became more aware of climate change, Congress began considering strategies to limit greenhouse gas emissions. In the mid-1990s, organizations of skeptics (often funded by industry), such as the George C. Marshall Institute, responded that there was simply not enough evidence to justify pricey interventions, and many Americans agreed. The Senate, for example, passed the Byrd-Hagel Resolution 95–0, stating that climate science was too uncertain for the United States to agree to emissions limits unless developing countries did the same.[22]

While global warming skeptics doubted the credibility of the scientific establishment, anti-vaccine activists questioned the integrity of leading medical organizations. At a 1998 press conference, British gastroenterologist Andrew Wakefield blamed rising rates of autism on the vaccine for measles, mumps, and rubella (MMR), tapping into existing belief in the dangers of vaccines. Although researchers quickly discredited Wakefield, online access meant that similar conspiracy theories could rapidly catch on. By 1998, the number of worldwide internet users jumped to 147 million from just 16 million three years before.[23]

Skepticism about climate change or vaccines drew on longer-standing concerns about what many came to see as blind deference to scientific authorities. In 1972, reporters revealed that the Tuskegee Study on untreated syphilis denied informed consent to its predominantly black test subjects. In the 1970s, reporters also spread the word about the involuntary sterilization of women of color, the ongoing enforcement of eugenic sterilization laws, and nonconsensual Cold War experiments involving human exposure to radiation.[24]

While these varied critics exposed abuses committed in the name of science, conservative scholars condemned what they saw as bias in both the social and hard sciences. Starting in the mid-1960s, in the neoconservative journal *The Public Interest*, commentators like Peter Skerry questioned the accuracy of the scientific conclusions drawn by leading medical institutions and courts. By the mid-1990s, related arguments had spread well beyond the academy. Abortion foes, like other conservatives, argued that scientists put politics ahead of sterling research, burying or defunding studies that illuminated what was wrong with abortion.[25]

Groups like NRLC and AUL also emphasized what they described as scientific uncertainty about the safety of abortion. When it came to RU 486, one part of a two-pill protocol for medical abortion, pro-lifers insisted that there was too much uncertainty surrounding the safety of the drug. In 1995, in the quest to get approval from the Food and Drug Administration (FDA), researchers had begun clinical trials in the United States. However, researchers in Europe had already studied the drug, and 250,000 women in more than twenty countries had used it. Abortion foes nevertheless argued that the uncertainty surrounding the safety of medical (as opposed to surgical) abortion made it too risky. "American women still don't know how RU 486 will affect their fertility, their immune system or their future children," wrote Myrna Gutiérrez of AUL. At a 1997 Life Forum meeting, activist Mike Schwartz, the founder of self-proclaimed Planned Parenthood watchdog Life Decisions International, agreed that the pro-life "argument should be that these drugs hurt women."[26]

Groups like AUL and NRLC suggested that groups like ACOG concealed a connection between abortion and breast cancer just as they hid the dangers of RU 486. The abortion–breast cancer (ABC) campaign began in 1992 when Joel Brind, an endocrinologist at Baruch College in New York, read an article in *Science News* suggesting that women who got pregnant as teenagers had a lower chance of getting breast cancer. Curious about what happened if a woman terminated her pregnancy, Brind pored over the medical literature on the subject and concluded that abortion increased women's cancer risk. He drove to Congress to persuade lawmakers that he was right. Abortion opponents immediately took notice. "The information we have received is that this person has not previously identified as a pro-life person and is respected in his field of endocrinology," a colleague wrote to Doug Johnson of NRLC. "At one time, he was a very left-leaning liberal. He thus might be a good witness in some situations where his expertise is relevant."[27]

By the mid-1990s, Brind regularly wrote for *National Right to Life News*, and AUL promoted the ABC connection in informed consent laws. As part of the effort to connect abortion and breast cancer risk, Judith Koehler of AUL developed and circulated model legislation, complete with medical research and talking points. In a letter to Life Forum leader Connie Marshner, Clarke Forsythe called the ABC campaign "one of our most important and strategic initiatives." The science behind the ABC connection, however, was contested. A 1994 study by Janet Daling and her colleagues at the Fred Hutchinson Cancer Research Center in Seattle suggested that among those who had been pregnant at least once, women who had abortions had a 50 percent higher risk of breast cancer. However, some researchers argued that case-control studies like Daling's were deeply flawed. Such research depended on self-reporting from patients. As a result, researchers could not control other variables that might influence the result. Reporting bias could also create issues. Some researchers argued that women who had abortions but did not get breast cancer were less likely to respond to researchers' requests than those who had become sick.[28]

Between 1995 and 1998, several peer-reviewed studies addressed the ABC connection, concluding that there was a modestly increased risk for women after induced abortion. In 1997, however, a larger study published in the *New England Journal of Medicine* found no connection between abortion and breast cancer. Many thought that the 1997 article settled the question because it represented a cohort, rather than case-control, study. By contrast to case control studies (which relied on reporting from their subjects), the 1997 study followed women who had abortions, using medical records, to determine how many developed the disease. Soon, because of the 1997 study, the World Health Organization, the American Cancer Society, and the National Cancer Institute concluded that there was no evidence of a link between abortion and breast cancer. Nevertheless, abortion foes insisted that the medical establishment had political motives for discounting case-control studies.[29]

The leaders of the crisis pregnancy center (CPC) movement claimed to step in when groups like ACOG refused to inform women of the ABC connection. As early as the 1980s, CPCs had provided women with medical advice about abortion. In 1984, for example, a North Carolina center informed women that abortion would render them sterile in the future. But after they began to receive government funding, leaders of the CPC movement worked to establish the medical expertise of those who worked at pro-life pregnancy counseling centers. In 1996, the Welfare Reform Act earmarked $50 million for abstinence-only education – money for which CPCs were eligible. The following year, Thomas Glessner, the head of the National Institute of Family and Life Advocates (NIFLA), urged CPCs to become medical centers. Glessner argued that without claiming medical expertise, CPCs would be ineffective. "The number one reason women come to these centers is to find out if they're pregnant," he explained to his colleagues at a Life Forum strategy meeting. "A [non-medical] counseling center cannot give them a medical answer .... [We] lose a lot of women this way." By highlighting their medical credentials and showing women ultrasounds, CPC staff and advocates claimed the expertise to assess the costs and benefits of abortion.[30]

In the mid-1990s, antiabortion leaders argued that groups like ACOG, together with the media and many experts, refused to provide accurate information about the costs of abortion. Questioning the credibility and expertise of those who opposed them, AUL and NRLC disputed the basic facts about RU 486, abortion, and breast cancer. Independent but parallel conversations touched on everything from global warming to vaccines. Without joining these discussions, pro-life groups insisted that the safety of abortion was equally contested – and that many conventional authorities would not tell the truth.

As pro-lifers contested who had the competence to measure the costs and benefits of abortion, abortion-rights organizations had to reconsider time-tested strategies. Regardless of whether Clinton continued vetoing bans passed by Congress, similar statutes had spread in the states and seemed to damage the standing of the abortion-rights movement. Part of the problem was that pro-lifers had challenged the credibility of medical experts who insisted on the need for safe and legal abortions. While ACOG had once been the obvious source for medical questions surrounding abortion, abortion-rights leaders had to convince Americans where to place their faith all over again. A debate centered on the costs and benefits of abortion created disputes not only about the effects of abortion but also about the very definition of scientific expertise.

REESTABLISHING THE CREDIBILITY OF MEDICAL PROFESSIONALS

In the late 1990s, the leaders of abortion-rights groups privately lamented how badly the D&X battle was going. Late abortions had always been a difficult subject for abortion-rights supporters, and the line drawings of D&X, coupled with loaded descriptions of it, upset some voters who might have otherwise been sympathetic to abortion-rights. Ordinarily, attacking the lack of a health exception in D&X bans might have been effective. Polls, for example, showed that the vast majority of voters supported legal abortion if "a woman's physical health [was] endangered."[31] But groups like NRLC and AUL maintained that scientists could not agree on whether women ever needed D&X. Larger abortion-rights groups found themselves embroiled in a fight about whether experts thought D&X best protected women's health.

In 1997, however, abortion-rights leaders hoped that the fate of D&X might largely be an historical footnote. If women could take RU 486 at home with or even without a prescription, then legal restrictions – almost all of which regulated the conduct of physicians – might have less bite. However, the Supreme Court's latest decision, *Mazurek v. Armstrong*, made clear that states could steer all abortions into clinics or hospitals, the availability of RU 486 notwithstanding. Montana, like many states, required all abortions to be performed by a licensed physician. In *Mazurek*, in challenging Montana's law, the Center for Reproductive Law and Policy argued that Montana's law burdened women seeking abortions without benefitting them in any way. The brief further argued that Montana's law was a bill of attainder, a legislative act declaring someone guilty of a crime without a trial. According to the Center, pro-life activists in Montana had targeted and punished physician assistants who performed abortions. The Center further reasoned that the law had no legitimate purpose. According to the Center, the law reflected nothing more than a desire to outlaw abortion. In a brief opinion, *Mazurek* rejected this argument. The Court did not focus on the bill-of-attainder argument. When it came to the purpose of the law, *Mazurek* reiterated that "the Constitution gives the States broad latitude to decide that particular functions may be performed only by licensed professionals." Clarke Forsythe of AUL proclaimed *Mazurek* the most important legal development since the decision of *Casey* – a guarantee that states could channel abortions out of the home and into medical facilities. The Court's decision only made the D&X fight more important. State restrictions often made it harder for poor women to get abortions, pushing them to wait until later in pregnancy when some experts thought that D&X had safety advantages.[32]

Shortly after *Mazurek*, a public relations nightmare made it harder for abortion-rights supporters to credibly claim to measure the costs and benefits of partial-birth abortion. The media firestorm began with an unlikely culprit, Ron Fitzsimmons, a lobbyist for the National Coalition of Abortion Providers, a group of independent clinics. Fitzsimmons believed that abortion providers reinforced the stigma surrounding D&X by insisting that it was (and should be) rarely performed. Believing that abortion-rights groups like NARAL had deliberately underestimated the number of D&X surgeries performed each year, Fitzsimmons gave an interview to *American Medical News*, admitting that he had "lied through his teeth" when discussing D&X. Whereas Fitzsimmons had estimated that doctors performed only a few hundred procedures, he later suggested that the number ran into the thousands, especially in the second trimester. According to pro-lifers, Fitzsimmons demonstrated that the opposition routinely lied about the costs of abortion.[33]

While denouncing Fitzsimmons' remarks, larger abortion-rights organizations mostly stuck to arguments that women alone could competently evaluate the need for a particular abortion procedure. NCAP leaders maintained that there were constitutional and moral reasons to defer to women, particularly if the facts surrounding the costs and benefits of D&X were unclear. "In the end, we trust individuals to make difficult and complicated decisions about their own lives," explained a handout distributed by the group. The National Abortion Federation (NAF) put out a press release asserting that while no one knew exactly how many D&X procedures had been performed, common sense dictated that women who had faced tragic pregnancies were the most reliable sources of information about partial-birth abortion.[34]

Over time, however, larger abortion-rights groups sought out a better way to defuse claims about the facts of abortion. In a three-year strategic plan, NARAL responded to the campaign "to frame the debate around issues such as late abortion."[35] The plan's authors intended to reestablish the credibility of ACOG and the abortion-rights movement itself by "reposition[ing] the choice issue in public debate."[36] In the summer of 1997, NARAL elaborated on this idea. As NARAL President Kate Michelman explained, the group planned to return to the issue of "who decides" when there were complex moral and medical issues surrounding abortion.[37] In a climate of doubt, everyone would still agree on the importance of "keeping politicians out of reproductive health decisions."[38]

Planned Parenthood hired Democratic pollster Celinda Lake to research possible arguments about the costs and benefits of a D&X ban. "Absolutely do not try to point out inaccuracies in the other side's description of the procedure," Lake Research advised in its subsequent report. Instead of questioning the facts argued by the opposition, abortion-rights advocates were urged to tell the stories of "the real women who have suffered." Lake Research suggested the following message: "These abortions happen only in the most tragic and dire health circumstances, and only when it is medically necessary." Lake Research echoed what many pro-choice leaders already knew: Voters were uncomfortable with later abortions but inclined to doubt the media and politicians. Whatever questions anyone had about the medical establishment, many believed that politicians were even worse. "Voters believe that politicians should stay out of the decision," the report explained succinctly.[39]

But tapping into voters' dislike for politicians only went so far, and D&X bans enjoyed significant support. Even President Clinton privately asked staffers if the procedure had the health benefits supporters claimed.[40] In May 1997, ACOG came out in favor of Daschle's proposal even though NARAL and other abortion-rights groups opposed it. The American Medical Association put out a press release supporting the partial-birth ban favored by NRLC and concluded that the procedure was never medically necessary.[41]

Clinton again vetoed the Partial-Birth Abortion Ban Act in October, but abortion-rights leaders felt that they were losing ground with voters. In early 1998, abortion-rights organizations held a variety of summits about how to fend off the scientific claims made by the opposition. Discussion at *"Roe v. Wade* at 25: A Symposium on the Issues" centered on what the abortion-rights movement should do now that "the fetus [was] no longer abstract." Many present worried that because voters questioned doctors or women's moral compass, the public did not trust them to tell the truth about abortion. "When we avoid the [moral] issue, . . . people assume that we don't take abortion seriously," one attendee explained.[42]

Following the symposium, Planned Parenthood launched "Responsible Choices," a campaign to show that women and doctors deserved the power to resolve disputed scientific questions about the costs and benefits of abortion. "Our action agenda speaks to America's moral center—our shared faith in equality, respect for diversity, and compassion for the vulnerable," explained the organization's 1997–1998 annual report. "Responsible Choices" did not focus on the benefits of abortion for women or even on the facts about D&X or breast cancer. "Responsible Choices" instead urged voters to trust women and physicians to resolve contested scientific questions about the costs and benefits of abortion precisely because both groups understood the moral stakes of abortion.[43]

Just the same, it was hard to shake the grip abortion foes seemed to have on discussion of the costs and benefits of D&X. Longstanding discomfort with later abortion and a nagging distrust of elites (including medical ones) made partial-birth abortion a toxic issue for abortion-rights supporters. Lake Research completed a study of "Responsible Choices," and the results were not heartening for Planned Parenthood. The report indicated that while "'choice' and 'responsibility' [were] popular terms," "Responsible Choices" had not convinced many that D&X was medically valuable – or that pro-choice doctors or advocates were the best source of information about the procedure. Regardless of anything else, as the report put it, opponents of the ban seemed to be "losing the debate over the necessity of the procedure."[44]

For abortion-rights supporters, proving the need for a health exception had become surprisingly hard. Pro-lifers fielded their own experts, but larger antiabortion groups also fed into a populist undercurrent, successfully convincing some voters that they did not need experts to know that D&X was both unnecessary and wrong. When discussing abortion, these organizations at times asked voters to stay true to their own moral views of abortion and to trust women (and doctors) to do the same. But by framing abortion as an inherently subjective matter, pro-choice groups made it much more difficult to defeat a D&X ban. The more that facts became harder to separate from personal truth, the more inevitable a D&X ban came to seem.

DEFINING THE FACTS FOR A YOUNGER GENERATION

Questioning the facts surrounding a D&X ban became a focal point of debate as both sides rallied to recruit younger Americans. As a new millennium began, many younger Americans could not remember a time when abortion was illegal. For this reason, those under the age of forty did not hold always firm opinions on abortion and, pro-lifers hoped, might be open to arguments about the costs of D&X. Abortion-rights supporters, by contrast, worried that support for legal abortion would flag among voters too young to know what the world had been like before *Roe*. To reach younger Americans, pro-choice groups framed abortion as a moral and constitutional question that women should decide. Because they did not always emphasize the benefits of abortion or D&X, however, abortion-rights groups left an opening for pro-lifers who claimed that late abortion was as shameful as it was secretive.

The push to woo younger voters picked up intensity partly because of an existential threat to Bill Clinton's presidency. During the investigation of Clinton's failed Whitewater real estate deal, Kenneth Starr, the independent counsel charged with investigating the president, received a taped conversation in which a former White House intern, Monica Lewinsky, claimed that she had performed oral sex on the president.[45] In a January 1998 press conference, Clinton stated that he had never had sexual relations with Lewinsky. Believing that the president had lied under oath, the House of Representatives approved two articles of impeachment. The danger to abortion-rights seemed clear. A bloodied Democratic Party might struggle to hold the White House. Clinton seemed to be the only thing stopping a ban on partial-birth abortion from sailing through.[46]

Notwithstanding the popularity of D&X prohibitions, an outbreak of violence against abortion providers put off young voters. In 1997, the Army of God, a Christian terrorist organization, claimed responsibility for nail bombings of abortion clinics in Atlanta and Birmingham. Members of the Lambs of Christ, a group of traveling clinic blockaders, went even further. In 1998, James Charles Kopp, an activist affiliated with the group, murdered Dr. Barnett Slepian in his home in Buffalo, New York. When he was killed, Slepian had just returned from a memorial service for his father. The bullet only narrowly missed Slepian's son. The dreadful details of Slepian's killing damaged abortion opponents' image, especially with younger, undecided voters.[47]

The leaders of groups like NARAL believed that describing the benefits of abortion (or contesting the facts about D&X specifically) would not work to reach younger voters like those frightened by Slepian's murder. Instead, NARAL and Planned Parenthood focused on the issue of who should decide about abortion. At an August NARAL conference, attendees summarized research concluding "that Americans agree[d] with the other side on religion, [the idea that] abortion is murder, [that] restrictions [are desirable], [that] abortion is a manifestation of promiscuity, and [that] promiscuity is a manifestation of moral decline in America." NARAL leaders reasoned that voters indifferent to the facts about abortion would come around if they saw the issue as a moral right uniquely understood by women. NARAL emphasized the importance of "[r]eposition[ing] choice ... by highlighting that it is a mainstream American value and has a moral dimension." Instead of discussing the benefits of abortion (and of D&X), NARAL would emphasize that women had the right to make a decision – and that they made ethical, careful choices when exercising that right.[48]

The NARAL Foundation started a campaign, "Choice for America," to reach young people who had "become relatively complacent about the status of reproductive rights." As part of its campaign to defeat partial-birth abortion bans, NARAL would emphasize the "moral and ethical considerations involved in the abortion decision." The campaign described choice itself as a moral norm – a "fundamental American value as central to our way of life as the freedom of worship." "Choice for America" argued that at a time when it seemed harder than ever to know who was telling the truth, voters should hold fast to "women's moral capacity to make complex reproductive decisions."[49]

Even certain pro-lifers wondered if arguments about the costs of abortion would guarantee success for partial-birth abortion bans. At a major 1998 Life Forum strategy meeting, Mike Schwartz of Life Decisions International urged his colleagues to change their tactical plan. In his view, legal and political change would never be enough unless attitudes shifted. Schwartz argued that no states would criminalize abortion even if the Court overturned *Roe*. Rather than using arguments about the costs of abortion, Schwartz favored education and clinic protests. Clarke Forsythe of AUL responded that reversing *Roe* was indispensable – and that only arguments about the costs of abortion would increase pro-lifers' odds of success. "The challenge of public opinion over the next several decades is dispelling the notion of abortion as a necessary evil," Forsythe asserted. In his view, abortion foes had already established that abortion was evil since "most Americans [saw] the fetus as a human life, if not a full child." He advised his colleagues "to invest more in the second part: dispelling the myth that abortion is necessary." To do so, abortion foes would have to stress the costs of abortion for women as a way of "convincing Middle America that abortion is bad for women, or at least not good." Although Forsythe did not persuade everyone, larger pro-life groups saw no reason to change course. Like AUL members, NRLC leaders believed that emphasizing arguments about the facts about partial-birth abortion – especially its effects on women – would do the most to change public opinion, especially among the young.[50]

Soon, the Supreme Court took on questions about the facts of partial-birth abortion. When questioning the constitutionality of D&X bans, providers emphasized the laws' lack of a health exception. The Court had to consider whether the Constitution required such an exception – and whether the evidence indicated that one was necessary. In the political arena, by contrast, abortion-rights supporters asked voters to pay more attention to abstract values such as choice. This argument made some political sense, given that scientific arguments about the costs and benefits of D&X seemed to have gone nowhere. But by setting aside questions about who had the expertise to evaluate the safety of different abortion procedures, larger abortion-rights groups created an opportunity for the opposition. At times, when pro-lifers were questioning the accuracy of ACOG's position, theirs were the only voices many voters heard.

THE *STENBURG* CASE

The Supreme Court became embroiled in the debate about the evidence support-ing a health exception to D&X bans. The majority and dissent in the Court's first partial-birth abortion case, *Stenberg v. Carhart*, offered strikingly different conclu-sions about how the Court should address scientific disputes about the costs and benefits of abortion. The majority reasoned that because of the importance of women's health, the possibility that D&X had unique benefits made a health exception constitutionally necessary. By contrast, the Court's swing vote, Anthony Kennedy, dissented, insisting that lawmakers should have more latitude when scientific evidence was in dispute. The split in *Stenberg* guaranteed that pro-lifers would continue promoting D&X bans.

In the lead-up to *Stenberg*, abortion-rights supporters could not help but feel relieved. Clinton's widely expected political reckoning never came, and the presi-dent survived an impeachment vote. Nor did Republicans' electoral windfall in the 1998 midterms materialize. Democrats actually took control of the House. But even if the fight for a federal D&X ban stalled, abortion opponents had gained ground in the states. By 2000, NRLC had helped thirty-one states introduce such laws, and abortion-rights supporters questioned their constitutionality in court.[51]

In 2000, several circuit courts of appeal were considering challenges to NRLC model laws banning partial-birth abortion, and in February, the Supreme Court agreed to hear *Stenberg*, a Nebraska case. That state defined partial-birth abortion as "deliberately and intentionally delivering into the vagina a living unborn child, or a substantial portion thereof, for the purpose of performing a procedure that the person performing such procedure knows will kill the unborn child and does kill the unborn child." Nebraska outlawed this procedure unless a woman's life would be threatened by a physical disorder, illness, or injury if she carried a pregnancy to term. The state treated any violation of the law as a felony and automatically revoked the medical license of any doctor found guilty under the statute. Dr. Leroy Carhart, a physician who performed the procedure, sought a declaration that the law violated the Constitution.[52] In a 1998 ruling, Nebraska Judge Richard Kopf held that the law was unconstitutional as applied to Dr. Leroy Carhart and his patients. A three-judge panel of the Eighth Circuit Court of Appeals struck down the law in its entirety.[53]

In briefs before the Supreme Court, the Center for Reproductive Law and Policy first stressed that Nebraska's statute was either impermissibly vague or likely to encompass the most common second trimester abortion procedure, dilation and extraction (D&E), thereby "banning most pre-viability abortions." When it came to vagueness, the Center contended that the statute did not define crucial terms and thereby failed to give physicians notice of the conduct it prohibited. Moreover, the

Center insisted that as Nebraska defined the procedure, the elements of a partial-birth abortion also applied to almost all abortion methods, including D&E. The Center reasoned that even if the Court read the law to apply only to D&X, it would impermissibly limit women's control over their own reproductive care. The Center argued that *Roe* and *Casey* recognized a right for a woman not only to decide to terminate a pregnancy before viability but also to choose "her preferred method."[54]

Together with pro-life amici, Nebraska responded that the law did not extend to D&E partly because legislators had never suggested such an application. Moreover, Nebraska claimed the constitutional authority to outlaw any abortion technique under *Casey* so long as there were safe alternatives available. The government maintained that there was no convincing evidence that D&X had health benefits. "Where, as here, . . . opinions by medical witnesses are in disagreement, the decision regarding the regulation of medical procedures should be left to the state legislature," Nebraska argued.[55]

With a decision on *Stenberg* expected by the summer of 2000, both antiabortion and abortion-rights groups focused on the upcoming election. The presidential race again exposed divisions within the pro-life movement.[56] Absolutists expressed concerns about George W. Bush, the Republican nominee, because he had suggested that he favored rape and incest exceptions to abortion bans, even later in pregnancy. But Bush spoke proudly about his faith, and he enjoyed strong support from evangelical antiabortion organizations like Focus on the Family. All abortion foes preferred him to the Democratic nominee, Vice President Al Gore, a strong proponent of abortion-rights.[57]

NRLC lawyers did not hold out much hope for a victory in *Stenberg*. Nevertheless, antiabortion lawyers believed that even a loss could help the movement win back the White House. In a summer 2000 memo, NRLC lobbyist Doug Johnson explained that defeat in *Stenberg* could pay off on election day. "Whatever the Court does," he wrote, "the most important single point to get across in our response is the fact that Al Gore opposes state and federal bans on partial-birth abortion." NARAL leaders also emphasized the influence that the next president would likely have on the Supreme Court. "The outcome of the 2000 presidential election will determine whether the right to legal abortion remains secure for the next generation," the organization explained in an executive summary.[58]

In June, the Court issued a decision in *Stenberg*, striking down the Nebraska law. Recognizing "the division of medical opinion" present in the case, *Stenberg* reasoned that the Constitution still required a health exception. "[T]he uncertainty [present here] means a significant likelihood that those who believe that D&X is a safer abortion method in certain circumstances may turn out to be right," wrote Justice Stephen Breyer for the majority. "If so, then the absence of a health exception will place women at an unnecessary risk of tragic health consequences. If they are wrong, the exception will simply turn out to have been unnecessary."[59]

Stenberg also concluded that the disputed law encompassed D&E as well as D&X. Because both procedures required that a "substantial portion" of the fetus be drawn into the vaginal canal, and because the legislature had not explicitly exempted D&E, *Stenberg* held that Nebraska's law applied to procedures beyond D&X.[60]

Justice Anthony Kennedy, one of the authors of the *Casey* plurality, wrote an attention-getting criticism of the majority's reasoning. First, Kennedy stated that the Court had underestimated the importance of Nebraska's interest in regulating D&X. Kennedy attached special significance to the government's desire to forbid "medical procedures which, in the State's reasonable determination, might cause the medical profession or society as a whole to become insensitive, even disdainful, to life."[61] When it came to the uncertainty surrounding the safety of D&X, Kennedy insisted that states had the constitutional authority to "take sides in a medical debate, even when fundamental liberty interests are at stake and even when leading members of the profession disagree with the conclusions drawn by the legislature."[62]

Win or lose, the Court's decision fired up pro-lifers interested in a D&X ban. Polls indicated steady support for prohibition on partial-birth abortion. Kennedy's dissent suggested that the government should have the power to intervene when experts disputed the costs and benefits of partial-birth abortion. And with the 2000 election coming soon, the next president might have the opportunity to nominate a new Supreme Court justice who would agree.

Kennedy's *Stenberg* dissent seemed more consequential after George W. Bush won a historically close race, earning a potential chance to nominate new members of the Court. Only 537 votes separated the two candidates in Florida, the state that would determine the result. Al Gore requested that the votes be retallied by hand, and both candidates brought their cause to the courts. The Florida Supreme Court ordered a statewide recount. James Bopp Jr. of NRLC strategized with Bush's attorneys to develop an argument based on the Equal Protection Clause. This argument drew on a line of Supreme Court cases starting with *Reynolds v. Sims* (1964). *Reynolds* dealt with the right to vote. The Fifteenth, Nineteenth, and Twenty-Sixth Amendments all addressed that right, establishing that states could not abridge it on the basis of race, sex, or age for those over 18. The Court had also struck down certain discriminatory voting provisions under the Equal Protection Clause. In *Harper v. Virginia Board of Elections* (1966), for example, the Court held that a poll tax, a payment due before a person could register to vote, violated equal protection principles. *Reynolds* addressed a different question: how state apportionment of legislators affected the right to vote. The *Reynolds* Court held that under the Equal Protection Clause, states had to apportion legislative seats based primarily on population size. *Reynolds* gave rise to the famous "one person, one vote" principle. Bopp recommended using a similar theory in the case that would become *Bush v. Gore*. Bush's attorneys contended that Florida had diluted the votes of those in counties that did not perform a recount or that used a more rigorous standard to count the votes. Seven justices accepted this argument. The question of remedy proved far more divisive. By a 5–4 margin, the Court held that no constitutionally valid recount could be held before a state-mandated deadline. Believing there was not time for further recounting, the majority instead ended the recount with Bush ahead, handing him the election. With an ally in the White House, NRLC leaders knew that they could probably pass a partial-birth abortion ban. Moreover, if any sitting justices retired, Bush could replace them with judges who might be more sympathetic to the cause than the *Stenberg* majority had been.[63]

ABORTION RESEARCH GROWS

In the early 2000s, following Bush's election and Kennedy's *Stenberg* dissent, researchers on both sides expanded their efforts to gather or analyze scientific evidence about the costs and benefits of abortion. Abortion-rights groups had existing research groups of their own and had profited from the supportive positions taken by the American College of Obstetricians and Gynecologists. Nevertheless, in the 2000s, as pro-lifers foregrounded claims about the hazards of abortion, new research initiatives began. Pro-choice institutes gathered evidence not only on the safety of abortion but also on the negative effects of abortion restrictions. Antiabortion researchers tried to match this effort, founding their own organizations. But sometimes hobbled by a lack of funds and data, pro-lifers often claimed that the scientific establishment ignored any politically inconvenient results.

Angela Lanfranchi, one of those involved in the science and politics of abortion, had always wanted to be a doctor. As a medical student working at the Columbia Hospital For Women's neonatal intensive care unit, she was shocked when physicians rushed in a child born alive during a saline abortion. Lanfranchi remembered thinking it was crazy that her colleagues were "jumping around trying to save this kid while the doctor the floor below was trying to kill it." The inconsistency she saw convinced her that "something was wrong."[64]

Lanfranchi became a breast surgery specialist. After hearing a press conference on the link between abortion and breast cancer, she was skeptical but wanted to look further into the idea. On the intake form she gave to patients, she soon saw a pattern involving abortion and breast cancer risk. After further researching the issue, Lanfranchi came to an unshakable conclusion that abortion put women in danger.[65] With Joel Brind and two other physicians, Lanfranchi founded the Breast Cancer Prevention Institute, an organization committed to studying breast cancer risks. She believed to the bottom of her heart that experts withheld information about abortion because the truth was politically incorrect.[66]

Tracy Weitz also worked at the intersection of abortion politics and research. Not long after graduating from college, Weitz took a job as a manager of an abortion clinic. The work stoked a lifelong interest in the medical side of reproductive health. After completing a Ph.D. in medical sociology at the University of California–San

Francisco, Weitz took on several leadership roles at the university, eventually founding Advancing New Standards in Reproductive Health (ANSIRH) there in 2002. Under Weitz's guidance, ANSIRH prioritized questions about the safety of abortion, women's experiences of the procedure, and racial and economic disparities affecting access.[67]

Professionals like Weitz and Lanfranchi warred not only about the need for D&X but also about breast cancer and RU 486. Abortion-rights organizations had a head start in disseminating professional research. Founded in 1968, Planned Parenthood's Guttmacher Institute had long published peer-reviewed abortion studies. But in the 2000s, the Buffett Foundation, the William and Flora Hewlett Foundation, the David and Lucile Packard Foundation, the John Merck Fund, and the Educational Foundation of America funded additional abortion-related research. The Buffett Foundation alone provided $40 million to the Guttmacher Foundation and nearly $30 million to Gynuity Health Projects, which focused on medical abortion. Abortion opponents developed their own research organizations, such as the Breast Cancer Prevention Institute, but pro-lifers lamented a lack of funding and poor access to data.[68]

Often, pro-lifers made progress not by publishing their own studies but by sowing doubt about existing research. Justice Kennedy's *Stenberg* dissent suggested that even scientific uncertainty should give legislators more freedom to restrict abortion. And even if scientific authorities sided with the opposition, pro-lifers could still make progress by questioning those authorities. Abortion opponents deployed this strategy with RU 486 and breast cancer. After approving RU 486 in 2000, in June, the FDA considered a series of restrictions on who could prescribe the drug.[69] Organizations from the National Cancer Institute to the American Cancer Society had concluded that there was no connection between abortion and breast cancer. AUL and NRLC replied that scientific institutions would simply not acknowledge convincing evidence about the dangers of abortion. AUL pursued laws requiring women to hear about a link between abortion and breast cancer. By 2001, eleven states had passed such a statute. AUL leaders believed that a breast cancer warning "could cause many abortion-minded women to seek one of the many alternatives." In the context of breast cancer or RU 486, pro-lifers insisted that the possibility of a threat to women's health justified restrictions on abortion.[70]

Abortion-rights supporters accused the opposition of peddling sham science. In a widely distributed debate manual, for example, NARAL insisted that there was no uncertainty at all when it came to breast cancer and abortion. The manual emphasized that "[t]he *New England Journal of Medicine*, the National Breast Cancer Foundation, the American Cancer Society, and the World Health Organization [had] all concluded that no link ha[d] been established between abortion and breast cancer."[71]

In dealing with D&X, the manual asserted that antiabortion politicians neither understood nor cared about how to measure the costs and benefits of abortion.

A Massachusetts NARAL affiliate circulated similar claims. "The most effective response to the so-called 'partial-birth' abortion attack goes back to the key question of 'Who decides,'" the affiliate stated. "The answer is the patient, in consultation with her doctor, not politicians or the government." Abortion-rights supporters reasoned that the opposition simply spread falsehoods. "Women should be informed, not misinformed," the NARAL debate manual reasoned.[72]

Antiabortion activists continued promoting restrictions centered on the risks of RU 486, breast cancer, and D&X even when expert organizations rejected their conclusions. AUL, NRLC, and allied research organizations insisted that evidence on the safety of abortion was incomplete or misunderstood. Pro-life researchers suggested that authorities buried the truth about the hazards of abortion to suit their political allies. Groups like NARAL and Planned Parenthood worked with new and established research organizations to suggest that no one with any credibility doubted the safety of abortion. At the same time, in the political arena, abortion-rights activists tried to direct the dialogue back to constitutional liberties. Scientific evidence, leaders of groups like NARAL believed, would do little to motivate donors or voters. But the very emphasis put on placating popular majorities alienated some who supported legal abortion. Some feminists worried that rather than seeking reproductive justice for all women, the abortion-rights movement often demanded no more than voters were willing to give them.

ABORTION-RIGHTS STRATEGIC DIVISIONS

By 2002, a federal ban on D&X was back on track, and abortion-rights supporters disagreed about how to stop it. Women of color and reproductive justice advocates worried that larger abortion-rights groups had returned to alienating arguments about choice. These feminists also thought that the movement had at times prioritized short-term success over the kind of meaningful social change that would make progress possible on a broad reproductive justice agenda. The emphasis put on winning seemed particularly shortsighted in the context of a D&X ban. While seeking to defeat pro-lifers' proposal, groups like NARAL and NAF insisted that late abortions were rare and performed only in grave circumstances. Perhaps abortion-rights activists could delay passage of a prohibition, but in the meantime, the stigma surrounding late abortion seemed strong, and public support for a ban had not wavered. The terrorist attacks of September 11, 2001 postponed major congressional action on divisive issues like abortion. NRLC instead prioritized a proposed ban on human cloning and the Unborn Victims of Violence Act, a federal law that treated a child in utero as a victim for the purpose of sixty federal violent crimes. Others proposed federal laws that they hoped would smooth the way for a ban on partial-birth abortion. In September 1998, Hadley Arkes, a pro-life professor from Amherst College, proposed a federal law defining a person in the federal code to include an unborn child. Writing in the *Crisis*, a lay Catholic magazine, Arkes called for "a bill to protect the child born alive, and [to] install this premise—that the claim of the child to the protection of the law cannot pivot on the question of whether anyone happens to 'want' her." Arkes argued that his bill would aid the passage of a a ban on partial-birth abortion by "counter[ing]" the conclusion of certain lower courts that bans on the procedure were unconstitutional. He worked with Professors Robert George of Princeton and Michael Uhlmann of Claremont McKenna College to win congressional supporters for his proposal. Although NRLC lobbyist Doug Johnson worried that the bill would be a distraction from the partial-birth-abortion battle, Arkes prevailed, and Congress passed the Born-Alive Infants Protection Act of 2002. Arkes saw the bill as the promising start of a strategy centered more on natural law arguments – claims that the founders of the Constitution relied on underlying moral principles and rights that predated the document and even the nation itself.[73]

Between 2002 and 2003, however, larger antiabortion groups returned to familiar arguments about the costs of abortion. AUL championed a connection between abortion and breast cancer. The group still insisted that claims about the costs of abortion would mean the end for *Roe*. At a 2002 AUL symposium, attendees spoke about the importance of "[m]olding arguments for Middle America" by "assembling the latest data" and "putting the emphasis on the impact on women." A media consulting firm, Creative Research Communication, proposed a similar messaging strategy. "Many of the promises made by the pro-abortion movement have simply failed to materialize," CRC contended. "At the same time, the impact on women has become clear—sterility, complications with future pregnancies, depression, and other medical problems are all linked to abortion." Armed with similar arguments, Doug Johnson of NRLC worked with Representative Steve Chabot (R–OH) to introduce a new partial-birth abortion ban that addressed some of the concerns raised in *Stenberg*. First, the law defined "partial-birth abortion" more narrowly. Republicans in Congress also made findings suggesting that D&X was never medically indicated and in fact posed risks for women's health. In 2003, George W. Bush signed into law the federal Partial-Birth Abortion Ban Act.[74]

To defuse the threat of a partial-birth abortion ban, larger pro-choice groups went back to tested claims about "who decides." Polls and focus groups demonstrated that arguments about freedom of choice packed a punch. For this reason, in 2003, NARAL officially changed its name to NARAL Pro-choice America and announced a campaign to educate younger voters about abortion.[75] Planned Parenthood also reformulated its message to win the trust of younger voters. Lake, Snell, and Perry Associates, Celinda Lake's new political strategy research firm, advised members to stress that Planned Parenthood provided education and preventative services, both of which were popular. "The best positioning for abortion uses the terms freedom of choice and responsible decision-making," the organization advised. Planned Parenthood reinforced the idea that individual voters' opinions were as good as those of experts. Making D&X a question of individual moral decision-making seemed strategically savvy but made it even harder for medical organizations like ACOG to influence debate.[76]

These choice arguments also left cold many of the women of color who led reproductive justice groups. In 2000, the National Network of Abortion Funds (NNAF)), a group founded in 1993 to improve reproductive health access for low-income and diverse women, launched a two-year public education effort to improve access. The following year, Patricia Ireland of the National Organization for Women (NOW) launched the Emergency Action for Women's Lives, a series of events calling attention to the Bush Administration's positions on reproductive issues. But the themes of the Emergency Action, such as "Supporting *Roe v. Wade*" or "Endorsing Privacy in Medical Decision-Making," fell flat with many women of color. "The reproductive rights movement in its current state does not even begin to adequately address the unique concerns of not just Black women, but women collectively," wrote Toni Bond (later Toni Bond Leonard) of NNAF. Whereas groups like NARAL pursued a single-issue agenda, reproductive justice activists called for rights to everything from safe housing and good jobs to access to contraception and sex education and adequate prenatal care. Nevertheless, reproductive justice organizations sometimes worked closely with larger abortion-rights groups. For example, in 2004, when the Feminist Majority Foundation, NARAL, Planned Parenthood, and NOW announced a March for Women's Lives, several member groups urged SisterSong, a leading reproductive justice collective, to participate, and Loretta Ross, the group's national coordinator, helped to direct the march.[77]

Despite this collaboration, reproductive justice groups still resented what they saw as a strategy that put political caution ahead of the needs of women of color. These activists thought that rather than highlighting a full range of social justice and reproductive health issues, larger groups fiercely defended an increasingly hollow win in *Roe*. And rather than talking about the ways that women benefitted from abortion and other needed services, larger groups fell back on empty arguments about choice. While organizations like NARAL remained predominantly white, new reproductive justice groups formed in states from Pennsylvania to California, many of them affiliating with SisterSong.[78]

The D&X conflict also exacerbated tactical divisions among abortion foes. While some antiabortion lawyers thought that their side simply repeated arguments that the Supreme Court had already rejected, grassroots activists saw the partial-birth abortion campaign as a sign of everything that was wrong with arguments about the costs of abortion. By deemphasizing rights-based arguments, the argument went, larger pro-life groups had become both uninspiring and ineffective.

ANTIABORTION STRATEGIC DIVISIONS

Notwithstanding the passage of the Partial-Birth Abortion Ban Act, some abortion foes saw a strategy centered on the costs of the procedure (and of abortion) as futile or worse. In 2000, Harold Cassidy was still litigating a case, *Donna Santa Marie v. McGreevey*, on behalf of women who wanted to bring wrongful death actions following an abortion. Cassidy argued that doctors had performed abortions without explaining that the procedure ended the life of a whole, separate human being, thereby denying patients' informed consent. As Cassidy stated at a confidential 1998 Life Forum meeting, those leading the *Donna Santa Marie* litigation "hope[d] to establish the fact that there is a separate, complete, unique human being [present] throughout the gestational period."[79]

Donna Santa Marie was central to an alternative litigation strategy forged by Cassidy and his allies – one that did not stress claims about the costs and benefits of abortion. In November 1997, Cassidy and Professor Robert George, a prominent legal scholar from Princeton, hosted the first meeting of the National Foundation for Life, a group that hoped to spearhead a different approach to the courts. Early supporters included the National Institute of Family and Life Advocates (NIFLA), a network of CPCs, Jay Sekulow's American Center for Law and Justice, and University Faculty for Life, a group of professors opposed to abortion. Rather than emphasizing arguments about the costs of abortion, the Global Project, a major legal initiative of the National Foundation for Life, would reinvigorate rights-based claims – particularly, the contention that *Roe* violated the rights of both women and unborn children. Cassidy explained this approach as a different way to attack *Casey*. There, the plurality had held that nothing about the practice of abortion had changed since 1973. Cassidy hoped to refute this claim by "assembling a team of scientists and doctors who ... established that new recombinant DNA technology establishes that life begins at conception." Cassidy also argued that the Court had never addressed the possibility that abortion violated women's rights. As a brochure for the National Foundation for Life explained: "the fact that a mother-child relationship exists was not considered by either *Roe* or *Casey*."[80]

While working on the Global Project, Cassidy received a call from Norma McCorvey, the "Roe" in *Roe v. Wade*, who told him that she would do anything to reverse *Roe v. Wade*. Within a matter of weeks, Sandra Cano, the named plaintiff in *Doe v. Bolton*, also contacted Cassidy. He passed the request on to Allan Parker, a former trial attorney who had cofounded the conservative Justice Foundation. Parker agreed to represent McCorvey and Cano, and he filed an amicus curiae brief on their behalf in *Donna Santa Marie*. While *Donna Santa Marie* was pending, Parker launched Operation Outcry, a project asking "each woman who has suffered in any way from abortion to fill out [an] 'Affidavit' form giving the personal facts surrounding her abortion." Parker and Cassidy thought that the strategy used by larger groups still neglected the ways that abortion harmed women – not simply by harming them but by stripping them of rights.[81]

The Third Circuit Court of Appeals rejected Donna Santa Marie's wrongful death challenge in 2002, but Cassidy and Parker were undeterred. While Parker continued working on Operation Outcry, Cassidy brought a lawsuit on behalf of

Rosa Acuna, a woman who claimed that her doctor told her that her abortion would simply remove "blood" rather than killing a "living human being" – a statement Acuna felt was contravened when she had to have surgery to remove parts of the unborn child missed during the original procedure. In her wrongful death claim, Acuna contended that a reasonably prudent patient "would want to know whether the proposed procedure would terminate the life of an existing human being."[82]

Cassidy and Parker were not alone in believing that the time had come for a new, overarching strategy for the pro-life movement. One of those interested in creating a more cohesive coalition was Raymond Ruddy, a conservative Catholic donor who had made a fortune at his Boston-based company, Maximus Inc., a private business that contracted with the government to provide health and welfare services. As a thought experiment, Ruddy had tried to diagram the chain of command and structure of the pro-life movement and found that he could not do it. Later, Ruddy received a similar chart for Planned Parenthood and concluded that it was "massive, well-organized, [and] well-funded." He commissioned Chuck Donovan, a former NRLC member and current Family Research Council employee, to conduct a study of Planned Parenthood. Donovan delivered his conclusions in the fall of 2002, urging pro-lifers to "establish a national organization, or a federation of existing and new organizations, with Planned Parenthood's scope of action." In a parallel but unrelated effort, pro-lifers did try to build a more coordinated coalition. As of 2003, the newly formed Culture of Life Leadership Coalition's (CLLC) executive committee included Harold Cassidy, Jeffrey Ventrella of the Alliance Defense Fund, a Christian nonprofit that funded conservative litigation, Pia de Solenni of the Family Research Council, Michael Schwartz of Concerned Women for America, and Mary Cunningham Agee, a former Wall Street executive and founder of a network of pro-life support services for pregnant women. The CLLC soon developed a message based on what members saw as the costs of abortion for women.[83]

The Coalition's Legal Working Group (LWG), for example, proposed to "end . . . legal abortion" by using the argument that "abortion harms women." The LWG planned to initiate medical malpractice lawsuits on behalf of women who regretted abortions, to defend medical providers and pharmacists who did not want to provide abortions or contraceptive services, to litigate on behalf of CPCs, and to defend abortion restrictions. As part of these campaigns, lawyers would highlight "inherent conflicts of interest between the abortion industry and pregnant women." The public relations working group agreed on the importance of focusing on the costs of abortion for women. The group planned to change the minds of those who thought that "abortion [was] good or necessary for women" but admitted that the message proposed was "temporary" – a stand-in for claims about fetal rights.[84]

Nevertheless, in the short term, the coalition proposed a message that "women deserve better than abortion." In the context of partial-birth abortion, for example, activists would argue that "children deserve a chance to be born" and that "women deserve better than the pain and suffering of partial-birth abortion." However, internal tensions roiled the coalition, some of them concerning the involvement of NRLC. While that group's general counsel had participated in coalition meetings, other NRLC members had not, and some within NRLC felt slighted. In any case, by 2004, the coalition disbanded after members felt that they could not develop a cohesive enough strategy in time for a major summit.[85]

In South Dakota, Harold Cassidy tried to emphasize claims about women who lost a constitutionally protected right to a relationship with their unborn children. In 2004, Tom Monaghan, the CEO of Domino's Pizza, brought Cassidy in for a meeting at the Thomas More Law Center, a group he had founded in 1998, and asked Cassidy if he would be willing to help lawmakers in South Dakota defend an abortion ban that they planned to advance. Cassidy thought it was too soon to try to criminalize abortion, but he wanted to contribute what he could to the South Dakota project. He helped assemble witnesses for a hearing in the state, including four women who had had abortions. During the hearing, Cassidy had the impression that lawmakers had not considered what he saw as the physical and psychological damage done by abortion, the risk of suicide it created, or women's right to preserve their relationship with their children. Although the bill did not pass, Cassidy became a valued consultant for some South Dakota legislators and pregnancy help centers.[86]

South Dakota's repeated attempts to ban abortion made the divisions in the pro-life movement more visible than ever.[87] Pro-lifers renewed a fight about whether limited restrictions – and the cost-based arguments tied to them – deserved support. Judie Brown of American Life League (ALL), an organization not affiliated with the Cultural Life Leadership Coalition, mocked the strategy behind the federal Partial-Birth Abortion Ban Act. By focusing on access and the costs of abortion, as Brown saw it, pro-lifers had passed a "bill [that] will not ban anything and probably will not stop one abortion." Brown's complaints may not have been surprising. As Ted Olsen wrote in *Christianity Today*, ALL had often served as the proverbial "wet blanket at the pro-life party."[88]

But debate about partial-birth abortion revealed that a larger group of pro-lifers were fed up with incremental restrictions, especially when laws explicitly authorized abortions in cases of rape, incest, or a threat to the woman's life. One of these activists, Dan Becker, a pastor at Little River Church in Georgia and an NRLC member, became the political action committee director for Georgia Right to Life (GRL), an NRLC affiliate. In 2000, GRL announced that it would endorse political candidates only if they favored abortion bans with no exceptions. Michigan and Tennessee affiliates adopted similar endorsement criteria. GRL promoted an explicitly faith-based, Christian approach, arguing that it would work better than a strategy centered on arguments about abortion's costs. As Becker would write later, "a Personhood approach produces outstanding political and legislative gains, while accomplishing a dramatic shift in public opinion."[89]

The D&X struggle again showed how those on both sides questioned the wisdom of focusing so much on the costs and benefits of abortion. Reproductive justice advocates argued that by focusing on who decides about partial-birth abortion, prochoice leaders did not explain why women needed D&X or any other health service. On the antiabortion side, focusing on arguments about the costs of abortion seemed either unethical or pointless. These divisions spoke to the broader downsides of stressing the costs and benefits of abortion. Notwithstanding their tactical advantages, these claims sometimes buried the underlying values that had inspired many to mobilize.

GONZALES AND THE JURISPRUDENCE OF UNCERTAINTY

When the Center for Reproductive Rights (the former Center for Reproductive Law and Policy) and other abortion-rights litigators challenged the federal Partial-Birth Abortion Ban Act in federal court, both sides again clashed about who should measure the costs and benefits of abortion when the scientific facts were in dispute. The Supreme Court agreed to address the constitutionality of the federal ban in two consolidated appeals. Doctors who performed second trimester abortions filed two separate suits in Nebraska and California, and both district courts concluded that the law was unconstitutional and blocked enforcement of it. The Courts of Appeals for the Eighth and Ninth Circuit affirmed, and the Supreme Court agreed to hear the challenge to the Partial-Birth Abortion Ban Act.[90]

James Bopp Jr. and Thomas Marzen of NRLC applied for a grant from the Alliance Defense Fund (ADF), by then one of the major sources of financial support for conservative litigation. By 2004, ADF had total revenue of nearly $18 million and in 2007 alone spent nearly $4 million on litigation. Bopp and Marzen's application offered insight into the value pro-life lawyers saw in litigating bans on partial-birth abortion.[91]

Bopp and Marzen predicted that the Court would strike down the federal law. *Stenberg*, after all, had come down only a few years before. The two explained that the case would still allow abortion foes to "explore the outer legal limits of the ability of the government to restrict abortion practice." Bopp and Marzen further hoped that the litigation would "educate the voting public [about] the radical nature of the abortion liberty and . . . identify political figures as radical supporters of the abortion liberty."[92] To prevail, abortion foes would have to show that the federal statute differed from the one struck down in *Stenberg*. Prior to passing the Act, Congress had held extensive hearings and found no need for a health exception. More witnesses, including experienced obstetricians and gynecologists, testified in favor of the ban.[93]

Congress' findings aside, professional medical organizations had more fully embraced D&X since 2000. Instructors at some medical schools taught about the procedure, and it appeared in medical textbooks. In 2004, the *American Journal of*

Obstetrics and Gynecology published a study by Dr. Stephen Chasen and his colleagues that concluded that D&X might be the safest procedure for women under certain circumstances. Chasen found that D&E, the alternative to D&X, more often caused serious complications. Doctors almost exclusively used D&X later in pregnancy when the rate of complications would usually increase. Nevertheless, the Chasen study found that the overall rate of complications associated with the two procedures was quite similar. On this basis, the study concluded that D&X was safer than other options. There were reasons that this conclusion might make sense: For example, Chasen suggested that D&X required fewer passes with sharp instruments and might lower the odds of uterine perforation. Nevertheless, like Congress' findings, the Chasen study was limited. Critics pointed to the relatively small sample included. As importantly, Chasen's study was not a randomized, controlled trial, the gold standard in medicine.[94]

A shakeup on the Court undermined earlier predictions about a challenge to the Partial-Birth Abortion Ban Act. In the winter of 2005, the news broke that Chief Justice William Rehnquist was battling cancer. While the Bush Administration vetted possible replacements, Sandra Day O'Connor, one of the Court's swing votes, announced she was leaving the bench to help her husband fight Alzheimer's disease. A few weeks later in 2005, Bush nominated John Roberts, a judge on the DC Circuit Court of Appeals, to replace O'Connor. Roberts did not have a long track record, but there were some signals that he might be more sympathetic to the antiabortion movement than O'Connor was. While O'Connor had helped craft the compromise in *Casey*, Roberts had signed an antiabortion brief during his time as a staff attorney in the George H. W. Bush Administration.[95]

Rehnquist lost his battle with cancer in early September. Bush elevated Roberts to the position of Chief Justice, and a month later, he chose Samuel Alito, a judge on the Third Circuit Court of Appeals, to take O'Connor's place. Alito also appeared to be a potential ally for abortion opponents. For example, when *Casey* was in the lower courts, Alito was the only judge who dissented from part of the Third Circuit's opinion striking down a spousal involvement requirement.[96]

With Alito and Roberts on the Court, NRLC hosted a discussion with government attorneys and antiabortion amici about how to approach *Gonzales v. Carhart*, especially when it came to measuring the costs and benefits of abortion. Many of the conservative Christian groups attending the amicus meeting had recently grown dramatically. In 2000, Mathew Staver of Liberty Counsel had sold his private law practice and formed a partnership with well-known evangelist Jerry Falwell Sr. and his Liberty University. The partnership allowed Liberty Counsel to expand considerably. For example, in 2006, a year before Falwell's death, Liberty University provided $600,000 to Staver's organization. As Jay Sekulow and Pat Robertson's American Center for Law and Justice (ACLJ) grew, the group also took on a more ambitious agenda. Other organizations were relatively new, such as the Thomas More Society (founded in 1997, and not to be confused with the Tom Monaghan's

Michigan-based Thomas More Law Center), a public interest litigation firm created by attorney Tom Brejcha during the defense of antiabortion protesters in *NOW v. Scheidler.*[97]

Those present at the *Gonzales* meeting broadly agreed that resolving claims about scientific uncertainty about the costs and benefits of abortion would likely decide the case. Paul Linton, who had recently become special counsel for the Thomas More Society, worried that Roberts and Alito would not be eager to overrule a case decided so recently. In Linton's view, antiabortion attorneys had to distinguish *Stenberg* by highlighting "the weight to be given Congressional findings [and] the significance of the different factual record." Clarke Forsythe of AUL thought that the most important thing would be to win over Justice Anthony Kennedy. To do so, Forsythe wanted to argue that "[n]o significant medical authority demonstrates that ... D&X would be the safest procedure."[98] Walter Weber of ACLJ agreed that the two most urgent questions facing the Court were "[w]hat the standard for government action in the face of medical disagreement should be" and "[h]ow the Court [has] dealt with contrary medical views in prior abortion cases." Ultimately, at the March 2006 conference, those present attached profound importance to the same questions.[99]

When the parties briefed *Gonzales* before the Supreme Court, questions about who could resolve scientific disputes about the costs and benefits of D&X ran through the case. The Center for Reproductive Rights and Planned Parenthood emphasized that there was more evidence of the benefits of D&X than there had been at the time that *Stenberg* was litigated. Together with amici, the Center contended that D&X was safer than any other alternative in certain circumstances. When it came to resolving uncertainty, amici opposing the act pointed to the superior credentials of those who saw safety advantages in using D&X for some women. In its brief, the American College of Obstetricians and Gynecologists highlighted the support of "an array of skilled physicians with impeccable credentials and vast clinical experience," "leading medical texts and peer-reviewed studies; [and] the curricula of leading medical schools."[100]

Most abortion opponents conceded that there was considerable uncertainty surrounding the need for D&X but emphasized that Congress deserved deference when the facts were disputed. After all, lawmakers could hold more extensive hearings and gather more evidence than the courts could. "As the evidence before Congress and the lower courts aptly demonstrates, there is some disagreement within the medical community about whether 'partial-birth abortion' is an accepted, safe and ethical medical procedure," claimed the pro-life Liberty Counsel. "In such cases, Congress and state legislatures are permitted to 'take sides' in the debate and are to be given wide latitude with regard to their final decision."[101] ACLJ contended that childbirth was safer than any abortion, even early in pregnancy. Operation Outcry elaborated on this argument in a brief on behalf of Sandra Cano and other women who experienced post-abortion regret. The brief detailed familiar assertions about the physical and psychological risks of abortion, arguing that the safety of abortion was uncertain notwithstanding the criticisms of major medical and psychological organizations.[102]

In April 2007, the Court voted five to four to uphold the federal Partial-Birth Abortion Ban Act. The majority opened with a graphic description of D&X. As *Gonzales* described it, a physician would dilate the cervix, remove all but the head of the fetus, force "scissors into the base of the skull," introduce "a suction catheter into this hole and evacuate . . . the skull contents." After describing partial-birth abortion, Justice Kennedy's majority opinion addressed whether the law was unconstitutionally vague. *Gonzales* noted that whereas the law in *Stenberg* required that a "substantial part" be outside a woman's body, the Partial-Birth Abortion Ban Act prohibited only those procedures that took place when either the head or the fetal trunk past the navel moved outside the woman's body. The Court also pointed to the fact that prosecutors had to prove intent. Under the law, a physician would not face punishment unless he intended to deliver a fetus beyond the prohibited point. For these reasons, the Court concluded that the law gave physicians enough notice about what they were not allowed to do. The Court reasoned that the "anatomical landmarks" defining a partial-birth abortion also ensured that the statute did not extend to D&E.[103]

Gonzales turned next to whether the law created an undue burden under *Casey*. The Court first discussed whether the federal statute had a valid purpose. Kennedy stated that the law validly "express[ed] respect for the dignity of human life." The *Gonzales* Court also demonstrated the influence of arguments about post-abortion regret mentioned in Sandra Cano's amicus brief. "Respect for human life finds an ultimate expression in the bond of love the mother has for her child," Kennedy wrote. "While we find no reliable data to measure the phenomenon, it seems unexceptionable to conclude some women come to regret their choice to abort the infant life they once created and sustained." Citing the brief submitted on behalf of women suffering post-abortion regret, *Gonzales* suggested that some physicians might not tell women in detail about what D&X involved. Outlawing D&X made sense because of the government's interest in "ensuring so grave a choice is informed." *Gonzales* also stated that Congress had a legitimate interest in maintaining public respect for the medical profession. "The State's interest in respect for life is advanced by the dialogue that better informs the political and legal systems, the medical profession, expectant mothers, and society as a whole of the consequences that follow from a decision to elect a late-term abortion," the majority explained.[104]

The Court next took up the question of whether the statute failed because it had no health exception. *Gonzales* highlighted "documented medical disagreement [about] whether the Act's prohibition would ever impose significant health risks on women." *Gonzales* recognized that the evidence contradicted some of Congress's findings. Nonetheless, the Court held that lawmakers had "wide discretion to pass legislation in areas where there is medical and scientific uncertainty."[105]

Justice Ruth Bader Ginsburg wrote a scathing dissent. She chastised the Court for ignoring substantial evidence that D&X was the safest procedure for women. Ginsburg especially took the Court to task for assuming that women would regret abortions. "The solution the Court approves, then, is *not* to require doctors to inform women, accurately and adequately, of the different procedures and their attendant risks," she wrote. "Instead, the Court deprives women of the right to make an autonomous choice, even at the expense of their safety."[106]

Gonzales created a blueprint for later antiabortion initiatives. Abortion foes would target later abortions, claiming that the science concerning fetal pain, fetal viability, or the safety of abortion was unsettled. As long as someone contested the scientific costs and benefits of abortion, antiabortion legislatures might have more power to regulate. And pro-lifers would echo Justice Kennedy's arguments about abortion and regret, contending that women had been wrong to rely on abortion.

THE POLITICS OF SCIENCE

At the height of the partial-birth abortion conflict, many questioned the line between science, spin, and deceit. Since the early 1980s, abortion foes had set aside a campaign to change the Constitution to focus on the overturning of *Roe*. As part of this strategy, larger pro-life groups sometimes played down fetal-rights claims. Instead, abortion foes stressed what they described as the costs of abortion. In the context of D&X, those on opposing sides contested what made scientific claims about the costs and benefits of abortion both reliable and relevant.

Forming their own expert organizations, abortion opponents contended that groups from ACOG to the American Cancer Society simply repeated what was politically correct. At the same time, antiabortion activists and lawyers defined new sources of expertise, including women who regretted abortion and lay people observing the abortion debate. Abortion-rights groups insisted that preeminent medical organizations, rather than voters or politicians, should make medical decisions. After 2007, disputes about science continued to shape the abortion wars. Laws involving fetal pain gained attention, as did regulations of abortion clinics claiming to protect women's health. The abortion debate reflected creeping doubt about whether any authority in America reliably told the truth.

Debate about partial-birth abortion illuminated how common ground in the abortion debate was becoming harder and harder to find. Rather than arguing only about core values, those on opposing sides came to disagree about who counted as an expert and what kind of evidence deserved attention. The result was not a change in the fundamental rights either side sponsored. For strategic purposes, both sides sometimes deemphasized those rights when lobbying politicians, going to court, or speaking to the media. But doing so only further polarized the conflict. Often, opposing activists saw one another not only as wrong but as fundamentally dishonest.

7

Polarization, Religious Liberty, and the War on Women

In 2018, news came that turned the American abortion debate upside down. For thirty years, Anthony Kennedy had often cast the deciding vote in abortion cases. But at the end of June, the long-serving justice announced his retirement. With his departure, the Court seemed likely to veer sharply away from protecting abortion-rights. Since the 2016 campaign, President Donald J. Trump had pledged to nominate pro-life judges to the Supreme Court. Leonard Leo, the executive vice president of the Federalist Society, a group of conservative and libertarian lawyers, supplied a list of potential nominees. Leo's role was telling. He himself was vocally opposed to abortion, and the Federalist Society selected only judges expected to overturn *Roe*. Trump's eventual pick, Judge Brett Kavanaugh of the DC Circuit Court of Appeals, had indeed criticized *Roe v. Wade* in a 2017 speech and dissented from an opinion allowing an immigrant minor to be released from detention to end her pregnancy. With Kavanaugh on the Court, it seemed likely that the Court would undo *Roe v. Wade* or substantially undercut abortion-rights.[1]

Between the decision of *Gonzales* and the announcement of Kennedy's retirement, claims about the costs and benefits of abortion remained at the center of legal conflict even as the broader struggle shifted in unpredictable ways. In 2008, Barack Obama, the first pro-choice president since Bill Clinton, revived the issue of national health care reform. Two years later, a backlash to Obama's proposal helped to give Republicans unparalleled control of state legislatures. The leaders of the self-proclaimed Tea Party passed a record number of abortion restrictions, many of them tied to claims about the societal costs of the procedure. Seizing on the Tea Party's hostility to the Obama health care bill, abortion-rights supporters highlighted the benefits of abortion for women's health and accused the opposition of misogyny. In the Obama era, those on opposing sides more often questioned the motives of those with whom they disagreed.

In the 2010s, the Court also made claims about the costs and benefits of abortion even more central to the conflict. In 2016, in *Whole Woman's Health v. Hellerstedt*, a short-handed Court held that the undue burden test required courts to weigh both the benefits and burdens created by abortion restrictions. The Court's decision was a welcome surprise for abortion-rights supporters. The justices struck down a Texas law that would have forced the closure of most clinics in the state. *Whole Woman's Health* suggested that the undue burden test required some scrutiny of abortion regulations. But *Whole Woman's Health* only deepened factual disputes about abortion. Both sides invested more in creating and collecting evidence about the effects of the procedure and of laws regulating it.

After Kavanaugh's confirmation, many believed the reversal of *Roe* to be inevitable, if not imminent. Opposing movements prepared for the state battles that would unfold if the justices no longer recognized a right to choose. Often over the objections of incrementalists, lawmakers pursued extreme solutions, with some states criminalizing all abortions, even in cases of rape or incest. Abortion-rights supporters demanded equally sweeping protections in states with pro-choice majorities. These ambitious campaigns notwithstanding, both sides continued stressing arguments about the costs and benefits of abortion, this time, fighting over the fate of *Roe* and *Casey*. Dialogue about the costs and benefits of abortion, it seemed, might dictate the fate of the 1973 decision.

ABORTION IN THE 2008 ELECTION

The election of Barack Obama, a Democratic senator from Chicago, catapulted health care reform to the top of the national agenda. Opposition to both Obama and his reform proposal crystallized pro-lifers' anger about what they perceived as violations of religious liberty. Abortion-rights supporters responded by accusing their opponents of bias against women. Party politics had already sorted pro-choice and pro-life Americans into camps that took different positions on a variety of social issues. But in the Obama era, abortion increasingly became entangled with the politics of religious liberty, further estranging those in opposing movements from one another.

In the lead-up to the 2008 election, some grassroots abortion opponents continued to resist a strategy centered on the costs of abortion. In South Dakota, the quest for an outright abortion ban had picked up steam since December 2005 when a state task force endorsed it. In March 2006, South Dakota lawmakers voted to criminalize all abortions unless a woman's life was at risk. Noting the additions of John Roberts and Samuel Alito to the Supreme Court, State Senator Julie Bartling, one of the key sponsors of the bill, insisted that it was time "to protect the rights and lives of unborn children." The South Dakota push reflected the impatience of certain pro-lifers who wondered if arguments about the costs of abortion would ever work. Despite his doubts about the timing of the proposal, Harold Cassidy tried to maximize the chances of success for the South Dakota ban even though he had nothing to do with drafting it. By contrast, groups like National Right to Life

Committee (NRLC) and Americans United for Life (AUL) thought that the bill would backfire. Daniel McConchie of AUL labeled the bill a "long-shot type of situation."[2]

In any case, in November, South Dakota voters repealed the measure by referendum partly because of pro-life divisions about exceptions for rape, incest, or threats to a woman's health or life. This setback did not discourage absolutists. In March 2007, Dan Becker's Georgia Right to Life sponsored a state constitutional amendment outlawing abortion and recognizing fetal rights. Although the resolution went nowhere, Kristi Burton, a homeschooled college student, almost singlehandedly pursued a similar agenda in Colorado. Burton fought for Amendment 48, a state-constitutional initiative that defined a constitutionally protected person as "any human being from the moment of fertilization." Burton and her colleagues expressed skepticism of incremental legislation. "The goal is to restore legal protection to preborn babies from the moment they are conceived, which is the only way we're going to stop abortion," stated Leslie Hanks, the vice president of Burton's group. Although Burton's attempt fell short, personhood champions tried to build a nationwide effort, and a new group, Personhood USA, formed to support organizations interested in personhood proposals.[3]

Strategies centered on the costs of abortion splintered the antiabortion movement before the 2008 election. But with a deeply unpopular war in Iraq, a frightening recession, and the prospect of national health care reform, the candidates did not spend much time discussing reproductive health. Believing that campaign-finance laws would make it impossible for pro-lifers to influence any election, NRLC had clashed with John McCain, the Republican nominee, over his proposed Bipartisan Campaign Finance Reform Act. NRLC, which relied heavily on its PAC and played a major role in elections, opposed limits on election spending. Nevertheless, all abortion opponents believed that an Obama victory would be devastating. The Illinois Democrat had enjoyed the support of leading abortion-rights organizations for much of the 2008 election season. Indeed, during the primary, NARAL Pro-choice America endorsed Obama over his main opponent (and the presumptive frontrunner), Senator Hillary Clinton (D–NY), as early as May 2008.[4]

Obama's election stunned abortion foes[5] and ignited violence among antiabortion extremists. In June 2009, Scott Roeder murdered Dr. George Tiller, a Kansas abortion provider who had survived a previous attempt on his life. Roeder entered Tiller's church, where the doctor was serving as an usher, and shot him in the head at point-blank range. Roeder had ties to David Leach, a member of the violent Army of God, a Christian terrorist organization, as well to the Montana Freemen, an armed anti-government militia. Members of NRLC and AUL again condemned the horrific killing but struggled with the fallout from Roeder's crime.[6]

Harold Cassidy labored away at the alternative approach he had helped to develop in South Dakota. The state had passed an informed consent law requiring doctors to make a state-mandated disclosure about the increased risk of suicide or psychological distress following an abortion. The statute further asserted that "abortion [would] terminate the life of a whole, separate, unique, living human being" and that a "pregnant woman [had] an existing relationship with that unborn human being and that the relationship enjoys protection under the United States Constitution and under the laws of South Dakota." When a court heard a challenge to the law, Cassidy represented two South Dakota pregnancy help centers as intervenors. By that time, Cassidy received support from the Alliance Defense Fund (ADF), a major Christian conservative nonprofit that funded litigation and trained attorneys, for his work in *Planned Parenthood of Minnesota, South Dakota, North Dakota v. Rounds.*[7]

Although Cassidy's strategy centered on rights-based claims, questions about the facts of abortion became central to the litigation. After bringing suit, Planned Parenthood charged that South Dakota's law dealt in emotion rather truth. As Cecile Richards, the head of the Planned Parenthood Federation of America, asserted: "ideology has no place in the doctor's office." In a brief, Cassidy responded that the disclosures were "unquestionably truthful and accurate." For example, Cassidy pointed to federal and South Dakota law as evidence that women had a protected relationship with the unborn children they carried. A district court enjoined enforcement of the law that Cassidy defended, but in June 2008, the Eighth Circuit Court of Appeals reversed, allowing the South Dakota law to go into effect. Later, a three-judge panel of the Eighth Circuit upheld all of the law's disclosure requirements but one involving an increased risk of suicide. To the surprise of some commentators, the court rejected Planned Parenthood's claims that the mandated disclosures were ideological claims rather than matters of scientific fact. In 2012, the full Eighth Circuit upheld even the suicide disclosure, again suggesting that the law made true statements of scientific fact.[8]

As Cassidy's effort reflected, Obama's election called new attention to a lasting strategic fracture in the antiabortion movement. Whereas groups like AUL and NRLC tried to expand on *Gonzales v. Carhart*, Cassidy believed that existing strategies would never dismantle abortion-rights. Without endorsing Cassidy's strategy, personhood proponents also held a skeptical view of mainstream tactical approaches. These absolutists contended that arguments about the costs of abortion stood in tension with the fundamental right that their movement had long championed. As important, personhood proponents argued that their movement need not choose between political pragmatism and a refusal to compromise. Becker and his allies believed that highlighting fetal rights – and refusing to settle for exceptions to abortion bans – could work as a political strategy if voters truly held politicians to account. By contrast, Becker and his allies worried that emphasizing claims about abortion's harms inadvertently suggested that the legality of the procedure depended on complex policy calculations rather than unchanging moral norms. Working in the courts, Cassidy also thought that pro-lifers could emphasize rights-based claims rather than emphasizing the effects of abortion. Cassidy maintained that the Court had not considered new evidence that a fetus was a human being or that women had a right to preserve a relationship with their unborn child. For some time, many abortion foes had seen a strategy based on claims about the costs of abortion as the only way to win. Soon, more activists would believe that there were other paths to victory.

Despite ongoing challenges from some abortion opponents, claims about the costs of abortion had staying power. If anything, *Gonzales* only increased the appeal of these contentions. There, the Court seemed to allow lawmakers more latitude when experts contested the science underlying an abortion restriction, even in cases in which elite medical organizations sided against abortion foes. Groups like AUL and NRLC believed that *Gonzales* proved that Justice Kennedy, the Court's swing voter, saw merit in claims about the costs of abortion. AUL stressed that *Gonzales* only increased the importance of "legislation designed to protect women from the negative consequences of abortion." In 2010, Denise Burke of AUL argued that "[m]ounting evidence of abortion's negative impact" might prompt even ambivalent Americans to reconsider their positions.[9]

Obama's election encouraged abortion foes to prioritize state restrictions. Under President Bush, Congress had passed not only the federal Partial-Birth Abortion Ban Act but also the Born-Alive Victims Protection Act, a statute extending legal person-hood to any child born alive, and the Unborn Victims of Violence Act, a statute treating a fetus injured or killed in utero by a third party as a victim of sixty federal crimes of violence. The Court, however, encouraged pro-lifers to focus as much on the states. Clarke Forsythe of AUL told his allies that *Gonzales* "restor[ed] deference to state legislatures." Many pro-life groups agreed with Forsythe that the Court's opinion encouraged the movement to focus on winning battles in state legislatures. Obama's win made victories at the state level even more important. A Democratic president would veto any federal antiabortion law, and Democrats had made major gains in Congress in any case. AUL began issuing state legislative reports and raised the profile of *Life List*, an annual ranking of pro-life states, to encourage states to compete with one another to pass the most regulations. Successful state laws proved the sophistication and influence of the pro-life movement at a time when the Democratic Party seemed ascendant. "We are making progress, state by state and law by law," Burke asserted. By 2010, following a backlash to Obama's signature reform, state legislatures would become more important to antiabortion strategy than even Burke could have anticipated.[10]

THE AFFORDABLE CARE ACT AND THE TEA PARTY

Barack Obama had run on a promise to transform American health care, and abortion-rights groups like NARAL Pro-choice America hoped that his reform bill would allow them to drive home arguments about the health benefits of abortion.

Although Obama's Patient Protection and Affordable Care Act (ACA) ultimately became law, the anger triggered by the bill significantly influenced the abortion conflict. The Tea Party movement, a complex coalition of grassroots activists, Republican establishment operatives and donors, and mostly white, older voters, despised the ACA. By the end of the 2010 elections, the GOP controlled an impressive number of state legislatures. These Republican lawmakers would weave claims about the costs of abortion into an ever-growing number of restrictions.

Abortion-rights supporters initially hoped that Obama would push their favored reforms. NARAL Pro-choice America, Planned Parenthood, and the National Organization for Women (NOW) revived the Freedom of Choice Act (FOCA), a bill that would codify abortion-rights and limit the access restrictions that states could pass. Abortion-rights supporters also pledged to restore abortion funding for the poor.[11] But Obama did not want to expend political capital on the abortion issue when it finally seemed possible to pass a federal health care bill expanding coverage.[12]

The ACA promised to reconfigure the health insurance market. The law expanded coverage for those with preexisting conditions, allowed younger Americans to stay longer on their parents' plans, and mandated that most Americans who did not already have insurance purchase coverage or pay a penalty. The law also punished employers with fifty or more workers who refused to offer coverage to workers, created a public option – under which parties could buy subsidized coverage from a federal agency – and put in place regulated state insurance exchanges. Given that the pro-life and pro-choice movements contested the relationship between abortion and health care, the two sides demanded to know whether the bill would cover procedures to end a pregnancy.[13]

Obama maintained that the bill was "abortion neutral" – that is, the law said nothing about abortion one way or the other. Pro-lifers responded that both the public option and the exchanges would allow states to choose to cover abortion and use federal funds to do so. Representative Bart Stupak (D–MI) and Representative Joseph Pitts (R–PA), both abortion opponents, proposed an amendment that would prevent any federal plan from covering abortion except in cases of rape, incest, or a threat to a woman's life. Ultimately, however, Stupak and his allies brokered a deal with President Obama whereby they withdrew the amendment in return for an executive order barring federal abortion funding under the ACA. Under the executive order, women could still purchase abortion coverage but could not use federal dollars to do so.[14]

Following the passage of the ACA, some pro-lifers experimented with new tactics. Rather than explicitly discussing the costs of abortion, some grassroots activists highlighted what they described as wrongdoing by Planned Parenthood. Planned Parenthood offered a variety of other services, including cancer screenings and testing for sexually transmitted diseases. Indeed, its annual reports explained that abortion comprised only 3 percent of all the services Planned Parenthood offered in

2011. Nevertheless, as the number of abortions declined nationwide, Planned Parenthood established itself as the largest national provider, and pro-lifers had more reason to target the organization.[15]

Attacks on Planned Parenthood had a long history. Congressional efforts to defund and discredit Planned Parenthood began during the Reagan Administration. In 1985, James Sedlak, a retired IBM engineer from upstate New York, organized Stop Planned Parenthood (STOPP) after he failed to prevent a clinic from opening in his hometown. Sedlak circulated a guide on how to deprive Planned Parenthood of local and state congressional funding. By 1992, he captured the attention of absolutists leading the American Life League, who helped to expand and streamline STOPP. In the mid-2000s, a concerted attack on Planned Parenthood captured the support of more abortion foes. In 2006, Lila Rose, a college student at the University of California, Los Angeles, released a video that seemed to show Rose, masquerading as a fifteen-year-old girl, seeking an abortion at Planned Parenthood. Rose claimed Planned Parenthood had ignored the statutory rape she had reported. Rose continued releasing videos, founding a group, Live Action, that would help to lead the fight against Planned Parenthood. In the years to come, larger groups like AUL and NRLC made claims about the criminality and dishonesty of Planned Parenthood leaders a central argument against legal abortion. These arguments sharpened divisions between those in the abortion wars. Rose and her allies insisted that the opposition harbored amoral profiteers with no respect for the law.[16]

Like Lila Rose, Shawn Carney, then a student at Texas A&M University, looked for new ways to protest abortion. In 2004, Carney and three other abortion opponents launched the first 40 Days for Life, a campaign of prayer, fasting, and vigils to end abortion. Three years later, 40 Days for Life had reached eighty-nine cities in thirty-three states. Carney and Rose claimed to speak for a new and bigger pro-life generation. Younger abortion foes might have overestimated the shift in public opinion, but for the first time, a 2009 Gallup poll showed that a majority of Americans identified as pro-life. Although abortion-rights supporters had allies in the White House and Congress, abortion opponents believed that they would soon regain control. Few could predict how quickly that moment would arrive.[17]

By 2010, anger about the ACA helped to give rise to a political movement that would change the terrain of the abortion wars. The so-called Tea Party got its start in February 2009 when CNBC reporter Rick Santelli condemned President Obama's emerging foreclosure relief plan. Believing that the administration had bailed out undeserving homeowners, Santelli invited angry "capitalists" to a "tea party" – a reference to the Boston Tea Party that preceded the Revolutionary War – to protest the move. After administration officials responded on air to Santelli's criticism, the media fanned the flames, and protesters responded to Santelli's request. By the spring of 2010, the protests had exploded. Anger about the ACA helped to fuel the Tea Party movement. Tea Partiers believed that ACA short-changed older, white

Americans by limiting their choice of health care and burdening a weak economy while funding new programs for groups that Tea Partiers saw as less deserving.[18]

Grassroots Tea Partiers, many of them older, middle-class, white Americans, mostly approved of Medicare and Social Security but opposed "big government" when it provided benefits to those perceived as undeserving, including immigrants, low-income, nonwhite Americans, and the young. The wealthy donors and advocacy groups who claimed the Tea Party mantle often held different priorities, including tax cuts for the wealthy, deregulation of business, and even the privatization of the Medicare and Social Security programs on which many grassroots activists depended. Nevertheless, both grassroots and elite Tea Party members shared a hatred of President Obama and his signature reform, the Affordable Care Act, which critics derisively labeled "Obamacare." The legislators who rode the Tea Party wave into office overwhelmingly identified as pro-life, and the prospects for legislation restricting abortion seemed brighter after the Tea Party flexed its political muscle.[19]

The Susan B. Anthony List (SBAL) and other larger pro-life groups aided the Tea Party takeover. SBAL's growth was impressive. In 1998, SBAL had spent less than $200,000 to help elect its favored candidates. By 2008, that number was closer to $700,000. By 2010, the group's nonprofit arm had an operating budget of $7 million. SBAL's evolution reflected the growing reliance of the pro-life movement on the GOP. The group began with the stated goal of electing pro-life women to Congress. But by the 2010s, SBAL worked extremely closely with the GOP – and often on behalf of male candidates. In 2010, Marjorie Dannenfelser, the organization's leader, announced a campaign, Votes Have Consequences, to defeat candidates who had ultimately cast a vote for Obama's bill. Many of the twenty-five lawmakers targeted by SBAL were pro-life Democratic women. By 2012, SBAL focused on competitive races and the presidential election – an effort that primarily helped Republicans. The SBAL still occasionally worked with Democrats but, like NRLC and AUL, almost always allied with the GOP.[20]

The leaders of SBAL and other antiabortion PACs could hardly believe their luck in 2010. The Republican Party gained sixty-three seats in the House of Representatives, six in the Senate, and 680 in state legislatures. Eight more anti-abortion governors took over.[21] Following the Tea Party wave, state legislatures passed a seemingly endless number of restrictions. Many of these laws built on the model that AUL and NRLC lawyers had crafted after *Casey* and *Gonzales*. Members of these groups had argued that lawmakers should step in to protect women from abortion even if experts disputed the evidence. In the states, Republican lawmakers were all too happy to spread the message that abortion had powerful costs.

TEA PARTY RESTRICTIONS

The Tea Party did not primarily bill itself as an antiabortion force. Indeed, abortion-rights supporters complained that since the 2010 election had focused on economic issues, Tea Party Republicans did not have a mandate to heavily restrict abortion. Regardless of what voters had in mind, the Tea Party wave began a new chapter of the conflict. States passed a record number of abortion restrictions each year after Tea Partiers took office – eighty-nine laws in 2010, compared to seventy-seven in 2009 and only thirty-three in 2008.[22]

At first, many of the new abortion restrictions directly related to the ACA. In 2009, thirteen states passed or considered bills that would bar the new insurance exchanges from covering abortion.[23] Later, AUL emphasized measures said to protect women from abortion providers who would cost them their health. Some of these laws gained support during the criminal trial of Dr. Kermit Gosnell, a Philadelphia abortion doctor later convicted of murder. Following Gosnell's 2011 arrest, prosecutors charged him with several counts of murder: one involving a woman who had died in his care and three involving infants who had been born alive and thereafter killed by Gosnell. Gosnell's gruesome story reinforced claims that abortion damaged women's physical health as well as their mental well-being, and larger pro-life groups stepped up efforts to pass onerous clinic regulations.[24]

Often, however, AUL's campaign for clinic regulations targeted Planned Parenthood. AUL's model legislation guide, *Defending Life*, proposed laws designed to shutter most abortion clinics.[25] Between 2011 and 2012, AUL also compiled a nearly 200-page report, "The Case for Investigating Planned Parenthood," that AUL said provided "evidence of systemic financial irregularities within the abortion giant." A few years later, the Center for Medical Progress (CMP), an antiabortion group known for undercover recordings, began releasing videos that supposedly showed Planned Parenthood workers contemplating the illegal sale of fetal tissue and generally treating fetal remains with disrespect. Although critics asserted that the videos were heavily edited, the CMP footage fed into efforts to defund Planned Parenthood. Extremists also took note, and at the end of 2015, in a brutal attack, Robert Lewis Dear Jr. shot and killed three people at a Colorado Springs, Colorado, Planned Parenthood, injuring nine more.[26]

In singling out Planned Parenthood, pro-lifers reworked claims about the costs of abortion for women. In the 1990s and early 2000s, larger antiabortion groups had primarily pushed mandatory counseling laws said to tell women about the risks of the procedure. Rather than just informing women about what pro-lifers described as the risks of abortion, new restrictions actually forced clinics to close. And instead of just playing up what pro-lifers saw as the dangers of the abortion procedure for women, AUL and its allies attacked the ethics of both specific abortion providers and some of the voters who supported them. Opposing activists had always insulted and denigrated one another, but the campaign to defund Planned Parenthood made attacks on named organizations and specific individuals one of the most visible dimensions of the antiabortion campaign.

If AUL tried to find an effective answer to *Casey*'s conclusion that women relied on abortion, NRLC relied on contested scientific claims about the costs of abortion for unborn children. Under the guidance of Mary Spaulding Balch, NRLC's director of state legislation, the group championed a law that would ban all abortions after twenty weeks – the point at which the organization claimed that unborn children could experience pain. Much as leading physicians' groups questioned the medical conclusions underlying Congress's partial-birth abortion ban, medical experts contested the science underlying NRLC's fetal pain law. A 2005 *Journal of the American Medical Association* article summarized then-available research and concluded that unborn children would not be able to experience pain as early as twenty weeks' gestation. The American College of Obstetricians and Gynecologists took a firm position that fetal pain was not possible until later in pregnancy. Pro-lifers sided with other researchers who asserted that fetal pain was possible as early as the eighteenth week. Moreover, abortion opponents argued that because of the Supreme Court's decision in *Gonzales*, scientific uncertainty was not an obstacle for lawmakers seeking to ban all abortions at or after twenty weeks. The fetal pain debate again raised questions about who had the expertise to measure the costs and benefits of abortion.[27]

Fetal pain laws also attacked what pro-lifers viewed as a weakness of *Casey*: the conclusion that states could ban abortion only after fetal viability. If the Court allowed states to ban abortion when some (but not all) experts believed that fetal pain was possible, then other medically contested justifications could also pass muster, and the states could ban abortion earlier in pregnancy.[28] In 2010, Nebraska became the first state to pass such a law, and NRLC attorneys soon hoped for many more.[29] AUL also sponsored fetal pain laws, relying on arguments about the costs of abortion for women. The states that passed twenty-week abortion bans claimed to protect both women and unborn children. AUL described these laws as "Mothers' Health and Safety Acts" or "Women's Late-Term Pregnancy Health Acts," statutes intended to eliminate fetal pain and to prevent the complications that women suffered more often in later-term abortions.[30]

With the expansion of conservative online media outlets, pro-lifers more vigorously contested who had the competence to measure the medical costs and benefits of abortion. Founded by conservative activist Andrew Breitbart in 2007, *Breitbart*, a news aggregator, grew after his 2012 death. With the help of Breitbart's successor, Steve Bannon, *Breitbart* relaunched as a tabloid-style site. *Breitbart* started a broader conservative media explosion, with outlets like the *Daily Caller* (founded 2010) and the *Blaze* (2011) offering a right-leaning view of the news. The Pew Research Foundation found that liberals and conservatives increasingly got their information from different sources, with many conservatives getting their news from a single outlet. As more Americans questioned the reliability of both the mainstream media and certain medical organizations, those on either side less often agreed about the facts of abortion – and about who had the expertise to evaluate them.[31]

Just as political polarization intensified, the cleavage in the abortion debate deepened. In 2011, state lawmakers shattered previous records, passing 135 restrictions. Fighting about the costs and benefits of abortion had not led to any effort to seek middle ground. Even if experts disagreed about the science surrounding an abortion restriction, groups like AUL and NRLC hoped to use that uncertainty to give sympathetic legislators more room to regulate. Groups like NARAL and Planned Parenthood responded by insisting that many of the new restrictions rested on unquestionably specious claims, not real science. Those on opposing sides more often (and more fully) embraced different sources of information.[32]

Pro-lifers' attack on Planned Parenthood further polarized the discussion. While abortion foes accused the abortion provider of financial misdeeds and moral failures, Planned Parenthood and its allies used the opposition campaign to reframe their own message. In the 2012 election, groups like Planned Parenthood and NARAL often argued that pro-lifers and their GOP allies took no interest in the well-being of women or anyone else who needed medical care. When it came to questioning the character of those on the other side, abortion-rights supporters could be just as fierce as their opponents.

THE WAR ON WOMEN

Larger abortion-rights groups used the attack on Planned Parenthood to renew arguments about the benefits of abortion for women seeking equal citizenship. Because Planned Parenthood provided a variety of services, abortion-rights supporters contended that the opposition fought to deprive women of both beneficial health care and a chance at a good career or education. In 2012, groups like NARAL Pro-choice America and Planned Parenthood claimed to defend the victims of a "war on women."

Arguments about a war on women caught on after a period of struggle for larger pro-choice groups. Although they seemed to be in a position of strength, abortion-rights supporters took a drubbing in the early years of the Obama Administration. Halfway through the 2010 election cycle, for example, NARAL managed to raise just over $500,000. The organization's polling also revealed a dangerous "intensity gap" in the commitments of younger pro-life and pro-choice voters. Among those in their twenties or thirties, more than 51 percent of those opposed to abortion described the issue as very important, compared to only 26 percent of those who supported abortion-rights. For some time, larger abortion-rights groups struggled to close this gap, experimenting with claims that "recognized the moral complexity" of the issue.[33]

But the attack on Planned Parenthood and the Affordable Care Act created new tactical opportunities. Because Planned Parenthood offered medical services beyond abortion, the organization and its allies framed the opposition as both anti–health care and anti-woman. So too did controversial comments made by prominent Republican candidates. Representative Todd Akin, a Republican Senate candidate from Missouri, gave an interview in which he stated that women could not get pregnant as a result of "legitimate rape" because the female body had "ways to shut that whole thing down." Richard Mourdock, an Indiana Republican campaigning for Senate, likewise stated during a speech that when women became pregnant as a result of rape, it was "something that God intended to happen." Mourdock and Akin's comments formed part of pro-choice groups' claims that pro-lifers had retrograde or even hostile attitudes toward women. The argument made headway. In 2011, Planned Parenthood's number of fans on Facebook surged by over 992 percent after Congress proposed defunding the organization, and the organization's online gifts grew by 500 percent. That year, NARAL added 1,000 subscribers a day to its active email list.[34]

Connecting abortion to both affordable health care and equality for women, groups like Planned Parenthood, NARAL Pro-choice America, and NOW helped to make the issue central to the 2012 election. Candidates and outside groups poured nearly $17 million into advertising, much of which spotlighted what abortion-rights supporters described as a Republican "war on women." In the 2012 season, EMILY's List, a group committed to the election of women who supported abortion-rights, spent more on the election than did any other single-issue group.[35]

"War on women" claims might have seemed familiar. In the 1990s, abortion-rights supporters in groups like Planned Parenthood had used national health care reform to stress claims about the health benefits of access to legal abortion. In 2012, by contrast, NARAL Pro-choice America and Planned Parenthood linked claims about the health benefits of abortion to arguments about equality for women. But rather than emphasizing the opportunities that legal abortion afforded women, these groups primarily questioned the motives of those who claimed to be pro-life. Feminists had accused abortion foes of misogyny for decades, but "war on women" claims spotlighted pro-lifers' intentions and character. Just as pro-lifers described Planned Parenthood and its supporters as corrupt, ghoulish, and morally bankrupt, NARAL Pro-choice America and Planned Parenthood emphasized claims about abortion foes' hatred of women. Those on both sides insisted that voters could not trust their opposition to say anything true about the costs and benefits of abortion.

ABORTION AND RELIGIOUS FREEDOM

"War on women" accusations gained attention partly because of a reinvigorated debate about birth control and religious liberty. When the ACA mandated coverage of certain contraceptives, some employers objected, and antiabortion groups like AUL and NRLC spoke out against what they described as an attack on religious freedom. While absolutist groups like Judie Brown's American Life League had denounced birth control and taken an explicitly religious stance since the 1970s, larger antiabortion groups had often avoided any public discussion of religious faith or contraception. By contrast, after 2012, AUL and NRLC leaders foregrounded the burdens on religious believers in describing the costs of both abortion and the ACA. But attitudes toward the contraceptive mandate, like the definition of religious freedom, showed that agreement of any kind was hard to find.

The religious freedom struggle escalated in 2011 when the Obama administration added eighteen forms of female contraception to the list of preventative services made available under the Affordable Care Act without a co-pay. A failure to provide coverage resulted in a $100 per day penalty for each affected individual. Initially, the contraceptive mandate exempted churches but not religious nonprofit businesses. As a result, the exemption did not cover a wide group of actors, including religious universities, hospitals, and for-profit businesses. Citing faith-based objections, some religious employers refused to subsidize what they saw as abortion-inducing drugs, including the birth control pill, the morning-after pill, and IUDs. These employers believed that these contraceptives were abortifacients because they blocked the implantation of a fertilized egg. The American College of Obstetricians and Gynecologists (ACOG) treated none of these birth control methods as abortifacients. According to ACOG, emergency contraception prevented ovulation, while copper IUDs either stopped fertilization or blocked implantation. Regardless, some employers felt that the government had trampled on their religious freedom.[36]

With the contraceptive mandate in court, religious-liberty arguments gained a broader audience. The well-publicized *Manhattan Declaration: A Call of Christian Conscience* (2009), a manifesto of conservative Christian principles developed by legal scholar Robert George and evangelical leader Chuck Colson, called on conservative Christians to defend three interrelated principles: "the sanctity of human life, the dignity of marriage as a union of husband and wife, and the freedom of religion." As religious-liberty arguments became more visible, larger antiabortion groups increasingly adopted them. AUL contended that the contraceptive mandate covered abortifacients and would set a precedent that could "coerce pharmacists to dispense RU 486, to coerce medical students to participate in abortion training, and to coerce doctors to participate in surgical abortions." NRLC similarly asserted that the contraceptive mandate would allow the Department of Health and Human Services to define anything as a "preventative service," including surgical abortion.[37]

NRLC and AUL had previously steered clear of any issue related to contraception because the opposition frequently accused pro-lifers of being anti-sex and anti–birth control. Moreover, given the role of Catholics in early pro-life activism, larger antiabortion groups had to fight off accusations that their movement was a front for the Catholic Church. These arguments stung partly because pro-lifers were divided on the issue of birth control. While some believed that contraception would lower the abortion rate, others thought that widely available birth control fueled irresponsible sex and increased the number of abortions. Some pro-lifers believed that popular forms of birth control were themselves abortifacients. For many reasons, beginning in the late 1960s, pro-life groups distanced themselves from the

Church's stance on contraception. The contraceptive mandate changed the willingness of antiabortion groups to speak out about birth control. While still not taking a public stand on contraception writ large, groups like NRLC and AUL vocally condemned the contraceptive mandate and sometimes described specific forms of birth control as abortifacients.[38]

In the 2010s, pro-lifers also more often defined themselves as defenders of religious liberty. Starting in the late 1980s, conservative Christian lawyers affiliated with the American Center for Law and Justice or Liberty Counsel linked opposition to abortion with Christian faith, as did members of the clinic-blockade movement and staff at many crisis pregnancy centers. For the most part, however, larger groups like NRLC and AUL still emphasized secular arguments. By contrast, during the fight over the contraceptive mandate, NRLC and AUL members defined themselves as champions of religious liberty. Groups like NARAL and Planned Parenthood responded that sexism, not religious freedom, defined the debate. Planned Parenthood, NARAL Pro-choice America, MoveOn.org, and the Service Employees International Union formed the Coalition to Protect Women's Health, which described the opposition as "people who voted against birth control and vote against health care." As NARAL Pro-choice America explained: "[A]nti-choice extremists who are opposed to birth control for ideological reasons have worked to restrict access to contraception."[39]

Facing criticism from religious leaders, the Obama Administration subsequently broadened the mandate's exemption. The new version permitted certain religious nonprofit corporations to opt out if they filled out a form stating their objections. This would allow the corporation to avoid directly covering those services. Instead, the insurer would bypass the employer and directly provide coverage. Because the new exemption still left out for-profit corporations, several closely held businesses, including Hobby Lobby, a home decor and craft chain, contended that the contraceptive mandate violated the Religious Freedom Restoration Act (RFRA), a 1993 federal statute dealing with the freedom of religion. After the Supreme Court retreated from strong enforcement of the Free Exercise Clause of the First Amendment, RFRA wrote an earlier, more protective standard into federal law. Under RFRA, the government could not substantially burden the free exercise of religion unless it had a compelling purpose and used the least restrictive means of achieving its aim. The Supreme Court eventually agreed to address whether the ACA violated RFRA.[40]

In 2014, in *Burwell v. Hobby Lobby Stores, Inc.*, one of several consolidated cases, the Supreme Court sided with Hobby Lobby and other religious businesses. In a 5–4 decision, the Court first held that closely held corporations (firms whose stock is held by a small number of people) counted as "persons" under RFRA and could thus rely on the statute to make a claim. The Court further concluded that the penalties for noncompliance constituted a serious burden under RFRA. Even assuming that the government had a compelling interest in expanding the contraceptive mandate, the Court reasoned that the administration had not used the least restrictive means of achieving its goal.[41]

Hobby Lobby was a controversial decision. Critics argued that the Court's decision defined religious conscience far too broadly and offered no limiting principle. Some wondered if as a result, religious employers could deny their workers access to AIDS drugs or refuse to hire workers of a certain race or sex. Nor did *Hobby Lobby* end challenges to the contraceptive mandate. A group of religious universities, businesses, and other entities argued that even compliance with the exemption impermissibly burdened religion under RFRA. In *Zubik v. Burwell* (2016), the Supreme Court avoided a decision on the merits of this argument. In supplemental briefing, the parties had agreed that insurance companies could provide direct coverage without any notice from employers. The Court remanded to see if lower courts could adopt a similar solution that balanced religious liberty and the availability of contraceptive coverage. However, pro-lifers and their allies continued emphasizing that the contraceptive mandate, like laws expanding abortion access, would cost conservative Christians the freedom to act on their religious beliefs.[42]

In the mid-2010s, partly because of debates about religious liberty, arguments about the costs and benefits of abortion became more closely tied to the fight about gay, lesbian, bisexual, transgender, and queer (LGBTQ+) rights. When efforts to secure marriage equality began in the mid-1990s, a backlash followed. In 1996, Congress passed the federal Defense of Marriage Act, defining marriage in all federal laws as between one man and one woman. Cases continued in state courts. In 2003, in *Goodridge v. Department of Public Health*, the Massachusetts Supreme Judicial Court held that denying same-sex couples the right to marry violated the state constitution. As more states authorized same-sex marriage, Americans gradually acclimated to the idea, a fact reflected by poll data. In 2013, in *Windsor v. United States*, the Supreme Court struck down the Defense of Marriage Act. Two years later, in *Obergefell v. Hodges*, the Supreme Court concluded that bans on same-sex marriage violated the federal Constitution. Anthony Kennedy's majority relied on arguments about the evolution of a right to marry and about equal protection for gay and lesbian couples.[43]

After *Obergefell*, abortion politics became even more intertwined with the issues of religious liberty and sexual orientation. Conservative Christians worried that the *Obergefell* Court had put religious liberty at risk. "The agenda is not tolerance for different beliefs and lifestyles," Denny Burk wrote in *The Federalist*, a conservative online magazine. "The agenda is a demand that everyone get on board with the moral revolution or be punished." Christian business owners especially worried about being forced to serve same-sex couples. The issue made national news in 2015 when Kim Davis, a clerk in Kentucky, refused to issue a marriage license to a same-sex couple, citing her religious liberty. A series of court cases followed. Florists, bakers, adoption agencies, and other business owners claimed that serving gay individuals or same-sex couples ran counter to their most deeply held religious beliefs. When states applied civil rights statutes to these service providers, conservative organizations and think tanks proclaimed that both religious liberty and freedom of speech faced an existential threat. Business owners claimed that the law compelled them to speak a message that violated their most deeply held beliefs. LGBTQ+ advocates responded that business owners sought a license to discriminate. These activists insisted that business owners' speech was not at issue when customers hired them – no one would understand a business' services to reflect the beliefs of the business owner rather than the customer. And these advocates maintained that after *Obergefell*, courts had to consider weighty interests in equal treatment for same-sex couples.[44]

Although some abortion foes did not participate directly in discussions of religious liberty for conservative Christian business owners, the pro-life movement did promote expansive religious-liberty laws and endorse the cause of other groups seeking religious liberty. AUL, for example, introduced model legislation that broadened the definition of a conscientious objector to include businesses and individuals who merely scheduled abortions or cleaned rooms where abortions were performed. By invoking conscience and religious liberty, AUL fought for a variety of model laws covering providers, pharmacists, hospitals, health plans, employers, and other health care workers who objected to abortion, contraception, or other medical services. NRLC made support for expansive conscience legislation a key metric for determining support of members of Congress. Groups like NARAL and the Center for Reproductive Rights responded that pro-lifers sought to "limit women's ability to access reproductive health care, under the guise of protecting religious liberty."[45]

While groups on both sides of the abortion conflict staked out positions on issues such as the contraceptive mandate, LGBTQ+ discrimination, and conscience, the debate became more polarized. Abortion foes argued that the opposition waged a war on religious liberty. Abortion-rights supporters, in turn, portrayed their opponents' positions on same-sex marriage or birth control as proof that pro-lifers discriminated against women and LGBTQ+ Americans. In part, this widening breach reflected a growing chasm between the American left and right. But more and more, those on either side also saw the facts about the costs and benefits of abortion in radically different terms.

REPRODUCTIVE JUSTICE AND #SHOUTYOURABORTION

After 2010, groups like NARAL and Planned Parenthood again stressed claims about the benefits of abortion, seeking to dispel the stigma surrounding abortion. At the same time, by making claims about the benefits of abortion, some grassroots activists wanted to advance a reproductive justice framework that highlighted the reasons that women needed a variety of services beyond abortion. Women of color continued to press for an approach that included support for women who wanted to raise children as well as control when and how they bore them. To varying degrees, abortion-rights groups adopted reproductive justice claims, even if they prioritized abortion over other issues. Starting in 2014, for example, Planned Parenthood at times rejected the pro-choice label, suggesting that it did not "reflect the full range of women's health and economic issues now being debated."[46] The National Organization for Women likewise adopted a reproductive justice agenda, seeking support for access to "abortion, birth control, pre-natal care, maternity leave, child care and other crucial health and family services." Women of color continued to launch their own reproductive justice initiatives. For example, in 2018, Black Women for Wellness, Black Women's Health Imperative, New Voices Pittsburgh, SisterLove, Inc., and SPARK Reproductive Justice Now asked veteran activist Marcela David for help forming In Our Own Voice: National Black Women's Reproductive Justice Agenda, a new policy-based organization that fought to give all women "complete economic, social, and political power and resources to make healthy decisions about [their] bodies, [their] families, and their communities."[47]

Others worked more directly to combat the stigma surrounding abortion. These efforts had a history. For example, in 2000, the National Coalition of Abortion Providers (NCAP) launched the Abortion Conversation Project, an effort to start dialogue about abortion to make the procedure seem less shameful. A similar effort began in 2015 after the House (but not the Senate) passed a law defunding Planned Parenthood. Amelia Bonow, a Seattle native who had had a positive abortion experience at Planned Parenthood, responded by going on Facebook and sharing the benefits she experienced from abortion. Lindy West, one of Bonow's friends, took a screenshot of her post, went to Twitter, and added the hashtag #ShoutYourAbortion. The campaign grew quickly, and users mentioned the hashtag over 100,000 times in a twenty-four-hour period. Within days, NARAL and Planned Parenthood were advising Bonow and her colleagues on how to refine Shout Your Abortion (SYA).[48] SYA – and the response to it – were a reminder of the growing gulf between those on either side of the abortion debate. Antiabortion lawmakers labeled the campaign "macabre." Some started a competing dialogue on Twitter, #ShoutYourAdoption, or accused Bonow and West of trivializing the issue.[49]

In the 2010s, arguments about the costs and benefits of abortion remained at the center of national discourse. Pro-life groups contended that the procedure cost women their psychological health, forced unborn children to suffer tremendous pain, and took away the rights of conservative Christians to act in accordance with their religious beliefs. Pro-choice organizations responded that abortion had important benefits, both in terms of the health outcomes women achieved and the life goals that many could pursue. Ironically, while the debate seemed more and more sharply divided, abortion itself was increasingly rare. By 2014, the abortion rate dipped to 14.6 per 1,000 women – lower than at any point since 1973. The reasons for this decline were unclear. Access to contraception and personal ambivalence about abortion might have been factors. But abortion regulations likely played a part as well. Abortion foes passed more restrictions between 2011 and 2013 than in the entire previous decade. Although the pace slowed after 2013, 288 restrictions – fully 27 percent of those passed between 1973 and 2016 – were introduced since 2010.[50]

The ongoing prominence of claims about the costs and benefits of abortion had certainly not made it any easier to seek compromise. Even as the number of abortions declined, abortion foes tried to break previous records for the number of restrictions passed in a given year. Those on opposing sides bitterly contested the effects of legal abortion on everything from women's health to religious liberty. And few could agree on how either to resolve claims of scientific uncertainty or to determine the basic facts about the procedure. With tensions escalating, pro-life leaders hoped that the Supreme Court would give lawmakers free rein to pass restrictions.

WHOLE WOMAN'S HEALTH AND THE UNDUE BURDEN STANDARD

The Supreme Court's next major abortion case arose out of what Charmaine Yoest of AUL called a strategy of "challenging and exposing the abortion industry."[51] Groups like AUL had not only played up claims about the costs of abortion but also sought to paint abortion providers as dishonest and irresponsible. In 2013, to further this strategy, AUL encouraged Texas lawmakers to adopt two related pieces of model legislation, the Women's Health Protection Act and the Abortion Providers Privileges Act, that could put clinics out of business. One provision demanded that abortion providers have admitting privileges at a hospital within thirty miles. The Women's Health Protection Act required abortion clinics to comply with regulations governing ambulatory surgical centers (ASCs). Some of these rules, such as the overhaul of existing buildings or the construction of new ones, would require expensive changes. The costs of abortion for women supposedly justified both measures.[52]

In 2013, after Texas passed both provisions, a group of abortion providers challenged the constitutionality of the admitting-privileges measure. The district court enjoined enforcement of the law, but the Fifth Circuit Court of Appeals reversed only days later.[53] Following a trial on the merits,[54] the Fifth Circuit upheld the admitting-privilege requirement.[55] A week after the Fifth Circuit's decision, providers challenged the ambulatory surgical center (ASC) provisions. Whole Woman's Health, the named plaintiff, also tweaked its challenge to the admitting-privileges requirement, questioning the constitutionality of the law only as it applied to facilities in McAllen and El Paso.[56] The district court enjoined enforcement of the two provisions,[57] and the Fifth Circuit again reversed.[58]

When the Supreme Court agreed to hear the case, abortion foes expected the Court to equate the undue burden standard with the least exacting form of judicial review: rational basis. "[T]he State is not required to *prove* the positive impact of HB 2 in order for a court to determine that the requirement has a rational basis (and is, thus, not an undue burden)," AUL argued in its Supreme Court brief.[59] NRLC similarly contended that under *Casey*, an undue burden must rise to the level of an "'absolute obstacle' ... or 'severe limitation' ... such as a 'complete prohibition' before it would be unconstitutional." If the undue burden standard required so much deference to state legislators, it would not matter much that the Court had preserved *Roe*. When states could constitutionally pass almost any restriction, then abortion-rights would mean very little.[60]

Abortion-rights supporters insisted that many restrictions would fail the undue burden standard. These attorneys contended that under *Casey*, courts had to consider both the benefits and costs of the law. Abortion-rights attorneys further reasoned that even a minimally burdensome law could be unconstitutional if it served no useful purpose. "The standard gives real substance to the urgent claims of the woman to retain the ultimate control over her destiny and her body, while permitting laws that are designed to inform her decision," the Center for Reproductive Rights argued.[61]

The two sides also disagreed about what had caused so many Texas abortion clinics to close. Abortion-rights supporters relied on studies completed by the Texas Policy Evaluation Project, organized in 2011 at the University of Texas-Austin by doctors, demographers, and public health experts. The project received financial support from the Susan Thompson Buffett Foundation, a major donor to abortion-rights causes, and its members included Daniel Grossman, the new head of Advancing New Standards in Reproductive Health, a leading research center supportive of abortion-rights.[62]

Since 2007, abortion opponents had tried to expand their capacity for research. In 2011, the Susan B. Anthony List founded the Charlotte Lozier Institute as an alternative to abortion-rights research groups. Texas and pro-life organizations cited evidence collected by sympathetic researchers, but as many abortion opponents realized, supporters of abortion-rights had an advantage in research funding and access to data. To overcome this hurdle, groups like NRLC and AUL relied on *Gonzales v. Carhart*, the Court's 2007 partial-birth abortion decision. Abortion opponents argued that under *Gonzales*, courts had to defer to legislatures when both sides presented scientific evidence. NRLC and AUL asserted that since there was a disagreement about whether the Texas law (HB2) benefitted women, courts should trust that lawmakers got it right.[63]

The Court that heard *Whole Woman's Health* was short-handed. Earlier in 2016, Antonin Scalia, one of the Court's most outspoken conservatives, had died unexpectedly during a Texas hunting trip. To replace him, Barack Obama had nominated Merrick Garland of the DC Circuit Court of Appeals. Even though many viewed Garland as a moderate, the Republicans who controlled the Senate refused to hold a vote on the confirmation. The eight-member Court nevertheless managed to reach a decision on the merits. In a 5–3 decision, the Court began by holding that earlier litigation had not barred providers from challenging either one or both provisions of HB2. The Court then turned to the meaning of the undue burden standard. Under *Casey*, as the majority reasoned, "courts consider the burdens a law imposes on abortion access together with the benefits those laws confer." In other words, courts would have to examine evidence about whether a law really served its stated purpose. The majority further rejected the idea that after *Gonzales*, courts should broadly defer to factual findings made by legislatures. Instead, "evidence and argument presented in judicial proceedings" would play a central role in determining the constitutionality of a law.[64]

The Court applied this test to the two challenged provisions of HB2. *Whole Woman's Health* credited evidence that abortion very rarely resulted in any complications that would require hospitalization. Texas asserted that the admitting-privilege provision would guarantee continuity of care, but the Court could not find a single incident in which the provision would have led to a better outcome. The Court further reasoned that the law would significantly burden women by forcing the closure of all but a handful of clinics. *Whole Woman's Health* pointed to the timing of clinic closures as well as to reasons that abortion providers might have been unable to maintain admitting privileges. For example, because complication rates were extremely low, providers would not admit the minimal number of patients required to maintain privileges at certain hospitals.[65]

The Court saw no more merit in the ASC provision.[66] *Whole Woman's Health* concluded that the law provided no benefit. According to the majority, the rare cases in which complications arose often started well after a woman left a clinic, when an ASC provision would add no value. Moreover, many abortions were medical, not surgical, and would be unchanged by any of the requirements of the Texas law. When it came to the effects of the law, the Court found that it would reduce the number of open clinics to seven or eight. The Court accepted the district court's conclusions that existing clinics could not expand to address any unmet need, at least not without diminishing the quality of services they provided.[67]

Whole Woman's Health certainly gave the undue burden standard more bite. The decision required that at a minimum, laws that claimed to help women actually deliver some benefit. In dicta, the Court stressed that abortion was safe. Moreover, *Whole Woman's Health* treated laws as burdensome when they lowered the quality of care women received or made abortions difficult or inconvenient. Previous decisions, by contrast, had required a more absolute obstacle.

Nevertheless, the decision hardly put abortion-rights on safe ground. By making each abortion case turn on its own specific facts, the Court opened the door for restrictions that differed only slightly from the one passed in Texas. Nor did the Court spell out clearly whether (or how) *Whole Woman's Health's* approach would apply to laws that claimed to protect an unborn child rather than a woman. And the Court reasoned that *Whole Woman's Health* could easily be reconciled with *Gonzales*, leaving questions about what made scientific disputes uncertain and when, if at all, the Court would defer to lawmakers.

The undue burden standard had always been both a blessing and a curse for those on both sides. As *Whole Woman's Health* showed, the rule could force states to confront the real-world effects of abortion restrictions. At the same time, the standard remained extraordinarily vague and subjective. At times, for abortion-rights supporters, the undue burden standard seemed to be a time bomb, available whenever justices wished to narrow abortion-rights. Soon, that bomb seemed ready to go off.

TRUMP'S TRIUMPH

In the summer of 2016, it appeared that the Court would only continue to expand abortion-rights. At the time, many expected Hillary Clinton to have an easy path to victory in the presidential election. Clinton, a former senator and secretary of state, had fended off a surprising challenge from Senator Bernie Sanders, a self-described Democratic-Socialist from Vermont. Sanders denounced income inequality and endorsed the idea of a universal, free college education. Ultimately, Clinton's experience, ties to major donors, and establishment connections proved too much for Sanders. On the Republican side, Donald Trump, a real estate mogul whom few gave a chance at the start of the election season, had defeated a group of more experienced rivals. But Trump seemed to have political liabilities that could cost him at the polls. In the summer of 2016, political commentators widely predicted that the Republican nominee would not rebound from several controversial remarks. On the campaign trail, he had made racially inflammatory comments about Latinos and African-Americans. Later, a leaked video showed Trump bragging to Billy Bush, the host of the television program *Access Hollywood*, about forcibly grabbing women's genitals. Fortunately for the GOP nominee, Clinton battled scandals of her own. Before becoming secretary of state in 2009, Clinton had set up a private email server that she used for both official and unofficial communications. The FBI had investigated whether Clinton had violated federal law by handling state business on the server. After concluding in July 2016 that no reasonable prosecutor would pursue charges against Clinton, the FBI nonetheless announced that it was reopening the investigation – eleven days before the election.[68]

On election night, Trump shocked many by losing the popular vote but winning the Electoral College. Republicans also secured majorities in both houses of Congress. The 2016 election, however, was not in many ways a referendum on legal abortion. The unpopularity of both candidates made a difference, as did Trump's appeal to older, mostly blue-collar whites anxious about globalization, jobs, immigration, and the country's changing racial composition. Nevertheless, Trump's commitment to the pro-life movement seemed to matter. Voters understood that the next president would select Scalia's replacement. Exit polls showed that seven in ten voters viewed the selection of a new Supreme Court justice as an important factor. For some of these voters, the prospect of overturning *Roe* might have been crucial.[69]

Moreover, many of the beliefs that had reshaped the abortion debate – including skepticism of scientific authorities and the mainstream media – helped to pave the way for Trump's win. Trump had endorsed several online conspiracy theories, including those spread by the anti-vaccine movement. He gained special notoriety for publicizing the theory of the so-called birther movement, which argued that Barack Obama was neither a Christian nor a US citizen (and because of the latter, not qualified to be president). Both before and after his election, Trump appealed to Americans who believed that the government, the scientific establishment, and the media concealed the truth from ordinary people.[70]

Trump's victory also revealed the importance of a conservative media ecosystem anchored by *Breitbart*. Those on both sides of the aisle relied on Twitter and Facebook or partisan websites for political information. Scholars Yochai Benkler, Robert Faris, Hal Roberts, and Ethan Zuckerman argued that many of the stories consumed by Trump supporters contained misleading half-truths, logical leaps, and bald-faced lies. By contrast, Trump ran on the idea that the political establishment and media outlets were dishonest and thoroughly corrupt.[71]

The fake news debate further exposed cracks that had appeared in earlier discussions of partial-birth abortion or a claimed abortion–breast cancer connection. Abortion foes had increasingly argued that groups like the American College of Obstetricians and Gynecologists and the mainstream media could not competently measure the costs and benefits of abortion because they put political correctness ahead of the truth. Supporters of abortion-rights often emphasized that the abortion debate turned not on objective facts but on the subjective needs and values of individual women. Over the course of the 2016 election, those contesting the abortion wars, like many other Americans, relied on different sources of information and questioned whether established organizations could reliably measure the costs and benefits of abortion.

Fights about who could be trusted only intensified after the election, especially after the president gained the opportunity to reshape the Supreme Court. In 2017, Trump nominated Neil Gorsuch, a judge on the Tenth Circuit Court of Appeals, to replace Antonin Scalia. In April 2017, a Republican-controlled Congress abolished the Supreme Court filibuster, a rule that required sixty votes before a nominee could advance. After the vote, the Senate pushed through Gorsuch's nomination by a 52–48 vote. Although Gorsuch had never directly addressed abortion in his ten years on the bench, pro-lifers expected him to move the Court closer to overturning *Roe*. Gorsuch had penned a book on euthanasia, writing that "the intentional taking of life by private persons is always wrong" – language many read as code for opposition to abortion. More important, the Federalist Society had vetted Gorsuch, likely with the expectation that he would reverse the 1973 decision.[72]

With Gorsuch on the Court and Trump in the White House, crisis pregnancy centers (CPCs) stood to make important gains. Trump announced changes to Title

X regulations governing family planning funding that channeled money away from licensed medical clinics and toward CPCs. The regulations barred any organization from receiving support from Title X, a program funding family planning for the poor, from making abortion referrals. The regulations further required any recipient performing abortions to financially and physically separate their family planning practice. Believing that the regulations compromised physicians' ability to give the best medical advice, Planned Parenthood announced its withdrawal from the Title X program – a step that would cost the organization roughly $60 million a year. CPCs, by contrast, were poised to receive far more federal support. After the regulations became final, the Trump Administration stood ready to award $5.1 million in grants to Obria, a CPC chain that offered natural family planning and abstinence-only sex education. The Supreme Court also gave CPCs a boost in *National Institute of Family and Life Advocates (NIFLA) v. Becerra*. That case involved a California law regulating CPCs. Licensed clinics had to notify women of the availability of free or low-cost state-provided abortion services. Unlicensed centers had to inform women that they were not qualified medical providers. California argued that its law protected women from misinformation. NIFLA, however, argued that the California law violated the Free Speech Clause of the First Amendment, and the Court agreed.[73]

Writing for a majority of five, Justice Clarence Thomas concluded that the unlicensed-clinic provision unduly burdened the speech of clinic staff. The lower courts had upheld the law by viewing it as a regulation of professional speech, akin to the antiabortion informed consent regulations already upheld in *Casey*, which required doctors to share information such as details of fetal development and the availability of child support. At times, members of the Court had implied that professional speech received less protection than certain forms of political expression. In theory, the government had more latitude to regulate the speech of doctors to ensure public safety. But the status of professional-speech doctrine remained unclear, and the Court did not think that it applied to the California law. The Court also at times gave states more power to regulate "factual, noncontroversial information." Thomas asserted that because abortion was so divisive, the state's mandated disclosure was anything but uncontroversial. The Court struck down the California law. Gorsuch's nomination proved consequential: He provided the fifth vote for Thomas' majority.[74]

Nevertheless, Gorsuch's nomination seemed to be an afterthought after Anthony Kennedy announced his retirement in June 2018. Many wondered if Kennedy's exit spelled the end for *Roe*. Commentators assumed that Chief Justice John Roberts and Justices Samuel Alito, Neil Gorsuch, and Clarence Thomas would all vote to reverse *Roe* or undermine abortion-rights. Trump had said as much of his nominees on the campaign trail, promising that the overruling of *Roe* would happen "automatically" if he got the chance to shape the Court. In replacing Kennedy, President Trump selected Brett Kavanaugh, a judge on the DC Circuit Court of Appeals.

Kavanaugh's nomination hit a snag when Dr. Christine Blasey Ford, a California professor, accused the nominee of attempting to sexually assault her in high school. Other accusers subsequently came forward. Ford's testimony triggered painful memories for victims of sexual assault or harassment, some of whom had spoken out as part of the #MeToo movement, a campaign against sexual violence and harassment. For Trump supporters, by contrast, Ford's testimony sent a chilling reminder of how even an accusation of wrongdoing could cost men their careers. Although the accusations against Kavanaugh stalled his nomination, a Republican Senate majority had the votes to put him on the Court. Kavanaugh's hearings seemed to expand an existing gender gap, with abortion-rights supporters increasingly defining themselves as women's defenders. Whatever his confirmation symbolized, Kavanaugh seemed likely to join an anti-*Roe* majority. Like Gorsuch, Kavanaugh had been vetted by the Federalist Society, and during his time on the DC Circuit Court of Appeals, had defined an undue burden in narrow terms. It appeared that there would be five votes to revolutionize abortion doctrine.[75]

Following Kavanaugh's nomination, some pro-lifers asserted that claims about the costs of abortion were too cautious. These absolutists called for a more immediate challenge to *Roe*, preferably one featuring claims about a right to life. Personhood proponents organized a new group, the National Personhood Alliance, an offshoot of Georgia Right to Life, to protect the "God-given, inalienable right to life of all innocent human beings as legal persons at every stage of their biological development." But voters had repeatedly rejected personhood measures, and other absolutists looked for a different tactical plan.[76] Faith2Action (F2A), a group founded in 2003 by former Ohio Right to Life leader and prominent evangelical activist Janet Folger Porter, promoted heartbeat bills, laws that banned all abortions after a doctor could detect fetal cardiac activity – usually around the sixth week of pregnancy. Faith2Action did not condone abortions before the sixth week but asserted that the Court would be more willing to accept a heartbeat bill than an outright ban.[77]

Heartbeat bills also reflected the importance of debate about who had the competence to measure the costs and benefits of abortion. Porter argued that the Court would uphold a six-week ban partly because of *Gonzales*'s holding on scientific uncertainty. Porter reasoned that if the Court allowed lawmakers to restrict abortion when experts disputed a scientific conclusion, the justices would uphold a more sweeping ban when a scientific assertion was beyond question. "The heartbeat law will simply allow the Supreme Court to move the line of protection from the arbitrary marker of viability to the 'consistent and certain' marker of heartbeat," F2A explained in 2019. Abortion-rights supporters responded that the very term "heartbeat bill" was unscientific and misleading (a fetus did not have a fully-formed heart until later in pregnancy) – and said that such laws denied women equality and autonomy.[78]

Harold Cassidy still defended South Dakota's anti-coercion mandatory-counseling law. Cassidy and his allies argued that abortion clinics routinely scheduled abortions without ensuring that women gave informed consent or had an established relationship with a physician. South Dakota responded by mandating that physicians screen women for coercion and pressure. The law further required that women wait seventy-two hours before having an abortion and visit one of several state-regulated pregnancy help centers to consult about the possibility of coercion as well as about sources of support for women who kept a child and ways to preserve a relationship with their unborn child. Those challenging the law contended that CPCs had a history of misleading women and would seek to shame women about their decisions. Federal courts initially enjoined the entire law, but at the time of this writing, only the mandatory third party counseling provision remains enjoined.[79]

With the Court expected to reverse *Roe*, those working in state legislators showed no interest in middle-ground solutions. Between 2011 and 2019, lawmakers had rarely introduced heartbeat bills, much less passed them. But in 2019, more than a dozen states considered heartbeat bills, and several passed. Other states considered laws that would outlaw abortion either immediately or as soon as the Court reversed *Roe*. Prominent groups, including March for Life and Students for Life, called on the GOP to reject rape and incest exceptions to abortion bans. Some even raised the possibility of criminally punishing women for ending pregnancies, although major state proposals did not clearly authorize the punishment of women. Absolutists in state legislatures certainly thought that the remaking of the Court improved their odds, but others wondered if President Trump had changed the political calculus. For decades, groups like NRLC and NARAL had worked to reach what some called the "mushy middle" – those without strong existing opinions on abortion. But Trump claimed to have won by energizing his base even if he had limited appeal to independents and other voters in the middle. GOP state legislatures believed that taking extreme positions on abortion might pay off just as much for them. Republican Georgia Governor Brian Kemp, the winner of a close election, stated that he relished the chance to "fight for life at the Capitol and the courtroom" by backing a heartbeat bill that also defined a fetus as a person after the sixth week of pregnancy. "The dynamic has changed," stated Eric Johnson, the head of a pro-life group that backed an outright ban in Alabama. "[W]e're at a point where we need to take a bigger and bolder step."[80]

Pro-choice lawmakers and attorneys wanted to go just as far in protecting abortion-rights. In 2019, New York passed a law allowing medical professionals who were not licensed physicians to perform abortions. The law further removed abortion from the criminal code and authorized the procedure at any point in pregnancy if a woman's health was at risk. Critics claimed that because the law did not define "health," New York had legalized abortion, as a leader of New York Right to Life stated, "well past when unborn children … suffer during the course of an abortion—and up to birth." Abortion-rights supporters denounced these claims as fearmongering, suggesting that voters should trust women and doctors to make responsible choices. Pro-lifers later used the New York law (as well as a similar failed measure from Virginia) as evidence that the opposition hoped to permit legal infanticide. Senator Ben Sasse (R–NE) proposed the Born-Alive Abortion Survivors Protection Act, a law that defined standard of care for infants born alive after abortion, and legislators introduced similar measures in the states. Abortion-rights supporters insisted that state and federal law already made infanticide illegal. Despite the controversy surrounding New York's law, states still considered broad protections for abortion-rights, even later in pregnancy. In 2019 alone, thirteen states introduced bills protecting rights, three of which reflected New York's approach. Abortion-rights supporters also won sweeping victories in state court. For example, in April 2019, rather than adopting the undue burden standard, the Kansas Supreme Court held that strict scrutiny, the most demanding standard, applied to any law that affected the state constitutional right to abortion.[81]

With many expecting the Court to overturn *Roe*, rights-based arguments certainly became more visible. The champions of absolute bans and heartbeat statutes highlighted claims about fetal personhood and a fundamental right to life. Groups like NARAL defended a right to choose that seemed to be in imminent peril. But arguments about the costs and benefits of abortion still played a crucial role. "Having an abortion did not free or empower [women]," argued one supporter of a heartbeat law. "It left them with a lifetime of regret." Planned Parenthood still showcased arguments about "medical and social health benefits [that women gained] since abortion was made legal in the United States."[82]

Over the course of several decades, claims about the costs and benefits of abortion had often set the terms of debate. Defending incremental restrictions, pro-lifers had played down arguments about a right to life. Instead, abortion foes described the benefits of laws limiting abortion and denounced what they described as the dangers of the procedure. Abortion-rights supporters often responded by asserting that the procedure protected women's health and allowed them to achieve equal citizenship. To be sure, larger abortion-rights groups at times fell back on rights-based claims, especially when trying to energize potential voters or donors. Absolutists, dissenting antiabortion attorneys, and blockaders also resisted claims about the costs of abortion, seeing them as unprincipled or unproductive.

Nevertheless, both sides often framed the conflict as a fight about whether abortion helped or harmed women, families, or the larger society. As this question preoccupied pro-choice and pro-life advocates, the chasm between the two sides widened. Indeed, as both sides prepared for the probability that the Court would overturn *Roe*, state legislatures gravitated to more extreme solutions. These deepening divisions were not surprising. Neither movement let go of the constitutional right it defended. Now, however, in disputing the costs and benefits of abortion, those on opposing sides also disagreed about the effects of abortion and who could legitimately measure them. And soon, it seemed that the conflict would escalate again. Each movement would fight to determine what abortion politics looked like when the Court no longer recognized abortion as a constitutional right.

Conclusion

Since 1973, commentators have often suggested that legal and political debate about abortion in America has almost never changed. Abortion-rights activists and attorneys champion a right to choose while pro-lifers defend a right to life, and neither side has considered a compromise. To be sure, the two sides never came close to reaching a consensus on abortion at any point. Nor is there any reason to imagine that any middle ground solution would have been possible. The foundational constitutional claims of the pro-choice and pro-life movements have remained constant. But the legal history of abortion in America has been far more complex than a clash of constitutional absolutes. Between 1973 and 2019, those on opposing sides often focused on whether abortion harmed or helped women or the communities in which they lived.

The rise of claims about the costs and benefits of abortion was not inevitable. In the 1970s, as hearings on an antiabortion amendment dragged on, leaders of groups like AUL and NRLC sought to buy time. These groups pushed incremental restrictions that would lower the abortion rate and burnish the reputation of antiabortion groups. But right-to-life claims did not make sense for those defending funding bans since these laws did not formally prevent a single abortion. To justify these restrictions, NRLC leaders instead emphasized claims about the harm done by abortion. While abortion-rights supporters initially dismissed these laws as unconstitutional, ACLU and Planned Parenthood attorneys later retooled their arguments in court by stressing the real-world costs of laws that restricted access to abortion but did not formally criminalize it.

The fight about funding laws foreshadowed a broader shift in the terms of the debate. In the early 1980s, a profoundly fragmented pro-life movement failed to make progress on a constitutional amendment even though their allies controlled the White House and Congress. Once NRLC and AUL gave up on the amendment campaign, incremental restrictions – once a stopgap solution – became the centerpiece of the effort to influence Supreme Court nominations and ensure that the justices reversed *Roe*. And as these laws became the focal point of pro-life organizing, arguments about the costs of abortion changed the course of the debate.

Although their importance ebbed and flowed, claims about the costs and benefits of abortion played a crucial part in the struggle of the next several decades. In the late 1980s, when many expected a reconfigured Court to set aside a right to abortion, groups like NRLC and AUL hoped that family involvement laws would give conservative justices a perfect test case. While these groups emphasized arguments about the costs of abortion for the family, the ACLU, NARAL, and Planned Parenthood fused claims about the benefits of abortion with arguments about equal treatment for women. Abortion-rights attorneys emphasized that restrictive laws stripped young women of emerging opportunities to pursue a career or education. Related arguments helped convince the Court to continue recognizing a constitutional right to abortion. *Casey*'s new rule, the undue burden test, made arguments about the costs and benefits of specific restrictions the touchstone of constitutional analysis.

After *Casey*, groups like NARAL and Planned Parenthood stressed claims about the health benefits of abortion to raise money, lobby for the coverage of abortion in national health care reform, and explain why some seemingly modest regulations unduly burdened women. To regain influence in pro-life circles, groups like AUL and NRLC sharpened claims about the costs of abortion for women's health. By the mid-1990s, when abortion foes pursued legislation outlawing a procedure they called partial-birth abortion, the debate turned not only on whether abortion harmed or helped women but also on who had the expertise to measure the procedure's effects.

Fights about the costs and benefits at times served as a proxy for battles about the clashing constitutional rights at issue in the abortion battle. But the shift in the terms of debate was significant. The abortion dialogue of the past several decades may foreshadow what will happen if the Court overturns *Roe* – when discussion centers on the effects of abortion rather than on what the Constitution has to say.

IF ABORTION IS NO LONGER A CONSTITUTIONAL RIGHT

Following the retirement of Anthony Kennedy, commentators widely predicted the demise of abortion-rights. Many have speculated that if the Court overturns *Roe*, the conflict may eventually deescalate. Commentators as different as Ruth Bader Ginsburg and Antonin Scalia have argued that by recognizing a constitutional abortion right, the Court short-circuited a process of compromise unfolding at the state level. By awarding one side a sweeping victory, *Roe* supposedly radicalized abortion opponents who felt disenfranchised by the Court's decision. And rather than searching for arguments that would resonate with more Americans, abortion-rights groups tenaciously defended the victory they had already secured.[1] We often believe that the conflict spiraled when the courts intervened. During policy discussions of abortion, legislators could arrive at solutions that allowed for some but not all abortions. By contrast, a right to choose or a right to life was absolute, a stark claim that left no room for negotiation.[2]

However, the recent history of the abortion conflict gives us reason to be deeply skeptical of claims that overturning *Roe* will make the abortion battle less polarized, even in the long term. As an initial matter, it seems wrong to blame the 1973 decision for the ugliness of the conflict. Scholars have shown that abortion became a wedge issue well before the Court intervened. In the immediate aftermath of *Roe*, those on both sides considered compromises on everything from pregnancy discrimination to fetal rights. By the early 1980s, these middle ground solutions had come to seem politically impossible, but the shift reflected factors beyond the Court's decision, including political party realignment and the rise of the Religious Right and the New Right.[3]

The history of the abortion struggle of recent decades offers more perspective on what has (and has not) deepened the divisions in the abortion debate. Between 1973 and the present, the abortion conflict has often put center stage the kind of policy matters that *Roe* supposedly made obsolete. Most abortion opponents still would outlaw all or most abortions if it was politically possible to do so. But for decades, pro-lifers have had little choice but to focus on laws limiting access to abortion. In defending these laws, pro-lifers have emphasized claims about their benefits – and the costs of abortion itself.

Since the abortion debate has centered on questions involving the real-world consequences of abortion and access to it, we might have expected divisions to begin healing. Access restrictions seem to allow for the possibility of compromise. There are degrees of access that women could have, depending on their age, needs, aspirations, health, mental well-being, and financial circumstances. In theory, opposing activists could have entered into a more productive discussion of whom abortion helps and when. Those on different sides of the debate could have struck bargains that regulate abortion without outlawing it altogether.

But a focus on incremental restrictions has done nothing to make the conflict less bitter. As an initial matter, opposing activists still hold irreconcilable foundational beliefs about the Constitution. Debating the policy consequences of abortion has not and will not convince many to alter their basic values. Nor, in all likelihood, would a decision overturning *Roe* make any difference to the constitutional absolutes defended by either side. Many abortion foes would not be completely satisfied with anything less than the recognition of a right to life that would require, rather than allow, the states to criminalize abortion. If *Roe* is gone, abortion-rights supporters would simply resume the fight for recognition of a sweeping right to choose in state legislatures and in state and federal courts.

Discussion of the costs and benefits of abortion has further polarized the conflict. If anything, as opposing movements delved into the costs and benefits of abortion, those on either side found new sources of disagreement. Pro-choice and pro-life activists at times clashed about what counted as a cost or benefit. Those on either side did not reach a consensus about when teenagers should be independent, how the government should aid the poor, or what the best system of health care delivery would be. Opposing movements further fought about who could fairly and competently measure the costs and benefits of abortion. As a result, pro-choice and pro-life activists increasingly questioned one another's honesty and competence. Pro-choice and pro-life activists have looked to different experts and collected distinct evidence. Abortion-rights and antiabortion activists have not only fought for different constitutional principles. Those on each side have also believed in irreconcilable narratives about abortion and issues related to it.

The history studied here suggests that the polarization of the abortion debate reaches much deeper than anything that can be explained by the Court's intervention. Overturning *Roe* will not make anything better. Clashing movements likely will still defend their vision of the Constitution, hoping to eventually reverse any outcome reached by the Court. And clashes reach beyond the right to choose and the right to life. Those on opposing sides do not agree on the facts about the safety of abortion or the effects of legal restrictions. We have only begun to understand what makes the abortion conflict so intractable.

THE UNPREDICTABILITY OF THE CONFLICT

We have also fundamentally overestimated our ability to anticipate what is coming next in the abortion conflict. In 2018, when it seemed likely that the Court would undo or gut *Roe*, many felt that Kennedy's exit had shaken up a debate that had not changed in some time. Commentators called Kennedy's retirement a "game changer" – and not just because President Trump transformed the Supreme Court. Prior to Kennedy's departure, reporters, activists, and scholars decried what scholar Eileen McDonagh calls the "abortion deadlock." Neither side could reach its substantive goal. Pro-lifers failed in their quest for a constitutional abortion ban, and supporters of abortion-rights contended with a never-ending stream of restrictions. Nor, it seemed to many, did anyone make new arguments. Abortion foes championed a right to life, and supporters of legal abortion defended values involving autonomy, privacy, sex equality, and choice.[4]

If the Court undoes or substantially alters abortion-rights, the abortion debate will certainly change. Some states will almost certainly criminalize all or most abortions. At the time of this writing, four have "trigger laws" designed to ban abortion as soon as the Court reverses *Roe*. Other states have already tried to criminalize all or most abortions, and more onerous laws will follow. Abortion-rights attorneys will look for other ways to protect legal abortion, including state constitutional law and federal and state statutes. And a campaign to reinstate federal constitutional protection for abortion will almost inevitably begin. These changes could have an unforeseen impact on both the party politics of abortion and the core arguments in the debate.

To many, it seems that after a long period of stasis, the abortion battle will finally and fundamentally change.

This picture of the abortion debate is not incorrect so much as it is incomplete. The overturning of *Roe* would have a revolutionary effect on abortion law and politics. However, as this recent history of the struggle makes clear, the debate has already been far more fluid and unpredictable than many observers suggest. Fights about abortion have mirrored much more than core arguments about choice and life. Instead, battles about incremental restrictions consistently reflected a complex set of beliefs about issues only tangentially related to abortion. The abortion struggle offered a window into disagreements about poverty, personal responsibility, welfare reform, maturity, parenthood, marriage, the health care system, and the trustworthiness of the media and the government.

Most Americans have remained profoundly conflicted about abortion itself, with views that would not fit well in either the pro-choice or pro-life movement. But as opposing sides contest the costs and benefits of abortion, the spotlight turns to related issues that also divide the public, from the social safety net to the structure of the family. Even if public opinion on legal abortion remains remarkably consistent, views on what it means to be pro-life or pro-choice have changed dramatically, as have the restrictions that dominate debate.

Regardless of what happens to *Roe v. Wade*, we would be wrong to think we are coming to the end of an era of stability and stalemate. What we have seen as an unchanging set of arguments and entitlements has been anything but predictable. This history further cautions against any confident predictions about the future. Because the abortion debate has often centered on policy arguments about the costs and benefits of abortion, we often have fought about how the government should operate, how society should care for the poor, how Americans should receive health care, how teenagers should become adults, how the law should handle religious-liberty claims, and how women in America flourish. We should expect the conflict to continue turning on values and tactics that would be hard to anticipate today.

THE UGLINESS OF THE CONFLICT

The recent story of the abortion debate is not, for many, a happy one. Neither movement has won anything lasting. For pro-lifers, frustrations have consistently run high. In recent decades, abortion foes have pursued a decision overturning *Roe*. While that goal has been elusive, pro-lifers actually want much more than the Court will likely ever deliver: recognition of a right to life and the criminalization of all or most abortions. Abortion-rights supporters, by contrast, have witnessed the steady erosion of a constitutional principle, and women in many states already have extremely limited access to abortion. Regardless of the fate of *Roe*, neither movement is likely to be any more content. The abortion battle will drag on even if the Court temporarily delivers a clear win for one side. If the Court reverses *Roe*, opposing sides will simply fight heated battles in each state. The kind of absolute constitutional protection demanded by both sides will not likely arrive with the overruling of *Roe*, and any victory, no matter how sweeping, will simply trigger a new round of fighting. Those who have witnessed the debate at a distance have no more reason for optimism. For most Americans, the recent history of the abortion conflict is a tale of hopeless polarization, personal hatreds, and political dysfunction. While the terms of the abortion debate may change, it never becomes any less ugly.

History offers no easy solutions for those hoping for a more productive discussion of abortion in America. But the story of recent decades suggests that we can no longer look so exclusively at the Supreme Court in explaining how bad things have become. Nor does the decision to treat abortion as a constitutional right account for the dismal state of the abortion battle. Politicians, grassroots activists, attorneys, and ordinary voters also have themselves to blame.

To some degree, the growing divide in the abortion debate reflects the polarization of both American party politics and media. As both movements have strengthened their reliance on a single party, the growing divisions between the Republican and Democratic Parties affected the abortion struggle. But both movements have profited strategically from taking polarized positions on the costs and benefits of abortion. Grassroots activists and lawyers have hoped to gain an advantage in fundraising or rallying the base by taking more extreme positions on the real-world effects of abortion. And by taking sharply different positions on the costs and benefits of abortion, both movements hope to motivate voters and ensure the loyalty of a party worried about maintaining the allegiance of single-issue voters. Far from bringing opposing movements closer together, discussing the policy consequences of abortion has pushed the two sides further apart. The conflict will continue to escalate if we believe the Supreme Court bears most of the responsibility for the state of the abortion debate – or if we expect things to improve automatically if the Court removes itself from the equation.

The time has come to reconsider why we have arrived at such an impasse. The stakes are high, for the abortion debate has always reflected other battles that define American culture. The abortion fight has shaped and reflected national conversations about health care, the needs of the poor, the role and size of government, the fortunes of the family, and the value and meaning of scientific expertise. We should expect future discussions of abortion to be no less meaningful. Regardless of the fate of *Roe v. Wade*, the legal history of abortion will still tell a story about what kind of country the United States has been and will become.

Notes

INTRODUCTION

1 Sarah McCammon, "With Higher Stakes in the Abortion Debate, Activists March on Washington," *NPR*, January 18, 2019, www.npr.org/2019/01/18/686260253/with-higher-stakes-in-the-abortion-debate-activists-march-on-washington, accessed March 28, 2019. For Mancini's statement, see Jeanne Mancini, "March for Life: Science Has Changed since *Roe v. Wade*, Now Abortion Laws Must Change," *USA Today*, January 18, 2019, www.usatoday.com/story/opinion/2019/01/18/march-life-revisit-abortion-decision-roe-wade-medical-discoveries-column/2593096002, accessed March 28, 2019. On the framing of the 2019 March for Life, see Michelle Boorstein, Julie Zauzmer, and Marisa Iati, "Trump and Pence Give Surprise Addresses at March for Life," *Washington Post*, January 18, 2019, www.washingtonpost.com/religion/2019/01/18/march-life-says-its-pro-science-despite-medical-consensus-favoring-abortion-access, accessed March 1, 2019; Julie Zauzmer, "The Abortion Issue Is More Polarized than Ever, Leading Some to View March for Life as a Republican Rally," *Washington Post*, January 17, 2019, www.washingtonpost.com/religion/2019/01/17/abortion-issue-is-more-polarized-than-ever-leading-some-view-march-life-republican-rally, accessed March 1, 2019; Mary Ziegler, "The Abortion Wars Have Become a Fight Over Science," *New York Times*, January 22, 2019, www.nytimes.com/2019/01/22/opinion/abortion-roe-science.html, accessed March 1, 2019. For the Georgia law, see House Bill 481, www.legis.ga.gov/Legislation/20192020/187013.pdf, accessed May 24, 2019. For the Alabama law, see "Alabama Abortion Law Passes: Read the Bill," *AL.com*, May 16, 2019, www.al.com/news/2019/05/alabama-abortion-ban-passes-read-the-bill.html, accessed May 24, 2019.

2 For Dworkin's argument about rights as trumps, see Ronald Dworkin, *Taking Rights Seriously* (Cambridge, MA: Harvard University Press, 1977), xi, 133, 188. For Tribe's argument, see Laurence H. Tribe, *Abortion: The Clash of Absolutes* (Cambridge, MA: Harvard University Press, 1992). For analysis of the influence and limits of Dworkin's theory, see Ashutosh Bhagwat, *The Myth of Rights: The Purposes and Limits of Constitutional Rights* (New York: Oxford University Press, 2010), 25–34. Other theorists have created alternatives to Dworkin's theory or questioned its accuracy as a description of American

constitutional law. Some scholars emphasize that constitutional jurisprudence treats rights not as a trump but as an important value balanced against competing considerations. See T. Alexander Aleinikoff, "Constitutional Law in the Age of Balancing," *Yale Law Journal* 96 (1987): 943–952. Certainly, when it comes to abortion law, this interpretation has merit. Nevertheless, opposing activists, politicians, and lawyers sometimes defined rights as trumps, even as constitutional jurisprudence shifted. The arguments studied here center on the public rhetoric of rights.

3 See Tribe, *The Clash of Absolutes.*

4 For scholarship on the differences between consequence- and rights-based arguments, see Note, "Rights in Flux: Nonconsequentialism, Consequentialism, and the Judicial Role," *Harvard Law Review* 130 (2017): 1436–1457; Richard M. Fallon Jr., "Individual Rights and the Powers of Government," *Georgia Law Review* 27 (1993): 368–371. For Scanlon's argument, see T. M. Scanlon, "Rights, Goals, and Fairness," in *Consequentialism and Its Critics* ed. Samuel Scheffler (New York: Oxford University Press, 1988), 74–85.

5 See Richard A. Posner, *Law, Pragmatism, and Democracy* (Cambridge, MA: Harvard University Press, 2003), 79, 124–127 (discussing *Roe* as a decision that had the effect of stifling "potentially worthwhile social experimentation"); Jeffrey Rosen, *The Most Democratic Branch: How the Courts Serve America* (New York: Oxford University Press, 2006), 96 ("[W]hen the Supreme Court struck some of these abortion restrictions down in the late 1970s and '80s, it finally energized abortion opponents who otherwise would have had to make their case in the political arena"); *Planned Parenthood of Southeastern Pennsylvania v. Casey,* 505 U.S. 833, 1001–1005 (1992) (plurality decision) (Scalia, J., dissenting); Ruth Bader Ginsburg, "Some Thoughts on Autonomy and Equality in Relation to *Roe v. Wade,*" *North Carolina Law Review* 63 (1985): 382–386; Robin West, "From Choice to Reproductive Justice: De-constitutionalizing Abortion-Rights," *Yale Law Journal* 118 (2009): 1394, 1394–1404.

1 *ROE V. WADE* AND THE RISE OF RIGHTS ARGUMENTS

1 On the commercialization and spread of abortion in the 1840s, see James C. Mohr, *Abortion in America: The Origins and Evolution of National Policy, 1800–1900* (New York: Oxford University Press, 1979), 126–127; Leslie J. Reagan, *When Abortion Was a Crime: Women, Medicine, and the Law in the United States, 1867–1973* (Berkeley: University of California Press, 1997), 10; Janet Farrell Brodie, *Contraception and Abortion in Nineteenth-Century America* (Ithaca, NY: Cornell University Press, 1994), 254–257.

2 See Mohr, *Abortion in America,* 145–189; Reagan, *When Abortion Was a Crime,* 10–13; Laurence H. Tribe, *Abortion: The Clash of Absolutes* (New York: W. W. Norton, 1992), 30.

3 Horatio Storer, *Why Not? A Book for Every Woman* (Boston: Lee and Shepherd, 1868), 85. For more on concerns about immigration and "race suicide," see Sara Dubow, *Ourselves Unborn: A History of the Fetus in Modern America* (New York: Oxford University Press, 2010), 26–32; Reagan, *When Abortion Was a Crime,* 9–13; Kristin Luker, *Abortion and the Politics of Motherhood* (Berkeley: University of California Press, 1984), 10–23.

4 On the spread of abortion bans and the continuing practice of abortion in the period, see Reagan, *When Abortion Was a Crime,* 10–15; Brodie, *Contraception and Abortion,* 254–255; Dubow, *Ourselves Unborn,* 32–40.

5 For Taussig's argument, see Frederick Taussig, *Abortion, Spontaneous and Induced: Medical and Social Aspects* (St. Louis, MO: Mosby, 1936), 448. On the changes to abortion practice in the 1930s and 1940s, see Reagan, *When Abortion Was a Crime*, 10–25; Luker, *Abortion and the Politics of Motherhood*, 192.

6 Lawrence Lader, "The Scandal of Abortion Laws," *New York Times*, April 25, 1965, SM32.

7 *NARAL Speaker and Debater's Notebook* excerpt (nd, c. 1972), NARAL, Carton 7, 1972 Debating the Opposition Folder. On the spreading use of psychiatric indications for abortion, see C. Lee Buxton, "One Doctor's Opinion of Abortion," *American Journal of Nursing* 68 (1968): 1026–1028; Herbert Packer and Ralph Gampell, "Therapeutic Abortion: A Problem in Law and Medicine," *Stanford Law Review* 11 (1959): 417–455.

8 On the thalidomide controversy, see Leslie J. Reagan, *Dangerous Pregnancies: Mothers, Disabilities, and Abortion in Modern America* (Berkeley: University of California Press, 2010), 60–63; Mary Ann Glendon, *Abortion and Divorce in Western Law* (Cambridge, MA: Harvard University Press, 1987), 12.

9 See "U.S. Mother Seeks Aid from Sweden," *New York Times*, August 5, 1962, 64; "Mother Loses Round in Legal Battle for Abortion," *New York Times*, July 31, 1962, 9; "Mother, Rebuffed in Arizona, May Seek Abortion Elsewhere," *New York Times*, August 1, 1962, 9.

10 See Reagan, *Dangerous Pregnancies*, 57; Dubow, *Ourselves Unborn*, 65.

11 Ruth Lidz, "Review: More Light on Abortion," *Family Planning Perspectives* 4 (1971): 5–7. For Force's argument: Robert Force, "Legal Problems of Abortion Reform," *Administrative Review* 19 (1967): 371. For Planned Parenthood's 1964 discussion, see "Need New Abortion Laws," *Science Newsletter*, December 1964, 397; see also "Abortion Laws Condemned," *Science News*, 1966, 320.

12 For Mahoney's statement: Dennis Mahoney, "Therapeutic Abortions–The Psychiatric Indication–A Double-Edged Sword," *Dickinson Law Review* 72 (1968): 288–289. For the other scholar's comment: John G. Herbert, "Is Legalized Abortion the Solution to Criminal Abortion?," *University of Colorado Law Review* 37 (1964): 291; see also Martin Tolchin, "Doctors Divided on Issue," *New York Times*, February 27, 1967, 23.

13 For McDonagh's statement: Patricia Krizmis, "Abortion Bill Proposal Hit by Six Bishops," *Chicago Tribune*, March 21, 1969, D20. For Ford's statement: Linda Greenhouse, "Constitutional Question: Is There a Right to Abortion?" *New York Times*, January 25, 1970, 200.

14 David J. Garrow, *Liberty and Sexuality: The Right to Privacy and the Making of Roe v. Wade* (Berkeley: University of California Press, 1998), 221. For more on the early reform campaign, see Suzanne Staggenborg, *The Pro-choice Movement: Organization and Activism in the Abortion Conflict* (New York: Oxford University Press, 1991), 34–50; Reagan, *When Abortion Was a Crime*, 221–239. For the ALI proposal: American Law Institute, Model Penal Code: Abortion (1959).

15 Daniel K. Williams, *Defenders of the Unborn: The Pro-life Movement before Roe v. Wade* (New York: Oxford University Press, 2016), 55.

16 For mentions in early legal treatises, see Christopher G. Tiedeman, *Treatise on State and Federal Control of Persons and Property in the United States Considered from Both a Civil and Criminal Standpoint*, vol. 1 (New York: F. H. Thomas Law Book Co., 1900), 36; Walter S. Cox, *Lessons in Laws for Women*, vol. 1 (New York: Brentano's, 1901), 257. For examples of the later medical manuals, see Patrick Finney and Patrick O'Brien, *Moral Problems in Hospital Practice: A Practical Handbook* (New York: Read Press, 1956);

Edwin Healy, *Medical Ethics*, vol. 1 (Chicago: Loyola University Press, 1956), 193; Emmanuel Hayt et al., *Law of Hospital and Nurse*, vol. 1 (New York: Hospital Textbook Co., 1958), 263.

17 "Abortion Change Gains in Georgia," *New York Times*, February 12, 1967, 64. For McEntegart's pastoral letter, see "Catholics to Hear Attack on Abortion," *New York Times*, February 25, 1968, 56; see also Marcie Rasmussen, "Abortion Reforms Gain in States," *Atlanta Journal-Constitution*, February 6, 1967, 8; "Public Hearing on Abortion Law to Be Held Today," *Atlanta Journal-Constitution*, January 6, 1968, 6. For arguments made by Catholic attorneys about fetal rights in California, see "Group Opposed to Legal Abortions," *Sun Reporter*, March 1, 1969, 1; Walter Trinkaus, "Letter to the Editor," *Los Angeles Times*, March 25, 1972, B4.

18 For a sample of these constitutional arguments, see William J. Kenealy, "Law and Morals," *Catholic Lawyer* 9 (1963): 201–203; Robert M. Byrn, "Abortion in Perspective," *Duquesne Law Review* 5 (1966): 134–135; David Louisell, "The Practice of Medicine and the Due Process of Law," *UCLA Review* 16 (1968–1969): 234; A. James Quinn and James A. Griffin, "The Rights of the Unborn," *Jurist* 3 (1971): 578.

19 Lynn Lilliston, "Mothers Fight for Right to Life," *Los Angeles Times*, February 23, 1967, C1.

20 On the early antiabortion movement, see Williams, *Defenders of the Unborn*; Mary Ziegler, *After Roe: The Lost History of the Abortion Debate* (Cambridge, MA: Harvard University Press, 2015), 38–50.

21 Greenhouse, "Constitutional Question," 200. For more on the shift from reform to repeal, see *Before Roe v. Wade: Voices That Shaped the Supreme Court's Ruling* eds. Reva B. Siegel and Linda Greenhouse (New Haven, CT: Yale University Press, 2010), 127–197. On the repeal movement, see Keith Monroe, "How California's Abortion Law Isn't Working," *New York Times*, December 29, 1968, SM10; see also Martin Tolchin, "Doctors Divided on Issue," *New York Times*, February 27, 1967, 1; Robert McFadden, "Flaws in Abortion Reform Found in an 8-State Study," *New York Times*, April 13, 1970, 1. For Kimmey's statement: Siegel and Greenhouse, *Before Roe v. Wade*, 33–34.

22 See Facts and Figures on Abortion of Interest to All Americans (1972), PPFA II, Box 93, Folder 84. On Planned Parenthood's endorsement, see Morris Kaplan, "Abortion and Sterilization Win Support of Planned Parenthood," *New York Times*, November 14, 1968, 50; Meeting Minutes, Planned Parenthood-World Population Board of Directors (disseminated February 8, 1969), PPFA I, Box 49, Folder 9. On ZPG's work on abortion, see Ziegler, *After Roe*, 99–105. For more on abortion-rights arguments before *Roe*, see Reva B. Siegel and Linda Greenhouse, "The Unfinished Story of *Roe v. Wade*," Yale Law School, Public Law Research Paper, June 2018.

23 On NOW's abortion endorsement, see NOW National Conference Minutes (November 18–19, 1967), 2–6, BFP, Carton 43, Folder 1544. On WONAAC, see Staggenborg, *The Prochoice Movement*, 26; Ann M. Valk, *Radical Sisters: Second-Wave Feminism and Black Liberation in Washington* (Urbana: University of Illinois Press, 2008), 205; Reagan, *When Abortion Was a Crime*, 257–334.

24 For the court's decision in *Abele v. Markle*, see 342 F. Supp. 224 (D.Conn. 1972). For the California Supreme Court's decision, see *People v. Belous*, 458 P.2d 194 (Cal. 1969). For more on pre-*Roe* litigation, see Garrow, *Liberty and Sexuality*, 273–330.

25 On the early years of NRLC, see Ziegler, *After Roe*, 38–42; Williams, *Defenders of the Unborn*, 94–97. For more on the early work of NRLC, see National Meeting: Right to Life Movement Agenda (July 31–August 3, 1970), ACCL, Box 4, 1970 National Right to Life Committee Folder; National Right to Life Committee Board of Directors Meeting Minutes (December 9, 1972), 3, ACCL, Box 4, 1972 National Right to Life Committee Folder; Martin McKernan, NRLC Legal Counsel, Legal Report (c. 1970), 3–4, ACCL, Box 4, 1970 National Right to Life Committee Folder.

26 On the early years of AUL, see Ziegler, *After Roe*, 38–42. For more on AUL's early activities, see Fundraising Letter (April 17, 1974), AUL, Executive File, Folder 91; Fundraising Letter (September 1, 1972), AUL, Executive File, Folder 91; Dr. Joseph Stanton to AUL Officers et al. (December 14, 1972), GHW, Box 404, Folder 4; "Statement of George Huntston Williams, Chairman of Americans United for Life" (November 19, 1971), 2, AUL, The Executive File, Folder 91; Informational Letter to AUL Members (June 19, 1972), AUL, The Executive File, Folder 91; George Huntston Williams to AUL Members of Board et al., "Progress Report on AUL" (August 3, 1972), AUL, The Executive File, Folder 91.

27 On the Minnesota and New York organizations, see Ziegler, *After Roe*, 38–43; Williams, *Defenders of the Unborn*, 154–156, 176, 186. For Rockefeller's veto, see William E. Farrell, "Government Vetoes Abortion Repeal as Not Justified," *New York Times*, May 14, 1972, www.nytimes.com/1972/05/14/archives/governor-vetoes-abortion-repeal-as-not-justified-tells-legis lature.html, accessed March 29, 2019.

28 See *Poe v. Ullman*, 367 U.S. 497, 502 (1961). On the effort to launch another round of constitutional litigation, see "Connecticut Clinic to Test Birth Law," *New York Times*, October 27, 1961, 10; Richard H. Parke, "Birth Clinic Tests Connecticut Law," *New York Times*, November 3, 1961, 37. For more on *Poe*, see Garrow, *Liberty and Sexuality*, 145–200; Leigh Ann Wheeler, *How Sex Became a Civil Liberty* (New York: Oxford University Press, 2012), xi–xxxiii; N. E. H. Hull and Peter Hoffer, *Roe v. Wade: The Abortion-Rights Controversy in American History* (Lawrence: University of Kansas Press, 2010), 82–83.

29 *Griswold v. Connecticut*, 381 U.S. 479, 485–486 (1965). For Goldberg's opinion, see ibid., 495 (Goldberg, J., concurring). For contemporary reaction to the *Griswold* decision, see "High Court Bars Curbs on Birth Control," *New York Times*, June 8, 1965, 1; Sydney H. Schanberg, "Legislature Voids Birth Control Ban, in Effect for 84 Years," *New York Times*, June 17, 1965, 1.

30 *Eisenstadt v. Baird*, 405 U.S. 438, 446–455 (1972). For a sample of scholarly reaction to the decision, see Gerald Gunther, "The Supreme Court 1971 Term–Foreword: In Search of Evolving Doctrine on a Changing Court: A Model for a Newer Equal Protection," *Harvard Law Review* 86 (1972): 1–48; Philip B. Kurland, "1971 Term: The Year of the Stewart-White Court," *Supreme Court Review* 1972 (1972): 181–329.

31 For examples of early arguments about privacy and choice, see Statement of Wilma Scott Heide on Abortion (1971), WSH, Box 14, Folder 11; NARAL Executive Committee Meeting Minutes (July 12–13, 1974), 2, NARAL, Carton 1, 1974 Executive Committee Minutes. For more on the importance of privacy arguments, see Garrow, *Liberty and Sexuality*, 529–590; Greenhouse and Siegel, *Before Roe v. Wade*, 109–146.

32 On equality arguments made before *Roe*, see Greenhouse and Siegel, *Before Roe v. Wade*, 39–44, 140–147; Ziegler, *After Roe*, 14–23, 104.

33 For Hodgson's statement: Jane E. Hodgson, "The Law and Reality in 1970," *Mayo Alumnus* (1970), 1–4. For Friedan's statement: Betty Friedan, "Abortion: A Woman's Civil Right" (1969), BFP, Carton 43, Folder 1457. This chapter later discusses additional arguments about the consequences of unplanned pregnancy for women.

34 On the diversity of the population-control movement, see Simone Caron, *Who Chooses? American Reproductive History since 1830* (Gainesville: University Press of Florida, 2008), 150–151, 153–155, 160–163; Matthew James Connelly, *Fatal Misconception: The Struggle to Control World Population* (Cambridge: Harvard University Press, 2008), 240–248; Thomas M. Shapiro, *Population Control Politics: Women, Sterilization, and Reproductive Choice* (Philadelphia: Temple University Press, 1985); Donald Critchlow, "Birth Control, Population, and Family Planning: An Overview," in *The Politics of Abortion and Birth Control in Historical Perspective* ed. Donald T. Critchlow (University Park: Pennsylvania State University Press, 1996), 1–22; Staggenborg, *The Pro-choice Movement*, 113. For further arguments about the costs of criminal abortion laws, see Larry Lader to NARAL Board Members Re: The Damage to the Abortion Movement from the Second Hour of the TV Report on the American Commission on Population Control (1972), NARAL Carton 7, Debating the Opposition Folder. For NARAL's debate manual, see 1972 NARAL Debate Manual, 1–6; see also Pamphlet, "Legal Abortion Means" (n. d., ca. 1972), NARAL, Carton 7, Debating the Opposition Folder.

35 See Brief for the Appellants, 109, *Roe v. Wade*, 410 U.S. 113 (1973) (Nos. 70–18, 70–40); see also Motion for Leave to File Brief and Brief Amici Curiae, 34, *Roe v. Wade*, 410 U.S. 113 (1973) (Nos. 70–18, 70–40); Motion for Leave to File Brief Amici Curiae, 16, *Roe v. Wade*, 410 U.S. 113 (1973) (Nos. 70–18, 70–40).

36 On the early litigation in *Roe* and *Doe v. Bolton*, see *Roe v. Wade*, 314 F. Supp. 1217 (N.D. Tex. 1970); *Doe v. Bolton*, 319 F. Supp. 1048 (N.D. Ga. 1970).

37 On early drafts of *Roe*, see Garrow, *Liberty and Sexuality*, 549–576; Bernard Schwartz, *Decision: How the Supreme Court Decides Cases* (New York: Oxford University Press, 1996), 232; Michael Graetz and Linda Greenhouse, *The Burger Court and the Rise of the Judicial Right* (New York: Simon and Schuster, 2016), 140–141; see also Clarke Forsythe, *Abuse of Discretion: The Inside Story of Roe v. Wade* (New York: Encounter Books, 2013). For the Court's decision in *Vuitch*, see *United States v. Vuitch*, 402 U.S. 62 (1971).

38 *Roe v. Wade*, 410 U.S. 113, 116, 130–135 (1973). *Roe* also dealt with arguments about whether the Court had jurisdiction to hear the case. One issue involved whether the case was moot because some of the women involved in challenging the law had already terminated their pregnancies. Another turned on whether all of the plaintiffs in the case had standing to bring a challenge. The Court held that neither concern defeated jurisdiction in the case. See ibid., 116–130. Standing doctrine spoke to when a party could bring a suit in court. Generally, the doctrine required that a party had faced or would face concrete harm that a court could redress.

39 Ibid., 147–151.

40 Ibid., 152–156.

41 Ibid., 156–159.

42 Ibid., 159–163.

43 See ibid., 163–165. On the decision in *Doe v. Bolton*, see *Doe v. Bolton*, 410 U.S. 179 (1973).

44 For a recollection of pre-*Roe* support for a fetal life amendment, see, e.g., Statement of Senator John Ashcroft (June 5, 1998), in Congressional Record: 144 Cong. Rec. 11264 (1998)(statement of Sen. Aschcroft).

45 NRLC Ad Hoc Strategy Meeting Minutes (February 11, 1973), 1–12, ACCL, Box 4, 1973 National Right to Life Committee Folder.

46 See "Memorandum on Progress" (September 1973), ACCL, Box 4, 1973 National Right to Life Committee Folder 2.

47 Resolution Number Three (1973), ACCL, Box 4, 1973 National Right to Life Committee Folder 2. For more on antiabortion opposition to a states-rights proposal, see Robert Byrn to Edward Golden, Strategy Memorandum (February 20, 1973), ACCL, Box 4, 1973 National Right to Life Committee Folder 2; Dennis Horan to NRLC Board of Directors et al. (January 19, 1974), 2, ACCL, Box 4, 1974 National Right to Life Committee Folder; Abortion Part II: Testimony on S. 119 and S. 130 Before the Subcommittee on Constitutional Amendments of the Senate Judiciary Committee, 93d Congress 2d Sess. (1974) 366–367 (Statement of Representative G. William Whitehurst).

48 See National Committee for a Human Life Amendment, "Human Life Amendment: Major Texts," https://web.archive.org/web/20071202101135/http://www.nchla.org/datasource/idocuments/HLAmajortexts.pdf, accessed September 15, 2017.

49 On scholars' views about the problems with antiabortion amendments circulating in the mid-1970s, see Joseph Witherspoon to NRLC Executive Committee (August 14, 1973), ACCL, Box 4, 1973 National Right to Life Committee Folder 3; Robert Sassone to Marjory Mecklenburg (November 8, 1973), ACCL, Box 4, National Right to Life Committee Folder 3; National Right to Life Committee Board of Directors Meeting Minutes (December 2, 1973), ACCL, Box 4, National Right to Life Committee Folder 3; Nellie Gray to the National Right to Life Board of Directors (December 8, 1973), ACCL, Box 4, National Right to Life Committee Folder 1; Joseph Witherspoon to Dr. Joseph Stanton (December 21, 1973), ACCL, Box 4, National Right to Life Committee Folder 1.

50 On the formation and early work of March for Life, see Nellie Gray to the National Right to Life Committee Board of Directors (February 10, 1974), ACCL, Box 8, 1974 National Right to Life Committee Folder; *March for Life Program: Five Years of Pro-life Action for a Human Life Amendment* (Washington, DC: March for Life, 1978); Barbara Gamarekian, "Leader of 'March for Life' Sees Issue as Apocalyptic," *New York Times*, March 13, 1981, A18. On the early work of ACCL, see William Hunt and Joseph Lampe, "Strategy Considerations for ACCL Involvement in Abortion and Related Issues" (1974), ACCL, Box 8, 1974 National Right to Life Committee Folder; American Citizens Concerned for Life, Model Letter in Support of the Pregnancy Discrimination Act (1977), 1, ACCL, Box 15, ACCL Folder 1; American Citizens Concerned for Life, "Philosophy and Objectives" (1978), ACCL, Box 15, ACCL Folder 1. On the early work of Birthright, see Williams, *Defenders of the Unborn*, 154–157.

51 On the start of the hearings, see Linda Charlton, "Start of Life Debated at Abortion Hearing," *New York Times*, May 21, 1974, 33. For arguments on the movement's diversity, see Abortion Part I: Testimony on S. 119 and S. 130 before the Senate Subcommittee on Constitutional Amendments of the Senate Judiciary Committee, 93d Congress 2d Sess. (1974) 287–288 (Statement of Rabbi David Bleich); Ibid., 329–331 (Statement of Pastor Robert Holbrook). For the movement's biological arguments, see Abortion Part III:

Testimony on S. 119 and S. 130 before the Senate Subcommittee on Constitutional Amendments of the Senate Judiciary Committee, 93d Cong., 2d Sess. (1974) 428–432 (Statement of Representative Lawrence Hogan); Abortion Part II: Testimony on S. 119 and S. 130 before the Senate Subcommittee on Constitutional Amendments of the Senate Judiciary Committee, 93d Cong. 2d Sess. (1974) 452 (Statement of Dr. William Colliton, Jr.).

52 Brief of Amicus Curiae for the United States Catholic Conference, 16–17, *Planned Parenthood of Central Missouri v. Danforth*, 428 U.S. 52 (1976) (Nos. 74–1151, 74–1419); see also Brief as Amicus Curiae for Dr. Eugene Diamond and Americans United for Life, 27–28, 35–37, *Planned Parenthood of Central Missouri v. Danforth*, 428 U.S. 52 (1976) (Nos. 74–1151, 74–1419). For Witherspoon's statement: Testimony before the House Subcommittee on Civil and Constitutional Rights of the House Judiciary Committee, 94th Cong. 2d Sess. (1976) 26 (Statement of Professor Joseph Witherspoon).

53 On the claimed influence of pro-lifers on elections in the late 1970s, see Dolores Barclay and Victoria Graham, "Abortion: It Ends Political Lives, Too," *Chicago Tribune*, February 15, 1976, 1; John Herbers, "Anti-abortionists' Impact Felt in Elections across the Nation," *New York Times*, June 20, 1978, A1; Dave Andrusko, "Pro-life Gains, President, 10 Senators and More," *National Right to Life News*, November 19, 1980, JRS, 1980 National Right to Life News Box; "National Right to Life PAC Proclaims Victories," *National Right to Life News*, November 18, 1980, JRS, 1980 National Right to Life News Box.

54 On *Edelin*, see Frank Susman to Judy Mears, Jimmye Kimmey, et al. (January 18, 1975), 1–4, ACLU, Box 1355, *Edelin v. Massachusetts*; Commonwealth's Motion in Opposition to Defendant's Motion to Dismiss (February 1975), 48–49, ACLU, Box 1355, *Edelin v. Massachusetts*; see also Lawrence Altman, "Doctor Guilty in Death of a Fetus," *New York Times*, February 16, 1975, A1; John Kifner, "Abortion Foe Cites Role," *New York Times*, February 17, 1975, 41.

55 For the Massachusetts Supreme Judicial Court's decision, see *Com. v. Edelin*, 359 N.E.2d 4 (Mass. 1976). On the immediate reaction to the matter within the antiabortion movement, see Mildred Jefferson, "Lifelines," *National Right to Life News*, February 1977, JRS, 1977 National Right to Life News Box.

56 On the rise of pro-life incrementalism, see Ziegler, *After Roe*, 38–67; Reva B. Siegel, "Dignity and the Politics of Protection: Abortion Restrictions Under *Casey/Carhart*," *Yale Law Journal* 117 (2008): 1707–1712; David J. Garrow, "Significant Risks: *Gonzales v. Carhart* and the Future of Abortion Law" *Supreme Court Review* 2007 (2007): 34–42.

2 THE HYDE AMENDMENT AND ITS AFTERMATH

1 Dexter Duggan, interview with Mary Ziegler, January 13, 2017.

2 Ibid. For examples of Duggan's writings on abortion, see Clipping, Dexter Duggan, "Aborting Court Ignorance," *Orange County Register*, August 4, 1985, DDP, on file with the author; Dexter Duggan, "Law Professors Evaluate June 20 Rulings," *National Right to Life News*, September 1977, 2, JRS, 1977 National Right to Life News Box; Dexter Duggan, "Malice Seen in Abortions for the Poor," *National Right to Life News*, October 1977, 2, JRS, 1977 National Right to Life News Box.

3 Duggan, interview.

4 Duggan, interview. For more on Duggan's tax protest, see Dexter Duggan to William F. Buckley Jr. (April 5, 1973), DDP, on file with the author; Dexter Duggan to Chief of the Correspondence Section for the Internal Revenue Service (June 4, 1973), DDP, on file with the author; "Pro-lifers Deny Government's Right to Tax for Abortions," *National Right to Life News*, May 1975, 5, JRS, 1975 National Right to Life News Box.

5 Karen Mulhauser, interview with Mary Ziegler, January 6, 2017. For more on Mulhauser's activism, see Johanna Schoen, *Abortion after Roe* (Chapel Hill: University of North Carolina Press, 2015), 97; Mary Ziegler, *After Roe: The Lost History of the Abortion Debate* (Cambridge, MA: Harvard University Press, 2015), 123–124, 138–139, 213–215; Suzanne Staggenborg, *The Pro-choice Movement: Organization and Activism in the Abortion Conflict* (New York: Oxford University Press, 1991), 84, 88, 96, 107.

6 Mulhauser, interview.

7 Ibid. This chapter later discusses at greater length the Hyde Amendment and NARAL's strategy to defeat it.

8 See Ziegler, *After Roe*, 96–157; Daniel K. Williams, *Defenders of the Unborn: The Pro-life Movement before Roe v. Wade* (New York: Oxford University Press, 2016), 113–116; Schoen, *Abortion after Roe*, 72.

9 On the rise and fall of the welfare-rights movement, see Premilla Nadasen, *Rethinking the Welfare Rights Movement* (New York: Routledge, 2012); Felicia Kornbluh, *The Battle for Welfare Rights: Politics and Poverty in Modern America* (Philadelphia: University of Pennsylvania Press, 2007); Martha F. Davis, *Brutal Need: Lawyers and the Welfare-Rights Movement, 1960–1973* (New Haven, CT: Yale University Press, 1993); Elizabeth Bussiere, *(Dis)Entitling the Poor: The Warren Court, Welfare Rights, and the American Political Tradition* (University Park: Pennsylvania State University Press, 1997). On Nixon's guaranteed-income plan, see Bruce Steensland, *The Failed Welfare Revolution: America's Struggle over Guaranteed Income Policy* (Princeton, NJ: Princeton University Press, 2008), 79–159; Davis, *Brutal Need*, 139; Marissa Chappell, *The War on Welfare: Family, Poverty and Politics in Modern America* (Philadelphia: University of Pennsylvania Press, 2010), 59–124.

10 On changing attitudes toward welfare, see Steensland, *The Failed Welfare Revolution*, 110–159; Chappell, *The War on Welfare*, 100–124; Kornbluh, *The Battle for Welfare Rights*, 161–183. On the timing and causes of political party polarization, see James E. Campbell, *Polarized: Making Sense of a Divided America* (Princeton, NJ: Princeton University Press, 2016), 119–170; Sean M. Theriault, *Party Polarization in Congress* (New York: Cambridge University Press, 2008), 4–30; Nolan McCarty, Keith Poole, and Howard Rosenthal, *Polarized America: The Dance of Ideology and Unequal Riches* 2nd ed. (Cambridge, MA: MIT Press, 2016), 5–50.

11 See Dan Andriacco, "More on Black Genocide," *National Right to Life News*, October 1974, 8, JRS, 1974 National Right to Life News Box; see also NRLC Pamphlet, "Abortion … Where Does It End?" (1975), ACCL, Box 8, 1975 NRLC Folder; NRLC Press Release, NRLC Press Release (March 6, 1974), ACCL, Box 8, 1974 NRLC Folder; see also "Appeals Court Holds Missouri Welfare Law Unconstitutional," *National Right to Life News*, January 1975, 4, JRS, 1975 National Right to Life News Box.

12 For pro-life arguments on the consequences of abortion funding, see Dexter Duggan to Chief of the Correspondence Section for the Internal Revenue Service, 1; "Pro-lifers Deny

Government's Right to Tax for Abortions," *National Right to Life News*, 5. For abortion-rights claims about the consequences of abortion funding, see NARAL Newsletter (July 1976), 4, NARAL, Box 41, Folder 10; NARAL, Memo, "Arguments against the Hyde Amendment" (nd, ca. 1976), NARAL, Box 41, Folder 10.

13 This chapter later discusses the constitutional debate about the consequences of funding restrictions.

14 Lee Gidding to NARAL Board of Directors (February 7, 1973), 1–2, NARAL, Carton 1, 1973–1974 Executive Committee Folder. For more on this attitude, see NARAL Executive Committee Meeting Minutes (February 5, 1973), NARAL, Carton 1, 1973–1974 Executive Committee Minutes Folder; NARAL Executive Committee Meeting Minutes (March 27, 1973), NARAL, Carton 1, 1973–1974 Executive Committee Meeting Minutes Folder. For recollections of movement attitudes after *Roe*: Mulhauser, interview; Frances Kissling, interview with Mary Ziegler, January 11, 2017; Carolyn Buhl, interview with Mary Ziegler, January 27, 2017.

15 See Edward Weinstock et al., "Legal Abortions in the United States since the 1973 Supreme Court Decisions," *Family Planning Perspectives* 17 (1974–1975): 24–31. For more on access issues in the period, see Schoen, *Abortion after Roe*, 30–56. On the abortion rate by race, see Christopher Tietze, "Legal Abortion in the United States: Rates and Ratios by Race and Age, 1972–1974," *Family Planning Perspectives* 9 (1977): 13–14. On the death rate in illegal abortions by race, see Willard Cates Jr. and Roger Rochat, "Illegal Abortions in the United States, 1972–1974," *Family Planning Perspectives* 8 (1976): 87.

16 Lee Gidding to NARAL Directors et al. (February 7, 1973), 1–2, NARAL, Carton 1, 1973–1974 Executive Committee Folder. For more on NARAL's focus on access, see NARAL Executive Committee Meeting Minutes (March 4, 1973), NARAL, Carton 1, 1973–1974 Executive Committee Folder; Board of Directors Minutes (October 1, 1973), NARAL, Carton 1, 1973–1974 Executive Committee Folder.

17 Policy Statement, NOW Task Force on Reproduction and Population (November 1973), NOW, Box 54, Folder 24.

18 Judith Atkinson to Editor of NARAL Newsletter (nd, ca. 1977), NARAL, Box 48, Folder 4. On the Tallahassee dispute, see Linda Curtis to Karen Mulhauser (July 12, 1977), NARAL, Box 48, Folder 4; Linda Curtis to Louise Tyrer (July 12, 1977), NARAL, Box 48, Folder 4; Feminist Women's Health, Press Release, "Feminists Urge Radical Change of Planned Parenthood Decision Makers" (nd, ca. July 1977), NARAL, Box 48, Folder 4; Summary of Report for Planned Parenthood Board of Directors Meeting, June 1977, Tallahassee Feminist Women's Health Center (May 31, 2977), NARAL, Box 48, Folder 4.

19 See Planned Parenthood Federation of America Executive Committee Meeting Minutes (October 11, 1977), NARAL, Box 48, Folder 4. For more on the Medical Rights Fund, see Kenyon Burke to Margot Krupp (May 11, 1977), NARAL, Box 48, Folder 4; B.T. Hollins to Executive Committee (February 23, 1977), NARAL, Box 48, Folder 4.

20 Nancy Gertner, interview with Mary Ziegler, March 1, 2017; John Reinstein, interview with Mary Ziegler, March 1, 2017. For more on Gertner's background and career, see Nancy Gertner, *In Defense of Women: Memoirs of an Unrepentant Advocate* (Boston: Beacon, 2011).

21 See NARAL, Status of ACLU/NARAL Lawsuits as of February 11,1974 (February 1974), NARAL, Carton 1, 1974–1975 Executive Committee Folder. For more on the Haverhill

case, see *Doe v. Hale Hospital*, 500 F.2d 144 (1st Cir. 1974). For the New Jersey case, see *Doe v. Bridgeton Hospital Association*, 366 A.2d 641 (N.J. 1976). For more on the early work of the RFP, see Leigh Ann Wheeler, *How Sex Became a Civil Liberty* (New York: Oxford University Press, 2012), 160–171.

22 On poor women's relative lack of access to abortion services, see Schoen, *Abortion after Roe*, 4–42. These differences were particularly pronounced when abortion was a crime. See Mark A. Graber, *Rethinking Abortion: Equal Choice, the Constitution, and Reproductive Politics* (Princeton, NJ: Princeton University Press, 1996), 58; Leslie J. Reagan, *When Abortion Was a Crime: Women, Medicine, and Law in the United States, 1867–1973* (Berkeley: University of California Press, 1997), 368; Rhonda Copelon and Sylvia Law, "'Nearly Allied to Her Right to Be'–Medicaid Funding for Abortion: The Story of *Harris v. McRae*," in *Women and the Law Stories* eds. Elizabeth M. Schneider and Stephanie Wildman (New York: Foundation Press, 2011), 220–221.

23 *King v. Smith*, 392 U.S. 309 (1968). On the role of lawyers in the welfare-rights movement, see Davis, *Brutal Need*, 34–69; Kornbluh, *The Battle for Welfare Rights*, 37–84; Bussiere, *(Dis)Entitling the Poor*, 7–19. For the Court's decision in *Goldberg*, see *Goldberg v. Kelly*, 397 U.S. 254 (1970). For the Court's decision in *Shapiro*, see *Shapiro v. Thompson*, 394 U.S. 618 (1969). On the campaign to reform AFDC in the period, see Steensland, *The Failed Welfare Revolution*, 73–104; Davis, *Brutal Need*, 138; Bruce J. Schulman, *The Seventies: The Great Shift in American Culture, Society, and Politics* (New York: Da Capo, 2001), 32–40. On the declining support for FAP, see Jennifer Erkulwater, *Disability Rights and the American Social Safety Net* (Ithaca, NY: Cornell University Press, 2006), 76–77; Steensland, *The Failed Welfare Revolution*, 149–190; Kornbluh, *The Battle for Welfare Rights*, 137, 152–153.

24 On the defeat of welfare rights in the Supreme Court in the 1970s, see Kornbluh, *The Battle for Welfare Rights*, 7; Kaaryn S. Gustafson, *Cheating Welfare: Public Assistance and the Criminalization of Poverty* (New York: New York University Press, 2011), 30–31. For the Supreme Court decisions holding that the Constitution did not protect welfare rights, see *Lavine v. Milne*, 424 U.S. 577, 584 n.9 (1976); *San Antonio Independent School District v. Rodriguez*, 411 U.S. 1 (1973); *Jefferson v. Hackney*, 406 U.S. 535 (1972); *James v. Valtierra*, 402 U.S. 137 (1971); *Lindsey v. Normet*, 405 U.S. 56, 74 (1972); *Dandridge v. Williams*, 397 U.S. 471 (1970).

25 On inflation in the 1970s, see Thomas Borstelmann, *The 1970s: A New Global History from Civil Rights to Economic Inequality* (Princeton, NJ: Princeton University Press, 2011), 60; Alan S. Binder, "The Anatomy of Double-Digit Inflation in the 1970s," in *Inflation: Causes and Effects* ed. Robert E. Hall (Chicago: University of Chicago Press, 1982), 261–265. On the influence of fuel shocks and other price increases, see Meg Jacobs, *Panic at the Pump: The Energy Crisis and the Transformation of American Politics in the 1970s* (New York: Farrar, Straus, and Giroux, 2016); Meg Jacobs, "The Conservative Struggle and the Energy Crisis," in *Rightward Bound: Making America Conservative in the 1970s* eds. Bruce J. Schulman and Julian E. Zelizer (Cambridge, MA: Harvard University Press, 2008), 193–208.

26 Martin Gilens, *Why Americans Hate Welfare: Race, Media, and the Politics of Antipoverty Policy* (Chicago: University of Chicago Press, 1999), 125. On the employment rate in the 1970s, see Bureau of Labor Statistics, Labor Force Statistics from the Current

Population Survey: Unemployment Rate, https://data.bls.gov/timeseries/LNU04000000?
years_option=all_years&periods_option=specific_periods&periods=Annual+Data, accessed
January 26, 2017. On wage stagnation, see Borstelmann, *The 1970s*, 61–63; Schulman, *The
Seventies*, 4–12; Joseph A. McCartin, "The Turnabout Years: Public Sector Unionism and
the Financial Crisis," in *Rightward Bound: Making America Conservative in the 1970s* eds.
Bruce J. Schulman and Julian E. Zelizer (Cambridge, MA: Harvard University Press,
2008), 210–227. On increasing layoffs and competition, see Borstelmann, *The 1970s*, 81,
133–134.

27 On the state-action doctrine in constitutional law, see Mark Tushnet, *Weak Courts, Strong
Rights: Judicial Review and Social Welfare Rights in Comparative Constitutional Law*
(Princeton, NJ: Princeton University Press, 2008), 177–208; William M. Wiecek, *The Birth
of the Modern Constitution: The United States Supreme Court, 1941–1953* (New York:
Cambridge University Press, 2006), 67, 628–638.

28 For examples of the laws on public facilities and funding, see "State Laws Challenged,"
National Right to Life News, August 1974, 11, JRS, 1974 National Right to Life News Box;
"Elective Abortion Funding Comes under State Fire," *National Right to Life News*,
September 1977, 7, JRS, 1977 National Right to Life News Box; Alice L. Hartle, "Appellate
Court Finds Hospital Abortion Refusal Unconstitutional," *National Right to Life News*
March 1974, 5, JRS, 1974 National Right to Life News Box.

29 For the most part, lawsuits brought against private hospitals did not succeed. See *Doe
v. Bridgeton Hospital Association*, 366 A.2d 641 (N.J. 1976). For other courts rejecting a
similar argument applied to private hospitals, see *Doe v. Bellin Memorial Hospital*, 479
F.2d 756 (7th Cir. 1973); *Watkins v. Mercy Medical Center*, 364 F. Supp. 799 (D. Idaho
1973); *Barrett v. United Hospital*, 376 F. Supp. 791 (S.D.N.Y. 1974); *Ascherman
v. Presbyterian Hospital of Pacific Medical Center*, 507 F.2d 1103 (9th Cir. 1974); *Greco
v. Orange Memorial Hospital Corporation*, 513 F.2d 873 (5th Cir. 1975).

30 For examples of the movement's early constitutional arguments, see William J. Kenealy,
"Law and Morals," *Catholic Lawyer* 9 (1963): 201–203; Robert M. Byrn, "Abortion in
Perspective," *Duquesne University Law Review* 5 (1966): 134–135; Thomas L. Shaffer,
"Abortion, the Law, and Human Life," *Valparaiso University Law Review* 3 (1967–1968):
106; Robert M. Byrn, "Abortion on Demand: Whose Morality?" *Notre Dame Law Review*,
46 (1970–1971): 26–27; David Louisell, "The Practice of Medicine and the Due Process of
Law," *UCLA Law Review* 16 (1968–1969): 234. On the history of the pro-life movement,
see Williams, *Defenders of the Unborn*, 130–200; Ziegler, *After Roe*, 48–52; Keith Cassidy,
"The Right to Life Movement: Sources, Development, and Strategies," in *The Politics of
Abortion and Birth Control in Historical Perspective* ed. Donald T. Critchlow (University
Park: Pennsylvania State University Press, 1996), 139–142.

31 Meeting Minutes, NRLC Ad Hoc Strategy Meeting (February 11, 1973), 4, 5–7, ACCL,
Box 4, 1973 NRLC Folder 1. For more on the organization's early strategy discussions, see
Dennis Horan to NRLC Board of Directors et al. (January 19, 1974), 2, ACCL, Box 4,
1974 NRLC Folder 2; Joseph Witherspoon to NRLC Executive Committee (August 14,
1973), ACCL, Box 4, 1973 NRLC Folder 1; Robert Sassone to Marjory Mecklenburg
(November 8, 1973), ACCL, Box 4, 1973 NRLC Folder 2; National Right to Life Commit-
tee Board of Directors Meeting Minutes (December 2, 1973), ACCL, Box 4, 1973 NRLC
Folder 2. Interestingly, welfare-rights supporters also invoked a "right to life," one that

covered basic necessities. For discussion of "right to life" rhetoric in the welfare-rights movement, see Debussiere, *(Dis)Entitling the Poor*, 109–110. For an earlier argument of this kind, see A. Delafield Smith, *The Right to Life* (Chapel Hill: University of North Carolina Press, 1955).

32 On the Church Amendment and its significance, see Sara Dubow, "'A Constitutional Right Rendered Utterly Meaningless': Religious Exemptions and Reproductive Politics, 1973–2014," *Journal of Policy History* 27 (2015): 1–25; Rebecca Kluchin, *Fit to Be Tied: Sterilization and Reproductive Rights in America, 1950–1980* (Piscataway, NJ: Rutgers University Press, 2011), 143–144; Patricia Miller, *Good Catholics: The Battle over Abortion in the Catholic Church* (Berkeley: University of California Press, 2014), 184. For the *Commonweal* statement: "Abortion: Next Round," *Commonweal*, March 23, 1973, 98.

33 Letter from Brenda Feigen Fasteau, Coordinator, Women's Rights Project, ACLU, to Representative Mr. Marlin D. Schneider (August 28, 1973), BAP, Box 10, Folder 4.

34 "Hospital to Appeal," *National Right to Life News*, March 1974, 5, JRS, 1974 National Right to Life News Box. For more on pro-life concern about the hospital suits, see Hartle, "Appellate Court," 4; "High Court Refuses Hospital Appeal," *National Right to Life News*, December 1974, 2, JRS, 1974 National News Box; "ACLU Guidelines Tell You How to Sue Your Local Hospital," *National Right to Life News*, July 1975, 11, JRS, 1975 National Right to Life News Box; "Court Rules against Hospital," *National Right to Life News*, December 1975, 2, JRS, 1975 National Right to Life News Box.

35 For White's estimate, see Ray White to Board of Directors (November 1974), ACCL, Box 8, 1974 NRLC Folder 1. For more on the movement's interest in funding, see NRLC, "Senate Votes to Prohibit Federal Funding for Abortion" (October 1974), ACCL, Box 8, 1974 NRLC Folder 1. On the relative abortion rates of Medicaid-eligible and Medicaid-ineligible women, see Jacqueline Darroch Forrest, Christopher Tietze, and Ellen Sullivan, "Abortion in the United States, 1976–1977," *Family Planning Perspectives* 10 (1978): 275.

36 See Ziegler, *After Roe*, 101–152.

37 On Kennedy's work, see Florynce Kennedy, *Color Me Flo: My Hard Life and Good Times* (Englewood Cliffs, NJ: Prentice Hall, 1976), 147. For more on nonwhite feminists' support of reproductive rights before *Roe*, see Jennifer Nelson, *Women of Color and Reproductive Rights* (New York: New York University Press, 2003); Jennifer Nelson, *More than Medicine: A History of the Feminist Women's Health Movement* (New York: New York University Press, 2015), 182–200; Reagan, *When Abortion Was a Crime*, 243; Laura Briggs, *Reproducing Empire: Race, Sex, Science, and U.S. Imperialism in Puerto Rico* (Berkeley: University of California Press, 2003).

38 For Clements' statement: "Two Views on Legal Abortions," *Jet*, March 22, 1973, 20. For Craven's statement: Erma Craven, "Abortion, Poverty, and Black Genocide: Gifts to the Poor?" in *Abortion and Social Justice* eds. Thomas W. Hilgers and Dennis J. Horan et al. (New York: Sheed and Ward, 1972). For Jackson's statement: Robert Johnson, "Legal Abortion: Is It Genocide, or a Blessing in Disguise?" *Jet*, March 22, 1973, 15. For more on the "black genocide" argument, see Ziegler, *After Roe*, 92–125; Donald T. Critchlow, *Intended Consequences: Birth Control, Abortion, and the Federal Government in Modern America* (New York: Oxford University Press, 1999), 142–145; Nelson, *Women of Color*, 78–89.

39 On the Roncallo Amendment, see Bea Blair, Executive Report (1974), NARAL, Carton 1, 1974 Executive Committee Folder; Alice Hartle, "Abortion Exclusion Fails in House,"

National Right to Life News, August 1974, 1, JRS, 1974 National Right to Life News Box; Janet Grant, "House Members Explain 'No' Vote on Amendment," *National Right to Life News*, September 1974, 12, JRS, 1974 National Right to Life News Box.

40 See White to Board of Directors, 1. On the movement's frustration with the pace of the constitutional amendment campaign, see "Human Life Amendment Hearing in House" (October 1974), ACCL, Box 8, 1974 NRLC Folder. On the movement's struggles in the period, see Ziegler, *After Roe*, 30–52; Williams, *Defenders of the Unborn*, 221–245.

41 On the relatively low levels of polarization in the 1970s, see Campbell, *Polarization*, 119; Sean M. Theriault, *The Gingrich Senators: The Roots of Partisan Warfare in Congress* (New York: Oxford University Press, 2013), 36; Matthew Levendusky, *The Partisan Sort: How Liberals Became Democrats and Conservatives Became Republicans* (Chicago: University of Chicago Press, 2009), 13–23.

42 Andriacco, "More on Black Genocide," 8; see also NRLC Pamphlet, "Abortion . . . Where Does It End?" 2; March 1974 NRLC Press Release, 1; see also "Appeals Court Holds Missouri Welfare Law Unconstitutional," 4.

43 On the war-tax protests, see William Conrad Gibbons, *The U.S. Government and the Vietnam War: Executive and Legislative Roles and Relationships, Part IV* (Princeton, NJ: Princeton University Press, 1995), 426–450. On coverage of the protests from the time, see Morris Kaplan, "Writers Protest Vietnam War Tax," *New York Times*, September 17, 1967, 8; "Peace, Not Piece," *Off Our Backs*, May 16, 1970, 5; Bill Kovach, "Protest Diverts Telephone Taxes," *New York Times*, February 28, 1971, 7.

44 For Grasso's statement: Letter to Ella Grasso from William Whelan, Executive Director, Connecticut Catholic Conference (March 16, 1973), LGP, Box 69, Folder 7. For the bishops' pamphlet: Dubow, "A Constitutional Right," 9–10 (quoting The Bishops of Connecticut, "Your Conscience and Abortion," September 1974).

45 "Pro-lifers Deny Government's Right to Tax for Abortions," *National Right to Life News*, June 1975, 5, JRS, 1975 National Right to Life News Box. On Danninger and Houle's protests, see Michael McKee, "Two Kinds of Tax Resistance: The Symbolic and the Practical," *National Right to Life News*, March 1977, 7, JRS, 1977 National Right to Life News Box. On Reilly's protest: "IRS Ignores Tax Deduction by Protester," *National Right to Life News*, April 1975, 11, JRS, 1975 National Right to Life News Box.

46 For Duggan's letter to Buckley: Duggan to Buckley, 1–2. On Buckley's response, see Buckley to Duggan, 1. For Duggan's letters to the IRS, see Duggan to Chief, Correspondence Section, 1; Dexter Duggan to Louise Taylor, Internal Revenue Service, 1–2.

47 "Pro-lifers Deny Government's Right," 5.

48 Ibid.

49 On the relative unpopularity of pro-life tax protests, see Duggan to Buckley, 1–2; "Tax Protesting," 7.

50 Roanne Shamsky, Political Strategy Committee, to the California Democratic Health and Welfare Committee (October 29, 1979), PWP, Box 22, Folder 1. For Biden's statement: "HEW Funding Bill Delayed," *National Right to Life News*, November 1974, 11, JRS, 1974 National Right to Life News Box. For Pastore's statement: ibid.

51 On the failure of the Bartlett Amendment, see Marjorie Hunter, "Senate Upholds U.S. Abortion Funds," *New York Times*, April 11, 1975, 28. On the NRLC explanation for the defeat, see Alice Hartle, "Senator Bartlett to Pursue HEW Funding Ban," *National Right*

to Life News, January 1975, 1, JRS, 1975 National Right to Life News Box. On the abortion-rights movement's response to the defeat, see NARAL Executive Committee Minutes (April 11–12, 1975), NARAL, Carton 1, 1974–1975 Executive Committee Minutes Folder. On Liebman and Scott's argument against the proposal, see Anne Scott and Jan Liebman to Legislative Coordinator Re: Labor HEW Appropriation (September 1974), NOW, Box 54, Folder 27. The Bartlett Amendment never passed. As the chapter shows, a similar measure, the Hyde Amendment, had more success.

52 On the conflict within NARAL immediately after legalization, see Staggenborg, *The Pro-choice Movement,* 72–75.

53 NARAL Executive Committee Meeting Minutes (November 21, 1975), NARAL, Carton 1, 1974–1975 Executive Folder. For the convention message: 1975 NARAL Convention, 1. For recollections of the movement's focus on the constitutional amendment: Roger Craver, interview with Mary Ziegler, August 15, 2016; Kissling, interview; Sylvia Law, interview with Mary Ziegler, July 22, 2016; Al Gerhardstein, interview with Mary Ziegler, May 16, 2016; Mulhauser, interview.

54 NOW, Abortion Action Program (1974), NOW, Box 54, Folder 26.

55 See note 60 and text accompanying.

56 ACLU Reproductive Freedom Project, "The Abortion Controversy: A Doctor's Guide to the Law" (April 1975), on file with the author. For similar claims, see NARAL: Questions and Answers (1976), NARALMO, Box 1, Pamphlet Folder; "Abortion under Attack: Legislative Alert" (September 1974), NOW, Box 54, Folder 26; NOW, "Right to Choose Update" (Fall 1974), NOW, Box 2, Folder 42.

57 On the reasons for party polarization in the 1970s, see Campbell, *Polarized,* 119–170; Theriault, *Party Polarization,* 4–30; McCarty, Poole, and Rosenthal, *Polarized America,* 5–50. On the abortion issue in the 1976 presidential election, see Critchlow, *Intended Consequences,* 204; Robert Mason, *Richard Nixon and the Quest for a New Majority* (Chapel Hill: University of North Carolina Press, 2014), 229–231; Marjorie J. Spruill, *Divided We Stand: The Battle over Women's Rights and Family Values That Polarized American Politics* (New York: Bloomsbury, 2017), 70–94.

58 On the influx of socially and fiscally conservative Republicans in the mid-1970s, see Steven Schier and Todd E. Eberly, *American Government and Popular Discontent: Stability without Success* (New York: Routledge, 2013), 69–75; Joseph A. Aistrup, *The Southern Strategy Revisited: Top-Down Advancement in the American South* (Lexington: University of Kentucky Press, 1996), 119; Matt Grossman and David Hopkins, *Asymmetric Politics: Ideological Republicans and Interest Group Democrats* (New York: Oxford University Press, 2016), 218–284; Paul Boyer, "The Evangelical Resurgence in American Protestantism," in *Rightward Bound: Making America Conservative in the 1970s* eds. Bruce J. Schulman and Julian E. Zelizer (Cambridge, MA: Harvard University Press, 2008), 48.

59 Janet Grant, "Pro-life Strength Shown in Hyde Amendment," *National Right to Life News,* September 1976, 1; see also Laurence H. Tribe, *Abortion: The Clash of Absolutes* (New York: W. W. Norton, 1992), 158–160; *Congressional Record* S. 27674 (Daily Edition, August 22, 1977), 22.

60 NARAL Newsletter (July 1976), 4, NARAL, Box 41, Folder 10. On the evaluation of the Court's latest decision, see ibid., 2. For Werner's statement on the possibility of losing on

the Hyde Amendment: Carol Werner to NARAL Board Members et al. (July 30, 1976), NARAL, Box 41, Folder 10; see also Carol Werner to Congressional Staff (July 1976), NARAL, Box 41, Folder 10.

61 NARAL, Memo, "Arguments against the Hyde Amendment" (n. d., ca. 1976), NARAL, Box 41, Folder 10.

62 For Bartlett and Dole's statements: "HEW Funding," 12–13. On pro-life perceptions of the veto, see "Ford Makes a Point of Supporting Hyde Provision in Veto Message," *National Right to Life News*, September 1976, 4, JRS, 1976 National Right to Life News Box. For more on the veto, see Donald T. Critchlow, "When Republicans Became Revolutionaries: Conservatives in Congress," in *The American Congress: The Building of Democracy* ed. Julian E. Zelizer (New York: Houghton Mifflin Harcourt, 2004), 708–794; Critchlow, *Intended Consequences*, 202–205.

63 "HEW Funding," 12–13.

64 For the regulation challenged in *Maher*: Connecticut Welfare Department, Public Assistance Program Manual, Vol. 3, c. III, § 275 (1975). For the lower court litigation in *Maher*, see *Roe v. Norton*, 408 F. Supp. 660 (D. Conn. 1975); *Roe v. Norton*, 408 F. Supp. 660 (2d. Cir. 1975). On the lower court litigation in *Beal*, see *Doe v. Beal*, 523 F. 2d 611 (3d Cir. 1975); *Doe v. Wohlgemuth*, 523 F. 2d 611 (1975). On the lower court litigation in *Poelker*, see *Doe v. Poelker*, 515 F.2d 541 (8th Cir. 1975); *Doe v. Poelker*, 527 F.2d 605 (8th Cir. 1976).

65 On Horan's early interest in litigation, see Dennis Horan to NRLC Policy Committee (September 5, 1973), 1–3, ACCL, Box 8, 1973 NRLC Folder. On Horan's early work on the abortion issue, see John Gorby and Dennis Horan, "The Legal Case for the Unborn," in *Abortion and Social Justice*, eds. Thomas W. Hilgers and Dennis J. Horan (New York: Sheed and Ward, 1972): 105–141; Americans United for Life, Meeting Minutes (March 10–11, 1972), 4, 6–7, AUL, Executive File Box Folder 91. For discussion of Rosenblum's early work, see Nick Thimmesch, "Right to Life Fights for Human Values," *Chicago Tribune*, June 17, 1973, A6; "Victor Rosenblum, 1925–2006," *Chicago Tribune*, March 15, 2006, http://articles.chicagotribune.com/2006-03-15/news/0603150265_1_anti-abortion-mr-rosenblum-law-schools, accessed January 28, 2017. On AUL's new emphasis on litigation, see David Mall to AUL Board of Directors, "First Quarterly Report" (February 28, 1975), GHW, Box 5, Folder 6. On the creation of the Legal Action Project and its first cases, see James Bopp Jr. to Mary Hunt (June 25, 1978), 1–4, JBP, Matter Boxes, File 143; James Bopp Jr. to Legal Liaison Committee Re: Report of the Progress of the Legal Action Project (February 1, 1978), JBP, Matter Boxes, File 143; James Bopp Jr. to Richard A. Bradley (July 2, 1979), JBP, Matter Boxes, File 144.

66 See *Planned Parenthood of Central Missouri v. Danforth*, 428 U.S. 52, 61–64 (1976).

67 See Brief of the Appellees, 13–15, <u>*Maher v. Roe*</u>, 432 U.S. 464 (1977) (No. 75–1440). For more on the unconstitutional-conditions doctrine and its relevance in the 1970s, see Kathleen M. Sullivan, "Unconstitutional Conditions," *Harvard Law Review* 102 (1989): 1422–1428; Richard A. Epstein, "Foreword: Unconstitutional Conditions, State Power, and the Limits of Consent," *Harvard Law Review* 102 (1988): 103–120; Cass R. Sunstein, "Why the Unconstitutional Conditions Doctrine Is an Anachronism (with Particular Reference to Religion, Speech, and Abortion)," *Boston University Law Review* 70 (1990): 595–600. For examples of cases relying on the doctrine, see *Speiser v. Randall*, 357 U.S. 513, 526

(1958); *Perry v. Sindermann*, 408 U.S. 593, 597 (1972). For similar amicus arguments, see Motion for Leave to File Brief Amici Curiae and Annexed Brief for the American Public Health Association et al., 9–33, *Maher v. Roe*, 432 U.S. 464 (1977) (No. 75–1440).

68 Brief of Appellees, 13–15.

69 Ibid. (citation and quotation omitted). The Court subsequently issued a second opinion in *Bellotti*. See *Bellotti v. Baird*, 443 U.S. 622 (1979).

70 See Motion for Leave to File Brief and Brief Amicus Curiae, Americans United for Life, 1–6, *Poelker v. Doe*, 432 U.S. 519 (1977) (No. 75–442). For more on AUL's arguments in the earlier stages of the *Poelker* litigation, see Janet Grant, "Pro-lifers Ask Supreme Court to Lift Injunction on Hyde Amendment Provision," *National Right to Life News*, January 1977, 1, JRS, 1977 National Right to Life News Box; "Legal Update," *National Right to Life News*, December 1979, 13, JRS, 1979 National Right to Life News Box; Patrick Truman "Legal Update," *National Right to Life News*, December 1979, 13, JRS, 1979 National Right to Life News Box; Letter to AUL Members (1978), AUL, Executive File Box, Folder 92.

71 Brief of Appellees, 14–15. For Connecticut's argument in *Maher*, see Brief of the Appellant, 13–20, *Maher v. Roe*, 432 U.S. 464 (1977) (No. 75–1440).

72 *Maher v. Roe*, 432 U.S. 464, 473-474 (1977). For more on the reasoning and significance of *Maher*, see Serena Mayeri, *Reasoning from Race: Feminism, Law, and the Civil Rights Movement* (Cambridge, MA: Harvard University Press, 2011), 193; Ziegler, *After Roe*, 66, 132; Samuel Walker, *Presidents and Civil Liberties from Wilson to Obama: A Story of Poor Custodians* (New York: Cambridge University Press, 2012), 355–356.

73 See *Maher v. Roe*, 432 U.S. 464, 479 (1977).

74 Ibid., 480. For the decisions in *Beal* and *Poelker*, see *Poelker v. Doe*, 432 U.S. 519 (1977); *Beal v. Doe*, 432 U.S. 438 (1977).

75 For the NRLC statement: National Right to Life Committee Press Release (June 20, 1977), ACCL, Box 8, 1977 NRLC Folder. For abortion foes' analysis: Duggan, "Law Professors Evaluate June 20 Rulings," 2; see also Richard Stith, "Supreme Court Decisions Allow Government to Be Pro-life," *National Right to Life News*, January 1978, 4, JRS, 1978 National Right to Life News Box.

76 Pam Lowry, interview with Mary Ziegler, May 31, 2017. For more on Lowry's work: Jean Weinberg, interview with Mary Ziegler, May 24, 2017. For an example of Lowry's work, see Pamphlet, Dr. Kenneth Edelin Defense Fund (n. d., ca. 1975), PLL, on file with the author.

77 Weinberg, interview. For more on "Impact '80," see Staggenborg, *The Pro-choice Movement*, 96; Heather Munro Prescott, *The Morning After: A History of Emergency Contraception in the United States* (Piscataway, NJ: Rutgers University Press, 2011), 66–67.

78 NARAL, Model Letter to Member of U.S. Senate (June 23, 1977), NARAL, Box 41, Folder 10. On the debate and passage of the Hyde Amendment in 1977, see "House Votes to Ban Using U.S. Funds for Abortion," *Chicago Tribune*, June 18, 1977, A3; Martin Tolchin, "House Bars Medicaid Abortions and Funds for Enforcing Quotas," *New York Times*, June 18, 1977, 49; Adam Clymer, "Senate Vote Forbids Using Federal Funds for Most Abortions," *New York Times*, June 30, 1977, 1.

79 For Wattleton's statements: Judy Klemesrud, "Planned Parenthood's New Head Takes a Fighting Stand," *New York Times*, February 3, 1978, A14. On the decision to move

Planned Parenthood into politics, see Faye Wattleton, *Life on the Line* (New York: Ballantine, 1996), 205–215.

80 "Summary of Reproductive Task Force Meetings, April 28 & 29, 1979" (April 1979), 1, NOW, Box 49, Folder 22; see also "Summary of Conference Call Meeting, August 19, 1979" (August 31, 1979), NOW, Box 49, Folder 22. On NOW's focus on the ERA, see Mayeri, *Reasoning from Race*, 30–37.

81 On the founding of CARASA, see Nelson, *Women of Color*, 135; Ziegler, *After Roe*, 147–148; Jael Silliman, Marlene Gerber Fried, Elena Gutiérrez, and Loretta Ross, *Undivided Rights: Women of Color Organize for Reproductive Justice* 2d ed. (Chicago: Haymarket, 2016), 43. On the early work of NWHN, see NWHN, "Position Paper on Abortion Adopted by the National Women's Health Network Board" (June 4, 1978), 1–2; JoAnne Fischer to Eleanor Smeal (February 13, 1979), 1–2, BSP, Carton 3, Folder 142. For examples of the early work of CARASA, see "Defend Women's Right to Choose–Draft Outline for CARASA" (n. d., c. 1979), 1, MTP, Box 8, CARASA Folder. For more on CARASA's focus on a multi-issue agenda and a more radical understanding of choice, see Notes on Strategy for Steering Committee Meeting (March 18, 1978), MTP, Box 8, CARASA Steering Committee Folder (contending that CARASA had forced other groups to make concessions because of "its people, [its] activism, and clear and consistent politics"); Meredith Tax, "R2N2 Fights Right to Life and Hyde," *CARASA News*, June 1979, 1, MTP, Box 8, CARASA News Folder 2; "Reports from the Triannual Meeting," *CARASA News*, July/August 1979, 1, MTP, Box 8, CARASA News Folder 2.

82 For the statement on the effects of the Hyde Amendment: Nelson, *Women of Color*, 152. On mainstream organizations' use of similar arguments, see Ziegler, *After Roe*, 147–155. For more on the racial politics of the Hyde Amendment, see Mayeri, *Reasoning from Race*, 243; Laura R. Woliver, *The Political Geographies of Pregnancy* (Urbana: University of Illinois Press, 2002), 86.

83 "House Bans," 13; see also Tolchin, "House Bans Funds," 49; Clymer, "Senate Bans," 1.

84 For Carter's positions during the campaign, see David E. Rosenbaum, "Democrats Adopt a Platform Aimed at Uniting Party," *New York Times*, June 16, 1976, 1; David E. Rosenbaum, "Welfare Is a Major Issue for Carter," *New York Times*, April 3, 1977, 1. On Carter's waning commitment to reform, see David E. Rosenbaum, "Carter to Give Plan on Welfare Soon," *New York Times*, April 28, 1977, 19; David E. Rosenbaum, "Senators Fighting Carter on Welfare," *New York Times*, October 3, 1977, 1; Austin Scott, "'Welfare Mess' Defies Solution," *Los Angeles Times*, September 20, 1978, B30.

85 See Dan Thomasson, "The Cost to Taxpayers Annually Has Been Put at $3 Billion," *New York Times*, September 5, 1976, B6; Nancy Hicks, "Senate Committee Votes to Tighten the Medicaid Rules to Prevent Abuses and Fraud," *New York Times*, September 15, 1976, 26. For the *New York Times*'s position, see Rosenbaum, "Welfare Is a Major Issue," 1. On Reagan's take on the issue, see David E. Rosenbaum, "Ford-Reagan Aims Alike, but Tactics Are Different," *New York Times*, February 9, 1976, 57. On opposition to busing among whites, see Timothy J. Meagher, "Racial and Ethnic Relations in America, 1965–2000," in *Race and Ethnicity in America: A Concise History* ed. Ronald H. Bayor (New York: Columbia University Press, 2003), 218. For more on opposition to busing and its effect on race relations, see Ronald P. Formisano, *Boston against Busing: Race, Class, and Ethnicity in the 1960s and 1970s* (Chapel Hill: University of North Carolina

Press, 1991). On the *Bakke* case and hostility to affirmative action, see Terry H. Anderson, *The Pursuit of Fairness: A History of Affirmative Action* (New York: Oxford University Press, 2004), 150–164. For the *Bakke* decision, see *Regents of the University of California v. Bakke*, 438 U.S. 265 (1978).

86 On the House vote in late November, see John H. Averill, "House Rejects Abortion Plan," *Los Angeles Times*, November 30, 1977, B1. On the Senate vote, see "Abortion Proposal Rejected by Senate," *Atlanta Journal–Constitution*, December 7, 1977, 2A.

87 Brief of Intervening Defendants-Appellees James L. Buckley, Jesse A. Helms, Henry J. Hyde, and Isabella Pernicone, *Harris v. McRae*, 448 U.S. 297 (1980) (No. 79–1268). For more arguments about the abuse of medical exceptions to the funding bans, see "Peggy Grant, "House-Senate Debate Down to the Wire," *National Right to Life News*, December 1977, 1, JRS, 1977 National Right to Life News Box; Robert Krebsbach to James Bopp Jr. (September 28, 1978), JBP, Matter Boxes, File 141.

88 "Bitter House-Senate Battle Ends for Now," *National Right to Life News*, January 1978, 1, JRS, 1978 National Right to Life News Box.

89 For the ACLU's argument: ACLU Campaign for Choice (1977), RHS, Box 1, Folder 19. For the Planned Parenthood pamphlet: Planned Parenthood Justice Institute, Fundraising Letter (October 9, 1978), RHS, Box 1, Folder 19; see also NOW, Model Letter to Representative (June 13, 1979), NOW, Box 54, Folder 26.

90 See Departments of Labor and Health, Education, and Welfare Appropriations: Testimony before the Senate Labor and HEW Appropriations Committee, Subcommittee on Labor and HEW Appropriations, 96th Congress, 1st Session (1979), 230–234 (Statement of Mamie Williams of RCAR). For a similar argument, see Departments of Labor and Health, Education, and Welfare Appropriations: Testimony before the House Appropriations Committee, Subcommittee on Labor and HEW Appropriations, 96th Congress 2d Sess. (1980), 196–202 (Statement of Suellen Lowry). For the RCAR pamphlet: RCAR, "It's Hyde Again" (1979), RHS, Box 1, Folder 19. For more on the influence and history of RCAR, see Staggenborg, *The Pro-choice Movement*, 59–60, 74–89, 101–104, 144–145; Samuel A. Mills, "Abortion and Religious Freedom: The Religious Coalition for Abortion-Rights and the Pro-choice Movement, 1973–1989," *Journal of Church and State* 33 (1991): 569–591.

91 On home price inflation in the 1970s, see Yanek Mieczkowski, *Gerald Ford and the Challenges of the 1970s* (Lexington: University of Kentucky Press, 2005), 105; Michael Stewart Foley, *Front Porch Politics: The Forgotten Heyday of American Politics in the 1970s and 1980s* (New York: Macmillan, 2013), 237–245; Louis Hyman, *Debtor Nation: The History of America in Red Ink* (Princeton, NJ: Princeton University Press, 2011), 221–225.

92 See Wallace Turner, "Tax Question Divides Voters in California," *New York Times*, April 13, 1978, A24; "The Jarvis-Gann Proposal," *Wall Street Journal*, April 25, 1978, 24; William Wong, "Taxes Boil over in California," *Wall Street Journal*, February, 27, 1978, 16.

93 For Jarvis's statement: "Californian Jarvis Fights Tax Dragon," *Atlanta Journal-Constitution*, June 4, 1978, 18C. For more on Jarvis's views on race and welfare, see David O. Sears and Jack Citrin, *Tax Revolt: Something for Nothing in California* (Cambridge, MA: Harvard University Press, 1982), 187, 200; Solon Simmons, *The Eclipse of Equality: Arguing America on "Meet the Press"* (Palo Alto, CA: Stanford University Press, 2013), 175; Antoine J. Banks, *Anger and Racial Politics: The Emotional Foundation of Racial Attitudes in America* (New York: Cambridge University Press, 2014), 1–5.

94 See Adam Clymer, "Reagan Urges Party to Support Tax Cuts," *New York Times*, June 25, 1978, 27. On the Proposition 13 vote, see Richard Bergholz, "Voters Deliver Tax Message in Proposition 13 Landslide," *Los Angeles Times*, June 7, 1978, A7; Wallace Turner, "California Voters Approve a Plan to Cut Property Taxes \$7 Billion," *New York Times*, June 7, 1979, A1. On the spread of similar revolts, see Adam Clymer, "California Vote Seen as Evidence of U.S. Tax Revolt," *New York Times*, June 8, 1978, AS23; David Johnston, "Even Washington State Has Tax Revolt," *Los Angeles Times*, June 25, 1978, M1.

95 See 439 U.S. 479 (1979). For more on *Colautti*, see Bonnie Steinbock, *Life Before Birth: The Moral and Legal Status of Embryos and Fetuses* 2d ed. (New York: Oxford University Press, 2011), 187; David Garrow, *Liberty and Sexuality: The Right to Privacy and the Making of Roe v. Wade* (Berkeley: University of California Press, 1998), 631.

96 443 U.S. 622 (1979). For more on *Bellotti*, see Garrow, *Liberty and Sexuality*, 631–637; Helena Silverstein, *Girls on the Stand: How Courts Fail Pregnant Minors* (New York: New York University Press, 2007), 21–33.

97 For recollections of Copelon and Law's case: Sylvia Law, interview with Mary Ziegler, June 22, 2016. For recollections of the litigation strategy leading to the case: Gertner, interview; Reinstein, interview. For more on the litigation, see Copelon and Law, "Nearly Allied to Her Right to Be," 220–225; Ira Glasser, "Abortion Funding: A Case of Religious War," *Los Angeles Times*, January 7, 1979, E5.

98 Brief of Appellees, 121.

99 Ibid., 93.

100 NARAL Newsletter (April 1978), JBP, Matter Boxes, File 306. For the argument made in Copelon and Law's brief, see Brief of Appellees, 133–136.

101 Brief Amici Curiae of NOW et al., 6, 8, 46, 62, 66, *Harris v. McRae*, 448 U.S. 297 (1980) (No. 79–1268). The Supreme Court sometimes permitted parties with a strong interest in the litigation but no direct involvement in a specific case to submit a brief as a "friend of the court" or amicus curiae. NOW's was one such brief.

102 James Bopp Jr., interview with Mary Ziegler, June 14, 2015. For more on Bopp's journey, see Mark Bennett, "Terre Haute's James Bopp Jr. a Conservative Titan," *Washington Times*, June 29, 2014, www.washingtontimes.com/news/2014/jun/29/terre-hautes-jim-bopp-jr-a-conservative-titan, accessed June 27, 2017; Peter Overby, "The 'Country Lawyer' Shaping Campaign Finance Law," NPR, June 22, 2011, www.npr.org/2011/06/22/137318888/the-country-lawyer-shaping-campaign-finance-law, accessed June 12, 2017. For Bopp's memo on the possible outcomes in *McRae*, see James Bopp Jr., "Alternatives of the United States Supreme Court in the Abortion Funding Cases" (June 1, 1980), JBP, Matter Boxes, File 168. For NRLC's brief in *McRae*'s companion case, see Brief Amicus Curiae of the National Right to Life Committee, 5–14, *Williams v. Zbaraz*, 448 U.S. 358 (1980) (No. 79–4).

103 Brief of Intervening Defendants-Appellees James L. Buckley et al., 35, *Harris v. McRae*, 448 U.S. 297 (1980) (No. 79–1268).

104 Ibid., 17.

105 On Reagan's embrace of small-government politics, see Gil Troy, *Morning in America: How Reagan Invented the 1980s* (Princeton, NJ: Princeton University Press, 2005), 37–42; Doug Rossinow, *The Reagan Era: A History of the 1980s* (New York: Columbia University

Notes to pages 53–55233

Press, 2015), 5; Gary Orren, "Fall from Grace: The Public's Loss of Faith in Government," in *Why People Don't Trust Government* eds. Joseph Nye Jr. et al. (Cambridge, MA: Harvard University Press, 1997). On the decline in public trust, see Gallup, "Trust in Government," www.gallup.com/poll/5392/trust-government.aspx, accessed February 1, 2017. On Watergate and its impact on perceptions of the government, see Marc Hetherington, *Why Trust Matters: Declining Political Trust and the Demise of Political Liberalism* (New York: Oxford University Press, 2005), 23–24; Borstelmann, *The 1970s*, 45.

106 On the reasons for declining trust in government, see Borstelmann, *The 1970s*, 40–47; Orren, "Fall from Grace," 166; Hetherington, *Why Trust Matters*, 12.

107 See Ronald Reagan, Inaugural Address (January 21, 1981), www.presidency.ucsb.edu/ws/? pid=43130, accessed January 31, 2017. On Carter's support for deregulation, see Kim McQuaid, *Uneasy Partners: Big Business in American Politics, 1945–1990* (Baltimore, MD: Johns Hopkins University Press, 1994), 151–153; W. Carl Biven, *Jimmy Carter's Economy: Policy in an Age of Limits* (Chapel Hill: University of North Carolina Press, 2002), 154–162. On Reagan's successful attack on "big government," see Adam Clymer, "Reagan off to a Fast Start," *New York Times*, November 18, 1979, E4. On the history of neoliberalism, see Daniel Stedman Jones, *Masters of the Universe: Hayek, Friedman, and the Birth of Neoliberal Politics* (Princeton, NJ: Princeton University Press, 2012).

108 *Harris v. McRae*, 448 U.S. 297, 318–322 (1980).

109 Ibid., 316–317.

110 See David Stockman, *The Triumph of Politics: How the Reagan Revolution Failed* (New York: Harper and Row, 1986), 9; David Stoesz and Howard Jacob Karger, *Reconstructing the American Welfare State* (Lanham, MD: Rowman and Littlefield, 1992), 51; Michael Camasso, *Family Caps, Abortion, and Women of Color: Research Connection and Political Rejection* (New York: Oxford University Press, 2007), 7; Chappell, *The War on Welfare*, 225.

111 On state funding for abortions between 1980 and 1981, see Rachel Benson Gold, "Publicly Funded Abortions in FY 1980 and FY 1981," *Family Planning Perspectives* 14 (1982): 204–207. For the 2018 number, see "State Abortion Funding under Medicaid" (July 1, 2018), www.guttmacher.org/state-policy/explore/state-funding-abortion-under-medicaid, accessed July 18, 2018. On Planned Parenthood's sliding-scale fee and its spread, see "Abortion Clinics: An Evaluation," *New York Magazine*, July 24, 1972, 24; "Planned Parenthood Girds for New Siege over 'Children by Choice,'" *Chicago Tribune*, March 8, 1981, B4. On the spread of abortion funds, see Peggy Dobbie, "After a Decade of Choice, What Lies Ahead? Abortion Fund Established," *Women Wise*, March 31, 1983, 1; Sharman Stein, "Groups Offer Place for Poor to Turn for Abortion Aid," *New York Times*, June 9, 1989, A14.

112 David Gaetano, "Pro-life Gains: President, 10 Senators, and More," *National Right to Life News*, November 10, 1980, 7, JRS, 1980 National Right to Life News Box. On Elwell and Bopp's campaign to influence the 1980 GOP platform, see Williams, *Defenders of the Unborn*, 241; Right to Life of Michigan Board Meeting Minutes (April 2, 1980), RLM, Box 1, Administrative Board Minutes Folder; Jo Freeman, "Republicans: Feminists Avoid a Direct Confrontation," *In These Times*, July 30, 1980, 5. On the rise of the Moral Majority, see Daniel K. Williams, *God's Own Party: The Making of the Christian Right* (New York: Oxford University Press, 2010), 174–182; Laura Kalman, *Right Star Rising:*

A New Politics, 1974–1980 (New York: W. W. Norton, 2010), 263–284. On the alignment of the pro-life movement and the GOP, see Ziegler, *After Roe*, 216–222; Williams, *Defenders of the Unborn*, 245–253.

113 John C. Willke, "We Have a Bill," *National Right to Life News*, February 23, 1981, 1, 4, JRS, 1981 National Right to Life News Box; James Bopp Jr., "The Abortion Funding Proscription Bill," *National Right to Life News*, February 23, 1981, JRS, 1981 National Right to Life News Box.

3 LAUNCHING A QUEST TO REVERSE *ROE*

1 Paige Comstock Cunningham, interview with Mary Ziegler, October 23, 2014. For more on Cunningham's work in the period, see Marlene Cimons, "Groups on Both Sides of Issue Condemn Attack," *Los Angeles Times*, December 31, 1994, A20; Barbara Brotman, "Bill Seeks to Narrow Grounds for Abortion of 'Viable' Fetus," *Chicago Tribune*, March 12, 1990, 2; Chris Reidy, "Abortion Skirmishes Start Early," *Orlando Sentinel*, September 9, 1989, D8.

2 Cunningham, interview.

3 Judy Goldsmith, interview with Mary Ziegler, December 5, 2014. For more on Goldsmith's work in NOW, see Maryann Barasko, *Governing NOW: Grassroots Activism in the National Organization for Women* (Ithaca, NY: Cornell University Press, 2004), 96–125; Deanna Rohlinger, *Abortion Politics, Mass Media, and Social Movements in America* (New York: Cambridge University Press, 2015), 82–86.

4 Goldsmith, interview.

5 Ibid.

6 Ibid.

7 On the Hatch Amendment dispute, see Dave Andrusko, "Hatch Could Pass This Session, Willke Says," *National Right to Life News*, December 21, 1981, 1, JRS, 1981 National Right to Life News Box; "From the President's Desk: The NRLC Board–A Hatch Endorsement!" *National Right to Life News*, December 21, 1981, 3, JRS, 1981 National Right to Life News Box; "President's Column: Beware of False Friends," *A. L. L. About Issues*, September 1981, WCX, ALL About Issues Folder; Judie Brown, "Down the Hatch: The Hatch Federalism Amendment Will Not Save Babies," *A. L. L. About Issues*, January 1982, WCX, ALL About News Folder; "Senator Hatch, No!" *A. L. L. About Issues*, January 1, 1982, WCX, ALL About Issues Folder.

8 On the rise and evolution of pro-life incrementalism, see Mary Ziegler, *After Roe: The Lost History of the Abortion Debate* (Cambridge, MA: Harvard University Press, 2015), 58–62, 90–91; Daniel K. Williams, *Defenders of the Unborn: The Pro-life Movement before Roe v. Wade* (New York: Oxford University Press, 2016), 263–267. For examples of arguments of this kind made in the period, see Doug Johnson to Faith Whittlesey (May 6, 1983), RRP, Morton Blackwell Papers, Box 14, NRLC Folder 1; NRLC Statehouse Update (August 12, 1983), 1–4, Morton Blackwell Papers, Box 14, NRLC Folder 1; Americans United for Life Board of Directors Meeting Minutes (March 30, 1984), MFJ, Box 13, Folder 6; "From the Executive Director's Desk," *AUL Newsletter*, Winter 1987, 7, SBL, Box 1, AUL Folder 2. On increased evangelical mobilization around the abortion issue, see Daniel K. Williams,

God's Own Party: The Making of the Christian Right (New York: Oxford University Press, 2010), 207.

9 For examples of arguments of this kind, see Minutes of Communications Committee Board Meeting (September 15, 1984), NARAL, Box 16, Folder 3; Nanette Falkenberg to Members of the Media (March 20, 1985), NARAL, Box 185, Folder 5; Louise Tyrer to PP Affiliate Directors et al. (February 1985), NARAL, Box 188, Folder 5; Mary Heffernan to NARAL Foundation (April 15, 1985), NARAL, Box 188, Folder 5.

10 *Planned Parenthood of Central Missouri v. Danforth*, 428 U.S. 52, 52–55 (1976).

11 Reginald Stuart, "Akron Divided by Heated Abortion Debate," *New York Times*, February 1, 1978, A10. For Hubbard's statement: Jane Hubbard, Letter to the Editor, "Should City Monitor Abortion?" *Akron Beacon Journal*, November 21, 1977, A6. For more on the Akron battle, see "Akron Abortion Proposal Could Fuel National Debate," *Chicago Tribune*, January 25, 1978, B2.

12 Roy Lucas to Robert McCoy (June 30, 1982), JHP, Box 14, Akron Folder. On the decline of hospital-based abortions and the rise of freestanding clinics, see Stanley K. Henshaw, Jacqueline Darroch Forrest, Christopher Tietze, and Ellen Sullivan, "Abortion Services in the United States, 1979 and 1980," *Family Planning Perspectives* 14 (1982): 5–8; Sara Seims, "Abortion Availability in the United States," *Family Planning Perspectives* 12 (1980): 88–101. On the decline in abortion providers between 1982 and 1985, see Stanley K. Henshaw, Jacqueline Darroch Forrest, and Jennifer Van Vort, "Abortion Services in the United States, 1984 and 1985," *Family Planning Perspectives* 19 (1987): 63–70.

13 For more on NRLC's financial struggles, see Dr. John Willke to Carolyn Gerster (December 12, 1978), JBP, Matter Boxes, File 140; Mary Reilly Hunt to Judie Brown (March 21, 1978), JBP, Matter Boxes, File 140; Robert Krebsbach to Mildred Jefferson (September 15, 1977), JBP, Matter Boxes, File 140. On Jefferson's conflict with NRLC before her ouster and after the founding of Right to Life Crusade, see Mary Reilly Hunt to Mildred Jefferson (1977), JBP, Matter Boxes, File 487; Mary Reilly Hunt to NRLC Board of Directors (July 25, 1978), JBP, Matter Boxes, File 487; Carolyn Gerster to Chapter Presidents (January 15, 1979), JBP, Matter Boxes File 487; Carolyn Gerster to State Leader (January 15, 1979), JBP, Matter Boxes, File 487.

14 James Bopp Jr. to NRLC Legal Liaison Committee (March 16, 1978), JBP, Matter Boxes, File 306. For more on NRLC's financial struggles, see James Bopp Jr. to Carolyn Gerster (August 30, 1979), JBP, Matter Boxes, File 141; Judie Brown to Carolyn Gerster (March 6, 1979), JBP, Matter Boxes, File 141. For more on the importance attached to informed consent bills, see Sandy Faucher to James Bopp Jr. (July 6, 1978), JBP, Matter Boxes, File 141; Richard Garnett to James Bopp Jr. (November 22, 1981), JBP, Matter Boxes, File 433. Bothell and NRLC ultimately agreed to dismiss the lawsuit.

15 See Stuart, "Akron Divided," A10.

16 Cheryl Swain to Jane Hodgson (November 23, 1977), JHP, Box 15, Akron File. On Hodgson's career in the abortion-rights movement, see Carole Joffe, *Doctors of Conscience: The Struggle to Provide Abortion before and after Roe v. Wade* (Boston: Beacon, 1995), 8–27; Leslie J. Reagan, *Dangerous Pregnancies: Mothers, Disabilities, and Abortion in Modern America* (Berkeley: University of California Press, 2010), 170–174; David J. Garrow, *Liberty and Sexuality: The Right to Privacy and the Making of Roe v. Wade* (Berkeley: University of California Press, 1998), 428–430.

17 Jane Hodgson, Testimony Presented to the Akron City Council, Re: Proposed Regulations Governing Abortion Clinics (February 4, 1978), JHP, Box 15, Akron File.

18 "Akron Council Passes Abortion Law," *Ellensburg City Record*, March 1, 1978, 6. On the other states that copied the Akron ordinance, see "Parts of Akron Abortion Law Are Struck Down by US Judge," *Pittsburgh Post-Gazette*, August 23, 1979, 6.

19 On the testimony in the *Akron I* trial, see Transcript Excerpt of Trial Testimony of Dr. Frederick Robbins, Dean of Case Western Reserve School of Medicine and recipient of 1954 Nobel Prize, in Joint Appendix at 207a, *City of Akron v. Akron Center for Reproductive Health*, 462 U.S. 416 (1983).

20 Judith Adamek to Akron City Council (January 16, 1978), JBP, Matter Boxes, File 306. On the factual arguments made by Bopp and his colleagues, see Raymond Adamek to James Bopp Jr. (July 19, 1978), JBP, Matter Boxes, File 306; James Bopp Jr., Notes, "Informed Consent Proof" (nd, ca. 1978), JBP, Matter Boxes, File 306; Dr. Myre Sim to Eugune Fife (nd, ca. 1978), JBP, Matter Boxes, File 306. For factual arguments made by the ACLU and its allies, see Affidavit of Lori Lee (April 14, 1978), JBP, Matter Boxes, File 306; NARAL Press Release, Pamphlet, "The Opponents of Abortion Have Succeeded in Their Campaign to ..." (1978), JBP, Matter Boxes, File 306; NARAL Brochure, "Akron Abortion Ordinance: What You Need to Know" (nd, ca. 1978), JBP, Matter Boxes, File 306.

21 For the trial court's decision, see *Akron Center for Reproductive Health, Inc. v. City of Akron*, 479 F. Supp. 1172, 1201–1207, 1215 (N.D. Ohio 1979). For commentary on it from the period, see William Hershey, "Parts of Akron Abortion Law Struck Down," *Akron Beacon Journal*, August 22, 1979, A1. For the Sixth Circuit's decision, see *Akron Center for Reproductive Health, Inc. v. Akron*, 651 F.2d 1198, 1206, 1208, 1210 (6th Cir. 1981). On the decision to appeal, see Jim Carney, "U.S. Appeals Court Voids Part of Akron Abortion Law," *Akron Beacon Journal*, June 13, 1981, A1.

22 On the decision of *Matheson*, see *H. L. v. Matheson*, 450 U.S. 398 (1981). On O'Connor's nomination and the rumors about her previous politics, see Harold O. J. Brown to Edwin Meese III (July 8, 1981), RRP, OA 2408, O'Connor Folder; Max Friedersdorf to Jim Baker, Edwin Meese, Michael Deaver, et al. (July 6, 1981), RRP, OA2408, O'Connor Folder; Merilee Melvin, Memorandum to Edwin Meese (July 6, 1981), RRP, OA2408, O'Connor Folder; Merilee Melvin, Memorandum to Edwin Meese (July 8, 1981), RRP, OA 2408, O'Connor Folder. On O'Connor's positions on abortion and the ERA, see Donald T. Critchlow, *The Conservative Ascendancy: How the GOP Right Made Political History* (Cambridge, MA: Harvard University Press, 2007), 199.

23 On the push for the human life bill, see Joan Beck, "The Pro-life Groups Turn to Congress on Abortion," *Chicago Tribune*, January 30, 1981, B2; "Abortion Foes Offer Bill," *Chicago Tribune*, February 11, 1981, 8; Jon Margolis, "The Abortion Struggle on Capitol Hill," *Chicago Tribune*, March 22, 1981, A2; Bernard Weinraub, "Abortion Becoming a Top Priority Issue in Congress," *New York Times*, March 13, 1981, A18. On the doubts raised about the constitutionality of the human life bill, see Testimony on S. 158, A Bill to Provide that Human Life Shall Be Deemed to Exist from Conception, before the Senate Judiciary Committee, Subcommittee on Separation of Powers, 97th Congress 1st Sess. (May 21, 1981), 242–56 (Statement of Prof. Laurence H. Tribe); Testimony on S. 158, A Bill to Provide that Human Life Shall Be Deemed to Exist from Conception, before the Senate Judiciary Committee, Subcommittee on Separation of Powers, 97th Congress 1st

Sess. (June 10, 1981), 515–519 (Statement of Prof. Norman Dorsen); Testimony on S. 158, A Bill to Provide that Human Life Shall Be Deemed to Exist from Conception, before the Senate Judiciary Committee, Subcommittee on Separation of Powers, 97th Congress 1st Sess. (May 21, 1981), 308–311 (Statement of Prof. Robert Bork).

24 David N. O'Steen, Confidential Memo, "A New Solution–Two Amendments" (1980), CRP, on file with the author. For more on O'Steen's proposal, see Ziegler, *After Roe*, 86. On Hatch's proposal, see "Hatch Introduces New Federalist Amendment," *National Right to Life News*, September 28, 1981, 1, JRS, 1981 National Right to Life News Box; Leslie Bennetts, "Antiabortion Forces in Disarray Less Than a Year after Victories in Elections," *New York Times*, September 22, 1981, B5.

25 On the founding of the American Life League, see, e.g., Carol Mason, *Killing for Life: The Apocalyptic Narrative of Pro-life Politics* (Ithaca, NY: Cornell University Press, 2002), 15; Richard M. Viguerie, *The New Right: We're Ready to Lead* (Falls Church, VA: Viguerie and Co., 1981), 102, 154; Judie Brown, *It Is I Who Have Chosen You: An Autobiography* (Stafford, VA: American Life League, 1997), 7, 15, 41. On the formation of Scheidler's group, see Lee Strobel, "Right to Life Groups Muster Forces," *Chicago Tribune*, June 20, 1974, N14; Brenda Stone, "After Two Years, an Ominous Future for Legal Abortion," *Chicago Tribune*, January 22, 1975, B1; Mitchell Locin, "Bill to Ban Tax-Paid Abortion Is Vetoed," *Chicago Tribune*, September 14, 1977, 3; Patrick Buchanan, "Fighting Planned Parenthood," *Chicago Tribune*, November 7, 1978, B4; "8 Abortion Foes Arrested at Clinic," *Chicago Tribune*, September 9, 1979, 10. On the Army of God and antiabortion extremism in the early 1980s, see Mason, *Killing for Life*, 22–26; Jennifer Jefferis, *Armed for Life: The Army of God and Anti-abortion Terror in the United States* (Santa Barbara, CA: Praeger, 2011).

26 See Judie Brown, "Senator Hatch, No!" *A.L.L. About News*, January 1982, 1, WCX, ALL about News Folder; Judie Brown to John Willke (February 19, 1982), JBP, Matter Boxes, File 300.

27 Brown, "Senator Hatch, No!" 1. For more on ALL's view of Hatch and the Human Life Bill, see Christopher Wolfe, "The Human Life Bill–Yes!" *A.L.L. About News*, February 1982, 6, WCX, 1982 ALL About News Folder. On the division about the Hatch Amendment within the NRLC, see Anthony Lauinger to Directors and State Officers of the National Right to Life Committee (February 12, 1982), JBP, Matter Boxes, File 300; John Willke, "The Healing Commences," *National Right to Life News*, April 11, 1982, 3, JRS, 1981 National Right to Life News; Helen DeWitt to Friend of Life, August 23, 1982, 1-3, JBP, Matter Boxes, File 300; NRLC Board of Directors Meeting Minutes (January 30, 1982), JBP, Matter Boxes, File 300. On the December 1981 vote, see Ziegler, *After Roe*, 87.

28 Brown to Willke, 2. For Brown's statement on an alternative strategy: Judie Brown, "Facing the Battle," *A.L.L. About News*, February 1982, WCX, ALL About News Folder.

29 NRLC Brochure, "The Hatch Amendment: Questions and Quotes" (nd, ca. 1982), JBP, Matter Boxes, File 178; see also James Bopp Jr., "The Power Granted Congress and the States by the Hatch Federalism Amendment" (January 8, 1982), JBP, Matter Boxes, File 300.

30 On the panel vote, see "Senate Panel OKs Antiabortion Amendment," *Chicago Tribune*, December 17, 1981, 5. On the filibuster and final vote, see Robert Pear, "Filibuster Starts Abortion Debate," *New York Times*, August 17, 1982, A18; Robert Pear, "Baker Sets Vote after Labor Day on Ending Filibuster on Abortion and School Prayer," *New York Times*,

August 21, 1982, 9; Steven V. Roberts, "Senate Kills Plan to Curb Abortion by a Vote of 47–46," *New York Times*, September 16, 1982, A1.

31 On the panel vote, see Bernard Weinraub, "Abortion Curbs Endorsed, 10–7, by Senate Panel," *New York Times*, March 11, 1982, A1. For Helms' statement: John Herbers, "Abortion Battle Moving to the States," *New York Times*, June 12, 1983, 27. On the conflict between Galebach, Helms, and Hatch, see James Baker to Michael Uhlmann (September 14, 1982), RRP, OA11299, Galebach Papers; Michael Uhlmann to Stephen Galebach (September 13, 1982), RRP, OA11299, Galebach Papers.

32 For the statement about access: Notes from 3/31/1982 Strategy Meeting with Roger Craver, NARAL, Box 70, Folder 4. On the budget shortfall, see Sue Kuhn to Nanette Falkenberg (November 29, 1982), NARAL, Box 70, Folder 1; Sue Kuhn to Nanette Falkenberg (October 26, 1981), NARAL, Box 70, Folder 1; Sue Kuhn to Nanette Falkenberg (July 21, 1982), NARAL, Box 70, Folder 1. On Craver's explanation of NARAL's fundraising difficulties, see Memo, Craver, Mathews, Smith to NARAL (November 12, 1982), NARAL, Box 70, Folder 1.

33 Lael Morgan, "A Push for Planned Parenthood," *Los Angeles Times*, January 21, 1980, OC10. On the ad campaign, see Patricia McCormack, "Planned Parenthood Mounts Ad Campaign," *Los Angeles Times*, October 10, 1980, C6.

34 On the decision of some affiliates not to perform abortions, see Tom Davis, *Sacred Work: Planned Parenthood and Its Clergy Alliances* (Piscataway, NJ: Rutgers University Press, 2005), 147. On the investigation, see Robert Pear, "Planned Parenthood Groups Investigated on Use of US Funds," *New York Times*, December 6, 1981, 30. On the Title X cuts, see Critchlow, *Intended Consequences*, 212.

35 On the rise and fall of R2N2, see Jael Silliman et al., *Undivided Rights: Women of Color Organizing for Reproductive Justice* 2d ed. (Chicago: Haymarket, 2016), 39–41; Ziegler, *After Roe*, 149–155. For a discussion of the early work of R2N2 on abortion, see R2N2 Abortion Task Force Paper Draft (July 20, 1981), 11, R2N2, Box 1, Abortion Task Force Folder.

36 For Rosoff's plea: Jeannie Rosoff to Interested Parties (November 1, 1982), NARAL, Box 81, Folder 5. On the emphasis put on the Hatch Amendment after its reintroduction, see Nanette Falkenberg to NARAL Member (nd, ca. 1983), NARAL, Box 70, Folder 3; Nanette Falkenberg to NARAL Sustaining Member (nd, ca. 1983), NARAL, Box 70, Folder 3. On the decision of some affiliates not to perform abortions, see Davis, *Sacred Work*, 147. On the investigation, see Pear, "Planned Parenthood," 30. On the Title X cuts, see Critchlow, *Intended Consequences*, 212.

37 On *Ashcroft* and the law challenged in that case, see Mo. Rev. Stat. 188.025 et seq.; *Planned Parenthood Association v. Ashcroft*, 483 F. Supp. 679, 699–701 (1980). On *Simopoulos* and the law challenged in that case, see Va. Code § 18.2–71 (1982); *Simopoulos v. Commonwealth of Virginia*, 277 S.E. 2d 194.

38 Sylvia Law, interview with Mary Ziegler, June 22, 2016. For more on Law's career and early work on the ACLU Reproductive Freedom Project, see Sylvia Law and Rhonda Copelon, "'Nearly Allied to Her Right to Be': The Story of *Harris v. McRae*," in *Women and the Law Stories* eds. Elizabeth Schneider and Stephanie Wildman (New York: Foundation Press, 2013), 219; Leigh Ann Wheeler, *How Sex Became a Civil Liberty* (New York: Oxford University Press, 2013), 277.

39 Law, interview. This chapter later discusses the *Akron I* decision in greater depth.
40 On Segedy and Destro's background and strategy, see Meaghan Winter, "How the Undue Burden Standard Eroded *Roe v. Wade*," *Slate*, March 17, 2016, www.slate.com/articles/double_x/cover_story/2016/03/how_the_undue_burden_concept_eroded_roe_v_wade.html, accessed September 7, 2018; Joseph Fiske Kobylka and Lee Epstein, *The Supreme Court and Legal Change: Abortion and the Death Penalty* (Chapel Hill: University of North Carolina Press, 1992), 235–242; Tracy A. Thomas, "The Struggle for Gender Equality in the Northern District of Ohio," in *Justice and Legal Change on the Shores of Lake Erie: A History of the United States District Court for the Northern District of Ohio* eds. Paul Finkelman and Roberta Sue Alexander (Athens: Ohio University Press, 2012), 168–170; Tracy A. Thomas, "Back to the Future of Regulating Abortion in the First Term" *Wisconsin Journal of Law, Gender, & Society* 29 (2014): 47–52.
41 James Bopp Jr., "Standards of Review for Abortion Legislation" (nd, ca. 1978), JBP, Matter Boxes, File 140.
42 Petition for a Writ of Certiorari for the City of Akron, 1, *City of Akron v. Akron Center for Reproductive Health, Inc.*, 462 U.S. 416 (1983) (No. 81–746).
43 Brief Amicus Curiae of Feminists for Life, *City of Akron v. Akron Center for Reproductive Health, Inc.*, 462 U.S. 416 (1983) (No. 81–746).
44 For Planned Parenthood's argument: Brief of Amici Planned Parenthood Federation of America et al. at 7–62, *City of Akron v. Akron Center for Reproductive Health, Inc.*, 462 U.S. 416 (1983) (No. 81–746). For Copelon's claim: Brief Amicus Curiae for Certain Religious Organizations, 8–33, *City of Akron v. Akron Center for Reproductive Health, Inc.*, 462 U.S. 416 (1983) (No. 81–746). For NAF's claim, see Brief Amicus Curiae for the National Abortion Federation, 3, *City of Akron v. Akron Center for Reproductive Health, Inc.*, 462 U.S. 416 (1983) (No. 81–746). For NOW and NARAL's brief: Brief Amici Curiae for the National Organization for Women et al., 14, *City of Akron v. Akron Center for Reproductive Health, Inc.*, 462 U.S. 416 (1983) (No. 81–746).
45 On the Hatch-Eagleton Amendment, see Steven V. Roberts, "Full Senate Gets Abortion Measure," *New York Times*, April 20, 1983, A12; Ellen Hume, "Anti-abortion Amendment Killed in Senate," *Los Angeles Times*, June 29, 1983, 1; Dorothy Collin, "Abortion Amendment Defeated," *Chicago Tribune*, June 29, 1983, 3. For Jepsen's statement: Dee Jepsen, Memorandum to Elizabeth Dole (January 12, 1983), RRP, Morton Blackburn Papers, Box 14, NRLC Folder 2. On Willke's prediction, see John Willke to NRLC Board of Directors and State Offices Re Upcoming Vote on Hatch-Eagleton (June 22, 1983), 1–2, RRP, Morton Blackwell Papers, Box 14, NRLC Folder 2.
46 *City of Akron v. Akron Center for Reproductive Health, Inc.*, 462 U.S. 416, 434, 444–445 (1983).
47 Ibid., 452–474 (O'Connor, J., dissenting).
48 See *Planned Parenthood Association of Kansas City, Missouri v. Ashcroft*, 462 U.S. 476, 480–486 (1983); *Simopoulos v. Virginia*, 462 U.S. 506, 512–520 (1983).
49 Memorandum, Janet Benshoof, ACLU Reproductive Freedom Project, "The New Supreme Court Abortion Decision: A Legal Analysis with Questions and Answers" (July 18, 1983), 1–12, PMP, Box 114, Folder 2040. On Benshoof's background, see Charles Cohn et al., "Testing Guam's Tough New Abortion Law, Janet Benshoof Is Arraigned for Giving Advice," *People*, April 9, 1990, http://people.com/archive/testing-guams-tough-new-abor

tion-law-janet-benshoof-is-arraigned-for-giving-advice-vol-33-no-14, accessed July 4, 2016. For more on Benshoof's early work at the RFP, see Janet Benshoof and Judith Levin to Women's Rights Liaisons and Lawyers, Affiliate Directors (July 16, 1979), JHP, Box 15, Akron Folder (discussing the RFP's work in parental involvement cases); Janet Benshoof, Linda Ojala, and Franz Jevne to Jane Hodgson et al. (July 22, 1983), JHP, Box 15, Akron Folder; Janet Benshoof, Suzanne Lynn, and Lourdes Soto, "New Supreme Court Decision: *H.L. v. Matheson*" (April 1, 1981), JHP, Box 15, Akron Folder.

50 Benshoof Memorandum, 1–2.

51 NARAL Voters' Campaign (nd, ca. 1983), NARAL, Box 218, Folder 12. On Falkenberg, see NARAL, "Nanette Falkenberg: Biography" (nd, ca. 1982), NARAL, Box 218, Folder 12; Memorandum, Nanette Falkenberg Re: Outcome of the 1984 Elections on the Abortion Issue (nd, ca. 1984), NARAL, Box 218, Folder 12.

52 Emily Tynes to NARAL Affiliates (September 6, 1984), NARAL, Box 218, Folder 12. For NARAL's take on *Akron I*, see Gail Harmon and William S. Jordan to Nanette Falkenberg (June 7, 1984), NARAL, Box 218, Folder 12.

53 On the rise in anti-clinic attacks, see Suzanne Staggenborg, *The Pro-choice Movement: Organization and Activism in the Abortion Conflict* (New York: Oxford University Press 1991), 130–134; Linda Gordon, *The Moral Property of Women: A History of Birth Control Politics in America* (Urbana: University of Illinois Press, 2002), 190; Sandra Morgen, *Into Our Own Hands: The Women's Health Movement in the United States, 1969–1990* (Piscataway, NJ: Rutgers University Press, 2002), 190–200. For Johnston's argument: Peg Johnston, "Pro-life Is Anti-life, Woman, Sex," *Hera*, July 31, 1985, 4. For an example of the NRLC response to the bombing, see Gerald M. Boyd, "Reagan Condemns Arson at Clinics," *New York Times*, January 4, 1985, A1.

54 See NRLC Statehouse Update (August 12, 1983), RRP, OA 9106, Galebach Papers. For a study of the law and politics of reproductive torts, see Dov Fox, *Birth Rights and Wrongs: How Medicine and Technology Are Remaking Reproduction and the Law* (New York: Oxford University Press, 2019).

55 On the attorneys' fees that AUL had to pay, see Deanna Silberman, "They're In It for Life," *Student Lawyer* 18 (1989): 30–35. On the conflict within AUL, see George Huntston Williams to AUL Board Members (September 20, 1977), AUL, Executive File, Folder 91; Patrick Trueman to Members of the Board (July 10, 1978), AUL, Executive File, Folder 91. On Marzen's work in AUL, see "To Be Born, to Die: Individual Rights in the 1980s," *American Bar Association Journal* 70 (1984): 27–29; Marcia Chambers, "Advocates for the Right to Life," *New York Times*, December 16, 1984, A94. Marzen went on to work on right-to-die issues. For an early example of Marzen's work on the issue, see Thomas J. Marzen, "In the Matter of Claire C. Conroy," *Issues in Law and Medicine* 1 (1985): 77–84. On his move, see Thomas Marzen to AUL members and Leaders (October 10, 1984), MFJ, Box 13, Folder 6. Marzen would later work at Bopp's law firm in Terre Haute, Indiana.

56 On the new generation of AUL lawyers, see Silberman, 30–35. For more on evangelical mobilization on abortion in the mid-1980s, see Lauren F. Winner, "Reaganizing Religion: Changing Political and Cultural Norms among Evangelicals in Ronald Reagan's America," in *Living in the 1980s*, eds. Gil Troy and Vincent Cannato (New York: Oxford University Press, 2009), 194; Williams, *God's Own Party*, 207.

57 On the AUL conference, see Steven Baer, Report of the Education Division (1984), MFJ, Box 13, Folder 6; AUL Board of Directors Meeting Minutes (March 30, 1984), MFJ, Box 13, Folder 6; AUL Fundraising Letter (May 21, 1984), MFJ, Box 13, Folder 6; Dennis Horan to Friend of AUL (February 28, 1984), MRX, Box 68, Folder 38; AUL Brochure, "Reversing *Roe v. Wade* Through the Courts" (nd, ca. 1984), MRX, Box 68, Folder 38. For O'Connor's statement, see *City of Akron v. Akron Center for Reproductive Health, Inc.*, 462 U.S. 416, 458 (1983).

58 Victor Rosenblum and Thomas J. Marzen, "Strategies for Reversing *Roe v. Wade* in the Courts," in *Abortion and the Constitution: Reversing Roe v. Wade through the Courts*, eds. Dennis J. Horan et al. (Washington, DC: Georgetown University Press, 1987), 199–203.

59 See ibid.

60 Ibid. On the focus on the reasons women terminate a pregnancy, see AUL May 1984 Fundraising Letter, 1. Chapter 4 further discusses these strategies.

61 Fundraising Letter (nd, ca. February 1984), JBP, Matter Boxes, File 433.

62 Jean Doyle to NRLC Sustaining Member (August 13, 1984), JBP, Matter Boxes, File 433. On Willke's return, see NRLC Fundraising Letter (July 8, 1984), JBP, Matter Boxes, File 433.

63 NRLC, Memorandum, "To Change a Nation: A Historic Media Project Authorized by the NRLC Educational Trust Fund" (nd, ca. 1984), JBP, Matter Boxes, File 433. For more on the media campaign, see July 1 Fundraising Letter, 1–3; NRLC Fundraising Letter (August 13, 1984), JBP, Matter Boxes, File 433. For more on NRLC's early media efforts, see "National Right to Life Educational Trust Launches Media Impact Campaign," *National Right to Life News*, August 1984, 1, JRS, 1984 National Right to Life News Box.

64 Memorandum, "To Change a Nation," 1–3. On the fundraising benefits created by the media initiative, see Mary Reilly Hunt to NRLC Executive Committee (July 10, 1984), JBP, Matter Boxes, File 433.

65 On the influence of *The Silent Scream*, see Staggenborg, *The Pro-choice Movement*, 128; Sara Dubow, *Ourselves Unborn: A History of the Fetus in Modern America* (New York: Oxford University Press, 2010), 156–161; Johanna Schoen, *Abortion after Roe* (Chapel Hill: University of North Carolina Press, 2015), 145–151. For Nathanson's background and the controversy surrounding his career, see Emma Brown, "Bernard Nathanson, Abortion Doctor, Who Became Antiabortion Advocate, Dies at 84," *Washington Post*, February 22, 2011, www.washingtonpost.com/local/doctor-who-performed-abortions-later-decried-the-procedure/2011/02/23/ABe5NUI_story.html, accessed August 17, 2018.

66 On the claims made in *The Silent Scream* involving fetal pain, see Betty Cuniberti and Elizabeth Mehren, "'Silent Scream': Abortion Film Stirs Both Friend and Foe," *Los Angeles Times*, August 8, 1985, 20; Elizabeth Mehren and Betty Cuniberti, "Meet the Vocal Exponent of 'The Silent Scream,'" *Los Angeles Times*, August 8, 1985, D1; Paul Houston, "'Silent Scream' Called Testament for Pro-life," *Los Angeles Times*, February 13, 1985, B6. For O'Steen and Falkenberg's comments: Dena Kleiman, "Debate on Abortion Focuses on Graphic Film," *New York Times*, January 25, 1985, B8. For Goldsmith's argument: Houston, "Silent Scream," 1. On the representational politics of *The Silent Scream*, see Rosalind Pollack Petchesky, "Fetal Images: The Power of Visual Culture in the Politics of Reproduction," *Feminist Studies* 13 (1987): 263–292; Valerie Harouni, "Fetal Politics: Abortion Politics and the Optics of Allusion," *Camera Obscura*

29 (1992): 130–149; Jessie Givner, "Reproducing Reproductive Discourse: Optical Technologies in the Silent Scream and Eclipse of Reason," *Journal of Popular Culture* 28 (1994): 229–244.

67 Ellen Hume, "Morality Struggle: Anti-abortionists Gain as Furor Spreads and Uneasiness Grows," *Wall Street Journal*, April 15, 1985, 1.

68 On the transformation of medical care, see John C. Burnham, *Health Care in America: A History* (Baltimore, MD: Johns Hopkins University Press, 2015), 410–417; Nancy Tomes, *Remaking the American Patient: How Madison Avenue and Modern Medicine Turned Patients into Consumers* (Chapel Hill: University of North Carolina Press, 2016), 329–350. On the medical malpractice crisis of the 1980s, see Frank A. Sloan, Randall R. Bovbjerg, and Penny B. Githens, *Insuring Medical Malpractice* (New York: Oxford University Press, 1991), 7; Rogan Kersh, "Medical Malpractice and the New Politics of Health Care," in *Medical Malpractice and the U.S. Health Care System* eds. William M. Sage and Rogan Kersh (New York: Cambridge University Press, 2006).

69 On the improvements in neonatal care and their impact on perceived viability, see Schoen, *Abortion after Roe*, 87; Sheldon Ekland-Olson, *Life and Death Decisions: The Quest for Morality and Justice in Human Societies* (New York: Routledge, 2013), 55; Carol A. Heimer and Lisa R. Staffen, *For the Sake of the Children: The Social Organization of Responsibility in the Hospital and the Home* (Chicago: University of Chicago Press, 1998), 40. For more on the politics of fetal images in the period, see Petchesky, "Fetal Images," 263–292; Carol A. Stabile, "The Traffic in Fetuses," in *Fetal Subjects, Fetal Positions* eds. Lynn M. Morgan and Meredith Wilson Michaels (Philadelphia: University of Pennsylvania Press, 1999), 136–152; Karen Newman, *Fetal Positions: Individualism, Science, and Individuality* (Palo Alto, CA: Stanford University Press, 1996).

70 On the spread of viability-related regulations, see Americans United for Life Board Meeting Report (March 1984), MFJ, Box 13, Folder 6; AUL 1984 Fundraising Letter, 1; Robert A. Jones, "Accent on Fetal Pain," *Los Angeles Times*, September 24, 1984, A1.

71 For examples of these arguments, see Hume, "Morality Struggles," 1; Houston, "Silent Scream," 1; Kleiman, "Debate on Abortion," 1.

72 On the White House picket, see "NOW Pickets Reagan on Abortion," *Los Angeles Times*, March 23, 1984, B11. On the vigils, see Marlene Cimons, "NOW to Hold Vigils at 25 Abortion Clinics in 18 States to Guard against Violence," *Los Angeles Times*, January 18, 1985, B25; Adrianne Goodman and Nancy Wride, "Abortion Anniversary: Clinics Tighten Security," *Los Angeles Times*, January 25, 1985, OC_A1. For recollections of NOW's work on reproductive rights: Goldsmith, interview; Mary Jean Collins, interview with Mary Ziegler, July 15, 2015.

73 Kim Gandy, interview with Mary Ziegler, May 25, 2016. For more on the march, see Robin Toner, "NOW Marches in Support of the Right to Abortion," *New York Times*, June 15, 1986, A21; Stephen Braun, "Feminists Out in Force," *Los Angeles Times*, March 17, 1986, A8. For more on the feminist energy surrounding the abortion-rights movement in the mid-1980s, see William Saletan, *Bearing Right: How Conservatives Won the Abortion War* (Berkeley: University of California Press, 2004), 35–42.

74 On the "squeal rule," see "900 Groups Oppose Birth Control Rule," *Los Angeles Times*, January 26, 1983, B2; "Quit Bugging Planned Parenthood," *Atlanta Journal-Constitution*, September 7, 1983, 10A. On the Mexico City policy, see Joan Radovich, "U.S. Acts to Ban

Abortion Funds Abroad," *Los Angeles Times*, July 14, 1984, A1; Susan Rasky, "Reagan Restrictions on Foreign Aid for Abortion Programs Leads to a Fight," *New York Times*, October 24, 1984, A20.

75 Louise Tyrer to PP Affiliate Directors et al. (February 1985), NARAL, Box 185, Folder 5. For more on Planned Parenthood's response to *The Silent Scream*, see Planned Parenthood Federation of America, "The Facts Speak Louder: Planned Parenthood's Response to *The Silent Scream*" (1985), on file with the author.

76 Nanette Falkenberg to Judy Goldsmith (February 1, 1985), NARAL, Box 229, Folder 11.

77 Mary Heffernan and Lynn Paltrow to Meeting Attendees (March 19, 1985), NARAL, Box 185, Folder 6. For the other concerns motivating the symposium: Mary Heffernan to NARAL Foundation (April 15, 1985), NARAL, Box 185, Folder 5. On the National Black Women's Health Project, see Silliman, Fried, Gutiérrez, and Ross, *Undivided Rights* 80–83, 100–103. On the National Latina Women's Health Project, see Marlene Gerber Fried, "Abortion in the United States–Legal but Inaccessible," in *Abortion Wars: A Half-Century of Struggle, 1950–2000* ed. Rickie Solinger (Berkeley: University of California Press, 1998), 208–227.

78 NARAL Strategy Weekend Second Day Session (March 1985), 1, 3–4, 6–8, NARAL, Box 185, Folder 5.

79 Nanette Falkenberg to Members of the Media (March 20, 1985), NARAL, Box 185, Folder 5. On the statement about women speaking out: Heffernan to NARAL Foundation, 1. For more on the launch of *Silent No More*, see Staggenborg, *The Pro-choice Movement*, 125–127; Saletan, *Bearing Right*, 37–40.

80 Memorandum, Impact of Focus on Women Strategy Weekend on "Silent No More," (April 29, 1985), NARALMA, Box 16, Folder 14. For Falkenberg's statement on hardship cases: Letter from Nanette Falkenberg to NARAL Leadership, *Re: Action* (nd, c. 1985), NARALMA, Box 16, Folder 14. On the letters collected as part of *Silent No More*, see Nadine Brozan, "Abortion-Rights: New Tactics," *New York Times*, May 6, 1985, C12.

81 On the spread of downsizing in the 1980s, see William S. Baumol, Alan S. Blinder, and Edward N. Wolff, *Downsizing in America: Causes and Consequences* (New York: Russell Sage Foundation, 2003), 1–10, 257–260; David B. Audrestsch and A. Roy Thurik, "Introduction," in *Innovation, Evolution, and Employment* eds. David B. Audretsch and A. Roy Thurik (New York: Cambridge University Press, 1999), 4–8.

82 Memorandum from Nanette Falkenberg, 1. On NARAL's goal of giving women a voice, see Press Release, NARAL, "Abortion: Silent No More" (March 20, 1985), NARALMA, Box 16, Folder 14.

83 On RCAR and NOW's outreach, see Staggenborg, *The Pro-choice Movement*, 144; Nelson, *More than Medicine*, 168; Silliman, Fried, Gutiérrez, and Ross, *Undivided Rights*, 82.

84 Catherine Davis, interview with Mary Ziegler, August 15, 2017.

85 Ibid.

86 Ibid. For more on Davis's work in the movement, see Shaila Dewan, "Anti-abortion Billboards on Race Split Atlanta," *New York Times*, February 6, 2010, A9; Shaila Dewan, "To Court Blacks, Foes of Abortion Make Racial Case," *New York Times*, February 27, 2010, A1. On the Restoration Project, see Paige Winfield Cunningham, "'Black Babies Matter': The Black Anti-abortion Movement's Political Problem," *Washington Examiner*,

September 28, 2015, www.washingtonexaminer.com/black-babies-matter-the-black-anti-abortion-movements-political-problems.

87 On Black Americans for Life, see Jacquin Sanders, "Anti-abortion Leader Doesn't Fit the Pattern," *St. Petersburg Times*, October 11, 1987, 1B; Richette Haywood, "How Will the Abortion Ruling Affect Blacks?" *Jet*, July 24, 1989, 14; "More Fuel for the Abortion Fire," *Black Enterprise*, October 1990, 31; Pamela Carr, "Which Way Black America? Anti-abortion," *Ebony*, October 1989, 134.

88 On the fight for the Pennsylvania Abortion Control Act, see Jil Clark, "Pennsylvania Legislature Passes Anti-abortion Bill," *Gay Community News*, January 9, 1982, 3; Jil Clark, "Governor's Veto Kills Abortion Control Bill," *Gay Community News*, January 30, 1982, 5; "Abortion Control Law Barred in Pennsylvania," *New York Times*, December 10, 1982, A16. On AUL's concerns about the Pennsylvania Abortion Control Act, see Edward Grant, "Abortion and the Constitution: The Impact of *Thornburgh* on the Strategy to Reverse *Roe v. Wade*," in *Abortion and the Constitution: Reversing Roe v. Wade through the Courts* eds. Dennis J. Horan et al. (Washington, DC: Georgetown University Press, 1987), 245–263.

89 For the Third Circuit's decision, see *American College of Obstetricians and Gynecologists v. Thornburgh*, 737 F.2d 283, 290–296 (3d Cir. 1984). On reaction to *Thornburgh* and the Supreme Court's decision to hear the case, see Linda Greenhouse, "Court to Hear Pennsylvania Abortion Appeal," *New York Times*, April 16, 1985, A23; Glen Elsasser, "High Court to Review State Abortion Law," *Chicago Tribune*, May 25, 1985, 4A.

90 For Kolbert's argument, see Brief for Appellees, 1–6, *Thornburgh v. American College of Obstetricians and Gynecologists*, 476 U.S. 747 (1986) (No. 84–495). For the ACLU's argument: Brief Amici Curiae of the American Civil Liberties Union et al., 28, *Thornburgh v. American College of Obstetricians and Gynecologists*, 476 U.S. 747 (1986) (No. 84–495).

91 Brief of the National Abortion-Rights Action League et al. as Amici Curiae, 20–24, *Thornburgh v. American College of Obstetricians and Gynecologists*, 476 U.S. 747 (1986) (No. 84–495).

92 Ibid., 20–27. For more on NARAL's strategy prior to *Thornburgh*, see Saletan, *Bearing Right*, 36–42.

93 See Brief Amici Curiae of the Center for Constitutional Rights et al., 22–25, *Thornburgh v. American College of Obstetricians and Gynecologists*, 476 U.S. 747 (1986) (No. 84–495).

94 For AUL's argument, see Brief of Drs. Eugene Diamond and Jasper Williams, 5–15, *Thornburgh v. American College of Obstetricians and Gynecologists*, 476 U.S. 54 (1986) (No. 84–1379); see also Brief of National Right to Life Committee, 16–20, *Thornburgh v. American College of Obstetricians and Gynecologists*, 476 U.S. 747 (1986) (No. 84–495); Brief Amici Curiae of Olivia Gans et al., 6–18, *Thornburgh v. American College of Obstetricians and Gynecologists*, 476 U.S. 747 (1986) (No. 84–495). This argument took center stage in earlier pro-life briefs, particularly in *Harris v. McRae*, the unsuccessful challenge to the Hyde Amendment. See Brief Amicus Curiae of the National Right to Life Committee, 4–15, *Williams v. Zbaraz*, 448 U.S. 358 (1980) (No. 79–4).

95 See Brief of the National Right to Life Committee in *Thornburgh*, 16–20.

96 Brief Amici Curiae of Olivia Gans et al., 6.

97 Brief for the United States as Amicus Curiae in Support of Appellants, 2, *Thornburgh v. American College of Obstetricians and Gynecologists*, 476 U.S. 747 (1986) (No. 84–495).

On AUL perceptions of the brief for the United States, see Grant, "Abortion and the Constitution," 245–263.

98 See *Thornburgh v. American College of Obstetricians and Gynecologists*, 476 U.S. 747, 751–759 (1986). On the significance of the Court's decision, see Garrow, *Liberty and Sexuality*, 652, 657, 662; Joseph Fiske Kobylka and Lee Epstein, *The Supreme Court and Legal Change: Abortion and the Death Penalty* (Chapel Hill: University of North Carolina Press, 1992), 255–257; James F. Simon, *The Center Holds: The Power Struggle within the Rehnquist Court* (New York: Simon and Schuster, 1995), 225–226.

99 For Johnson's comment: William K. Stevens, "Margin of Vote Is Called Key to Abortion Decision," *New York Times*, June 12, 1986, B12. For Willke's comment: Gailey, "Abortion Foe," 6.

100 On the 1986 election, see Linda Greenhouse, "A Turning Point on the Abortion Issue?" *New York Times*, November 13, 1986, B11; Bruce Buursma, "Voters Temper Religious Right," *Chicago Tribune*, December 5, 1986, A8; Robin Toner, "Abortion Foes Ponder Setbacks," *New York Times*, January 26, 1987, A22. For the Court's decision on family planning groups, see *Babbitt v. Planned Parenthood of Central and Northern Arizona et al.*, 479 U.S. 925 (1986). For contemporary reception of the decision, see Glen Elsasser, "High Court Removes a Barrier to Abortions," *Chicago Tribune*, November 4, 1986, 1; "Court Upholds Funds for Family Planning Clinic," *New York Times*, November 4, 1986, A27.

101 On Burger's retirement and the elevation of Rehnquist and nomination of Scalia, see Philip Hager, "Move to Provide New Conservative Strength," *Los Angeles Times*, June 18, 1986, D1; Stuart Taylor Jr., "Rehnquist and Scalia Take Their Places on Court," *New York Times*, September 27, 1986, 1. On Powell's retirement, see Glen Elsasser and Janet Cawley, "Powell Quits Supreme Court," *Chicago Tribune*, June 27, 1987, 1; Stuart Taylor Jr., "Powell Leaves High Court," *New York Times*, June 27, 1987, 1. On the significance of Bork's nomination, see Steven M. Teles, *The Rise of the Conservative Legal Movement: The Battle for Control of the Law* (Princeton, NJ: Princeton University Press, 2008), 169–177; Mark Tushnet, *A Court Divided: The Rehnquist Court and the Future of Constitutional Law* (New York: W. W. Norton, 2005), 336.

102 On the failure of Bork's nomination, see Al Kamen and Edward Walsh, "Senate Panel Votes 9–5 to Reject Bork," *Washington Post*, October 7, 1987, A1. On Bork's defeat in the Senate, see David Lauter, "Senate Vote Rejects Bork, 58–42," *Los Angeles Times*, October 23, 1987, 1; Linda Greenhouse, "Judge Bork Is Stepping Down to Answer Critics and Reflect," *New York Times*, January 15, 1988, A1. For the Court's decision in *Hartigan*, see *Hartigan v. Zbaraz*, 484 U.S. 171 (1987). For commentary on the decision from the period, see David Savage, "Abortion Splits High Court," *Los Angeles Times*, December 15, 1987, 1.

103 Guy Condon to Richard John Neuhaus (April 1988), RJN, Box 33, Folder 2. For Willke's statement: J. C. Willke, "From the President's Desk: Of Greatest Importance," *National Right to Life News*, September 12, 1988, 3, JRS, 1988 National Right to Life News Box. On Kennedy's confirmation, see Linda Greenhouse, "Senate, 97 to 0, Confirms Kennedy to High Court," *New York Times*, February 4, 1988, A1.

104 On the outcome of the 1988 election, see Helen Dewar, "Democrats Strengthen Control of Hill in Divided Government," *Washington Post*, November 10, 1988, A37; Robert

Shogan, "Sharp Partisan Split Threatens Bush Programs," *Los Angeles Times*, January 22, 1989, A1; Dan Balz, "Bush Given Painful Lesson about Divided Government," *Washington Post*, March 10, 1989, A1. On Bush's record and murky position on abortion in the period, see Gerald M. Boyd, "Bush Team Battles Foes of Abortion over Cabinet Job," *New York Times*, December 21, 1988, A1; Laura Sessions Stepp and Ann Devroy, "Bush Cites Abortion 'Tragedy' in Call to 67,000 Protesters," *Washington Post*, January 24, 1989, A1; David Lauter, "Bush Attempts to Distance GOP from Abortion Issue," *Los Angeles Times*, November 8, 1989, A22.

105 Grant, "Abortion and the Constitution," 258.

106 Chapter 4 further discusses Operation Rescue's bid for leadership of the pro-life movement.

107 Kate Michelman to NARAL Friends (December 21, 1988), NARAL, Box 204, Folder 8. On the strategic plan, see NARAL, Strategic Plan, 1987–1990 (nd, ca. 1987), NARAL, Box 204, Folder 8. Chapter 4 discusses abortion-rights supporters' disagreement about the strategy NARAL used.

4 *PLANNED PARENTHOOD V. CASEY*, THE FAMILY, AND EQUAL CITIZENSHIP

1 Rachael Pine, email interview with Mary Ziegler, August 3, 2018; Rachael Pine, interview with Mary Ziegler, April 8, 2016. For more on Pine's work on reproductive rights, see Susan Okie, "Court May Enter Debate on When Pregnancy Starts," *Washington Post*, May 28, 1989, A18; David G. Savage, "Courts to Decide If Clinics May Talk about Abortion," *Los Angeles Times*, May 30, 1990, 1; David G. Savage, "Abortion Opponents Expected to Press for Regulation Instead of Ban," *Los Angeles Times*, January 15, 1991, 1. For Pine's statement about *Hodgson* serving as an operational challenge, see Rachael Pine, "Speculation and Reality: The Role of Facts in Judicial Protection of Fundamental Rights," *University of Pennsylvania Law Review* 136 (1988): 655–727.

2 Pine, interview.

3 Edward Grant, interview with Mary Ziegler, March 30, 2016; Edward Grant, interview with Mary Ziegler, March 18, 2016. For more on Grant's work in AUL, see Philip Hager, "Dismiss Attempt to Reinstate Illinois Law," *Los Angeles Times*, May 1, 1986, 22; Cynthia Gorney, "Whose Body Is It, Anyway?" *Washington Post*, December 13, 1988, D1; Savage, "Abortion Opponents Expected to Press," 1.

4 Grant, interview.

5 Grant, interview. Chapter 5 further discusses pro-lifers' reaction to the *Casey* decision.

6 Grant, interview.

7 On early family involvement laws, see National Right to Life Committee Strategy Meeting (February 10, 1973), ACCL, Box 4, 1973 NRLC Folder. For more on the early restrictions championed by the movement, see "Governor Signs Missouri Bill," *National Right to Life News*, July 1974, 7, JRS, 1974 National Right to Life News Box; "Massachusetts Passes Law over Governor's Veto," *National Right to Life News*, September 1974, 2, JRS, 1974 National Right to Life News Box; "Michigan Citizens for Life Vows Abortion Law Enforcement," *National Right to Life News*, August 1975, 3, JRS, 1975 National Right to Life News Box. On the spread of such laws in the 1970s, see Terry Sollum and Patricia Donovan, "State

Laws and the Provision of Family Planning and Abortion Services in 1985," *Family Planning Perspectives* 17 (1985): 262–266; see also Missouri Right to Life, HCS-HB 492, "Parental Consent" (1979), JBP, Matter Boxes, File 111; Georgia Dullea, "Teen-Age Abortions without Family Consent Hang in the Balance," *New York Times*, June 22, 1976, 54.

8 For more on the history of the no-fault revolution, see Joanna L. Grossman and Lawrence M. Friedman, *Inside the Castle: Law and the Family in 20th-Century America* (Princeton, NJ: Princeton University Press, 2011), 159–192; Lawrence Friedman, *Private Lives: Families, Individuals, and the Law* (Cambridge, MA: Harvard University Press, 2004); Allen M. Parkman, *Good Intentions Gone Awry: No-Fault Divorce and the American Family* (Lanham, MD: Rowman and Littlefield, 2000). On women's rate of workforce participation, see United States Department of Commerce Bureau of Census, *A Statistical Portrait of Women in the United States* (Washington, DC: Government Printing Office, 1976), 26–28. On changing sexual mores, see Daniel C. Beggs & Henry A. Copeland, Special Ethic Accompanies College Sexual Revolution, *Chicago Tribune*, May 8, 1971, 2.

9 *Bellotti v. Baird*, 443 U.S. 622, 640, 644 (1979) (*Bellotti II*). For the Court's decision in *Bellotti I*, see *Bellotti v. Baird*, 428 U.S. 132 (1976). For the Court's decision in *Danforth*, see *Planned Parenthood of Central Missouri v. Danforth*, 428 U.S. 52 (1976).

10 See *H. L. v. Matheson*, 450 U.S. 398, 405–411 (1981). For more on movement responses to *Matheson*, see Janet Benshoof et al. to Abortion Providers et al., "New Supreme Court Decision: *H. L. v. Matheson*" (April 1, 1981), JHP, Box 5, Reproductive Freedom Project Folder.

11 *City of Akron v. Akron Center for Reproductive Health*, 462 U.S. 416, 439–440 (1983); see also Samuel Davis, *Children's Rights under the Law* (New York: Oxford University Press, 2011), 89–90; Deborah L. Rhode, *Justice and Gender: Sex Discrimination and the Law* (Cambridge, MA: Harvard University Press, 1989), 217–218.

12 See George Bishop to Ohio Right to Life (May 23, 1984), JBP, Matter Boxes, File 433. For the statute challenged in *Hodgson*, see Minn. Stat. §§ 144.343(2)–(7). For the trial in the Minnesota case, see *Hodgson v. Minnesota*, 648 F. Supp. 756 (D. Minn. 1986). For the Ohio law, see Ohio Rev. Code Ann. §§ 2919.12(D). For the lower court's decision in the case, see *Akron Center for Reproductive Health v. Rosen*, 633 F. Supp. 1123 (N.D. Ohio 1986). For the polls, see Lydia Saad, "Public Opinion about Abortion: An In-Depth Review," Gallup, January 22, 2002, https://news.gallup.com/poll/9904/public-opinion-about-abortion-indepth-review.aspx, accessed May 30, 2019.

13 See Deanna Silberman, "They're in It for Life," *Student Lawyer* 18 (1989): 30–35. For early discussion of Forsythe's work, see Jeff Lyon, "Limiting Government Interference: Baby Doe Decision Takes Some Heat Off of Medical Community," *Chicago Tribune*, June 15, 1986, D1; Barbara Brotman, "The Abortion Maze: Crazy Quilt of Laws among States Likely to Get Worse," *Chicago Tribune*, January 14, 1990, A1. For recollections of Forsythe's impact: Grant, March 18 interview; Grant, March 30 interview Myrna Gutiérrez, interview with Mary Ziegler, August 9, 2016; Laurie Ramsey Jaffe, interview with Mary Ziegler, September 18, 2016; Paige Comstock Cunningham, interview with Mary Ziegler, October 23, 2014. Forsythe went on to write a good deal about *Roe*, including a book that received considerable attention. See Clarke Forsythe, *Abuse of Discretion: The Inside Story of Roe v. Wade* (New York: Encounter Books, 2013).

14 On the 1988 election and pro-lifers' discomfort, see Laurence H. Tribe, *Abortion: The Clash of Absolutes* (New York: W. W. Norton, 1992), 172; Raymond Tatalovich, *The*

Politics of Abortion in Canada and the United States: A Comparative Study (New York: Routledge, 1997), 145. On Bush's shifting views on abortion, see "Media Outlets Examine Evolution of George H.W. Bush's Stances on Abortion, Family Planning," *Kaiser Daily Health Policy Report,* December 6, 2018, www.kff.org/news-summary/media-outlets-exam ine-evolution-of-george-h-w-bushs-stances-on-family-planning-abortion, accessed May 30, 2019.

15 NRLC Press Release, "GOP Platform Committee Urged to Adopt Pro-life Planks Again," (July 7, 1988), JBP, Matter Boxes, File 345; see also Anthony Lauinger to David O'Steen et al. (April 21, 1988), JBP, Matter Boxes, File 345; Dr. Jack Willke, Testimony before the Platform Committee (nd, ca. July 1988), JBP, Matter Boxes, File 345. For AUL's statement on the value of aligning with abortion foes: "In Brief," *Life Docket,* August 1988, SBL, AUL Folder 1.

16 On Condon's fundraising contributions, see Guy Condon, "Building a Fundraising System on a Tight Budget," *Fundraising Management* 18 (September 1986): 56–58. On AUL's work on parental involvement statutes, see "Supreme Court Calls for More Briefs in Parental Notification Case," *AUL Newsletter,* September 1987, 3, SBL, Box 1, AUL Folder 2. On AUL's connection with the DeMoss Foundation in the period, see Thomas Marzen to James Bopp Jr. (January 30, 1989), JBP, Matter Boxes, File 345; see also Janet Benshoof and Andrea Miller, *Tipping the Scales: The Christian Right's Legal Crusade against Choice* (New York: Center for Reproductive Law and Policy, 1998), 76–78.

17 For the statement made by the NRLC board member: Geline Williams, interview with Mary Ziegler, August 10, 2016. For more on NRLC's involvement in parental consultation politics, see Leslie Bond, "Multi-Million Suit Filed in Indiana after Teen Abortions," *National Right to Life News,* July 30, 1987, 5, JRS, 1987 National Right to Life News Box; Dave Andrusko, "Minnesota to Appeal Decision of Court of Appeals Overturning Parental Notification Law," *National Right to Life News,* September 10, 1987, 4, JRS, 1987 National Right to Life News Box; Leslie Bond, "Martinez Signs Parental Consent," *National Right to Life News,* July 7, 1988, 1, JRS, 1988 National Right to Life News Box; Dave Andrusko, "Pro-Abortionists Unsure Whether to Appeal Decision Upholding Parent Notification Law," *National Right to Life News,* August 25, 1988, 5, JRS, 1988 National Right to Life News Box.

18 Laurie Ann Ramsey to Richard John Neuhaus (July 23, 1987), RJN, Box 33, Folder 2.

19 For the statute challenged in *Hodgson*: Minn. Stat. §§ 144.343(2)–(7). For more on the movement's fight against parental involvement statutes, see Janet Benshoof, Linda Ojala, and Franz Jevne to Jane Hodgson et al. (July 22, 1983), JHP, Box 15, ACLU Reproductive Freedom Project Folder; Suzanne Lynn to Reproductive Freedom Project Advisory Committee Minors' Litigators "Re: *Orr v. Knowles; Epp v. Kerret*" (September 29, 1983), RHP, Box 5, ACLU Reproductive Freedom Folder. For more on parental involvement politics, see Carol Sanger, *About Abortion: Terminating Pregnancy in the Twenty-First Century* (Cambridge, MA: Harvard University Press, 2017), 170–201.

20 Janet Benshoof and Rachel Pine to ACLU Board et al., "Re: Trial of *Hodgson v. State of Minnesota*" (March 24, 1986), JHP, Box 5, ACLU Reproductive Freedom Project Folder.

21 Edward Fiske, "Role of Colleges Widens in Guiding Students' Lives," *New York Times,* February 22, 1987, 1. For the statement in the *Times,* see Kenneth Woodard and Arthur Kornaber, "Youth Is Maturing Later: So Revamp Higher Education," *New York Times,*

May 10, 1985, A31. For more on changing ideas of maturity in the period, see James E. Côté, *Arrested Adulthood: The Changing Nature of Maturity and Identity* (New York: New York University Press, 2000), 63–66; Gary Cross, *Men to Boys: The Making of Modern Immaturity* (New York: Columbia University Press, 2008), 138–158.

22 Jennifer Lowe, "Boomerang Kids: For One Reason or Another, Adult Children Are Flocking Back Home to the Family Nest," *Chicago Tribune*, November 29, 1987, M18. For more on anxieties about boomerang children in the period, see Andrew Marton, "The Boomerangers: Adult Children Back in the Fold," *Washington Post*, August 3, 1990, B5.

23 Benshoof and Pine to ACLU Board, 4–5.

24 See ibid.

25 Mark Lally, Draft Amicus Curiae Brief (September 1988), JBP, Matter Boxes, File 679. For more on the strategy of NRLC's Ohio affiliate, see Mark Lally to James Bopp Jr. (1988), JBP, Matter Boxes, File 679; Mark Lally and Susan Stechschulte to Anthony Celebrezze (August 30, 1988), JBP, Matter Boxes, File 679.

26 Benshoof and Pine to ACLU Board, 4–5. For more on *Hodgson*, see Bernard Schwartz, *Decision: How the Supreme Court Decides Cases* (New York: Oxford University Press, 1996), 31–35; Helena Silverstein, *Girls on the Stand: How Courts Fail Pregnant Minors* (New York: New York University Press, 2007), 90, 98, 142, 152–153; Patricia Boling, *Privacy and the Politics of Intimate Life* (Ithaca, NY: Cornell University Press, 1996), 92–94.

27 On Bork's opposition to the *Roe* decision, see Jack M. Balkin, "Introduction: *Roe v. Wade*: Engine of Controversy," in *What Roe v. Wade Should Have Said: The Nation's Top Legal Experts Rewrite America's Most Controversial Decision* ed. Jack M. Balkin (New York: New York University Press, 2005), 13–14; H. L. Pohlman, *Constitutional Debate in Action: Civil Rights and Liberties* 2d ed. (Lanham, MD: Rowman and Littlefield, 2005), 116; Andrew Hartman, *A War for the Soul of America: A History of the Culture Wars* (Chicago: University of Chicago Press, 2015), 153–155. On the mobilizing effect of Bork's defeat, see Steven M. Teles, *The Rise of the Conservative Legal Movement: The Battle for Control of the Law* (Princeton, NJ: Princeton University Press, 2008), 169–170; Damon Rule, *Overruled: The Long Battle for Control of the U.S. Supreme Court* (New York: Macmillan, 2014), 109; Mark Tushnet, *A Court Divided: The Rehnquist Court and the Future of Constitutional Law* (New York: W. W. Norton, 2005), 336. On the Kennedy nomination and opposition to it, see "Senate Panel Approves Kennedy for the High Court," *Wall Street Journal*, January 28, 1988, 1; "Senators OK Kennedy 97–0," *Los Angeles Times*, February 3, 1988, 1; Joseph Tybor, "Reagan Record on Judges Blasted," *Chicago Tribune*, February 4, 1988, 17. For the Sixth Circuit's decision in the Ohio case, see *Akron Center for Reproductive Health v. Slaby*, 854 F.2d 852 (6th Cir. 1988).

28 On the background of the case, see Tamar Lewin, "Woman Has Abortion, Violating Court's Order on Paternal Rights," *New York Times*, April 14, 1988, A26; "Abortion Dispute Sent to Indiana Lower Court," *Chicago Tribune*, April 15, 1988, 3; "Father's Rights at Issue in Abortion Cases," *Chicago Tribune*, April 15, 1988, 3. On the declining abortion rate, see Stanley K. Henshaw and Jennifer Van Vort, "Abortion Services in the United States, 1991 and 1992," *Family Planning Perspectives* 26 (1994): 100–112.

29 Richard Coleson to Paul Lewis Re: Fathers' Rights Case (July 28, 1988), JBP, Matter Boxes, File 1185.

30 See *In the Matter of the Unborn Child [H]*, Findings of Fact, Conclusions of Law, and Order, Vigo Circuit Court, 1988 Term (No. 84C018804 JP 185), 6a.

31 See Respondents' Brief in Opposition to Petition for a Grant of Certiorari, *Smith v. Doe* (No. 88–1837) (1988), 3–5, on file with the author.

32 Petition for Writ of Certiorari, 8, 16, *Smith v. Doe* (No. 88–1837), on file with the author.

33 For context on the broader fathers' rights movement, see Deborah Dinner, "The Divorce Bargain: The Fathers' Rights Movement and Family Inequalities," *University of Virginia Law Review* 102 (2016): 80–105. For arguments made on behalf of biological fathers' rights in adoption, see, for example, Brief for the American Civil Liberties Union as Amicus Curiae, *Caban v. Mohammed*, 441 U.S. 380 (1979) (No. 11). For more on the Court's unwed-father jurisprudence, see *Stanley v. Illinois*, 405 U.S. 645 (1972); *Caban v. Mohammed*, 441 U.S. 380 (1979); *Lehr v. Robertson*, 463 U.S. 248 (1983). On the complex arguments made by biological fathers in court, see Serena Mayeri, "Foundling Fathers: (Non-)Marriage and Parental Rights in the Age of Equality," *Yale Law Journal* 125 (2016): 2295–2391.

34 For the Highland, Indiana, letter: E. Byrne O'Malley to James Bopp Jr. (July 20, 1988), JBP, Matter Boxes, File 1185. For more on the reasons that men pursued such cases, see Martha Brannigan, "Suit to Argue Fathers' Rights in Abortion–One Plaintiff Petitioned the Supreme Court," *Wall Street Journal*, August 23, 1988, 29; see also David Savage, "Fathers' Appeal to Justices Asks Equal Rights to Children, Even Unborn," *Los Angeles Times*, September 25, 1988, A20.

35 For the South Carolina letter: Maggie Koestner of the Constitutional Legal Foundation to James Bopp Jr. (nd, ca. 1988), JBP, Matter Boxes, File 1185. On the statement of Bopp and Coleson's client: Brannigan, "Suits to Argue," 29. For more on the competing ideas embedded in the cases, see Lewin, "Woman Has Abortion," A26; Brannigan, "Suits to Argue," 29; Savage, "Fathers' Appeal," A20; Al Kamen, "Court: Husband Can't Veto Abortion," *Washington Post*, November 15, 1988, A5.

36 Marney Rich, "A Question of Rights: Birth and Death Decisions Put Women in the Middle of Legal Conflict," *Chicago Tribune*, September 18, 1988, F1. For the result of the study, see Jean Davidson, "Drug Babies Push Issue of Fetal Rights," *Los Angeles Times*, April 25, 1989, 1. On coverage of the crack epidemic, see Dorothy E. Roberts, *Killing the Black Body: Race, Reproduction, and the Meaning of Liberty* 2d ed. (New York: Vintage, 2017), 154; Ibram X. Kendi, *Stamped from the Beginning: The Definitive History of Racist Ideas in America* (New York: Perseus, 2016), 434–441; Doris Marie Provine, *Unequal under Law: Race in the War on Drugs* (Chicago: University of Chicago Press, 2007), 192.

37 For the statement about the strategic value of prosecutions of pregnant drug users: "ACLU Contests C-Section Delivery of Viable Fetus," *Life Docket*, August 1988, 2, SBL, Box 1, File 1.

38 On *Conn v. Conn*, see Richard Coleson to Raymond Dunn (August 1, 1988), JBP, Matter Boxes, File 1185; Coleson to Joyer, 1–3; *Conn v. Conn*, 526 N.E.2d 958 (Ind. 1988), cert. denied by 488 U.S. 955 (1988).*Conn v. Conn*, 526 N.E.2d 958 (Ind. 1988), *cert. denied by* 488 U.S. 985 (1988). For more on NRLC's fathers' rights litigation, see Coleson to Lewis, 1; Richard Coleson to Tom Condit (July 20, 1990), JBP, Matter Boxes, File 1185; Betty Bevovar to James Bopp Jr. (October 28, 1988), JBP, Matter Boxes, File 1185; Tom Glessner

to James Bopp Jr. (April 8, 1988), JBP, Matter Boxes, File 1185; Revised Fathers' Rights Litigation Kit (August 24, 1988), JBP, Matter Boxes, File 1185.

39 *Conn v. Conn*, 488 U.S. 955 (1988) (denying certiorari); *Doe v. Smith*, 486 U.S. 1308 (1988). On the cases working through the courts, see Coleson to Joyer, 2–4; "Father's Rights: An Issue Whose Time Has Come," *National Right to Life News*, May 5, 1988, 2, JRS, 1988 National Right to Life News Box. For the argument in the *Conn* certiorari petition: Petition for a Writ of Certiorari, 8–27, *Conn v. Conn* (1988) (No. 88–347), on file with the author. For the ACLU's argument in *Conn*: Respondents' Brief in Opposition, 25, *Conn v. Conn* (1988) (No. 88–347), on file with the author.

40 On the early organization of Operation Rescue, see James Risen and Judith L. Thomas, *Wrath of Angels: The American Abortion War* (New York: Basic Books, 1998), 181–182, 258–261; Daniel K. Williams, *God's Own Party: The Making of the Christian Right* (New York: Oxford University Press, 2010), 223–224; Ziad W. Munson, *The Making of Pro-life Activists: How Social Movement Mobilization Works* (Chicago: University of Chicago Press, 2008), 87–88. For Scheidler's book, see Joseph Scheidler, *Closed: 99 Ways to Stop Abortion* (Wheaton, IL: Ignatius Press, 1985).

41 For the Tunkels' statement: Holly Morris, "Reluctant Couple Converts to Activism," *Washington Post*, February 2, 1989, A10.

42 Randall Terry, "Higher Laws," *Rutherford Institute Magazine*, March–April 1987, 4. For Terry's statement on the political-legal strategy: Pamphlet, "Operation Rescue Atlanta: July 18–22, 1988, FWHC, Box 51, Operation Rescue Newsletter Folder. For more on these criticisms, see Pamphlet: Repentance and Rescue Atlanta (nd, ca. 1988), FWHC, Box 51, Operation Rescue Folder; Randall Terry, Letter to Operation Members (nd, ca. 1988), FWHC, Box 51, Operation Rescue Folder.

43 On the support received by Operation Rescue, see Sara Diamond, *Roads to Dominion: Right-Wing Movements and Political Power in the United States* (New York: Guilford Press, 1995), 250–255; Steven P. Miller, *The Age of Evangelicalism: America's Born-again Years* (New York: Oxford University Press, 2014), 40. On the Atlanta blockade, see Robert O. Self, "The Reagan Devolution: Movement Conservatives and the Right's Days of Rage, 1988–1994," in *Recapturing the Oval Office: Historical Approaches to the American Presidency*, eds. Brian Balogh and Bruce J. Schulman (Ithaca, NY: Cornell University Press, 2015), 82.

44 On people of color in the pro-life movement in the period, see "Pro-life Leaders Alienate Blacks," *Los Angeles Sentinel*, May 4, 1989, A1; Jacquin Sanders, "Anti-abortion Leader Doesn't Fit the Pattern," *St. Petersburg Times*, October 11, 1987, 1B; Terry Mattingly, "Abortion Foe Breaks Barriers," *Chicago Tribune*, August 3, 1990, S8. On Williams' position, see "Abortion Condemned by Doctor as Black Genocide," *Jet*, November 19, 1981, 39. On Johnny Hunter and Black participation in Operation Rescue, see Christine Spolar, "Abortion Foes' Mood Defiant," *Washington Post*, January 21, 1992, B1; Patricia Edmonds, "Face-Off in Buffalo: Abortion Protests to Begin," *USA Today*, April 21, 1992, 3A.

45 On women of color in larger organizations and smaller groups, see Dorothy Gilliam, "Women of Color: 1 Voice," *Washington Post*, April 10, 1989, D3; E. J. Dionne Jr., "Tepid Black Support Worries Advocates of Abortion-Rights," *New York Times*, April 16, 1989, A1; Sam Fullwood III, "Black Women Reluctant to Join Pro-choice Forces," *Los Angeles Times*, November 27, 1989, A1.

46 See Dionne, "Tepid Black Support," A1; Fullwood, "Black Women Reluctant," A1.

47 On the reasons that a single-issue, libertarian agenda alienated women of color, see Dionne, "Tepid Black Support," A1; Fullwood, "Black Women Reluctant," A1. On the pro-life movement's identification with the GOP, see Daniel K. Williams, *Defenders of the Unborn: The Pro-life Movement before Roe v. Wade* (New York: Oxford University Press, 2016), 235–250; Williams, *God's Own Party*, 268–275; Mary Ziegler, *After Roe: The Lost History of the Abortion Debate* (Cambridge, MA: Harvard University Press, 2015), 200–215. Black voters strongly supported the Democratic Party in the period as a rule; a CBS/*New York Times* exit poll found that 89 percent of black voters chose Democratic nominee Michael Dukakis in 1988. See "The Elections: CBS/NYT Poll," *New York Times*, November 10, 1988, www.nytimes.com/1988/11/10/us/the-elections-the-new-york-times-cbs-news-poll-portrait-of-the-electorate.html?mcubz=3. Latino voters also tended to choose the Democratic Party; 69 percent favored Dukakis in 1988, compared only to 30 percent who supported George H. W. Bush. Ibid.

48 On SOS and similar organizations, see Suzanne Staggenborg, *The Pro-choice Movement: Organization and Activism in the Abortion Conflict* (New York: Oxford University Press, 1991), 142; Suzanne Staggenborg, "Can Feminist Organizations Be Effective?" in *Feminist Organizations: Harvest of the New Women's Movement* eds. Myra Marx Ferree and Patricia Yancy Martin (Philadelphia: Temple University Press, 1995), 348; Katie Monagle and Annys Shin, "How We Got Here," *Ms.*, May 1995, 54; Joannie M. Schrof, "Feminism's Daughters," *US News and World Report*, September 27, 1993, 68–73. On the creation of a close coalition of leading abortion-rights groups in the period, see Staggenborg, *The Pro-choice Movement*, 142–143.

49 For the statement on creating evidence of numbers: NARAL Agenda (March 8, 1989), NARAL, Box 204, Folder 8. For Hickman-Maslin Research to NARAL Re: "Do's and Don'ts" (March 22, 1989), NARAL, Box 204, Folder 9. For more on NARAL's message, see William Saletan, *Bearing Right: How Conservatives Won the Abortion War* (Berkeley: University of California Press, 2004), 109–110.

50 Tamar Abrams, interview with Mary Ziegler, December 9, 2014. For more on Abrams' work, see Saletan, *Bearing Right*, 74–76, 80; Cynthia Gorney, "Beyond the *Webster* Case: Abortion Arguments and Predictions," *Washington Post*, April 9, 1989, W25; Chris Bull, "Feminists Gear Up for DC Action," *Gay Community News*, March 5–11, 1989, 1.

51 Abrams, interview.

52 Hickman-Maslin Research to NARAL "Re: Do's and Don'ts," 2. For more on the importance of voter strength, see Jackie Blumenthal and Podesta Associates to Nikki Heidepren (March 13, 1989), NARAL, Box 204, Folder 8. For the statement on changing the political climate, see Affiliate Development Department to Affiliates (December 25, 1988), NARAL, Box 204, Folder 8.

53 Operation Rescue Strategy Meeting Minutes (May 15, 1989), FWHC, Box 3, Operation Rescue Folder; see also Lynne Randall, "Operation Rescue: What You Can Do," National Abortion Clinic Defense Conference (October 1990), FWHC, Box 3, Operation Rescue Folder.

54 Richard Coleson, interview with Mary Ziegler, July 27, 2017. For more on Coleson's work, see James Bopp Jr. and Richard Coleson, "The Right to Abortion: Anomalous, Absolute, and Ripe for Reversal," *Brigham Young University Journal of Public Law* 3 (1989): 181–185;

James Bopp Jr. and Richard Coleson, "What Does *Webster* Mean?" *University of Pennsylvania Law Review* 138 (1989): 157–176; James Bopp Jr. and Richard Coleson, "*Webster* and the Future of Substantive Due Process," *Duquesne Law Review* 28 (1989): 281–288.

55 Coleson, interview.

56 Roger Evans, interview with Mary Ziegler, May 26, 2016. For more on Evans' work in the period, see Stephanie B. Goldberg, "Life after *Roe*," *American Bar Association Journal*, October 1989, 42; Henry J. Reske, "Is This the End of *Roe*? The Court Revisits Abortion," *American Bar Association Journal*, May 1992, 64–66; Cynthia Gorney, *Articles of Faith: A Frontline History of the Abortion Wars* (New York: Simon and Schuster, 1998), 412–413.

57 Evans, interview.

58 See Grant to AUL Legal Advisors, 2. On the Missouri statute, see *Webster v. Reproductive Health Services*, 492 U.S. 490 (1989).

59 Clarke Forsythe to James Bopp Jr. (April 12, 1989), JBP, Matter Boxes, File 837.

60 James Bopp Jr. and Burke Balch to NRLC State Affiliates, "Re: Six Possible *Webster* Scenarios" (June 16, 1989), GHWB, OA/ID 45272, Lee Liberman Files. For more on NRLC's views on the *Webster* case in the lead-up to a decision, see National Right to Life Committee, "Abortion: Questions and Answers" (1989), GHWB, OA/ID 45272, Lee Liberman Files.

61 On the growing political and legal involvement of Focus on the Family and the Family Research Council, see Dan Gilgoff, *The Jesus Machine: How James Dobson, Focus on the Family, and Evangelical America Are Winning the Culture War* (New York: Macmillan, 2008), 151–176. On the founding of CASE and its work with Free Speech Advocates, see Sara Diamond, *Not by Politics Alone: The Enduring Influence of the Christian Right* (New York: Guilford Press, 1998), 86; Hans J. Hacker, *The Culture of Conservative Christian Litigation* (Lanham, MD: Rowman and Littlefield, 2005), 22; Amanda Hollis-Brusky and Joshua C. Wilson, "Playing for the Rules: How and Why New Christian Right Public Interest Law Firms Invest in Secular Litigation," *Law and Policy* 39 (2017): 121–141; Amanda Hollis-Brusky and Joshua C. Wilson, "Lawyers for God and Neighbor: The Emergence of 'Law as a Calling' as a Mobilizing Frame for Christian Lawyers," *Law and Social Inquiry* 39 (2014): 416–448.

62 C. Boyden Gray and William Roper, Memorandum to the President (June 23, 1989), GHWB, OA/ID 45272, Lee Liberman Files. For more on the Bush Administration's attitude toward *Webster* before the Court issued a decision, see Memorandum, "*Webster* Possibilities" (April 26, 1989), GHWB, OA/ID 45272, Lee Liberman Files; Memorandum, "Suggested Presidential Responses to the *Webster* Decision," (June 21, 1989), 1–5, GHWB, OA/ID 45272, Lee Liberman Files.

63 See *Webster v. Reproductive Health Services*, 492 U.S. 490, 514–518, 525–528, 532–536. For analysis of the *Webster* decision, see David J. Garrow, *Liberty and Sexuality: The Right to Privacy and the Making of Roe v. Wade* (Berkeley: University of California Press, 1998), 680–699; David L. Faigman, *Laboratory of Justice: The Supreme Court's 200 Year Struggle to Integrate Science and the Law* (New York: Henry Holt, 2004), 223–226, 228; Tribe, *Abortion*, 109, 123, 141–142.

64 For Marshner's statement: Life Forum Meeting Minutes, October 4, 1996, PWP, Box 80, Folder 2. For more on this divide, see Marvin Olasky, "Pro-life Pivot," *World Magazine*, January 17, 2009, https://world.wng.org/2009/01/pro_life_pivot, accessed April 25, 2019.

65 See Americans United for Life Board of Directors Meeting Minutes (June 16, 1990), RJN, Box 2, Folder 33. On the AUL's move to Washington, DC, see Guy Condon to Mildred Jefferson (March 15, 1991), MFJ, Box 13, Folder 8. For more on AUL's growth after *Webster*, see Deanna Silberman, "Americans United for Life," *Chicago Tribune*, August 1, 1991, www.chicagoreader.com/chicago/americans-united-for-life/Content?oid=878008, accessed June 15, 2018. On NRLC's 1990 budget, see *U.S. Women's Interest Groups: Institutional Profiles* ed. Sarah Slavin (Westport, CT: Greenwood, 1995), 419. On AUL's new sources of funding, see Americans United for Life, Board of Directors Meeting Minutes, 4 (October 28, 1989), MFJ, Box 13, Folder 7. For more on antiabortion optimism after *Webster*, see David Andrusko, "NRLC '89 Spells Out Formula for Abortion-Free America," *National Right to Life News*, July 13, 1989, 6, JRS, 1989 National Right to Life News Box.

66 On the mobilization of conservative Christian lawyers, see Hacker, *The Culture of Conservative Litigation*, 58; Joshua C. Wilson, *The New States of Abortion Politics* (Palo Alto, CA: Stanford University Press, 2016), 51; Ann Southworth, *Lawyers of the Right: Professionalizing the Conservative Coalition* (Chicago: University of Chicago Press, 2008), 28; Steven P. Brown, *Trumping Religion: The New Christian Right, The Free Speech Clause, and the Courts* (Tuscaloosa: University of Alabama Press, 2002), 39–54. Andrew R. Lewis, *The Rights Turn in Conservative Christian Politics: How Abortion Transformed the Culture Wars* (New York: Cambridge University Press, 2017), 27–28, 118–121.

67 On Cassidy's background: Harold Cassidy, interview with Mary Ziegler, July 19, 2018. On the *Baby M.* case, see *In re Baby M.*, 537 A.2d 1227 (N.J. 1988); see also Bob Port, "Sterns to Get Custody of Baby M.," *St. Petersburg Times*, April 1, 1987, 1A. For more on Concerned United Birth Parents, see Rickie Solinger, *Beggars and Choosers: How the Politics of Choice Shapes Abortion, Adoption, and Welfare in the United States* (New York: Farrar, Straus, and Giroux, 2001), 103–139.

68 Cassidy, July 19 interview.

69 For coverage of the *Loce* case, see Lawrence Binda, "Trespass or Defending Life?" *Daily Record*, April 14, 1991, 1; "Fetus's 'Rights' An Issue in Appeal by Abortion Foes," *Asbury Park Press*, September 7, 1991, 20; "Baby M. Attorney Fights for New Cause," *Daily Record*, April 12, 1992, 10. On Loce's legal strategy, "Court Won't Hear Appeal on Abortion," *Courier News*, March 1, 1994, 6. For the elements of the necessity defense, see *United States v. Turner*, 44 F.3d 900, 902 (10th Cir.1995). For examples of the early use of the necessity defense, see Pamphlet, "In Need of Defense" (nd, ca. 1980), JCK, Box 1, Folder 2; Pamphlet, "She Trespasses Too?" (nd, ca. 1980), JCK, Box 1, Folder 2.

70 For Cassidy's perspective: Cassidy July 19, interview. On the *Loce* case and appeal, see "Judge Agrees with Pro-lifers, but Issues Trespassing Fines," *Courier-News*, April 30, 1991, 3; Ellen Gamerman, "Top Court to Hear Abortion Case," *Asbury Park Press*, January 19, 1994, A3. When Loce's attorneys asked the Supreme Court to take his case, Mother Teresa, the famous Catholic nun and missionary, granted Cassidy's request to submit an amicus brief in the case, see Brief of Amicus Curiae of Mother Teresa of Calcutta, in Support of Petitioners' Petitions for Writ of Certiorari, *Loce v. State* (Nos. 93–1148, 93–1149).

71 For Terry's statement on the efficacy of blockades see Randall Terry, "The *Webster* Decision: A Halting Step in the Right Direction," *Rescue News Brief*, August 1989, 5,

FWHC, Box 51, Operation Rescue Folder. On Operation Rescue's financial and legal troubles, see Jon A. Shields, *The Democratic Virtues of the Christian Right* (Princeton, NJ: Princeton University Press, 2009), 55–56; Williams, *God's Own Party*, 224–225. For Terry's statement about rescuing as many babies as possible: "From Randall's Desk: The Day of Distress Has Dawned," *Rescue News Brief*, August 1989, 4, FWHC, Box 51, Operation Rescue Folder.

72 Clarke Forsythe and Paige Comstock Cunningham to State Pro-life Leaders and Other Interested Parties (August 22, 1989), 1–9, RJN, Box 2, Folder 33; Americans United for Life, Conceptual Meeting Minutes (March 21, 1990), RJN, Box 2, Folder 33; Curt Walsh to Richard John Neuhaus (November 28, 1990), RJN, Box 2, Folder 33.

73 Dan Balz, "Idaho Votes a Virtual Ban," *Washington Post*, March 3, 1990, A1; see also "Minnesota Bill Limiting Abortions Loses Ground," *New York Times*, March 1, 1990, D26.

74 On the Idaho law, see Timothy Egan, "Anti-abortion Bill in Idaho Takes Aim at Land-mark Case," *New York Times*, March 22, 1990, A1. On NRLC's investment in similar laws, see Paul Houston, "Abortion Opponents to Press States to Legislate Wide-Ranging Curbs," *Los Angeles Times*, October 3, 1989, A3.

75 For Coleson's statement: Richard Coleson to Mike Aloi (August 8, 1989), JBP, Matter Boxes, File 768; see also Richard Coleson to Mike Aloi (August 14, 1988), JBP, Matter Boxes, File 1185; Coleson to Condit, 1–3. For more on Bopp and Coleson's reading of *Webster*, see Bopp and Coleson, "What Does *Webster* Mean?" 158; Bopp and Coleson, "*Webster* and the Future of Substantive Due Process," 272 ("Indeed, *Webster* was a de facto reversal of *Roe v. Wade*"); James Bopp, Jr. Richard E. Coleson, and Barry A. Bostrom, "Does the United States Supreme Court Have a Constitutional Duty to Expressly Reconsider and Overrule *Roe v. Wade?*" *Seton Hall Constitutional Law Journal* 1 (1990): 76.

76 Richard John Neuhaus to Clarke Forsythe (September 15, 1989), RJN, Box 33, Folder 2; see also Forsythe to Neuhaus, August 22, 1989, 1. On the aggressive strategies pursued by NRLC in the immediate aftermath of *Webster*, see "Idaho's Strict Abortion Bill Advances," *Los Angeles Times*, March 17, 1990, 22; Tamar Lewin, "States Testing the Limits on Abortion," *New York Times*, April 2, 1990, A14. For more on AUL's strategy in the period, see "Restoring Parents' Rights," *AUL Insights*, November 1990, 1, SBL, Box 1, AUL Folder 2; "3 Steps toward Protecting the Unborn," *AUL Forum*, September 1992, 2–3, SBL, Box 1, AUL Folder 1. On ALL's criticism, see American Life League, "The Abortion Debate: Is It Whether Babies Have Rights or Which Babies Have Rights?" (Fall 1990), JBP, Matter Boxes, File 1094; see also Burke Balch to James Bopp Jr. (September 20, 1990), JBP, Matter Boxes File 1094.

77 On the shrinking gap between men and women's rates of college attendance, see *What the 1990 Census Tells Us about Women: A State Fact Book* (Washington, DC: Population Reference Bureau, 1993), 9. On the shrinking wage gap between men and women over the course of the 1980s, see US Department of Labor, *Facts on Working Women*, No. 90–3 (October 1990), 1. On the increase in income inequality and its relationship to marriage rates and college graduation, see Lane Kensworthy and Timothy Smeeding, "The United States: High and Rapidly-Rising Inequality," in *Changing Inequalities and Social Impacts in Rich Countries: Thirty Countries' Experience* eds. Brian Nolan et al. (New York: Oxford University Press, 2014), 704; Paul Ryscavage, *Income Inequality in America: An Analysis of Trends* (New York: Routledge, 1999), 12–18.

78 See Linda Greenhouse, "Battle on Abortion Turns to Rights of Teen-Agers," *New York Times*, July 16, 1989, 1.
79 Brief of Petitioners, 20–22, *Hodgson v. Minnesota*, 497 U.S. 417 (1990) (No. 88–125).
80 Brief of Respondents, 9, *Hodgson v. Minnesota*, 497 U.S. 417 (1990) (No. 88–125).
81 Brief Amicus Curiae of the Elliot Institute for Social Sciences Research and the American Academy of Medical Ethics, 10, *Hodgson v. Minnesota*, 497 U.S. 417 (1990) (No. 99–125).
82 Brief Amici Curiae for the American Psychological Association et al., 21, *Ohio v. Akron Center for Reproductive Health*, 497 U.S. 502 (1990) (No. 88–805).
83 For Focus on the Family's argument: Brief Amici Curiae Focus on the Family and the Family Research Council, 25–27. For the Solicitor General's argument, see Brief for the United States as Amicus Curiae Supporting Respondents, 21, *Hodgson v. Minnesota*, 497 U.S. 417 (1990) (No. 99–125).
84 For an overview of sex-equality arguments made in favor of abortion-rights, see Balkin, "Introduction," 18–19; Erin Daly, "Reconsidering Abortion Law: Liberty, Equality, and the New Rhetoric of *Planned Parenthood v. Casey*," *American University Law Review* 45: 77–93 (1995); David H. Gans, "The Unitary Fourteenth Amendment," *Emory Law Journal* 56 (2007): 907–918; Ruth Bader Ginsburg, "Some Thoughts on Autonomy and Equality in Relation to *Roe v. Wade*," *North Carolina Law Review* 63 (1985): 375–386; Sylvia A. Law, "Rethinking Sex and the Constitution," *University of Pennsylvania Law Review* 132 (1984): 955–980; Reva B. Siegel, "Reasoning from the Body: A Historical Perspective on Abortion Regulation and Questions of Equal Protection," *Stanford Law Review* 44 (1992): 261–290.
85 Brief for Petitioners, 12–13.
86 See *Hodgson v. Minnesota*, 497 U.S. 417, 451 (1990).
87 For Planned Parenthood's argument, see Brief of Appellees, 16–39, *Ohio v. Akron Center for Reproductive Health*, 497 U.S. 502 (1990) (No. 88–805).
88 See *Hodgson v. Minnesota*, 497 U.S. 417, 440–458 (1990); *Ohio v. Akron Center for Reproductive Health*, 497 U.S. 502, 512–520 (1990).
89 *Hodgson v. Minnesota*, 497 U.S. 417, 448 (1990).
90 Bopp and Coleson, "A Legal Analysis," 1–8. On the Guam law, see "Guam OKs Most Restrictive US Abortion Bill," *Chicago Tribune*, March 16, 1990, 6; Jane Gross, "Guam Approves Bill Posing Challenge to Abortion Ruling," *New York Times*, March 16, 1990, A1. On the Idaho veto, see "Idaho Abortion Bill Is Vetoed," *Chicago Tribune*, March 31, 1990, A1; Timothy Egan, "Idaho Governor Vetoes Measure Intended to Test Abortion Ruling," *New York Times*, March 31, 1990, A1. On the Louisiana law, see Maralee Schwartz, "A Strict Abortion Ban Voted in Louisiana," *Washington Post*, June 15, 1990, A1. For Grant's view: Edward Grant, email interview, July 15, 2018.
91 On the Louisiana veto, see Michael Kennedy and Karen Tumulty, "Louisiana Governor Vetoes Abortion Bill," *Los Angeles Times*, July 27, 1990, 1; Maralee Schwartz, "Louisiana Governor Vetoes Severe Abortion Bill," *Washington Post*, July 7, 1990, A3. On the Souter nomination, see Jack Nelson, Robert Shogun, and Ronald Brownstein, "Bush May Avoid Bitter Confirmation Struggle," *Washington Post*, July 24, 1990, A1; Paul Houston, "Lawmakers' Reaction to Bush Choice Favorable but Cautious," *Los Angeles Times*, July 24, 1990, A14; Maureen Dowd, "A Swift Nomination," *New York Times*, July 24, 1990, A1. On the Utah law, see Tamar Lewin, "Strict Antiabortion Law Signed in Utah," *New York Times*, January 26, 1991, A10; Tamar Lewin, "Harsh Loophole in Utah Law," *New York*

Times, March 9, 1991, 8; "Suit by ACLU Challenges New Utah Anti-abortion Law," *New York Times*, April 7, 1991, 21.

92 See NRLC Press Release, "In Landmark Ruling, Supreme Court Upholds 'Wall of Separation' between Abortion and Contraception in Federally-Funded Birth Control Clinics" (May 23, 1991), JBP, Matter Boxes, File 973. For the decision in *Rust: Rust v. Sullivan*, 500 U.S. 173 (1991).

93 On Republicans' shifting stand on abortion, see Robert Shogan, "Republicans Debate Stand on Abortion," *Los Angeles Times*, May 27, 1992, 1; E. J. Dionne Jr., "Abortion Battle Cry Heard Within GOP," *Washington Post*, July 21, 1991, A4; Robert Pear, "The 1992 Election: The GOP Faces Fight over Abortion," *New York Times*, May 26, 1992, A1. For Atwater's statement: Robin Toner, "Atwater Urges Softer Abortion Line," *New York Times*, January 20, 1990, A10. On the polls suggesting a decline in absolute opposition to abortion, see John Dillon, "Abortion Issue Clouds Outlook for GOP in 1990," *Christian Science Monitor*, June 22, 1990, 1. On claims that *Webster* had given abortion-rights activists an advantage, see Maralee Schwartz and Paul Taylor, "Abortion Stock-Taking," *Washington Post*, July 1, 1990, A8; Dan Balz and Ruth Marcus, "In Year since *Webster*, Abortion Debate Defies Predictions," *Washington Post*, July 3, 1990, A1. For NRLC's model parental involvement law, see NRLC Parental Notice Law Revised (October 29, 1990), JBP, Matter Boxes, File 1094.

94 "KKK Law Invoked in Abortion Argument," *Pittsburgh Post-Gazette*, October 17, 1991, A1. For Tucci's statement about "blood money": Pamphlet, Operation Rescue National (February 8, 1991), FWHC, Box 58, Operation Rescue Folder. For more on Operation Rescue's tactics, see Anthony Lewis, "Abroad at Home: Right to Life," *New York Times*, March 12, 1993, A29; Sara Rimer, "Abortion Foes in Boot Camp Mull Doctor's Killing," *New York Times*, March 19, 1993, A12; Mimi Hall, "Not All Abortion Foes Protest at Clinics," *USA Today*, March 12, 1993, A3.

95 On the Thomas nomination, see Terry Atlas, "Bush Chooses Conservative for the Supreme Court," *Chicago Tribune*, July 2, 1991, D1; Jack Nelson, "A Conservative Black Picked for the High Court," *Los Angeles Times*, July 2, 1991, A1. On the spread of state laws restricting abortion, see Dan Balz, "Abortion-Rights Strategy," *Washington Post*, January 23, 1990, A23; Mimi Hall, "Abortion Fight Shifts Gears," *USA Today*, April 30, 1991, A3.

96 American Association of University Women, "Teen Women and Abortion: Myth Versus Reality" (1990), NOW, Box 96, Folder 13. For the arguments made by NAF and the National Women's Law Center, see NAF and National Women's Law Center, "The Judicial Bypass Procedure Fails to Protect Young Women" (1990), FWHC, Box 63, Parental Notification Talking Points Folder.

97 Harrison Hickman to Loretta Ucelli and Kate Michelman, "Re: Parental Consent/Notification Update" (February 12, 1991), FWHC, Box 63, Parental Notification Talking Points Folder.

98 Ibid. For the National Women's Law Center's position, see the National Women's Law Center and the National Abortion Federation, "Judicial Bypass Fails," 4–5.

99 For a summary of the scholarly criticism of *Roe*, see Mary Ziegler, *Beyond Abortion: Roe v. Wade and the Fight for Privacy* (Cambridge, MA: Harvard University Press, 2018), 18.

100 Kathryn Kolbert, interview with Mary Ziegler, April 15, 2016. For more on Kolbert's background and contributions, see Jan Crawford Greenburg, *Supreme Conflict: The*

Inside Story of the Struggle for the United States Supreme Court (New York: Penguin, 2007), 151–152; N. E. H. Hull and Peter Charles Hoffer, <u>Roe v. Wade: The Abortion-Rights</u> *Controversy in American History* 2d ed. (Lawrence: University of Kansas Press, 2010), 364; Saletan, *Bearing Right*, 145–147.

101 Linda Wharton, interview with Mary Ziegler, August 14, 2016. For more on Wharton's contributions, see Denis Clay, "State Abortion Control Act Challenged by Two Groups," *Philadelphia Herald*, February 8, 1994, 4B; Milo Geyelin and Arthur Hayes, "Pennsylvania to Appeal Decision on Abortion to High Court," *Wall Street Journal*, October 23, 1991, B8; Carol Ann Douglas, "States Act on Abortion," *Off Our Backs*, March 1990, 12.

102 For Benshoof's statement: David Margolick, "Seeking Strength in Independence, Abortion-Rights Unit Quits ACLU," *New York Times*, May 21, 1992, A20. For more on the Center for Reproductive Rights, see Carole Sugarman and Ruth Marcus, "Reproductive Law Unit Splits from ACLU," *Washington Post*, May 21, 1992, A23.

103 On the effort to stoke a pro-choice backlash to *Casey*, see Cynthia Gorney, "Endgame," *Washington Post*, February 23, 1992, www.washingtonpost.com/archive/lifestyle/magazine/1992/02/23/endgame/125da2a0-5886-41ce-9cad-13144b44cffa, accessed October 2, 2018; Alice Fleetwood Bartee, *Privacy Rights: Cases Lost and Causes Won before the United States Supreme Court* (Lanham, MD: Rowman and Littlefield, 2006), 230. On the early litigation of *Casey*, See Tamar Lewin, "Quiet Trial Could Lead to Major Abortion Ruling," *New York Times*, August 5, 1990, 24; David G. Savage, "Ruling Backs State Action on Abortion," *Los Angeles Times*, October 23, 1991, 10. For the Third Circuit's decision in *Casey*, see *Planned Parenthood of Southeastern Pennsylvania v. Casey*, 947 F.2d 682 (3d Cir. 1991). For the arguments made at trial, see Trial Record, 193a–201a, 301a, *Planned Parenthood of Southeastern Pennsylvania v. Casey*, No. 2:88-CV-03228 (1990), KKP, Box 9, *Casey* Trial Transcript Folder.

104 Kitty Kolbert and Linda Wharton to *Planned Parenthood v. Casey* Work Team, "Re: Amicus Organizing Effort" (December 10, 1991), 2–5, KKP, Box 1, *Casey* Notes and Memoranda Folder. On the strategy guiding the appeal in *Casey*, see Kitty Kolbert to Reproductive Freedom Project Attorneys (September 26, 1991), KKP, Box 1, *Casey* Notes and Memoranda Folder; Kitty Kolbert and Lynn Paltrow to Nadine Strossen et al., "Re: *Casey* Campaign" (December 24, 1991), KKP, Box 1, *Casey* Notes and Memoranda Folder.

105 Brief and Petitioners and Cross Respondents, 6, 32–33, *Planned Parenthood of Southeastern Pennsylvania v. Casey*, 505 U.S. 833 (1992) (Nos. 91–744, 91–902);.

106 Brief Amicus Curiae of 178 Organizations in Support of Planned Parenthood of Southeastern Pennsylvania, 12, *Planned Parenthood of Southeastern Pennsylvania v. Casey*, 505 U.S. 833 (1992) (Nos. 91–744, 91–902). For Kolbert and Wharton's argument: Brief for Petitioners and Cross-Respondents, 33. For explicit mentions of the Equal Protection Clause in the litigation of *Casey*, see Reply Brief for Petitioners and Cross-Respondents, 14–18, <u>Planned Parenthood of Southeastern Pennsylvania v. Casey</u>, 505 U.S. 833 (1992) (Nos. 91–744, 91–902).

107 "Agenda: Amici Conference" (January 23, 1992), JBP, Matter Boxes, File 1013; List of Issues for Amici Conference (January 1992), JBP, Matter Boxes, File 1013.

108 Brief Amicus Curiae of the National Right to Life Committee Supporting Respondents-Cross-Petitioners, 7, *Planned Parenthood of Southeastern Pennsylvania v. Casey*, 505 U.S. 833 (1992) (Nos. 91–744, 91–902). For similar arguments, see Brief Amicus Curiae

of the United States Catholic Conference, the Christian Life Commission, Southern Baptist Convention, and National Association of Evangelicals in Support of Respondents and Cross-Petitioners, 4, *Planned Parenthood of Southeastern Pennsylvania v. Casey*, 505 U.S. 833 (1992) (Nos. 91–744, 91–902).

109 For Focus on the Family's argument: Brief Amicus Curiae of Focus on the Family et al., 2, *Planned Parenthood of Southeastern Pennsylvania v. Casey*, 505 U.S. 833 (1992) (Nos. 91–744, 91–902); see also Brief of Feminists for Life et al. as Amicus Curiae, 12-28, *Planned Parenthood of Southeastern Pennsylvania v. Casey*, 505 U.S. 833 (1992) (Nos. 91–744, 91–902).

110 See Linda Greenhouse, "Both Sides in Abortion Argument Look Past Court to Political Battle," *New York Times*, April 20, 1992, A1.

111 On the abortion positions of Bush's opponents in the 1992 election, see David Lauter and Douglas Jehl, "Parties Seek Abortion's Middle Ground," *Los Angeles Times*, July 26, 1992, SDA1; Jean Latz Griffin, "Abortion Remains Most Divisive Issue," *Chicago Tribune*, October 19, 1992, D5; E. J. Dionne Jr., "Bush Appears in Danger of Losing Much Conservative Support to Perot," *Washington Post*, June 8, 1992, A1. On the administration's anxiety about *Casey*, see Jay Lefkowitz to the Chief of Staff et al. (June 25, 1992), GHWB, OA 45270, Lee Liberman Files; Memorandum, "Will *Roe v. Wade* Be Overruled?" (nd, ca. 1992), GHWB, OA 07867, Jay Lefkowitz Papers.

112 Lee Liberman, Memorandum, "Some Thoughts on Abortion Decision Scenarios," 2–4, (July 4, 1992), GHWB, OA/ID 45272, Lee Liberman Files.

113 *Planned Parenthood of Southeastern Pennsylvania v. Casey* 505 U.S. 833, 877 (1992) (plurality decision).

114 Ibid., 877–891.

115 Ibid., 898.

116 Ibid., 847–854.

117 Ibid., 856. For scholars' perceptions of the impact of *Casey*, see Anita L. Allen, "Autonomy's Magic Wand: Abortion and Constitutional Interpretation," *Boston University Law Review* 72 (1992): 683–698; Wendy K. Mariner, "The Supreme Court, Abortion, and the Jurisprudence of Class," *Journal of Public Health* 82 (1992): 1556–1562; Kathleen M. Sullivan, "Foreword: The Justices of Rules and Standards," *Harvard Law Review* 106 (1992): 26–34; Earl M. Maltz, "Abortion, Precedent, and the Constitution," *Notre Dame Law Review* 68 (1992): 11–32; Michael J. Gerhardt, "The Pressure of Precedent: A Critique of Conservative Approaches to Stare Decisis in the Abortion Cases," *Constitutional Commentary* 10 (1993): 67–78.

118 Kolbert, interview.

119 Ibid.

120 Grant, interview.

121 Ibid.

5 CONTESTING THE RELATIONSHIP BETWEEN ABORTION AND HEALTH CARE

1 David C. Reardon, interview with Mary Ziegler, April 22, 2016; David C. Reardon, interview with Mary Ziegler, April 25, 2016. For more on Reardon's career and contributions to the movement, see Pamphlet, The Elliot Institute, "Post-Abortion Trauma: Learning the Truth,

Telling the Truth" (nd, ca. 1993), NCAP, Box 3, Elliot Institute Folder; David C. Reardon, "The Abortion Suicide Connection," *The Post-Abortion Review*, Summer 1993, 1, NCAP, Box 3, Elliot Institute Folder; David C. Reardon, "JAMAGymnastics: Jumping through Hoops to Prove Abortion Is Safe," *The Post-Abortion Review*, Summer 1993, E5, NCAP, Box 3, Elliot Institute Folder. For examples of Reardon's published work, see David C. Reardon, *Aborted Women: Silent No More* (Chicago: Loyola University Press, 1987); David C. Reardon, *Making Abortion Rare: A Healing Strategy for a Divided Nation* (Springfield, IL: Acorn, 1996).

2 Reardon, April 22 interview; Reardon, April 25 interview.

3 Reardon, April 22 interview; Reardon, April 25 interview. For Reardon's book: Reardon, *Making Abortion Rare*.

4 Pam Maraldo, interview with Mary Ziegler, May 5, 2016. For more on Maraldo's influence and time in Planned Parenthood, see William Saletan, *Bearing Right: How Conservatives Won the Abortion War* (Berkeley: University of California Press, 2004), 222; Marie Fox, "A Woman's Right to Choose? A Feminist Critique," in *The Future of Human Reproduction: Ethics, Choice, and Regulation* eds. John Harris and Soren Holm (New York: Oxford University Press, 1998), 99; Donald T. Critchlow, *Intended Consequences: Abortion, Birth Control, and the Federal Government in Modern America* (New York: Oxford University Press, 1999), 233–236.

5 For more on the struggles Maraldo faced in her early tenure, including violence against abortion providers, see James Risen and Judy L. Thomas, *Wrath of Angels: The American Abortion War* (New York: Basic Books, 1998), 340–345; David S. Cohen and Kristen Connen, *Living in the Crosshairs: The Untold History of Antiabortion Terrorism* (New York: Oxford University Press, 2016), 4, 58, 76; David J. Garrow, *Liberty and Sexuality: The Right to Privacy and the Making of Roe v. Wade* (Berkeley: University of California Press, 1998), 702–712.

6 Tamar Lewin, "Planned Parenthood President Resigns," *New York Times*, July 22, 1995, A6; see also Lewin, "Planned Parenthood Travels a Rocky Path into Future," A1. On internal reaction to Maraldo's plans for changing Planned Parenthood, see Planned Parenthood of Georgia Meeting Minutes (April 1995), PPSE, Box 3, 1995 Folder; Planned Parenthood of Georgia Meeting Minutes (May 1995), PPSE, Box 3, 1995 Folder. For recollections of the reasons for Maraldo's exit: Jim LeFevre, interview with Mary Ziegler, April 26, 2016; Alex Sanger, interview with Mary Ziegler, May 13, 2016; Gloria Feldt, interview with Mary Ziegler, June 14, 2016; Mark Salo, interview with Mary Ziegler, August 11, 2016.

7 On the history of the early reproductive justice movement in the 1990s, see Loretta Ross and Rickie Solinger, *Reproductive Justice: An Introduction* (Berkeley: University of California Press, 2017), 60; Loretta Ross et al., *Undivided Rights: Women of Color Organize for Reproductive Justice* (Boston: South End Press, 2004), 50, 159.

8 For examples of the movement's new health-centered arguments, see Argument Manual, "Promoting Reproductive Choices: A New Approach to Reproductive Health" (nd, ca. 1994), RCD, Box 2, NARAL Folder 1; NARAL Foundation, "Talking About the Freedom to Choose" (nd, ca. 1996), NARALMA, Box 14, Folder 12; Rochelle Sharpe, "Abortion Coverage Looks Like the Bitter Pill for Some in Prescription for Health Care Reform," *Wall Street Journal*, May 11, 1993, A20; "Ad Blitz Planned on Women's Health Care," *Los Angeles Times*, April 4, 1994, 17. Jennifer Nelson, *More than Medicine: A History*

of the Women's Health Movement (Piscataway, NJ: Rutgers University Press, 2015), 213. For more on the reproductive justice activism of women of color in the period, see Ross et al., *Undivided Rights*, 48–54; Ross and Solinger, *Reproductive Justice*, 60–67; Dorothy Sue Cobble, Linda Gordon, and Astrid Henry, *Feminism Unfinished: A Short, Surprising History of American Women's Movements* (New York: W. W. Norton, 2014), 196.

9 On the spread of CPCs in the period, see "Guy Condon Takes the Helm at CAC," Action Line, January/February 1993, 1, PAW, Box 15, Folder 11. For more on the rebranding of Care Net, see Christian Action Council, Fundraising Letter (April 6, 1993), PAW, Box 15, Folder 11; Care Net Fundraising Letter (July 29, 1993), PAW, Box 15, Folder 11; "Christian Council Launches Care Net," Action Line, July/August 1993, 1–2, PAW, Box 15, Folder 12; Margaret Hartshorn, *Foot Soldiers Armed with Love: Heartbeat International's First Forty Years* (Virginia Beach, VA: Donning Company Publishers, 2011), 33; Lynn Smith, "Bowed, but Unbroken?" *Los Angeles Times*, March 22, 1993, 1; National Institute of Family and Life Advocates, History, https://nifla.org/about-nifla, accessed January 19, 2018. On the founding and early work of ADF, see "Pro-life Speech at Risk," *ADF Quarterly Briefing*, Spring 1994, 1, AUS, Carton 1, Folder 14; Alliance Defense Fund Brochure (nd, ca. 2001), AUS, Carton 1, Folder 14; "Victory! ADF Funded Cases Set Historic Precedents for America," *ADF Quarterly Briefing*, August 1995, 1, AUS, Carton 1, Folder 14.

10 This chapter later discusses the rise of woman-protective antiabortion arguments.

11 On the health care battle that defined the early years of Clinton's presidency, see Paul Starr, *Remedy and Reaction: The Peculiar American Struggle over Health Care Reform* (New Haven, CT: Yale University Press, 2011), 79–129; Theda Skocpol, *Boomerang: Health Care Reform and the Turn against Government* (New York: W. W. Norton 1997), 154–163; David Blumenthal and James Morone, *The Heart of Power: Health and Politics in the Oval Office* (Berkeley: University of California Press, 2010), 361–419.

12 On the rise and influence of HMOs in the period, see Jan Gregoire Coombs, *The Rise and Fall of HMOs: An American Health Care Revolution* (Madison: University of Wisconsin Press, 2005), 223–235; Bradford H. Gray, "The Rise and Decline of the HMO: A Chapter in US Health-Policy History," in *History and Health Policy in the United States: Putting the Past Back In* eds. Rosemary A. Stevens, Charles E. Rosenberg, and Lawrence R. Burns (Piscataway, NJ: Rutgers University Press, 2006); Colin Gordon, *Dead on Arrival: The Politics of Health Care in Twentieth-Century America* (Princeton, NJ: Princeton University Press, 2003), 147–151, 297–300.

13 On the failure of health care reform in the period, see Starr, *Remedy and Reaction*, 79–129; Skocpol, *Boomerang*, 154–163; Blumenthal and Morone, *The Heart of Power*, 361–419. On the Republican Revolution of 1994, see Heather Cox Richardson, *To Make Men Free: A History of the Republican Party* (New York: Basic Books, 2015), 312–316; Herbert F. Weisberg and Samuel C. Patterson, *The Great Theater: The American Congress in the 1990s* (New York: Cambridge University Press, 2011), 210–225; Thomas Mann and Norman J. Orenstein, *The Broken Branch: How Congress Is Failing America and How to Get It Back on Track* (New York: Oxford University Press, 2006), 79–106.

14 On Mann's story, see Adriane Pugh-Berman, "Spying on Right to Life," *Off Our Backs*, September 30, 1982, 19; Reardon, *Aborted Women*, 184. On the feminist women's health movement and its political allies, see Jennifer Nelson, *Women of Color and the Reproductive Rights Movement* (New York: New York University Press, 2005), 7; Johanna

Schoen, *Choice and Coercion: Birth Control, Sterilization, and Abortion in Public Health and Welfare* (Chapel Hill: University of North Carolina Press, 2005), 298; Rebecca M. Kluchin, *Fit To Be Tied: Sterilization and Reproductive Rights in America, 1950–1980* (Piscataway, NJ: Rutgers University Press, 2009), 134.

15 On the founding of Project Rachel, see Carrie Gress, "Celebrating 30 Years of Project Rachel," *The Catholic World Report*, September 14, 2014, www.catholicworldreport.com/Item/3373/celebrating_30_years_of_project_rachel.aspx, accessed Nov. 16, 2016; Laura Salsini, "Church Forgives Catholic Women Who Had Abortions," *Orlando Sentinel*, September 7, 1985, 7; Dan Tracy, "An Abortion Treatment," *Orlando Sentinel*, February 1, 1987, B1.

16 National Right to Life Educational Trust Fund Report (November 11, 1993), 22, JBP, Matter Boxes, File 1171. For more on interest in post-abortion trauma, see Vincent Rue, "Post-Abortion Trauma: Crisis or Sham?" *National Right to Life News*, January 15, 1987, 6, JRS, 1987 National Right to Life News Box; Alfred Moran to Planned Parenthood Affiliates, Other Interested Organizations, "Notes on 1985 National Right to Life Convention" (August 13, 1985), FWHC, Box 51, Operation Rescue Folder. For examples of Franz and other NRLC members' writing on post-abortion trauma from the period, see Wanda Franz, "What Is Post-Abortion Trauma?" *National Right to Life News*, January 15, 1987, 1, JRS, 1987 National Right to Life News Box; Olivia Gans, "An Outpouring of Mourning," *National Right to Life News*, January 15, 1987, 1, JRS, 1987 National Right to Life News Box; Leonard Dinegar, "BAL and AVA Developing Leaders with Help of NRLC," *National Right to Life News*, April 2, 1987, 6, JRS, 1987 National Right to Life News Box.

17 On the early years of American Victims of Abortion, see Terry Waiting, "Victims of Abortion," *Spectator*, March 14, 1987, 30; Marlene Cimons, "Koop Backed in Call for Research on Abortion Effects," *Los Angeles Times*, January 12, 1989, 21; Janet Cawley, "The Stakes Are High, and So Are Emotions," *Chicago Tribune*, April 26, 1989, 14.

18 Strategy Proposal, Guy Condon to Richard John Neuhaus (February 11, 1991), RJN, Box 2, Folder 34; see also Americans United for Life Conceptual Meeting Minutes (March 21, 1990), RJN, Box 2, Folder 33; Guy Condon to Richard John Neuhaus (March 8, 1991), RJN, Box 3, Folder 2; Guy Condon to Richard John Neuhaus (February 11, 1991), RJN, Box 3, Folder 2.

19 Richard John Neuhaus, Memo on August 22, 1991 Roundtable Convened by the National Conference of Catholic Bishops' Secretariat of Pro-life Activities (1991), RJN, Box 3, Folder 2.

20 Strategy Proposal, 2.

21 Ibid.

22 National Right to Life Handbook (1987), SBL, Box 2, Folder 7. For more on NRLC's arguments from the period, see Betty Cuniberti and Elizabeth Mehren, "'Silent Scream': Abortion Film Stirs Friend, Foe," *Los Angeles Times*, August 8, 1985, 1; T. R. Reid, "Antiabortion Groups Confer," *Washington Post*, June 22, 1987, A2; Adriane Pugh-Berman, "Right-to-Life Convention," *Off Our Backs*, September 30, 1985, 7.

23 David C. Reardon to C. Everett Koop (September 14, 1987), 2, DRP; see also David C. Reardon to Everett Koop (July 1, 1988), DRP.

24 C. Everett Koop to David Reardon (January 9, 1989), DRP; see also David Reardon to C. Everett Koop (April 5, 1989), DRP.

25 For a sample of the stories in the *Sun Times* exposé series, see Pamela Zekman and Pamela Warrick, "The Abortion Profiteers: Making a Killing at the Michigan Avenue Clinics," *Chicago Sun Times*, November 12, 1978, 1; "Big Kickbacks to Abortion Mills," *Chicago Sun Times*, November 20, 1978, 1; "Hotline Deceptions Sell Most Abortions," *Chicago Sun Times*, November 25, 1978, 4; "Meet the Profiteers: Men Who Profit from Women's Pain," *Chicago Sun Times*, November 13, 1978, 1.

26 See *Ragsdale v. Turnock*, 625 F. Supp. 1212, 1225–1227 (N.D. Ill. 1985). For more on the case, see Glen Elsasser, "Of 3 Other Cases, Illinois' May Be Crucial," *Chicago Tribune*, July 4, 1989, 1; Barbara Brotman, "Why Abortion Debate Focuses on *Ragsdale* Case," *Chicago Tribune*, September 17, 1989, 1.

27 On the importance AUL leaders attached to *Ragsdale*, see "Court May Pull Reins in on *Roe* in Three New Abortion Cases," *Life Docket*, July/August 1989, 2, SBL, Box 2, AUL Folder 2; "Last-Minute Settlement of *Ragsdale* Case Endangers Women's Health," *Life Docket*, November/December 1989, 2, SBL, Box 2, AUL Folder 1; "AUL Clients Choose Not to Appeal *Ragsdale* Settlement," *Life Docket*, June 1990, 2, SBL, Box 2, AUL Folder 2. For AUL's argument, see Brief Amici Curiae for Feminists for Life and the American Association of Pro-life Obstetricians and Gynecologists, *Turnock v. Ragsdale*, 492 U.S. 916 (1989) (No. 88-790).

28 For Lohr's statement: "Last-Minute Settlement in *Ragsdale* Case," 2. For more on the settlement and significance of *Ragsdale*, see Karen Tumulty, "Illinois Takes Center Stage in Abortion Battle," *Los Angeles Times*, July 17, 1989, 1; Dan Balz, Davis S. Broder, and Christopher B. Daly, "Abortion Case Proves Touchy for Illinois Candidate," *Washington Post*, September 3, 1989, A8; William E. Schmidt, "Both Sides in Illinois Try to Settle Suit on Abortion Standards," *New York Times*, October 17, 1989, A17; Bill Peterson, "Abortion-Rights Advocates Win 'Major Victory' in Illinois," *Washington Post*, November 23, 1989, A3.

29 On the rise of Operation Rescue and the energizing of movement absolutists, see Risen and Thomas, *Wrath of Angels*, 219; Paul Saurette and Kelly Gordon, *The Changing Voice of the Anti-abortion Movement: The Rise of "Pro-Woman" Rhetoric in Canada and the United States* (Toronto: University of Toronto Press, 2015), 297; Faye Ginsburg, "Rescuing the Nation: Operation Rescue and the Rise of Antiabortion Militance," in *Abortion Wars: A Half-Century of Struggle, 1950–2000*, ed. Rickie Solinger (Berkeley: University of California Press, 1998), 231–232. On absolutists' anger about post-*Webster* strategy, see Dr. John Willke, "From the President's Desk: All, Part, or Nothing?" *National Right to Life News*, November 30, 1989, 3; Marvin Olasky, "Pro-life Pivot," *World*, January 16–17, 2009, 1–3.

30 On pro-life feminism in the 1970s and 1980s, see Daniel K. Williams, *Defenders of the Unborn: The Pro-life Movement before Roe v. Wade* (New York: Oxford University Press, 2016), 239–260; Mary Ziegler, *After Roe: The Lost History of the Abortion Debate* (Cambridge, MA: Harvard University Press, 2015), 170–190. On the history of post-abortion support groups, see Sara Dubow, *Ourselves Unborn: A History of the Fetus in Modern America* (New York: Oxford University Press, 2010), 161; Johanna Schoen, *Abortion after Roe* (Chapel Hill: University of North Carolina Press, 2015), 139–150.

31 Kate Michelman to NARAL Friends Re: Emergency Mobilization Action (December 21, 1988), NARAL, Box 204, Folder 8. For more on this strategy shift, see Affiliate

Development Department to Affiliates (December 23, 1988), NARAL, Box 204, Folder 8; NARAL, "Overall Strategy, Capture the Climate/Politicize/Polarize the Battle" (November 17, 1988), NARAL, Box 204, Folder 8; David Schribman, "Abortion-Issue Foes, Preaching to the Converted in No Uncertain Terms, Step Up Funding Pleas," *Wall Street Journal*, December 26, 1989, 1; Nancy Zirkin and Ronee Schreiber to Division Campaign for Choice Coordinators (March 8, 1990), NOW, Box 96, Folder 14; Bob Bingaman and Betty Means to Grassroots Task Force–National Pro-choice Coalition, (April 2, 1990), NOW, Box 96, Folder 12.

32 On the professionalization of pro-choice organizations, see Suzanne Staggenborg, "The Consequences of Professionalization and Formalization in the Pro-choice Movement," in *Waves of Protest: Social Movements since the Sixties* eds. Jo Freeman and Victoria Johnson (Lanham, MD: Rowman and Littlefield, 1999), 99–134; Sue Thomas, "The National Abortion-Rights Action League PAC: Reproductive Rights in the Spotlight," in *Risky Business? PAC Decision-Making in Congressional Elections* eds. Robert Biersack, Paul S. Herrnson, and Clyde Wilcox (Armonk, NY: M. E. Sharpe, 1994), 117–130; Joshua C. Wilson, *The New States of Abortion Politics* (Palo Alto, CA: Stanford University Press, 2016), vii–1.

33 David Schribman, "Abortion-Rights Group to Stress Contraception in Campaign to Reduce Unwanted Pregnancies," *Wall Street Journal*, June 10, 1991, A6. On American Life League's position on birth control, see Judie Brown, "Unite for Life: A Unique Pro-life Perspective," *A. L. L. About News*, January 1999, PLN, Carton 1, Celebrate Life Folder. For more on conflict about birth control within the movement in the 1990s, see Sandra Faucher and David N. O'Steen, "The Imperative to Remain Consistently 'Single Issue,'" *National Right to Life News*, May 28, 1987, 1, JRS, 1987 National Right to Life News Box; Doug Johnson, "Why Is the NRLC a 'Single-Issue Organization?'" *National Right to Life News*, May 28, 1987, 3, JRS, 1987 National Right to Life News Box.

34 Maralee Schwartz and Dan Balz, "Abortion-Rights Movement Marks '*Webster*' Decision," *Washington Post*, July 3, 1991, A3.

35 For Bush's 1990 speech on health care reform: "Transcript of Bush's State of the Union Message to the Nation," *New York Times*, February 1, 1990, A1. On the debate about health care during the 1992 campaign, see David Lauter and Robert Rosenblatt, "Clinton Spells Out His Plan to Curb Health Care Costs," *Los Angeles Times*, September 25, 1992, A1; Robert Pear, "Democrats Call Bush's Health Plan Inadequate," *New York Times*, January 6, 1989, A1; Clifford Krauss, "Democrats Offer New Health Care Plan," *New York Times*, June 26, 1992, A10.

36 On early speculation about what the reform proposal would include, see Robert Pear, "Health Initiative Tilting Toward Price Regulation," *New York Times*, February 16, 1993, A14; Robert Pear, "2 Dozen Taxes Weighed to Pay for Health Care Plans," *New York Times*, February 17, 1993, A1; Philip J. Hilts, "A.M.A. Is Softening Stand on Changes in the Health System," *New York Times*, March 4, 1993, A1, 7; Robert Pear, "Health Aides Plan to Place Medicare under New System," A1.

37 On FOCA and its collapse, see Elaine S. Povich, "Abortion-Rights Bill Rejected by Moseley-Braun," *Chicago Tribune*, July 10, 1993, 14; Adam Clymer, "Abortion-Rights Supporters Are Split on US Measure," *New York Times*, April 2, 1993, A18; Kevin Merida, "Abortion Bill Overtaken by Health Reform," *Washington Post*, March 21, 1994, A1.

38 PPFA Board of Directors to PPFA Legal Division et al. (July 1, 1992), 1–5, NCAP, Box 9, NARAL Materials Folder. On the public response of Planned Parenthood, see Planned Parenthood Federation Annual Report 1992, 9 (1992), JBP, Matter Boxes, File 1067.

39 See Planned Parenthood Federation of America 1992 Services Report (1992), JBP, Matter Boxes, File 1067.

40 Nadine Brozan, "Planned Parenthood Finds a Roman Catholic at the End of Its Wide Search for a New President," *New York Times*, November 21, 1992, 20; see also Maralee Schwartz, John Yang, and Ann Devroy, "Planned Parenthood Shift," *Washington Post*, November 21, 1992, A14. For the pamphlet put out by Planned Parenthood, see Planned Parenthood Federation of America, "Planned Parenthood Is the Largest, Most Trusted Health Care Provider to Women and Adolescents" (1994), White House Health Care Task Force, Health Care Task Force, and Christine Heenan, "CMH [Christine M. Heenan] – Abortion," Clinton Digital Library, accessed August 15, 2019, https://clinton.presidentialli braries.us/items/show/40539.

41 NARAL, "Choices: Promoting Reproductive Justice, a New Approach to Reproductive Health" (1992), 1–3, NARALMA, Box 42, Folder 12.

42 NARAL, Confidential Strategic Plan Draft, 2 (September 1993), NARALMA, Box 28, Folder 16; see also NARAL Strategic Planning Notes (nd, ca. August 1993), NARALMA, Box 28, Folder 15; Bob Bingaman to NARAL Affiliate Directors (August 18, 1993), NARALMA, Box 28, Folder 15.

43 For discussion of this challenge, see "NARAL's 1992 Campaign," *NARAL News*, Winter 1992, 1, RCD, Box 2, NARAL News Folder; Elizabeth Mehren, "New Battle Lines: The Changing Face of the Abortion Conflict," *Los Angeles Times*, March 24, 1993, 1; Brozan, "Planned Parenthood Finds," 20.

44 On Griffin's crime and trial, see "Jury Sequestered in Murder Trial," *New York Times*, February 28, 1994, A13; Ana Puga, "Radicalizing Right to Life," *Boston Globe*, October 30, 1994, 26. On the activities of Operation Rescue National, see Anthony Lewis, "Abroad at Home: Right to Life," *New York Times*, March 12, 1993, A29; Sara Rimer, "Abortion Foes in Boot Camp Mull Doctor's Killing," *New York Times*, March 19, 1993, A12; Mimi Hall, "Not All Abortion Foes Protest at Abortion Clinics," *USA Today*, March 12, 1993, A3.

45 On Clinton's reversal of the gag rule, see Ann Devroy, "Clinton Cancels Abortion Restrictions of Clinton-Bush Era," *Washington Post*, January 23, 1993, A1; Robin Toner, "Settling in: Easing Abortion Policy," *New York Times*, January 23, 1993, 1; Carol Jouzaitis, "Clinton Lifts Abortion Gag Rule," *Chicago Tribune*, January 23, 1993, N1.

46 On NARAL's financial struggles after *Casey*, see Eliza Newlin Carney, "The Morning After," *National Journal* March 5, 1994, 521–525; Mehren, "New Battle Lines," 1. On similar difficulties faced by Planned Parenthood, see Schwartz et al., "Planned Parenthood Shift," A14; Felicity Barringer, "Planned Parenthood: Quiet Cause for Focus of Fury," *New York Times*, October 30, 1990, A16.

47 See Ross et al., *Undivided Rights*, 297. For more on the relationship between women of color activists and larger pro-choice organizations, see Suzanne Staggenborg, *The Pro-choice Movement: Organization and Activism in the Abortion Conflict* (New York: Oxford University Press, 1991), 144; Sherie M. Randolph, "Not to Rely Completely on the Courts: Florynce Kennedy and Black Feminist Leadership in the Reproductive Rights Battle," in

Toward an Intellectual History of Black Women ed. Mia Bay (Chapel Hill: University of North Carolina Press, 2015), 248.

48 On Women of Color Coalition, see Nelson, *More Than Medicine*, 210; see also Sandra Morgen, *Into Our Own Hands: The Women's Health Movement in the United States, 1969–1990* (Piscataway, NJ: Rutgers University Press, 2002), 68.

49 See note 50 and accompanying text.

50 Nelson, *More Than Medicine*, 213. For more on the founding of SisterSong: Ross et al., *Undivided Rights*, 48–54; Ross and Solinger, *Reproductive Justice*, 60–67; Dorothy Sue Cobble, Linda Gordon, and Astrid Henry, *Feminism Unfinished: A Short, Surprising History of American Women's Movements* (New York: W. W. Norton, 2014), 196.

51 For NAF's concern about the shortage of abortion doctors, see Conference Program, National Abortion Federation, "Who Will Provide Abortions?" (1990), FWHC, Box 3, NAF Folder; see also Ron Fitzsimmons to NCAP Member (December 3, 1992), NCAP, Box 1, Newsletter Folder; Tamar Lewin, "Hurdles Increase for Many Women Seeking Abortion," *New York Times*, March 15, 1992, 1. For more on concern about the shortage of doctors, see Sheryl Stolberg, "More Like War than Medicine," *Los Angeles Times*, March 20, 1993, A1; see also Elizabeth Field, "'Reproductive Rights Focus of Day-Long, October 24 Workshop Here," *New York Times*, September 28, 1986, A10; Gina Kolata, "Under Pressures and Stigma, More Doctors Shun Abortion," *New York Times*, January 8, 1990, A1. For the decline in the number of abortion providers, see Stanley K. Henshaw, "Abortion Incidence and Services in the United States, 1995 and 1996," *Family Planning Perspectives* 30 (1998): 263–270. On the number of students who had performed a first-trimester abortion, see Sheryl Stolberg, "More Like War than Medicine," *Los Angeles Times*, March 20, 1993, A1.

52 On Life Dynamics' campaign in the period, see Junda Woo, "Abortion Doctors' Patients Broaden Suits," *Wall Street Journal*, October 28, 1994, B12; Mark Crutcher, Letter to the Editor, "We Help the Women Abortion Doctors Butcher," *Wall Street Journal*, December 7, 1994, A7. On the increase in malpractice insurance for most abortion providers in the period, see Tamar Lewin, "A New Weapon in an Old War," *New York Times*, April 15, 1995, 1. For examples of Life Dynamics' work, see Life Dynamics, "Access: The Key to Pro-life Victory" (nd, ca. 1994), PLN, Crate 1, Life Dynamics Folder 1; Mark Crutcher, "Firestorm: A Guerilla Strategy for Pro-life America" (nd, ca. 1992), JBP, Matter Boxes, File 1067; "Firestorm Hits US!," *LDI Update*, April 1993, 1, REC, Pro-life Organizations Folder. On the inability of independent clinics to find coverage, see Barbara Carton, "Management: The Dollars and Cents of the Abortion Business," *Wall Street Journal*, January 16, 1995, B1. For Crutcher's statement: Mark Crutcher, "Firestorm: A Guerilla Strategy for Pro-life America," 1 (nd, ca. 1992), JBP, Matter Boxes, File 1067.

53 On efforts to address a physician shortage, see Lisa Belkin, "Planned Parenthood of New York Begins Abortion Training," *New York Times*, June 19, 1993, 23; Stolberg, "More Like War than Medicine," A1.

54 On the early work of NOW LDF, see Legal Momentum, History, www.legalmomentum.org/history, accessed May 25, 2018.

55 On the failed effort to reopen the record in *Casey*, see *Planned Parenthood of Southeastern Pennsylvania v. Casey*, 822 F. Supp. 227 (E.D. Pa. 1993); *Planned Parenthood of Southeastern Pennsylvania v. Casey*, 14 F.3d 848 (3d Cir. 1994); *Planned Parenthood of Southeastern Pennsylvania v. Casey*, 510 U.S. 1309 (1994).

56 Brief for Respondents, 35, *Bray v. Alexandria Women's Health Clinic*, 506 U.S. 263 (No. 90–985). On the earlier litigation of *Bray*, see *National Organization for Women v. Operation Rescue*, 726 F. Supp. 1483 (E.D.Va. 1989); *National Organization for Women v. Operation Rescue*, 914 F.2d 582 (4th Cir. 1990).

57 On the reasons for the decision to reargue *Bray*, see Laurence H. Tribe, *Abortion: The Clash of Absolutes* (New York: W. W. Norton, 1992), 250.

58 Brief of Petitioners, 10–11, 22, *Bray v. Alexandria Women's Health Clinic*, 506 U.S. 263 (1993) (No. 90–985).

59 Brief for Respondents, 20–30, *Bray v. Alexandria Women's Health Clinic*, 506 U.S. 263 (1993) (No. 90–985). More recently, the pregnancies of transgender men have complicated the argument that only women can become pregnant or seek abortion. See Jessi Hempel, "My Brother's Pregnancy and the Making of a New American Family," *Time*, September 12, 2016, http://time.com/4475634/trans-man-pregnancy-evan, accessed August 20, 2018.

60 *Bray v. Alexandria Women's Health Clinic*, 506 U.S. 263, 270 (1993).

61 Brief of Petitioners, 9–10, *National Organization for Women, Inc. v. Scheidler*, 510 U.S. 249 (1994) (No. 92–780). On the earlier litigation in *Scheidler*, see *National Organization for Women, Inc. v. Scheidler*, 765 F. Supp. 937 (N.D. Ill. 1991); *National Organization for Women, Inc. v. Scheidler*, 768 F.2d 912 (7th Cir. 1992). For recollections of the *Scheidler* litigation: Elaine Metlin, interview with Mary Ziegler, December 15, 2015. For the statement from NOW's complaint, see Brief of Respondents Joseph M. Scheidler et al. at 2, *National Organization for Women, Inc. v. Scheidler*, 510 U.S. 249 (1994) (No. 92–780) (citing plaintiffs' second amended complaint).

62 For Linton's argument, see Brief of Respondent Timothy Murphy, 14, *National Organization for Women, Inc. v. Scheidler*, 510 U.S. 249 (1994) (No. 92–780). For ACLJ's brief, see Brief for Respondents Randall Terry et al., 42, *National Organization for Women, Inc. v. Scheidler*, 510 U.S. 249 (1994) (No. 92–780). For Scheidler's brief: Brief of Respondents Joseph M. Scheidler et al., 7–8, *National Organization for Women, Inc. v. Scheidler*, 510 U.S. 249 (1994) (No. 92–780).

63 For the Court's decision in *Scheidler I*, see *National Organization for Women, Inc. v. Scheidler*, 510 U.S. 249, 257–263 (1994). In 2003, the case returned to the Supreme Court. Then, the Court held that NOW's RICO claim failed because there was inadequate proof that blockaders obtained or attempted to obtain property from those entering clinics. See *Scheidler v. National Organization for Women, Inc.*, 537 U.S. 393 (2003). On the early litigation in *Madsen*, see *Operation Rescue v. Women's Health Center*, 626 So.2d 664 (Fla. 1993).

64 Brief for Respondents, 12, *Madsen v. Women's Health Center, Inc.*, 512 U.S. 753 (1994) (No. 93–880). For Liberty Counsel's argument: Brief for Petitioners, 8, *Madsen v. Women's Health Center, Inc.*, 512 U.S. 753 (1994) (No. 93–880).

65 *Madsen v. Women's Health Center, Inc.*, 512 U.S. 753, 767–768 (1994).

66 For the Court's decision in *Schenck*, see *Schenck v. Pro-choice Network of Western New York*, 519 U.S. 357 (1997). For earlier litigation in the case, see *Pro-choice Network of Western New York v. Project Rescue*, 799 F. Supp. 1417 (W.D.N.Y. 1992); *Pro-choice Network of Western New York v. Schenck*, 67 F.3d 377 (2d Cir. 1995). For abortion-rights supporters' claims about the rationale for the injunction: Brief for the American College of Obstetricians and Gynecologists et al. at 5, *Schenck v. Pro-choice Network of Western*

New York, 519 U.S. 357 (1997) (No. 95–1065). For similar abortion-rights arguments, see Brief of the Feminist Majority Foundation et al. as Amici Curiae, 5–11, *Schenck v. Pro-choice Network of Western New York*, 519 U.S. 357 (1997) (No. 95–1065); Brief Amicus Curiae of the American Civil Liberties Union et al., 21–23, *Schenck v. Pro-choice Network of Western New York*, 519 U.S. 357 (1997) (No. 95–1065). For antiabortion arguments seeking to distinguish *Schenck* from *Madsen*, see Brief for Petitioners, 31–44, *Schenck v. Pro-choice Network of Western New York*, 519 U.S. 357 (1997) (No. 95–1065); Brief Amicus Curiae of Family Research Council, 9–15, *Schenck v. Pro-choice Network of Western New York*, 519 U.S. 357 (1997) (No. 95–1065).

67 On later clinic-access cases involving the First Amendment, see *Schenck v. Pro-choice Network of Western New York*, 519 U.S. 937 (1996); *Hill v. Colorado*, 530 U.S. 730 (2000). These cases continued in later decades. See *McCullen v. Coakley*, 573 S. U.S. 464 (2014).

68 Mike Lux to Ricki Seidman and Melanne Verveer (April 12, 1993), "HC – Abortion Working Group," *Clinton Digital Library*, https://clinton.presidentiallibraries.us/items/show/35001, accessed August 14, 2019.

69 NRLC, "The Clinton Plan: Everyone Pays for Abortion on Demand" (nd, ca. 1993), BCP, Box 8, Neera Tanden Files. On NARAL's call-in program: Martin and Glantz to Joe Velasquez (April 15, 1994), BCP, Box 8, Neera Tanden Files.

70 Abortion Clinic Violence: Testimony before the House Judiciary Committee, Subcommittee on Crime and Criminal Justice, 103d Congress 1st Sess. (1993), 100 (Statement of Walter Weber); see also Abortion Clinic Violence: Testimony before the House Judiciary Committee, Subcommittee on Crime and Criminal Justice, 103d Congress 1st Sess. (1993, 39 (Statement of Randall Terry) (contending that the law "singled out [pro-lifers] as a movement"); House Judiciary Committee, Subcommittee on Crime and Criminal Justice, 103d Congress 1st Sess. (1993), 120 (Statement of James McHugh) (reasoning that the law "single[d] out one group, pro-life protesters, for special penalties imposed on no one else").

71 Bebe Verdery to Planned Parenthood Public Affairs Offices Re: Pro-active Clinic Legislation (nd, ca. 1993), PCN, Box 29, Folder 1. For the feminist group's argument: New York Clinic Defense Fund Newsletter (July 3, 1994), PCN, Box 14, Folder 9; see also Brochure, Clinic Defense Fund (June 3, 1994), PCN, Box 14, Folder 9; Pamphlet, Women's Health Action and Mobilization (WHAM!) (nd, ca. 1993), MHP, Carton 1, Folder 2.

72 NARAL, "Choices Argument Manual" (nd, ca. 1993), 1, 5, 8, RCD, Box 2, NARAL Folder.

73 On Clinton's vow to repeal the Hyde Amendment, see Philip Hilts, "Clinton and Abortion: Limited Expectations," *New York Times*, December 13, 1992, 44; Dana Priest and Ann Devroy, "Clinton to Call for Federally-Funded Abortions," *Washington Post*, March 30, 1993, A7. Indeed, in the immediate aftermath of the election, some scholars argued that the abortion issue had made a significant difference to Clinton's campaign. See Alan Abramowitz, "It's Abortion, Stupid: Policy Voting in the 1992 Presidential Election," *Journal of Politics* 57 (1995): 176–186.

74 On Perot's campaign, see Ronald B. Rappaport and Walter J. Stone, *Three's a Crowd: The Dynamic of Third Parties, Ross Perot, and Republican Resurgence* (Ann Arbor: University of Michigan Press, 2008), 4–21; Kathleen Hall Jamison, *Packaging the Presidency: A History and Criticism of Presidential Campaign Advertising* (New York: Oxford

University Press, 1996), 507–512; Steven J. Rosenstone et al., *Third Parties in America: Citizen Response to Major Party Failure* 2d ed. (Princeton, NJ: Princeton University Press, 1996), 231–267. On the spotlight Perot shone on budgetary issues, see Stone and Rappaport, *Three's a Crowd*, 61–70; Micah Sifrey, *Spoiling for a Fight: Third-Party Politics in America* (New York: Routledge, 2003), 74–103.

75 Choices Argument Manual, 4.

76 On changing policy about RU 486 in the period, see Martin Gilens, *Affluence and Influence: Economic Inequality and Political Power in America* (Princeton, NJ: Princeton University Press, 2012), 111; Carol Joffe, *Doctors of Conscience: The Struggle to Provide Abortion before and after Roe v. Wade* (Boston: Beacon, 1996); Tribe, *The Clash of Absolutes*, 215–218.

77 John Schwartz, "Abortion Pill Nears Approval," *Washington Post*, September 19, 1996, www.washingtonpost.com/archive/politics/1996/09/19/abortion-pill-nears-approval/d2b5af70-918e-45ca-8e9c-9a3f591eec2e, accessed July 10, 2017. For the press release: NRLC Press Release, "Pro-lifers to Protest RU 486 Licensing" (June 18, 1993), JBP, Matter Boxes, File 1171. For more on NRLC's fight against RU 486, see David N. O'Steen to James Bopp Jr. et al. Re: Secondary Boycott of RU 486 Manufacturer (June 24, 1994), JBP, Matter Boxes, File 1203; Carol Long and Mary Spaulding Balch to State Affiliates Re: Post-*Casey* Candidate Questionnaire (March 21, 1994), JBP, Matter Boxes, File 1203. On the push to legalize RU 486 after Clinton's election, see William J. Eaton, "Abortion Pill Debated at House Hearing," *Los Angeles Times*, July 29, 1992, A4; William Drozdiak et al., "Possible Opening for RU 486," *Washington Post*, December 8, 1992, WH17; "RU 486: A Changing Tune at FDA," *Los Angeles Times*, December 20, 1992, 4. On the claim that RU 486 could be used to treat breast cancer, see Eaton, "Abortion Pill Debate," A4; "Abortion Pill Approved for Breast Cancer Test," *New York Times*, November 20, 1993, A20. For Dempsey's statement: Howard Libit, "RU 486 Advocates See Private Abortion Techniques Quieting the Public Debate," *Los Angeles Times*, July 6, 1993, 5.

78 On the history of the morning-after pill, see Heather Munro Prescott, *The Morning After: A History of Emergency Contraception in the United States* (Piscataway, NJ: Rutgers University Press, 2011). For coverage of the pill in the period, see Jan Hoffman, "The Morning-After Pill: A Well-Guarded Secret," *New York Times*, January 10, 1993, A10; Jane Meredith Adams, "Morning after Pill Rekindles Abortion Row," *Chicago Tribune*, May 9, 1994, 1. After 1999, there were ongoing conflicts about whether the morning-after pill would be available over the counter (OTC). By 2006, the pill was available to women 18 and older, but fights about the OTC availability of the drug continued.

79 NARAL, "Choices Argument Manual," 2, 5, 8., NARALMA, Box 42, Folder 14.

80 On the inclusion of abortion in the health care plan, see Dana Priest, "Health Plan Threatened by Abortion Coverage," *Washington Post*, May 19, 1993, A3. On the Ginsburg nomination, see Robin Toner, "Anti-abortion Group Maps Strategy," *New York Times*, June 27, 1993, A14; Edward Walsh, "Antiabortion Group Considers Its Options," *Washington Post*, June 27, 1993, A4.

81 On the stalling of FOCA, see Robin Toner, "Political Memo: Success Spoils Unity of Pro-choice Groups," *New York Times*, April 20, 1993, A18; Jon Sawyer," Moseley-Braun Rejects Abortion-Rights Bill," *St. Louis Post Dispatch*, July 10, 1993, 1B. On the Hyde Amendment vote in Congress, see Adam Clymer, "Abortion Foes Win Vote in House on

Abortion Funds for the Poor," *New York Times*, July 1, 1993, A1; Kevin Merida, "Hyde Amendment Curb Survives Bitter Abortion Debate," *Washington Post*, July 1, 1993, A1; Eric Pianin, "Senate Keeps Medicaid Abortion Limits," *Washington Post*, September 29, 1993, A1; David Rosenbaum, "Defying President, Senate Votes to Keep Medicaid Abortion Limits," *New York Times*, September 29, 1993, A16. On the passage of FACE, see "A Victory of Abortion-Rights," *New York Times*, May 14, 1994, 20; Elsa Brenner, "Can a New Law Curb Protests over Abortion?" *New York Times*, July 1, 1994, WC1; Robert Pear, "Abortion Clinic Workers Say Law Is Being Ignored," *New York Times*, September 23, 1994, A16.

82 For Perot's statement: "Perot Criticizes Clinton Proposal," *New York Times*, January 24, 1994, A12. On the proliferation of alternative plans, see Robert Pear, "House Panel Begins Deliberations on Health Care Bill," *New York Times*, March 9, 1994, A13; David Rodgers and Hillary Stout, "Clinton and Allies Must Soon Decide How Much of Health Plan Can Be Saved before Election," *Wall Street Journal*, May 19, 1994, A16.

83 NRLC, "Abortion and the National Health Plan" (June 3, 1993), JBP, Matter Boxes, File 1171. For more on NRLC's campaign against the Clinton proposal, see Mary Spaulding Balch to State Directors et al. (September 13, 1993), JBP, Matter Boxes, File 1171; NRLC Fundraising Letter (November 12, 1993), JBP, Matter Boxes, File 1171; NRLC Board Minutes (June 22–23, 1993), 3, JBP, Matter Boxes, File 1171. For Planned Parenthood's argument, see Guttmacher Institute, Press Release: "Abortion and Sterilization Better Covered Than Contraception by Majority of Insurance Plans," March 9, 1994, White House Health Care Task Force, Health Care Task Force, and Christine Heenan, "CMH [Christine M. Heenan] – Abortion," Clinton Digital Library, accessed August 15, 2019, https://clinton.presidentiallibraries.us/items/show/40539.

84 NRLC November 12, 1993 Fundraising Letter, 2; see also Jacki Ragan to NRLC Board of Directors (May 2, 1994), JBP, Matter Boxes, File 1203. On the governors' resistance, see Richard Berke, "Clinton Is Facing State Resistance on Health Plan," *New York Times*, August 15, 1993, 1; Richard Berke, "To Governors, All Eyes on Clinton's Fight Ahead," *New York Times*, August 17, 1993, A14. On the AMA's opposition, see Robert Pear, "Clinton's Health Plan: AMA Rebels over Health Plan in Major Challenge to President," *New York Times*, September 30, 1993, A1; "AMA Vows to Fight to Revise Health Plan," *Wall Street Journal*, October 1, 1993, B1.

85 On the history of HMOs and their predecessors, see Gray, "The Rise and Decline of the HMO," 309–341; Coombs, *The Rise and Fall of HMOs*, 43–170; Jeffrey Lobosky, *It's Enough to Make You Sick: The Failure of American Health Care* (Lanham, MD: Rowman and Littlefield, 2012), 23–27.

86 On the spread of for-profit HMOs, see Jennifer Klein, *For All These Rights: Business, Labor, and the Shaping of the Public-Private Welfare State* (Princeton, NJ: Princeton University Press, 2003), 270. On the growth of HMO enrollment, see Gordon, *Dead on Arrival*, 297. For more on the reasons for the expansion of HMOs, see Cara Lesser, Paul Ginsburg, and Kelly Devers, "The End of an Era: What Became of the Managed Care Revolution in 2001?" *Health Services Research* 38 (2003): 337–355; Jon Gabel, "Market Watch: Ten Ways That HMOs Have Changed during the 1990s," *Health Affairs*, May/June 1997, www.healthaffairs.org/doi/10.1377/hlthaff.16.3.134, accessed November 30, 2018.

87 On the dissatisfaction with HMOs in the period, see Milt Freudenheim, "Many Patients Unhappy with HMOs," *New York Times*, August 18, 1993, A1; George Anders and Hillary Stout, "Dose of Reform: With Congress Stalled, Health Care Is Shaped by the Private Sector," *Wall Street Journal*, August 26, 1994, A1; Gordon, *Dead on Arrival*, 170–175.

88 On physicians' opposition to HMOs, see Ron Winslow and Edward Fensenhal, "Losing Patients: Physicians Fight Back as Insurers Cut Them from Health Networks," *Wall Street Journal*, December 30, 1993, A1; Marlene Cimons, "Doctors Divided over the Prospect of Managed Care," *Los Angeles Times*, March 23, 1994, A1.

89 Robert Pear, "States Rebelling at Federal Order to Cover Abortion," *New York Times*, January 5, 1994, A1. See Irvin Molotsky, "Clinton to Require States to Finance Abortions for the Poor," *New York Times*, December 25, 1993, 1; Karen DeWitt, "Abortion Decision Sets Off Debate," *New York Times*, December 26, 1993, 23. For the arguments made by leaders of NARAL and Planned Parenthood, see "New Rules to Require States to Pay for Some Abortions," *Los Angeles Times*, December 25, 1993, A23; Dewitt, "Abortion Decision," 23; Pear, "White House Defends," A1.

90 For Richardson's letter and Hanley's response: "U.S. Insists on Some Medicaid Abortions," *New York Times*, March 26, 1994, 7. On the arrival of the issue in the courts, see Robert Pear, "Pennsylvania Defies U.S. Abortion Rule," *New York Times*, January 19, 1994, A12; "Suit Planned to Seek Abortion Payments," *New York Times*, April 3, 1994, 3; James Dao, "Court Rejects Requirement of Financing for Abortion," *New York Times*, May 6, 1994, B1; Robert Pear, "U.S. Judge Bars Colorado Limits on Public Money to Abortion," *New York Times*, May 7, 1994, 1.

91 For discussion of the Whitewater scandal from the period, see Jeff Gerth and Stephen Engelberg, "U.S. Investigating Links to Arkansas S.&L.," *New York Times*, November 2, 1993, A20; Gwen Ifill, "Clinton's Damage Control Is Faltering," *New York Times*, January 11, 1994, A14; Viveca Novak, "Whitewater Report by GOP Accuses Clinton Officials," *Wall Street Journal*, January 4, 1995, 6.

92 Kathleen Q. Seelye, "Killings Harden a Debate on Capitol Hill," *New York Times*, August 3, 1994, A19. On Clinton's comments and the pro-choice response, see Robin Toner, "House Democrats Support Abortion in Health Plans," *New York Times*, July 14, 1994, A1. On Hill and his later conviction, see Tamar Lewin, "Death of a Doctor: The Moral Debate," *New York Times*, July 30, 1994, 1; "Hill Defense to Argue Killing Abortion Doctor Justifiable," *Orlando Sentinel*, October 4, 1994, C1; "For Paul Hill, a Life Sentence," *St. Petersburg Times*, November 14, 1994, 8A.

93 William J. Eaton, "Battle Lines Are Drawn as Dole Assails Plan for Health Care," *Los Angeles Times*, January 26, 1994, WA2; see also Adam Clymer, "In GOP Response to Clinton, Dole Denies There Is a Crisis in Health Care," *New York Times*, January 26, 1994, A15; see also Rogers and Stout, "Clinton and Allies," A16; Adam Clymer, "Dole Plans to Fight Bills Requiring Employer Mandates," *New York Times*, June 12, 1994, 28.

94 Joe Soss, Richard Fording, and Sanford Schram, *Disciplining the Poor: Neoliberal Paternalism and the Persistent Power of Race* (Chicago: University of Chicago Press, 2011), 68. On the influence of welfare reform on the health care debate, see Boychuk, *National Health Insurance*, 80–86. Michael Meeropol, *Surrender: How the Clinton Administration Completed the Reagan Revolution* (Ann Arbor: University of Michigan Press, 2000), 248–252; Arlene Geronomis, "Teenage Childbearing and Personal Responsibility," in

Race, Poverty, and Domestic Policy ed. C. Michael Henry (New Haven, CT: Yale University Press, 2004), 480–500.

95 R. W. Apple Jr., "How Long a Majority? Despite Sweeping Gains for Republicans, History Suggests That Power Is Temporary," *New York Times*, November 10, 1994, www.nytimes.com/1994/11/10/us/1994-elections-congress-analysis-lasting-majority-despite-sweeping-gains-for.html, accessed March 19, 2019. On the Republican Revolution of 1994, see Herbert F. Weisberg and Samuel J. Patterson, *The Great Theater: The American Congress in the 1990s* (New York: Cambridge University Press, 1998), 80–115; James Campbell, *The Presidential Pulse of Congressional Elections* (Lexington: University of Kentucky Press, 1993), 7–12; Gregory Schneider, *The Conservative Century: From Reaction to Revolution* (Lanham, MD: Rowman and Littlefield, 2009), 193–202.

96 Care Net Brochure, "A Pregnant Woman in Distress Needs More than a Slogan" (nd, ca. 1995), PAW, Box 15, Folder 12. For Condon's statement on relying on elites: "Guy Condon Takes the Helm," 1, 4–6.

97 On the Birthright litigation, see *Birthright v. Birthright, Inc.*, 827 F. Supp. 1114 (D. NJ. 1993). On the founding of NIFLA, see "About NIFLA," https://nifla.org/about-nifla, accessed March 30, 2018. On NIFLA's early work, see Mimi Hall, "Priest Removed After Condoning Doctor's Slaying," *USA Today*, August 24, 1993, 6A. For more on interest in CPCs and maternity homes in the 1990s. Marianne Donadio, interview with Mary Ziegler, January 16, 2018.

98 On the founding of the Susan B. Anthony List, see Steve Ertelt, "Announcements: Susan B. Anthony List Seeks Support," *Life Communications*, July 1994, 4; Paul Saurette and Kelly Gordon, *The Changing Voice of the Anti-abortion Movement: The Rise of "Pro-Woman" Rhetoric in Canada and the United States* (Toronto: University of Toronto Press, 2016), 269.

99 "Pro-life Free Speech," 1; "Victory!," 1. On ADF and the Becket Fund, see Joshua C. Wilson and Amanda Hollis-Brusky, "Playing for the Rules: How and Why New Christian Right Public Interest Law Firms Invest in Secular Litigation," *Law and Policy* 39 (2017): 123–128. For more on these organizations, see Ann Southworth, *Lawyers of the Right: Professionalizing the Conservative Coalition* (Chicago: University of Chicago Press, 2008), 31–35; Joshua C. Wilson, *The New States of Abortion Politics* (Palo Alto, CA: Stanford University Press, 2016), 41–46. Other organizations, like the Becket Fund for Religious Liberty (founded in 1994), litigated a variety of religious-liberty cases. At first, the Becket Fund did not participate in cases involving abortion or even contraception. Later, however, the organization defended clinic protesters in *McCullen v. Coakley*. See Wilson and Hollis-Brusky, "Playing for the Rules," 123–128.

100 See ADF Brochure, 2. On the early cases funded by ADF, see ADF Brochure, "The Alliance Defense Fund's Amazing Seven Year Track Record of Victories," 2001, AUS, Box 1, Folder 14; "Victory," 2–3. For a sample of cases on which Liberty Counsel and ACLJ worked or contributed briefs in the mid-1990s, see *Pro-choice Network of Western New York v. Schenck*, 67 F.3d 377 (2d Cir. 1995); *Hsu by and through Hsu v. Rosalyn Union Free School District No. 3*, 85 F.3d 839 (2d Cir. 1996); *Muller by Muller v. Jefferson Lighthouse School*, 98 F.3d 1530 (7th Cir. 1996); *Doe v. Santa Fe School District*, 171 F.3d 1013 (5th Cir. 1999). For Crutcher's argument, see Mark Crutcher to America's Pro-life Leaders (November 6, 1992), REC, Pro-life Material Folder.

101 Harold Cassidy to James Bopp Jr. (October 9, 1992), JBP, Matter Boxes, File 1067.

102 "The Good News about *Planned Parenthood v. Casey*," *AUL Briefing Memo*, July 1992, 7, PLN, Carton 1, AUL Folder 1. For more on the reaction of AUL members to *Casey*, see Guy M. Condon, "*Casey* Crushes Democratic Choice, Clashes with Public Conviction," *AUL Forum*, September 1992, 1, MRX, Box 37, Folder 28. For recollections of the response to the decision: Grant, March 28 interview; Gutiérrez, interview; Cunningham, interview.

103 "Americans United for Life 1992 Legal and Education Highlights" (1992), 1, PLN, Carton 1, AUL Folder 1.

104 James Bopp Jr. to Burke Balch (July 9, 1992), JBP, Matter Boxes, File 1067; see also James Bopp Jr. and Richard Coleson, Memo to Whom It May Concern (July 8, 1992), JBP, Matter Boxes, File 1067.

105 Bopp to Balch, 2. For Balch's proposals: Burke Balch to State Lobbyists for State Affiliates (July 8, 1992), JBP, Matter Boxes, File 1067.

106 On the impact of Gunn's murder, see Deana A. Rohlinger, *Abortion Politics, Mass Media, and Social Movements in America* (New York: Cambridge University Press, 2015), 70, 235; Jennifer L. Jefferis, *Armed for Life: The Army of God and Anti-abortion Terror in the United States* (Santa Barbara, CA: ABC–CLIO, 2011), 108, 138–140; Risen and Thomas, *Wrath of Angels*, 340–355. For Michelman's statement, see Lynne Bumpus-Hooper, "Pro-choice Groups Push for Bill Guaranteeing Access to All Clinics," *Orlando Sentinel*, March 11, 1993, http://articles.orlandosentinel.com/1993-03-11/news/9303110009_1_abortion-clinics-anti-choice-terrorism-anti-abortion-activists, accessed November 8, 2016. For more on the battle to pass FACE, see Michael Wines, "Senate Approves Bill to Protect Abortion Clinics," *New York Times*, May 13, 1994, A1; "Bitter Debate on Outlawing Abortion Clinic Blockades," *New York Times*, March 22, 1993, B5; Abby Margolis Newman, "Protections Debated for Abortion Clinics," *New York Times*, May 9, 1993, CN4.

107 For examples of these arguments, see Stephen Labaton, "Law on Abortion Protesters Gets First Test," *New York Times*, June 14, 1994, A14; Newman, "Protections Debated," CN4; Eric Harrison and David Savage, "Doctor's Killing Raises Fears for Abortion-Rights Groups," *Los Angeles Times*, March 12, 1993, VYA1.

108 Americans United for Life April 1993 Board Meeting Minutes, 2–3, 4–5.

109 Ibid. For more on the push for "right to know" laws, see "Mississippi Halves Abortion Rate," *AUL Forum*, December 1992, 5, MRX, Box 38, Folder 42.

110 Massachusetts Citizens for Life, 1; see also NRLC Model Informed Consent Law for 1995 (December 15, 1994), JBP, Matter Boxes, File 1203; Long and Spaulding Balch to State Affiliates, 6.

111 "JAMAGymnastics: Jumping through Hoops to Prove Abortion Is Safe," 4–5.

112 Pamphlet, "Post-Abortion Trauma: Learning the Truth, Telling the Truth" (1993), 1–3, NCAP, Box 5, Trauma Folder.

113 See AUL October 1994 Board Meeting Minutes, 2–4.

114 On the formation of NCAP, see Ron Fitzsimmons to Peg Johnston (March 11, 1990), PJP, Box 2, NAF Feminist Caucus Folder. For more on NCAP and its early years, see Mimi Hall, "Abortion Debate Turns to Regulation of the Doctor," *USA Today*, July 7, 1994, 2A; Tonya Whitfield, "A Voice for Abortion Providers' Rights," *National Journal*, July 9, 1993, 1658.

115 Letter from Ron Fitzsimmons to NCAP Members (July 30, 1992), NCAP, Box 1, Folder 1; see also Letter from Peg Johnston to Nicki Nichols Gamble (March 15, 1990), PJP, Box 2, November Gang Folder.

116 NARAL, "The Road to the Back Alley: The Anti-choice Legislation Campaign of the 104th Congress," (1994), NARAL, Box 226, Folder 14; see also Debra Saunders, "Battle Lines Are Forming on Capitol Hill," *Atlanta Journal-Constitution*, July 14, 1995, A10.

117 Planned Parenthood, "Planned Parenthood Annual Report, 1994–1995, For 79 Years, Continuing the Legacy" (1994), PPSE, Box 3, Folder 4. For more on the financial circumstances of pro-choice groups in the period, see Scott McCartney, "How Newt Gingrich Helps to Raise Millions for Liberal Causes," *Wall Street Journal*, November 28, 1994, A1; Spencer Rich, "Congress's Antiabortion Blocs Gain," *Washington Post*, December 5, 1994, A1.

118 Tamar Lewin, "Planned Parenthood Head Resigns," *New York Times*, July 22, 1995, A6.

119 Gloria Feldt, interview with Mary Ziegler, June 14, 2016.

120 Feldt, interview. For more on Feldt's work in Planned Parenthood, see Tony Mauro, "If *Roe* Reversed, Turmoil for States," *USA Today*, April 25, 1989, 3A; "Planned Parenthood's President," *Orlando Sentinel*, April 10, 1996, A10; Kim Painter, "Former Teen Mother to Head Planned Parenthood," *USA Today*, April 10, 1996, 7D.

121 Sanger, interview.

122 Ibid. For more on Sanger's work in Planned Parenthood, see Mimi Hall, "Wattleton Quits Job at Planned Parenthood," *USA Today*, January 9, 1992, A2; Lewin, "Hurdles Increase," A1; Alex Witchel, "At Work with Alex Sanger: In His Grandmother's Footsteps," *New York Times*, March 15, 1995, C1.

123 Sanger, interview.

124 Lewin, "Planned Parenthood Travels," A1. On the worries of the Georgia affiliate, see Planned Parenthood of Georgia Board of Directors January Meeting Minutes, 2–3; Planned Parenthood of Georgia Board of Directors February Meeting Minutes, 2; Planned Parenthood of Georgia April Board of Directors Meeting Minutes, 2–3.

125 See Lewin, "Planned Parenthood Head Resigns," A6; Lewin, "Planned Parenthood Travels," A1.

126 Chapter 6 discusses this history in greater depth.

6 PARTIAL-BIRTH ABORTION AND WHO DECIDES THE COSTS AND BENEFITS

1 Donna Harrison, interview with Mary Ziegler, April 22, 2016. For more on Harrison's work, see Brian Calhoun and Donna Harrison, "Challenges to the FDA Approval of Mifepristone," *Annals of Pharmacotherapy* 38 (2004): 163–168; Donna Harrison and Margaret M. Gary, "Analysis of Severe Adverse Effects of Mifepristone as an Abortifacient," *Annals of Pharmacotherapy* 40 (2006): 191–197; Donna Harrison, "Yes, Plan B Can Kill Embryos," *Heartbeat International*, 2014, www.heartbeatinternational.org/about-us/itemlist/tag/abortion%20information, accessed July 31, 2017. Harrison also became known for her work on abortion pill reversal techniques, another disputed area of abortion science. See Ruth Graham, "A New Frontier in the War over Reproductive Rights: Abortion Pill Reversal,"

New York Times, July 18, 2017, www.nytimes.com/2017/07/18/magazine/a-new-front-in-the-war-over-reproductive-rights-abortion-pill-reversal.html, accessed August 4, 2017.

2 Harrison, interview. For the description of partial-birth abortion: 1995 Legislative Agenda, 104th Congress, "Our Message to Congress: Abortion Is the Issue" (June 19, 1995), JBP, Matter Boxes, File 1275.

3 Nancy Yanofsky, interview with Mary Ziegler, July 25, 2017. For more on Yanofsky's work, see Paula Span, "Choice Ads Target Young and Listless," *Washington Post*, December 3, 1998, D1; "New National Campaign Seeks to Close Access Gap in Women's Reproductive Health Care," *Celebrating Voices*, July 31, 2000, 10; John Schwartz, "Abortion-Rights Group Vows Suit over Web Name," *New York Times*, May 10, 2001, B5.

4 Yanofsky, interview.

5 For the Court's decision in *Stenberg*, see *Stenberg v. Carhart*, 530 U.S. 914 (2000).

6 For the Court's decision in *Gonzales*, see *Gonzales v. Carhart*, 550 U.S. 124 (2007).

7 For Haskell's paper, see Martin Haskell, "Dilation and Extraction for Second Trimester Abortion" (September 13, 1992), on file with the author. For more on NAF and its history, see Johanna Schoen, *Abortion after Roe* (Chapel Hill: University of North Carolina Press, 2015), 99–123; Lori Freedman, *Willing and Unable: Doctors' Constraints in Abortion Care* (Nashville, TN: Vanderbilt University Press, 2010), 27–30.

8 On the MCCL ad, see John Dombrink and Daniel Hillyard, *Sin No More: From Abortion to Stem Cells, Understanding Crime, Law, and Morality in America* (New York: New York University Press, 2007), 79–82; Sheldon Ekland-Olson, *Life and Death Decisions: The Quest for Morality and Justice in Human Societies* (New York: Routledge, 2013), 44–50.

9 On the NRLC campaign, see NRLC, "Stop FOCA Now! An Analysis and State Call to Action" (1992), JBP, Matter Boxes, File 1067. On the divisions surrounding FOCA, see Elaine S. Povich, "Abortion-Rights Bill Rejected by Moseley-Braun," *Chicago Tribune*, July 10, 1993, 14; Kevin Merida, "Abortion Bill Overtaken by Health Reform," *Washington Post*, March 21, 1994, A1.

10 For Long's view, see Carol Long, "Final 60 Day Report" (August 22, 1994), JBP, Matter Boxes, File 1203; see also NRLC Fundraising Letter (November 23, 1994), JBP, Matter Boxes, File 1203. For more on the significance of the 1994 election, see Scott H. Ainsworth and Thad E. Hall, *Abortion Politics: Strategic Incrementalism and Policy Change* (New York: Cambridge University Press, 2010), 58–66; John C. Green, "The Christian Right and the 1994 Election: An Overview," in *God in the Grassroots: The Christian Right in the 1994 Election* eds. Mark Rozell and Clyde Wilcox (Lanham, MD: Rowman and Littlefield, 1995), 1–18; Kerry N. Jacoby, *Souls, Bodies, Spirits: The Drive to Abolish Abortion since 1973* (Westport, CT: Praeger, 1998), xi.

11 NRLC Board of Director Meeting Minutes (January 21, 1995), JBP, Matter Boxes, File 1275. For more on why the D&X ban seemed strategically wise to NRLC members, see NRLC Fundraising Letter (June 1995), JBP, Matter Boxes, File 1203; Karen Mineau Huggard to David N. O'Steen and Darla St. Martin (September 4, 1996), JBP, Matter Boxes, File 1327.

12 For Schafer's statement: Partial-Birth Abortion Act: Testimony before the Senate Judiciary Committee, 104th Congress 1st Session (1995), 69 (Statement of Brenda Pratt Schafer). For Alvaré's statement: Ibid., 113.

13 Ibid., 160 (Statement of Colleen Costello). For more on Costello's role in the debate, see Patrice Apodaca, "The Politics of Heartbreak," *Los Angeles Times*, May 7, 1996, E1; Robin Abcarian, "Lifesaving Option or Criminal Conduct?" *Los Angeles Times*, November 26, 1995, E1.

14 For Robinson's statement: Partial-Birth Abortion Ban Act, 104–105 (Statement of J. Courtland Robinson). For Romer's statement, see ibid., 110 (Statement of Nancy Romer).

15 See Bill Clinton, Letter to Congress (April 10, 1996), Domestic Policy Council, Neera Tanden, and Subject Files, "Abortion-Abortion [2]," Clinton Digital Library, accessed August 15, 2019, https://clinton.presidentiallibraries.us/items/show/6590. For more on Clinton's veto, see Ann Devroy, "Late-Term Abortion Ban Vetoed," *Washington Post*, April 11, 1996, A1; Todd S. Purdum, "President Vetoes Measure Banning Type of Abortion," *New York Times*, April 11, 1996, A1.

16 Talking Points, Doug Johnson to State Officers (April 4, 1996), JBP, Matter Boxes, File 1325; see also NRLC Board of Directors Meeting Minutes (April 13–14, 1996), JBP, Matter Boxes, File 1325. For letters written to Clinton in opposition to his veto, see Robert Dole to Bill Clinton (February 28, 1996), Domestic Policy Council, Neera Tanden, and Subject Files, "Abortion-Abortion [2]," Clinton Digital Library, accessed August 15, 2019, https://clinton.presidentiallibraries.us/items/show/6590; Dr. Franklin Paschall et al. to Bill Clinton (June 5, 1996), Domestic Policy Council, Neera Tanden, and Subject Files, "Abortion-Abortion [2]," Clinton Digital Library, accessed August 15, 2019, https://clinton.presidentiallibraries.us/items/show/6590.

17 Pamphlet, PHACT, "Your Conscience Tells You This Is Wrong" (1996), PWP, Box 80, Folder 2. For PHACT's letter: PHACT, "The Activists Have Spoken, the Politicians Have Spoken. May We Say Something?" (1996), JBP, Matter Boxes, File 1325; see also "Just the PHACTs, Ma'am," *Life Insights*, July–August 1996, 1, JBP, Matter Boxes, File 1325.

18 "CBS *60 Minutes* on Partial-Birth Abortion: A Critique" (June 10, 1996), JBP, Matter Boxes, File 1325. For more on the organization's skepticism of the media, see NRLC Board of Directors Meeting Minutes (January 21, 1995), JBP, Matter Boxes, File 1275. For a prominent argument about media bias from the period, see Bernard Goldberg, *Bias: A CBS Insider Exposes How the Media Distorts the News* (Washington, DC: Regnery, 2001).

19 On the Senate vote, see Jessica Lee, "Senate Upholds Veto of Abortion Procedure Ban," *USA Today*, September 27, 1996, 4A.

20 For NRLC's argument against the Daschle bill, see statement by Douglas Johnson, Post-Election Press Conference, November 7, 1996, 1–2, JBP, Matter Boxes, File 1327; NRLC Fundraising Letter (December 6, 1996), JBP, Matter Boxes, File 1327; Press Release, Doug Johnson (November 5, 1998), JBP, Matter Boxes, File 1931; Press Release, "National Right to Life Committee Responds to Senator Daschle's Phony Ban," November 26, 1996, PWP, Box 80, Folder 2.

21 For Marshner's statement and the background of Life Forum, see Life Forum Meeting Minutes, October 4, 1996, PWP, Box 80 Folder 2. For Weyrich's statement: Life Forum Meeting Minutes, September 26, 1996, PWP, Box 80, Folder 2. For the other statement made on the GOP at Life Forum: Life Forum Meeting Minutes, September 26, 1996, PWP, Box 80, Folder 3; see also Joe Barrett to Mike Schwartz (September 15, 1997), PWP, Box 80, Folder 10 (complaining that many saw the pro-life movement as a "front

for the GOP"). For Weyrich's complaints about Gingrich, see: Life Forum Meeting Minutes, October 24, 1997, 3, PWP, Box 80, Folder 7. Dole had already moved to the left on abortion ahead of his defeat. See Katherine Q. Seelye, "Dole's Switch on Abortion Leads Quickly to Furor on GOP Right," *New York Times*, December 19, 1995, www.nytimes.com/1995/12/19/us/dole-s-switch-on-abortion-leads-quickly-to-furor-on-gop-right.html, accessed April 26, 2019; Elizabeth Kolbert, "Abortion, Dole's Sword in '74, Returns to Confront Him in '96," *New York Times*, July 8, 1996, www.nytimes.com/1996/07/08/us/politics-political-life-abortion-dole-s-sword-74-returns-confront-him-96.html, accessed April 26, 2019. On Dole's defeat, see Will Marshall, "Why Did Clinton Win?" *American Prospect*, March-April 1997, https://prospect.org/article/controversy-why-did-clinton-win, accessed April 26, 2019. For the Gallup poll, see Lydia Saad, "Public Opinion on Abortion: An In-Depth Review," Gallup, January 22, 2002, https://news.gallup.com/poll/9904/public-opinion-about-abortion-indepth-review.aspx, accessed May 31, 2019; see also Lydia Saad, "Americans Agree with Banning Partial Birth Abortion," Gallup, November 6, 2003, https://news.gallup.com/poll/9658/americans-agree-banning-partialbirth-abortion.aspx, accessed May 31, 2019.

22 See Karen Wright, "Heating the Global Warming Debate," *New York Times*, February 3, 1994, SM24. For examples of global warming skepticism, see William J. Broad, "Two Views from the Greenhouse," *New York Times*, July 5, 1998, BR21; Dixy Lee Ray, "Global Warming: Fact or Fiction?" *Chicago Tribune*, April 13, 1992, 119; William Nierenberg, "Talking Point: Global Warming: Look Before We Leap," *New Scientist* (March 9, 1991): 10; Frederick Seitz, *Global Warming and Ozone Hole Controversies: A Challenge to Scientific Judgment* (Washington DC: George C. Marshall Institute, 1994), 16–17, 22; Frederick Seitz, "Debate Spurs Science," *New York Times*, May 9, 1998, A10. On the Byrd-Hagel Resolution, see Paul R. Brewer and Andrew Pease, "Federal Climate Change Politics in the United States: Polarization and Paralysis," in *Turning Down the Heat: The Politics of Climate Policy in Affluent Societies* eds. Hugh Compston and Ian Bailey (New York: Palgrave-Macmillan, 2008), 88.

23 On the history of the anti-vaccine movement, see Paul A. Offit, *Deadly Choices: How the Anti-Vaccine Movement Threatens Us All* (New York: Basic Books, 2011), 60–72; Susan Jacoby, *The Age of American Unreason* (New York: Knopf, 2006), 219–223; Mark A. Largent, *vaccine: The Debate in Modern America* (Baltimore, MD: Johns Hopkins University Press, 2012); James Colgrove, *State of Immunity: The Politics of Vaccination in Twentieth-Century America* (Berkeley: University of California Press, 2006). On increasing access to the Internet, see Christopher S. Yoo, *The Dynamic Internet: How Technology, Users, and Businesses Are Changing the Network* (New York: Rowman and Littlefield, 2012), 15–23; see also Internet World Statistics, www.internetworldstats.com/emarketing.htm, accessed October 11, 2017.

24 For attacks on unquestioning deference to science in earlier periods and cases of human experimentation, see Eileen Welsome, *The Plutonium Files: America's Secret Medical Experiments in the Cold War* (New York: Random House, 1999); James H. Jones, *Bad Blood: The Tuskegee Syphilis Experiment* (New York: Simon and Schuster, 1993); Jennifer Nelson, *More than Medicine: A History of the Feminist Women's Health Movement* (New York: New York University Press, 2015).

25 For a sample of the work in *The Public Interest* on what commentators saw as the politicization of science and social science, see Peter Skerry, "The Class Conflict over Abortion," *The Public Interest* 52 (1978): 69–84; Daniel Patrick Moynihan, "Social Science and the Courts," *The Public Interest* 54 (1979): 12–31; Eleanor P. Wolf, "Social Science and the Courts: The Detroit Schools Case," *The Public Interest* 42 (1976): 102–120; Mark Snyderman and Stanley Rothman, "Science, Politics, and the IQ Controversy," *The Public Interest* 83 (1986): 79–97. For an argument that many environmental conclusions were not supported by relevant scientific evidence, see Bjorn Lomberg, *The Skeptical Environmentalist: Measuring the Real State of the World* (New York: Cambridge University Press, 2001).

26 Life Forum Meeting Minutes, October 24, 1997, 5, PWP, Box 80, Folder 7. For Gutiérrez's statement: Myrna Gutiérrez, "Letter to the Editor: RU 486 Side Effects Still Unknown," *New York Times*, March 9, 1995, A24. On the RU 486 clinical trial, see Beverly Winikoff, et al., "Acceptability and Feasibility of Early Pregnancy Termination by Mifepristone-Misoprostol: Results of a Large Multicenter Trial in the United States," *Archives of Family Medicine* 7 (1998): 360–378. On the French study, see André Ullman and Louise Silvestre, "RU 486: The French Experience," *Human Reproduction* 9 (1994): 126–130. For more on AUL's work on abortion and breast cancer, see Clarke D. Forsythe, "Abortion Laws: A Report from the States," *Wall Street Journal*, August 9, 1995, A9.

27 Tom Strahan to Doug Johnson (December 11, 1992), JBP, Matter Boxes, File 1067. For more on Brind's story, see Barry Yeoman, "The Scientist Who Hated Abortion," *Discover*, February 1, 2003, http://discovermagazine.com/2003/feb/feathated, accessed August 7, 2017; Wendy Parmet, "Beyond Privacy: A Population Approach to Reproductive Rights," in *Reconsidering Law and Policy Debates: A Public Health Perspective* ed. John G. Culhane (New York: Cambridge University Press, 2011), 22; Sara Dubow, *Ourselves Unborn: A History of the Fetus in Modern America* (New York: Oxford University Press, 2010), 162.

28 For AUL's model law, see Judith Koehler to Connie Marshner, June 5, 1996, Re: Abortion and Breast Cancer Press Packet, PWP, Box 80, Folder 1. For Forsythe's statement on the ABC campaign, see Clarke Forsythe to Connie Marshner, July 18, 1996, PWP, Box 80, Folder 1. For more on the ABC campaign, see The Abortion–Breast Cancer Act Legal Fact Sheet (nd, ca. 1996), PWP, Box 80, Folder 1. On the effort to publicize a connection between abortion and breast cancer, another issue where medical details were in dispute, see "Breast Cancer Emerges as Major Weapon in Fight against Abortion," *AUL Forum*, September 2000, 1, PLN, AUL Forum Boxes; "AUL Focuses on Women's Right to Know, Abortion–Breast Cancer Link," *AUL Forum*, Spring 1998, REC, AUL Folder; Joel Brind, "Denial Digs In Deeper as Evidence Mounts of Increased Incidence of Breast Cancer in Women Who've Aborted," *National Right to Life News*, January 1995, 8, JRS, 1995 National Right to Life News Box; Joel Brind, "The Abortion–Breast Cancer Connection Goes to Trial," *National Right to Life News*, September 28, 1998, 26, JRS, 1998 National Right to Life News Box; Joel Brind, "Making a Molehill Out of a Mountain," *National Right to Life News*, June 15, 1995, 10, JRS, 1995 National Right to Life News Box. For the Daling study, see Janet Daling et al., "Risk of Breast Cancer among Young Women: Relationship to Induced Abortion," *Journal National Cancer Institute* 86 (1994): 1584–1592. For a sample of other studies in this vein, see M. C. Pike, "Oral Contraceptive Use and Early Abortion as Risk Factors for Breast Cancer in Young

Women," *British Journal of Cancer* 43 (1981): 72–76; Joel Brind et al., "Induced Abortion as an Independent Risk Factor for Breast Cancer: a Comprehensive Review and Meta-Analysis," *Journal of Epidemiology and Community Health* 50 (1996): 481–496. On the issues with case control studies, see B. M. Lindefors-Harris et al., "Response Bias in a Case-Control Study: Analysis Utilizing Comparative Data Concerning Legal Abortions from Two Independent Swedish Studies," *American Journal of Epidemiology* 134 (1991): 1003–1008: E. F. Jones et al., "Underreporting of Abortion in Surveys of U. S. Women: 1976 to 1988," *Demography* 29: 113–126. Other studies found no evidence of reporting bias in Daling's work. See Mei-Tzu C. Tang et al., "Case-Control Differences in the Reliability of Reporting a History of Induced Abortions," *American Journal of Epidemiology* 151 (2000): 1139–1143.

29 On the 1996 studies, see P. A. Newcomb et al., "Pregnancy Termination in Relation to Risk of Breast Cancer," *Journal of the American Medical Association* 275 (1996): 283–287. For the 1997 study: Mads Melbye et al., "Induced Abortion and the Risk of Breast Cancer," *New England Journal of Medicine* 336 (1997): 81–85. On the position taken by the World Health Organization, the National Cancer Institute, and the American Cancer Society, see Rita Rubin, "Abortion and Breast Cancer," *USA Today*, March 1, 2001, D9.

30 Life Forum Meeting Minutes (January 23, 1997), 11, PWP, Box 80, Folder 3. On the evolution of CPCs in the period, see Karissa Haugeberg, *Women against Abortion: Inside the Largest Legal Reform Movement of the Twentieth Century* (Champaign: University of Illinois Press, 2017), 58–60. For more on NIFLA and the transition to medical clinic CPCs, see Steve Schwalm, "Conservative Spotlight: National Institute of Family and Life Advocates" *Human Events* 52 (1996): 9; Mary Meehan, "How Pregnancy Centers 'Love Them to Life,'" *Human Life Review*, Summer 2012, 44–56.

31 Gallup, "Abortion," *In Depth Topics: A to Z*, https://news.gallup.com/poll/1576/abortion.aspx, accessed March 20, 2019.

32 For the Court's decision in *Mazurek*, see *Mazurek v. Armstrong*, 520 U.S. 968, 973–974 (1997). For *Roe*'s holding on licensed physicians, see *Roe v. Wade*, 410 U.S. 113, 165 (1973). For the Center for Reproductive Law and Policy's argument, see Brief of Appellants, 29–32, *Mazurek v. Armstrong*, 520 U.S. 968 (1997) (No. 95–35962). On the predicted impact of *Mazurek* on medical abortion, see Lyle Denniston, "Doctors Only Abortion Law Upheld by Supreme Court," *Baltimore Sun*, June 17, 1997, 3A. For Forsythe's statement, see Life Forum Meeting Minutes (July 25, 1997), 6, PWP, Box 80, Folder 3.

33 For the *American Medical News* interview: David Stout, "An Abortion-Rights Advocate Says He Lied about the Procedure," *New York Times*, February 26, 1997, www.nytimes.com/1997/02/26/us/an-abortion-rights-advocate-says-he-lied-about-procedure.html, accessed August 8, 2017; see also Roy Rivenburg, "Partial Truths," *Los Angeles Times*, April 2, 1997, http://arti cles.latimes.com/1997-04-02/news/ls-44326_1_national-abortion-federation, accessed August 8, 2017. For discussion within NCAP about D&X: Ron Fitzsimmons to NCAP Members (February 17, 1997), NCAP, Box 3, Folder 3; see also Ron Fitzsimmons to NCAP (February 26, 1997), NCAP, Box 3, Folder 3.

34 For NCAP's statement: Ron Fitzsimmons to NCAP (February 26, 1997), 2. For the NAF press release, see National Abortion Federation Press Release (February 26, 1997), NCAP, Box 3, Folder 3. For more on the response to Fitzsimmons' comment, see Ron Fitzsimmons to NCAP (May 12, 1997), NCAP, Box 3, Folder 3; NAF Update on HR 1122 (May 23,

1997), NCAP, Box 3, Folder 3; Center for Reproductive Law and Policy Fundraising Letter (nd, ca. 1997), NCAP, Box 3, Folder 3.

35 NARAL, Fiscal Year '99 Goals (nd, ca. 1998), 1, NARAL, Box 94, Folder 7.

36 NARAL Three-Year Strategic Plan, 1997–2000 (1997), 1–3, NARAL, Box 94, Folder 7; see also Kate Michelman's Speech, San Francisco Power Luncheon, March 20, 1997, NARAL, Box 200, Folder 10.

37 Kate Michelman to Interested Parties (July 20, 1997), 1–4, Domestic Policy Council, Neera Tanden, and Subject Files, "Abortion-Choice-Reframing," Clinton Digital Library, accessed August 15, 2019, https://clinton.presidentiallibraries.us/items/show/6592. On the "Real Choices" initiative, see Mary Beth Maxwell to Joyce Cunha (November 28, 1993), NARALMA, Box 28, Folder 15; see also "Expanding the Meaning of 'Choice,'" *New York Times,* January 17, 1994, A16.

38 Michelman to Interested Parties, 3, 7.

39 Lake Research to Friends and Clients (September 17, 1996), FWHC, Box 3, Partial Birth Abortion Folder 3.

40 See John Hilley et al. to Bill Clinton (April 10, 1997), Domestic Policy Council and Elena Kagan, "Abortion Partial Birth-Notes and Memos," Clinton Digital Library, accessed August 15, 2019, https://clinton.presidentiallibraries.us/items/show/25759.

41 For the AMA's statement, see American Medical Association Press Release (May 14, 1997), Domestic Policy Council and Elena Kagan, "Abortion Partial Birth-Medical Statements," Clinton Digital Library, accessed August 16, 2019, https://clinton.presidentiallibraries.us/items/show/25758. For more on the AMA's stance, see P. John Seward of American Medical Association to Senator Rick Santorum (May 20, 1997), Domestic Policy Council and Elena Kagan, "Abortion Partial Birth-Medical Statements," Clinton Digital Library, accessed August 16, 2019, https://clinton.presidentiallibraries.us/items/show/25758. For ACOG's position, see American College of Obstetricians and Gynecologists' Statement of Policy (May 20, 1997), Domestic Policy Council and Elena Kagan, "Abortion Partial Birth-Medical Statements," Clinton Digital Library, accessed August 16, 2019, https://clinton.presidentiallibraries.us/items/show/25758.

42 "*Roe v. Wade* at 25: A Symposium" (1998), 1–18, RCD, Box 2, Planned Parenthood Foundation Meeting Folder.

43 On the Action's Fund 1998 spending plan, see Norah O'Donnell, "Matter of Choice? Abortion Debate Moves into the Campaign Arena," *Roll Call,* October 8, 1998, 1.

44 Planned Parenthood Federation of America National Survey October 1998: Executive Summary (1998), 1–17, JBP, Matter Boxes, File 1931.

45 On Kenneth Starr's investigation of Clinton, see Ken Gormley, *The Death of American Virtue: Clinton vs. Starr* (New York: Crown, 2010); Richard A. Posner, *An Affair of State: The Investigation, Impeachment, and Trial of President Clinton* (Cambridge, MA: Harvard University Press, 1999); Robert J. Spitzer, "The Presidency: The Clinton Crisis and Its Consequences," in *The Clinton Scandal and the Future of American Government* eds. Mark Rozell and Clyde Wilcox (Washington, DC: Georgetown University Press, 2000), 1–10.

46 On the impeachment trial and its impact on the 1998 election, see Peter Baker, *The Breach: Inside the Impeachment and Trial of William Jefferson Clinton* (New York: Simon and Schuster, 2000), 142–145; Gary C. Jacobson and Jamie L. Carson, *The Politics of*

Congressional Elections (Lanham, MD: Rowman and Littlefield, 2016), 209; Posner, *An Affair of State*, 251–258.

47 On the surge of antiabortion murder and violence, see Eyal Press, *Absolute Convictions: My Father, a City, and a Conflict that Divided America* (New York: Henry Holt, 2006), 220–223; Rickie Solinger, *Pregnancy and Power: A Short History of Reproductive Politics in America* (New York: New York University Press, 2005), 225.

48 Meeting Notes, NARAL Conference Expanding Choice for America (August 27–29, 1999), NARALMA, Box 51, Folder 9.

49 NARAL Foundation, "Choice for America" (1999), 1–3, RCD, Box 2, NARAL Folder. For more on Choice for America, see Mary Jacoby, "Abortion Debate Enlists Aid of Philanthropists," *St. Petersburg Times*, March 12, 2000, 1A; "$28 Million in Political Ads since January, Study Finds," *US Newswire*, April 27, 2001, 1.

50 Clarke Forsythe, "Pro-life Strategy Five Years after *Casey* and Clinton: A Response to Michael Schwartz's Strategy Analysis" (1998), 3, PWP, Box 80, Folder 10. For Schwartz's position, see Michael Schwartz, "Debunking the Myths that Keep Abortion Legal," Focus on the Family's *Citizen Magazine*, 1998, PWP, Box 80, Folder 10. On NRLC's view of the importance of the partial-birth abortion campaign, see NRLC Fundraising Letter (August 26, 1999), JBP, Matter Boxes, File 1934; National Right to Life Educational Trust Fundraising Letter (November 23, 199), JBP, Matter Boxes, File 1934.

51 On the number of state laws, see Center for Reproductive Rights, "So-Called 'Partial-Birth Abortion' Bans by State" (nd, ca. 2004), www.reproductiverights.org/sites/default/files/docu ments/pub_bp_pba_bystate.pdf, accessed October 4, 2018.

52 Neb. Rev. Stat. Ann. § 28–328(1) (Supp. 1999). On the litigation of D&X bans in the lead-up to *Stenberg*, see *Hope Clinic v. Ryan*, 195 F.3d 857 (7th Cir. 1999); *Planned Parenthood of Greater Iowa v. Miller*, 195 F.3d 386 (8th Cir. 1999); *Eubanks v. Stengel*, 224 F.3d 576 (6th Cir. 2000); *Planned Parenthood of Central New Jersey v. Farmer*, 220 F.3d 127 (3d Cir. 2000); *Summit Medical Associates, Inc. v. Pryor*, 180 F.3d 1326 (11th Cir. 1999).

53 On the early litigation of *Stenberg*, see *Carhart v. Stenberg*, 11 F. Supp. 2d 1099 (D. Neb. 1998); *Carhart v. Stenberg*, 11 F. Supp. 2d 1134 (D. Neb. 1998); *Carhart v. Stenberg*, 192 F.3d 1142 (8th Cir. 1999).

54 Brief of Respondent, 20–24, 33, *Stenberg v. Carhart*, 530 U.S. 914 (2000) (No. 99–830).

55 Brief for Petitioners, 46, *Stenberg v. Carhart*, 530 U.S. 914 (2000) (No. 99–830).

56 On absolutists' resentment of incrementalism, see Mary Ziegler, *After Roe: The Lost History of the Abortion Debate* (Cambridge, MA: Harvard University Press, 2015), 81–85; Michael W. Cuneo, "Life Battles: The Rise of Catholic Militancy within the American Pro-life Movement," in *Being Right: Conservative Catholics in America* eds. Mary Jo Weaver and R. Scott Appleby (Bloomington: University of Indiana Press, 1995), 283–285; Michael W. Cuneo, *The Smoke of Satan: Conservative and Traditionalist Dissent in Contemporary American Catholicism* (New York: Oxford University Press, 1997), 101–127.

57 On absolutists' skepticism of Bush, see "Judie Brown Asks George W. Bush to Clarify His Position on Life," *PR Newswire*, May 31, 2000, 1.

58 NARAL, "The Powers of the President: Reproductive Freedom and Choice, Executive Summary" (2000), JBP, Matter Boxes, File 1942. For Johnson's statement: Doug Johnson to NRLC Board and State Offices et al. Re: Impending Supreme Court Ruling in *Stenberg v. Carhart* (June 19, 2000), JBP, Matter Boxes, File 1942.

59 *Stenberg v. Carhart*, 530 U.S. 914, 937–938 (2000).

60 Ibid., 939–943.

61 Ibid., 961 (Kennedy, J., dissenting).

62 Ibid., 970. For contemporary discussion of the *Stenberg* decision, see Edward Walsh and Amy Goldstein, "Supreme Court Upholds Two Key Abortion-Rights," *Washington Post*, June 29, 2000, A1; Edward Lazarus, "Court Crackup," *Washington Post*, July 25, 2000, A23; George F. Will, "An Act of Judicial Infamy," *Washington Post*, June 29, 2000, A31; Philip J. Hilts, "The Reaction: Doctors Express Relief over Decision: Foes of Abortion Vow to Continue Their Fight," *New York Times*, June 30, 2000, A20.

63 On *Bush v. Gore* and the 2000 election, see Howard Gillman, *The Votes That Counted: How the Court Decided the 2000 Presidential Election* (Chicago: University of Chicago Press, 2001); Richard Hasen, *The Supreme Court and Election Law: Judging Equality from Baker v. Carr to Bush v. Gore* (New York: New York University Press, 2003), 41–61; Jeffrey Toobin, *Too Close to Call: The Thirty-Six-Day Battle to Decide the 2000 Election* (New York: Random House, 2001); Cass Sunstein, "Of Law and Politics," in *Bush, Gore, and the Supreme Court* eds. Cass Sunstein and Richard Epstein (Chicago: University of Chicago Press, 2001), 1–10. On the 2000 congressional races, see John Harwood, "Election 2000: Even as Election Ends, Battles Continue with Midterm Congressional Fight Ahead," *Wall Street Journal*, December 14, 2000, A16; Juliet Eilperin, "Hill Democrats Ready to Resist GOP Push," *Washington Post*, January 3, 2001, A1. For more on Bopp's vote-dilution argument: James Bopp Jr. and Richard E. Coleson, "Vote-Dilution Analysis in *Bush v. Gore*," *St. Thomas Law Review* 23 (2011): 461–482. For the Court's decision in *Reynolds v. Sims*, 377 U.S. 533 (1964).

64 Angela Lanfranchi, interview with Mary Ziegler, August 7, 2017. For more on the experiences of those working to document the ABC connection: Priscilla Coleman, interview with Mary Ziegler, August 2, 2017; Harrison, interview.

65 Lanfranchi, interview.

66 Lanfranchi, interview. For more on the Breast Cancer Prevention Institute, see Stephanie Simon, "Abortion Foes Seize on Reports of Cancer Link in Ad Campaign," *Los Angeles Times*, March 24, 2002, A26.

67 See Nina Martin, "Behind the Supreme Court's Decision, More than a Decade of Privately Funded Research," *Propublica*, July 14, 2016, www.propublica.org/article/supreme-court-abortion-decision-more-than-decade-privately-funded-research, accessed August 31, 2017; Nina Martin, "Amid Abortion Debate, the Pursuit of Science," *ProPublica*, January 7, 2014, www.propublica.org/article/amid-abortion-debate-the-pursuit-of-science, accessed September 1, 2017. For more on Weitz's work in the period, see Ann Hwang, "Exportable Righteousness, Expendable Women," *World Watch*, January/February 2002, 24–31; Bonnie Scott Jones and Tracy A. Weitz, "Legal Barriers to Second Trimester Abortions and Public Health Consequences," *American Journal of Public Health* 99 (2009): 623–630; Tracy A. Weitz and Susan Berke Fogel, "The Denial of Abortion Care: Information, Referrals, and Services Undermine Quality Care for U.S. Women," *Women's Health Issues* 20 (2010): 7–11.

68 See Nina Martin, "How One Abortion Megadonor Forced the Supreme Court's Hand," *Mother Jones*, July 14, 2016, www.motherjones.com/politics/2016/07/abortion-research-buf

fett, accessed July 20, 2017. For more on the research organizations created by those on each side of the abortion question, see Martin, "Amid Abortion Debate."

69 On the approval of RU 486 and the restrictions placed on the drug, see Daniel Grossman, "Fewer Rules, Fewer Late Abortions," *Los Angeles Times*, February 28, 2007, A9. In 2016, the FDA somewhat loosened regulations, allowing women to take RU 486 later into pregnancy and with fewer doctor's visits. See Sabrina Tavernise, "New FDA Guidelines Ease Access to Abortion Pill," *New York Times*, March 30, 2016, www.nytimes.com/2016/03/31/health/abortion-pill-mifeprex-ru-486-fda.html, accessed October 4, 2018.

70 For the AUL statement: "Breast Cancer Link Emerges as a Major Weapon in Fight against Abortion," *AUL Momentum*, September 2000, PLN, AUL Momentum Folder. For more on the movement's legal work on the issue, see Joel Brind, "Abortion and Breast Cancer: Bush's Election Sparks Backlash," *National Right to Life News*, April 2001, 4, JRS, 2001 National Right to Life News Box. On the laws backed by AUL, see Susan Milligan, "Some Push Link between Abortion, Cancer," *Chicago Tribune*, May 22, 2002, 2; Rubin, "Abortion and Breast Cancer," D9.

71 NARAL, "Talking about Freedom of Choice" (nd, ca. 2000), 3–4, NARALMA, Box 42, Folder 12.

72 NARAL Pro-choice Massachusetts, "Defending against Attacks" (nd, ca. 2003), NARALMA, Box 42, Folder 12; see also "Talking about Freedom of Choice," 3.

73 On NRLC's priorities in 2001, see NRLC Executive Committee Meeting Minutes (March 10, 2001), JBP, Matter Boxes, File 2264; Doug Johnson to James Bopp Jr. (April 18, 2001), JBP, Matter Boxes, File 2264. On the impact of the September 11 attack on abortion opponents, see Doug Johnson to NRLC Board of Directors (September 21, 2001), JBP, Matter Boxes, File 2264. On the effects of 9/11 on antiabortion terrorism, see John C. Green, "New and Old Evangelical Public Engagement: A View from the Polls," *The New Evangelical Social Engagement* eds. Brian Steensland and Philip Goff (New York: Oxford University Press, 2014), 136. On Arkes' strategy, see Hadley Arkes to Richard John Neuhaus (September 11, 1998), RJN, Box 3, Folder 27; Richard John Neuhaus to Hadley Arkes (June 22, 1998), RJN, Box 3, Folder 27; Hadley Arkes to Richard John Neuhaus (June 11, 1998), RJN, Box 3, Folder 27. For Arkes' article: Hadley Arkes, "Life Watch: The Adventures of Summer-Continued," *Crisis*, September 1, 1998, www.crisismagazine.com/1998/life-watch-the-adventures-of-summer-continued, accessed May 22, 2019.

74 Creative Research Communications, "The Beauty of Life, the Reality of Abortion" 1–2, (2002), PWP, Box 81, Folder 2. For the arguments stressed at the AUL forum, see Life Forum Meeting Minutes (September 2002), Box 81, Folder 2. On the effort to reintroduce a D&X ban, see Doug Johnson to James Bopp Jr. (June 19, 2002), JBP, Matter Boxes, File 2265; "U.S. Passes Ban on Partial-Birth Abortion," *National Right to Life News*, August 2002, 1, JRS, 2002 National Right to Life News Box.

75 Jennifer Lee, "Abortion-Rights Group Plans a New Focus and a New Name," *New York Times*, January 5, 2003, 1. For more on NARAL's 2003 framing of its work, see William Saletan, *Bearing Right: How Conservatives Won the Abortion War* (Berkeley: University of California Press, 2004), xiv.

76 Memorandum, Lake, Snell, and Perry Associates to Planned Parenthood Federation of America (2003), PPSE, Box 51, Folder 4; see also Planned Parenthood Federation of

America, "Message Kit" (September 2003), PPSE, Box 51, Folder 4; Planned Parenthood, "Mobilizing to Win" (Fall 2003), PPSE, Box 51, Folder 4.

77 Toni M. Bond, "Barriers between Black Women and the Reproductive Rights Movement," *Political Environments*, Winter/Spring 2001, 1; https://perma.cc/TU8U-8V99; see also Jennifer Frey, "Then and NOW: Patricia Ireland Reflects," *Washington Post*, July 19, 2001, C1. On the Emergency Action and perceptions of it among women of color, see Sarah Bollinger, "Feminists Mobilize for Choice," *Off Our Backs*, May 2001, 1.

78 For more on the work of reproductive justice activists in the period, see Loretta Ross and Rickie Solinger, *Reproductive Justice: An Introduction* (Berkeley: University of California Press, 2017), 67; Dorothy Roberts, *Killing the Black Body: Race, Reproduction, and the Meaning of Liberty* 2d ed. (New York: Vintage, 2016), xx.

79 Life Forum Meeting Minutes, July 10, 1998, 4, PWP, Box 80, Folder 10.. For more on Cassidy's background, see "Trial to Determine Fate of Abortion Ban," *New York Times*, September 9, 1998, B6; Patrick Mullaney, "A Father's Trial and the Case for Personhood," *Human Life Review* 27 (2001): 85–96. On Cassidy's background as a litigator, see Harold J. Cassidy: Chief Counsel, http://haroldcassidy.com/bio.html, accessed July 31, 2017.

80 Brochure, the National Foundation for Life, The Global Project (nd, ca. 1998), PWP, Box 80, Folder 3.

81 Kathleen Cassidy, "Post-Abortive Women Attack *Roe v. Wade*," *At the Center*, January 2001, www.atcmag.com/Issues/ID/16/Post-Abortive-Women-Attack-Roe-v-Wade, accessed July 24, 2018. For more on Operation Outcry and the Justice Foundation, see Reva B. Siegel, "The Right's Reasons: Constitutional Conflict and the Spread of Woman-Protective Antiabortion Argument," *Duke Law Journal* 57 (2008): 1641–1692. On Cano and McCorvey's involvement, see Affidavit of Sandra Cano, *Donna Santa Marie v. Whitman* (No. 99–2962); Affidavit of Norma McCorvey, *Donna Santa Marie v. Whitman* (No. 99–2962), www.epm.org/resources/2000/Mar/2/truth-about-roe-v-wade-according-jane-roe-norma-mc, accessed July 24, 2018.

82 For the statement from the *Acuna* suit, see *Acuna v. Turkish*, 808 A.2d 149, 153 (N.J. Super. A.D. 2002). On the Third Circuit's decision in *Donna Santa Marie*, see *Marie v. McGreevy*, 314 F.3d 136 (3d Cir. 2002).

83 On Ruddy's request and Donovan's report, see Statement of Purpose and Executive Summary, "Planned Parenthood and the Right to Life: Comparison of Organization and an Outline of a New Strategy to Stop Abortion," September 2002, JBP, Matter Boxes, File 2343; Charles Donovan, Executive Summary Notes, September 2002, JBP, Matter Boxes, File 2343. On the early work of the Culture of Life Leadership Coalition, see Letter to Culture of Life Leadership Coalition Leader (April 15, 2003), JBP, Matter Boxes, File 2343.

84 Presentation of Public Relations Group (April 29, 2003), 1–8, JBP, Matter Boxes, File 2343. For the conclusions of the Legal Working Group: Culture of Life Leadership Coalition Legal Working Group, Preliminary Report (2003), 1–14, JBP, Matter Boxes, File 2343.

85 Presentation of Public Relations Group (April 29, 2003), 1–8, JBP, Matter Boxes, File 2343. For the conclusions of the Legal Working Group: Culture of Life Leadership Coalition Legal Working Group, Preliminary Report (2003), 1–14, JBP, Matter Boxes, File 2343.

86 For Cassidy's recollections of the work in South Dakota: Harold Cassidy, interview with Mary Ziegler, July 19, 2018; Harold Cassidy, interview with Mary Ziegler, July 24, 2018. On

conflict within the Coalition, see James Bopp Jr. to Jeffrey Ventrella (May 3, 2004), JBP, Matter Boxes, File 2343; Harold Cassidy to James Bopp Jr. (May 3, 2004), JBP, Matter Boxes, File 2243; James Bopp to Harold Cassidy (May 3, 2004), JBP, Matter Boxes, File 2343. On Cassidy's proposed litigation project, see Paul Benjamin Linton to Harold Cassidy (June 15, 2004), JBP, Digital Files, Harold Cassidy Folder. On the 2004 South Dakota proposed ban, see Stephanie Simon, "South Dakota's Ban on Abortion Looks to the Future," *Los Angeles Times*, February 29, 2004, A38; "Governor Supports Bill to Ban Most Abortions in S. Dakota," *Los Angeles Times*, March 10, 2004, A20. For more on the South Dakota effort in 2004, see "South Dakota House Passes Bill Criminalizing Abortion," *US Newswire*, February 11, 2004, 1.

87 Rob Regier to Paul Benjamin Linton (December 21, 2004), 4, JBP, Digital Files, Harold Cassidy folder. For criticisms of the South Dakota approach, see Linton to Cassidy, 1–6; see also James Bopp Jr. and Richard Coleson, Memorandum to Whom It May Concern (August 7, 2007), http://operationrescue.org/pdfs/Bopp%20Memo%20re%20State%20HLA .pdf, accessed May 30, 2018.

88 Ted Olsen, "ALL or Nothing," *Christianity Today*, June 1, 2003, www.christianitytoday. com/ct/2003/juneweb-only/6-2-511.0.html, accessed May 30, 2018. For more on ALL's position on the partial-birth abortion strategy, see Judie Brown, "Partial Birth Abortion Ruling: Where Is the Victory?" American Life League, April 26, 2007, www.all.org/partial-birth-abortion-ruling-where-is-the-victory, accessed May 30, 2018.

89 Daniel C. Becker, *Personhood: A Pragmatic Guide to Prolife Victory in the Twenty-First Century and the Return to First Principles in Politics* (Apharetta, GA: TKS Publishing, 2011), 28. For Becker's recollections: Dan Becker, interview with Mary Ziegler, November 29, 2017.

90 For early litigation in the case, see *Carhart v. Ashcroft*, 331 F.Supp.2d 805 (D. Neb. 2004); *Carhart v. Ashcroft*, 413 F.3d 791 (8th Cir. 2005); *Planned Parenthood Federation of America v. Ashcroft*, 320 F.Supp.2d 957 (N.D. Cal. 2004); *Planned Parenthood Federation of America v. Ashcroft*, 435 F.3d 1163 (9th Cir. 2006).

91 On the Alliance Defense Fund and its influence, see Hans J. Hacker, *The Culture of Conservative Christian Litigation* (Lanham, MD: Rowman and Littlefield, 2005), 64; Ann Southworth, *Lawyers of the Right: Professionalizing the Conservative Coalition* (Chicago: University of Chicago Press, 2008), 163–194; Joshua C. Wilson, *The New States of Abortion Politics* (Palo Alto, CA: Stanford University Press, 2016), 30–42.

92 James Bopp Jr. and Tom Marzen, Alliance Defense Fund Grant Application (May 2, 2003), 1–5, JBP, Digital Records, Partial-Birth-Abortion Project File. ADF ultimately supported the litigation of *Gonzales*. See Alliance Defending Freedom, "*Gonzales v. Carhart*," http:// adflegal.org/detailspages/case-details/gonzales-v.-carhart, accessed December 3, 2018.

93 For Congress's findings, see 18 U.S.C. § 1531 (2000 ed., Supp. IV), p. 768.

94 On the medical textbooks mentioning D&X, see *Williams Obstetrics* eds. F. Gary Cunningham et al. (New York: McGraw-Hill, 2001); Philip G. Stubblefield, "First and Second Trimester Abortion," in *Gynecologic, Obstetric, and Related Surgery* eds. David H. Nichols and Daniel L. Clarke-Pearson 2d ed. (St. Louis, MO: Mosby, 2000), 1033, 1043; Maureen Paul, *A Clinician's Guide to Medical and Surgical Abortion* (New York: Churchill-Livingstone, 1999), 5–6, 107–108. For the Chasen study, see Stephen T. Chasen et al., "Dilation and Evacuation at or after Twenty Weeks: Comparison of

Operative Techniques," *American Journal of Gynecology and Obstetrics* 190 (2004): 1180–1183. For criticism of the Chasen study, see Brief Amici Curiae of the American College of Pro-life Obstetricians and Gynecologists et al., 23–25, *Gonzales v. Carhart*, 550 U.S. 124 (2007) (No. 05–380, 05–1382). Government witnesses relied on the Chasen study to suggest that D&X increased the risk of preterm birth and cervical incompetence – a conclusion vigorously disputed by statisticians who submitted an amicus brief in the case. See *National Abortion Federation v. Ashcroft*, 330 F. Supp.2d 436, 477 (S.D.N.Y. 2004); Amended Brief for Statisticians George Cobb et al., as Amici Curiae Supporting Respondents, *Gonzales v. Carhart*, 550 U.S. 124 (2007) (No. 05–380, 05–1382).

95 See Peter Baker, "Bush Nominates Roberts as Chief Justice," *Washington Post*, September 6, 2005, A1; Richard Stevenson, "Surprise Move: Critical Swing Justice–Bush's First Chance to Pick Justice," *New York Times*, July 2, 2005, A1; Linda Greenhouse, "Despite Rumors, Rehnquist Has No Plans to Retire Now," *New York Times*, July 15, 2005, A10.

96 See Elisabeth Bumiller and Carl Hulse, "Bush Picks U.S. Appeals Judge to Take O'Connor's Court Seat" *New York Times*, November 1, 2005, A1; Sheryl Gay Stolberg and Elizabeth Bumiller, "Congress Confirms Roberts as 17th Chief Justice," *New York Times*, September 30, 2005, A1; Adam Liptak, "Alito Vote May Be Decisive in Marquee Cases This Term," *New York Times*, February 1, 2006, A1.

97 On the expansion of Liberty Counsel and ACLJ, see Amanda Hollis-Brusky and Joshua C. Wilson, "Playing for the Rules: How and Why New Christian Right Public Interest Law Firms Invest in Secular Litigation" *Law and Policy* 39 (2017): 121–125.

98 Memo, "Jim: Supplemental Suggested Issues for PBA Conference from Clarke Forsythe" (nd, ca. 2006), JBP, Matter Boxes, File 2548. For Linton's suggestion: Paul Linton to Thomas Marzen (February 22, 2006), JBP, Digital Files, Partial Birth Abortion Project File.

99 For Weber's perspective: Walter Weber to Thomas Marzen (February 24, 2006), JBP, Matter Boxes, File 2548. On the agenda of the amici meeting, see "Partial Birth Abortion Amici Conference Agenda" (March 6, 2006), JBP, Matter Boxes, File 2548.

100 Brief of the American College of Obstetricians and Gynecologists, 1–3, *Gonzales v. Carhart*, 550 U.S. 124 (2007) (No. 05–380, 05–1382). For the Center's argument, see Brief for Respondents, 3–47, *Gonzales v. Carhart*, 550 U.S. 124 (2007) (No. 05–380, 05–1382); see also Brief of Planned Parenthood Respondents, 33–47, *Gonzales v. Carhart*, 550 U.S. 124 (2007) (No. 05–380, 05–1382); Brief of Amicus Curiae NARAL Pro-choice America Foundation et al., 3–4, *Gonzales v. Carhart*, 550 U.S. 124 (2007) (No. 05–380, 05–1382).

101 For Liberty Counsel's argument: Brief for Amici Curiae Jill Stanek et al., 20–21, *Gonzales v. Carhart*, 550 U.S. 124 (2007) (No. 05–380, 05–1382).

102 Brief of Sandra Cano et al., 6–30, *Gonzales v. Carhart*, 550 U.S. 124 (2007) (No. 05–380, 05–1382). For the abortion-rights response, see Brief for Institute for Reproductive Health Access et al., 2–27, *Gonzales v. Carhart*, 550 U.S. 124 (2007) (No. 05–380, 05–1382). For the American Center for Law and Justice's brief, see Amicus Brief of the American Center for Law and Justice et al., 3–26, *Gonzales v. Carhart*, 550 U.S. 124 (2007) (No. 05–380, 05–1382).

103 *Gonzales v. Carhart*, 550 U.S. 124, 146–156 (2007).

104 Ibid., 156–160.
105 Ibid., 162–167.
106 Ibid., 179–185 (Ginsburg, J., dissenting).

7 POLARIZATION, RELIGIOUS LIBERTY, AND THE WAR ON WOMEN

1 On Kennedy's retirement and perceptions of its significance, see Sarah McCammon, "Justice Anthony Kennedy's Retirement Could Reshape U.S. Abortion Debate," *NPR*, June 29, 2018, www.npr.org/2018/06/29/624416649/justice-anthony-kennedys-retirement-could-reshape-u-s-abortion-debate, accessed July 31, 2018; "Both Sides of the Abortion Debate Think That Justice Kennedy's Retirement Is a Game Changer," *Time*, June 27, 2018, http://time.com/5323890/anthony-kennedy-retirement-abortion-rights, accessed July 31, 2018; Julie Herschfeld Davis, "Departure of Kennedy, 'Firewall for Abortion-Rights,' Could End *Roe v. Wade*," *N.Y. Times*, June 27, 2018, www.nytimes.com/2018/06/27/us/politics/kennedy-abortion-roe-v-wade.html, accessed July 31, 2018. On Leonard Leo and the influence of the Federalist Society on Trump's pick, see "What Is the Federalist Society and How Does It Affect Supreme Court Picks?" *NPR*, June 28, 2018, www.npr.org/2018/06/28/624416666/what-is-the-federalist-society-and-how-does-it-affect-supreme-court-picks, accessed July 31, 2018; Jeffrey Toobin, "The Conservative Pipeline to the Supreme Court," *The New Yorker*, April 17, 2017, www.newyorker.com/magazine/2017/04/17/the-conservative-pipe line-to-the-supreme-court, accessed July 31, 2018. This chapter later discusses Kavanaugh's pre-2018 record on abortion.

2 Monica Davey, "Vote Due on South Dakota Bill Banning Nearly All Abortions," *New York Times*, February 22, 2006, A14; see also Evan Thomas and Martha Brant, "Reality Check for *Roe*," *Newsweek*, March 6, 2006, 44–45. For the Task Force's Report, see *Report of the South Dakota Task Force to Study Abortion, Submitted to the Governor and Legislature of South Dakota* (December 2005), 31–55. On the 2006 South Dakota abortion ban, see John Holusha, "South Dakota Governor Signs Abortion Ban," *New York Times*, March 6, 2006, www.nytimes.com/2006/03/06/politics/south-dakota-governor-signs-abortion-ban.html, accessed July 31, 2018; Monica Davey, "South Dakota Bans Abortion, Setting up a Battle," *New York Times*, March 7, 2006, www.nytimes.com/2006/03/07/us/south-dakota-bans-abor tion-setting-up-a-battle.html, accessed July 31, 2018. For Bartling's statement: "South Dakota Senate Oks Bill to Outlaw Abortions," *Los Angeles Times*, February 23, 2006, A16.

3 On Amendment 48, see Judith Graham and Judi Peres, "Rights for Embryos Proposed," *Chicago Tribune*, December 3, 2007, 1; Nicholas Riccardi, "Foes of Abortion Switch to States," *Los Angeles Times*, November 23, 2007, A1; "Pro-life Activists Push Personhood Initiatives," *Newsweek*, November 1, 2009, www.newsweek.com/pro-life-activists-push-per sonhood-initiatives-76951, accessed July 31, 2018. On Personhood USA, see Pema Levy, "Moment of Conception," *Prospect*, October 27, 2011, http://prospect.org/article/moment-conception, accessed July 31, 2018; Abigail Pesta, "Personhood USA's Keith Mason Eyes Election Day 2012," *Newsweek*, June 25, 2012, www.newsweek.com/personhood-usas-keith-mason-eyes-election-day-2012-65133, accessed July 31, 2018. On the Georgia Right to Life proposal, see Riccardi, "Foes of Abortion," A1; Graham and Peres, "Rights for Embryos," 1.

4 On the issues defining the 2008 election, see M. Margaret Conway, "The Scope of Participation in the 2008 Presidential Race: Voter Mobilization and Electoral Success,"

Winning the Presidency in 2008, ed. William J. Crotty (New York: Routledge, 2009; Michael Tesler and David O. Sears, *Obama's Race: The 2008 Election and the Dream of a Post-Racial America* (Chicago: University of Chicago Press, 2010), 17–52. On NARAL's endorsement, see Katherine Q. Seelye, "NARAL Picks Obama, and Uproar Breaks Out," *New York Times,* May 16, 2008, A20. On NRLC's spending in 2008, see National Right to Life Committee Outside Spending Summary 2008, Center for Responsive Politics, www.opensecrets.org/outsidespending/detail.php?cycle=2008&cmte=C00111278, accessed July 31, 2018.

5 For pro-life reaction to Obama's election, see David Crary, "Obama's Win Jolts Abortion Activists," *Orlando Sentinel,* November 12, 2008, A13; National Right to Life Committee Board of Directors Meeting Minutes (January 24–25, 2009), 1–3, MFJ, Box 7, Folder 7.

6 On Tiller's murder and the reaction to it, see Robin Abcarian and Nicholas Riccardi, "Abortion Doctor Fatally Shot," *Chicago Tribune,* June 1, 2009, 1; Peter Slevin, "Slaying Raises Fears on Both Sides of Abortion Debate," *Washington Post,* June 2, 2009, A1; Peter Slevin, "Abortion-Rights Activists Brace for Another Year of Challenges," *Washington Post,* June 10, 2009, A4. On Roeder's background, see "Roeder to Be Disciplined for 'Threats' in Calls to Army of God Member," *Rewire,* May 15, 2013, https://rewire.news/article/2013/05/15/roeder-to-be-disciplined-for-threats-in-call-to-army-of-god-member, accessed July 31, 2018; Peter J. Smith, "A Portrait of an Alleged Murderer: The Life of Suspected Tiller Killer Scott Roeder," *Life Site News,* June 2, 2009, www.lifesitenews.com/news/a-portrait-of-an-alleged-murderer-the-life-of-suspected-tiller-killer-scott, accessed July 31, 2018.

7 On ADF's involvement in *Rounds,* see Alliance Defending Freedom, *Planned Parenthood v. Rounds,* www.adflegal.org/detailspages/case-details/planned-parenthood-minnesota-v-rounds-1, accessed July 31, 2018; Alliance Defending Freedom, "Federal Court Upholds South Dakota Informed Consent Law," www.adflegal.org/detailspages/blog-details/allianceedge/2017/10/18/federal-court-upholds-south-dakota-informed-consent-law, accessed July 31, 2018. For the text of the South Dakota law: S.D. Cod. Law 34–23A–10.1.

8 For Cassidy's argument on appeal, see Brief on Appeal of Intervenors Alpha Center et al., 36–63, *Planned Parenthood of Minnesota, South Dakota, North Dakota v. Rounds,* 530 F.3d 724 (8th Cir. 2008) (No. 05–3093). For the statement in Cassidy's brief: ibid., 30. For Planned Parenthood's statement: "Eighth Circuit Issues Ruling in Planned Parenthood *v. Rounds*" (January 30, 2014), www.plannedparenthood.org/about-us/newsroom/press-releases/planned-parenthood-v-rounds, accessed May 1, 2019. For the district court's decision, see *Planned Parenthood of Minnesota, South Dakota, North Dakota v. Rounds,* 375 F.Supp.2d 881 (D.S.D. 2005). For the Eighth Circuit's decision, see *Planned Parenthood of Minnesota, South Dakota, North Dakota v. Rounds,* 530 F.3d 724 (8th Cir. 2008). For the Eighth Circuit's subsequent rulings in *Rounds,* see *Planned Parenthood of Minnesota, South Dakota, North Dakota v. Rounds,* 653 F.3d 662 (8th Cir. 2011), reversed in part by *Planned Parenthood of Minnesota, South Dakota, North Dakota v. Rounds,* 686 F.3d 889 (8th Cir. 2012) (en banc).

9 Denise M. Burke, "*Gonzales v. Carhart* One Year Later: Letting the People Decide" (April 23, 2010), https://aul.org/2010/04/23/gonzales-v-carhart-one-year-later-letting-the-people-decide, accessed March 4, 2019.

10 Barbara Veida, "Abortion Wars Return," *National Journal* 39 (2008): 28–32. On AUL's legislative reports, see "State Legislatures Continue Efforts to Protect Women from

Negative Effects of Abortion, AUL Report Reveals," *PR Newswire*, September 29, 2008, 1. For Burke's statement: Stephanie Simon, "Abortions Fall 25 Percent since All Time High in 1990," *Washington Post*, January 17, 2008, A8. For Forsythe's statement on restoring deference: Clarke Forsythe, "A New Dawn: *Gonzales v. Carhart* Begins a New Day in Abortion Law," April 23, 2010, https://aul.org/2010/04/23/a-new-dawn-gonzales-v-carhart-begins-a-new-day-in-abortion-law, accessed August 17, 2019.

11 On the abortion-rights movement's priorities in the aftermath of the 2008 election, see James Oliphant, "Abortion Laws on Democrats' Back Burner," *Los Angeles Times*, February 10, 2009, A14.

12 On the priority, or lack thereof, given to the abortion issue, see Oliphant, "Abortion Issue," A14. On the supposed odds of passing health care reform, see Jonathan Weisman and Greg Hitt, "Senator Defects to Democrats," *Wall Street Journal*, April 29, 2009, A1; Carl Hulse and Adam Nagourney, "Specter Switches Parties," *New York Times*, April 29, 2009, A1.

13 For the text of the act, see 42 U.S.C. § 18001 et seq. For more analysis of the law, see Benjamin Sommers et al., "The Affordable Care Act Has Led to Significant Gains in Health Insurance Access for Young Adults," *Health Affairs* 32 (2013): 165–174; Howard K. Koh and Kathleen G. Sebelius, "Promoting Prevention through the Affordable Care Act," *New England Journal of Medicine* 363 (2010): 1296–1299; Michael T. French et al., "Key Provisions of the Patient Affordable Care Act (ACA): A Systematic Review and Presentation of Early Research Findings," *Health Services Research* 51 (2016): 1735–1771.

14 On Obama's presentation of the ACA as abortion neutral, see Peter Steinfels, "In Health Care Battle, a Truce on Abortion," *New York Times*, September 12, 2009, A12; Linda Feldmann, "Abortion Wars Intensify over Health Care Reform," *Christian Science Monitor*, August 22, 2009, 25. On pro-life opposition, see Ricardo Alonso-Zalvidar, "Health Bill Allows Abortion Coverage," *Chicago Tribune*, August 6, 2009, 19. On the Stupak-Pitts Amendment, see David D. Kirkpatrick, "Abortion Fight Adds to Debate on Health Care," *New York Times*, September 29, 2009, A1; Philip Rucker, "Stupak's Decision to Retire Comes in Wake of Bruising Health Care Fight," *Washington Post*, April 10, 2010, A1. On the executive order, see "President Obama Signs Executive Order on Abortion," *PBS News Hour*, March 24, 2010, www.pbs.org/newshour/rundown/president-obama-to-sign-executive-order-on-abortion, accessed September 28, 2017. For pro-life views on the executive order, see Susan B. Anthony List, "AUL: Why Bart Stupak Is Wrong," March 30, 2010, www.sba-list.org/suzy-b-blog/aul-why-bart-stupak-wrong, accessed September 28, 2017; Matthew Clark, "Obama's Promise of No Abortion Funding in Obamacare Is Just a 'Magic' Trick," American Center for Law and Justice, 2010, https://aclj.org/obamacare/obama-promise-no-abortion-funding-obamacare-just-magic-trick, accessed September 28, 2017. For abortion-rights supporters' response to the executive order, see "President Obama Signs."

15 On Planned Parenthood's report on all the services offered in 2011, see Planned Parenthood, *Annual Report, 2011–2012*, 5, www.plannedparenthood.org/files/4913/9620/1413/PPFA_AR_2012_121812_vF.pdf. On Planned Parenthood's share of the national abortion market, see Stephanie Simon, "Extending the Brand: Planned Parenthood Hits Suburbia," *Wall Street Journal*, June 23, 2008, 1; Sandhya Somashekhar, "A 'Small' Part of Planned Parenthood," *Washington Post*, April 19, 2001, A1.

16 On Lila Rose and Live Action, see Stephanie Simon, "Currents: Facing a Tough Washington Climate, Abortion Foes Move Debate Online," *Wall Street Journal*, April 1, 2009, A19; Robin Abcarian, "Abortion Foe Goes Undercover," *Los Angeles Times*, April 26, 2009, A1. On earlier attacks on Planned Parenthood, see Mary Ziegler, "Sexing *Harris*: The Law and Politics of Defunding Planned Parenthood," *Buffalo Law Review* 60 (2012): 713–722.

17 On the Gallup poll, see Robin Abcarian, "51 Percent in U.S. Say They Are 'Pro-life,'" *Los Angeles Times*, May 16, 2009, A20; Lydia Saad, "More Americans 'Pro-life' than 'Pro-choice' for First Time," *Gallup News*, May 15, 2009, http://news.gallup.com/poll/118399/more-americans-pro-life-than-pro-choice-first-time.aspx, accessed September 26, 2017. On Forty Days for Life, see Forty Days for Life, "History," https://40daysforlife.com/history, accessed September 13, 2018; Krissah Thompson, "Antiabortion Forces' Rising Young Stars," *Washington Post*, January 22, 2014, C1; Elisabeth Parker, "Faithfully Taking A Stand," *Tampa Bay Times*, October 25, 2013, 1.

18 On the Tea Party, see Theda Skocpol and Vanessa Williamson, *The Tea Party and the Remaking of Republican Conservatism* (New York: Oxford University Press, 2013), 3–19; Charles S. Bullock III, "Conclusion: Evaluating Palin, the Tea Party, and Demint Influences," in *Key States, High Stakes: Sarah Palin, the Tea Party, and the 2010 Elections* ed. Charles S. Bullock III (Lanham, MD: Rowman and Littlefield, 2012), 211–227; Kate Zernike, *Boiling Mad: Inside Tea Party America* (New York: Macmillan, 2010); Nella Van Dyke and Davis S. Mayer, "Introduction," in *Understanding the Tea Party Movement* eds. Nella Van Dyke and Davis S. Mayer (New York: Routledge, 2016), 1–12.

19 Skocpol and Williamson, *The Tea Party*, 3–19; Bullock, "Conclusion: Evaluating Palin," 211–227; Van Dyke and Mayer, "Introduction," 1–12.

20 Sarah Jean Seman, "Susan B. Anthony List," *Human Events* 68 (2012): 24. On the operating budget, see Monica Potts, "Mission Aborted," *The American Prospect*, March 2012, 20–25. For SBAL's increase in election spending, see "Susan B. Anthony List: Election Spending by Cycle," www.opensecrets.org/pacs/lookup2.php?strID=C00332296, accessed August 17, 2019. On Votes Have Consequences: Potts, "Mission Aborted," 20–25.

21 On the Tea Party wave in 2010, see Charles S. Bullock, "Introduction: The 2010 Elections," in *Key States, High Stakes: Sarah Palin, the Tea Party, and the 2010 Elections* ed. Charles S. Bullock (Lanham, MD: Rowman and Littlefield, 2012), 1–10; Tim Storey, "GOP Makes Historic State Legislative Gains," *Rasmussen Reports*, December 10, 2010, www.rasmussenreports.com/public_content/political_commentary/commentary_by_tim_storey/gop_makes_historic_state_legislative_gains_in_2010, accessed September 14, 2018.

22 On the dramatic increase in abortion regulations, see "State Legislative Trends in 2010–Abortion Restrictions Once Again Dominate," Guttmacher Institute, January 2011, www.guttmacher.org/article/2011/01/state-legislative-trends-2010-abortion-restrictions-once-again-dominate, accessed July 31, 2018; "States Enact Record Number of Abortion Restrictions in 2011," Guttmacher Institute, January 5, 2012, www.guttmacher.org/article/2012/01/states-enact-record-number-abortion-restrictions-2011, accessed July 31, 2018.

23 On the abortion laws passed in the period, see John Leland, "Abortion Foes Advance Cause at State Level," *New York Times*, June 2, 2010, A10; Americans United for Life, "Defending Life 2010: Model Legislation" (2010), 163–287; "National Right to Life Committee Sets Legislative Strategy Conference to Capitalize on State Election Victories"

(November 9, 2010), www.nrlc.org/communications/releases/2010/release110910; National Right to Life Committee, Press Release, "Pain Capable Unborn Children Protected in Nebraska" (October 15, 2010), www.nrlc.org/communications/releases/2010/release101510, accessed September 27, 2017.

24 On Gosnell's crimes, see Larry Miller, "Gosnell Case Fuels Debate," *Philadelphia Tribune*, February 13, 2011, 1A; Eric Mayes, "Abortion Victim's Family Shaken by Clinic Tragedy," *Philadelphia Tribune*, January 25, 2011, 1A; Dinah Wisenberg Brin, "Abortion Doctor Accused of Murder," *Wall Street Journal*, January 20, 2011, A5.

25 For the 2010 edition of *Defending Life*, see Americans United for Life, *Defending Life 2010: Proven Strategies for a Pro-life America* (Washington, DC: Americans United for Life, 2010), www.aul.org/downloads/defending-life-2010.pdf, accessed July 31, 2018.

26 On the CMP and its influence, see Erik Eckholm, "Planned Parenthood Sues Abortion Foes," *New York Times*, January 15, 2016, A22; Christine Mai-Duc, "Backstory: An Anti-abortion Firestorm," *Los Angeles Times*, August 8, 2015, A2; Maria La Ganga, "Videos on Planned Parenthood Rouse Ire," *Los Angeles Times*, August 22, 2015, 1; Stephanie Armour, "Dueling Assessments of Planned Parenthood Videos," *Wall Street Journal*, August 28, 2015, A4. On Dear's attack on Planned Parenthood, see David Kelly, "The Nation: Clinic Reopens after Deadly Attack," *Los Angeles Times*, February 16, 2016, A6; "Motive of Attack under Scrutiny," *Los Angeles Times*, November 29, 2015, A6. For AUL's statement about defunding Planned Parenthood: "AUL Renews Call for Congressional Investigations into Planned Parenthood Finances and Tax Payer Abortion Funding," July 12, 2011, https://aul.org/2011/07/12/aul-renews-call-for-congressional-investigation-into-planned-parent hood-finances-and-taxpayer-abortion-funding, accessed December 10, 2018. For the text of the report, see Americans United for Life, *Special Report: The Case for Investigating Planned Parenthood* (Washington, DC: Americans United for Life, 2011).

27 For the *Journal of the American Medical Association* article, see Susan J. Lee et al., "Fetal Pain: A Systematic Multidisciplinary Review of the Evidence," *Journal of the American Medical Association* 294 (2005): 947–954. For the American College of Obstetricians and Gynecologists' position, see American College of Obstetricians and Gynecologists, "Facts Are Important–Fetal Pain" (July 2013), www.acog.org/-/media/Departments/Govern ment-Relations-and-Outreach/FactAreImportFetalPain.pdf, accessed September 26, 2017. On the view that fetal pain is possible earlier in pregnancy, see Doctors on Fetal Pain, "Fetal Pain: The Evidence," www.doctorsonfetalpain.com, accessed September 26, 2017. For more on the debate, Erik Eckholm, "Theory on Fetal Pain Is Driving Rules for Abortions," August 1, 2013, www.nytimes.com/2013/08/02/us/theory-on-pain-is-driving-rules-for-abortions.html, accessed August 18, 2019; Pam Belluck, "Complex Science at Issue in Politics of Fetal Pain," *New York Times*, September 17, 2013, A1.

28 On the strategic advantages of a fetal pain law, see Mary Spaulding Balch, JD, Director State Development Department to Whom It May Concern, Re: Constitutionality of the Model Pain-Capable Unborn Child Protection Act, July 2013, www.nrlc.org/uploads/state leg/PCUCPAConstitutionality.pdf, accessed September 26, 2017.

29 On Nebraska's law, see Monica Davey, "Nebraska, Citing Pain, Sets Limits on Abortion," *New York Times*, April 14, 2016, A16. On efforts to pass the Pain-Capable Unborn Child Protection Act in Congress, see Alexandra Desanctis, "Senate Fails to Pass 20-Week Abortion Ban," *National Review*, January 29, 2018, www.nationalreview.com/corner/abor

tion-ban-senate-vote-fails-pass-pain-capable-unborn-child-protection-act, accessed July 31, 2018; Sophie Tatum, "House Passes Ban on Abortion after 20 Weeks of Pregnancy," *CNN*, October 3, 2017, www.cnn.com/2017/10/03/politics/house-vote-abortion-after-20-week-ban/index.html, accessed July 31, 2018. On the number of twenty-week bans in 2018, see "State Policies on Later Abortion," Guttmacher Institute, August 1, 2019, www.guttmacher.org/state-policy/explore/state-policies-later-abortions, accessed August 18, 2019.

30 See Americans United for Life, *Defending Life 2019: From Conception to Natural Death* (Washington, Americans United for Life, 2019), 354–374. On the antiabortion regulations introduced in the period, see Audrey White and Becca Aaronson, "Anti-abortion Groups Push a New Round of Rules," *New York Times*, November 23, 2012, A25; Eric Zorn, "Old Scare Tactic a New Weapon in the Abortion Wars," *Chicago Tribune*, March 23, 2012, 1; Emily Bazelon, "Lifer: Charmaine Yoest's Cheerful War on Abortion," *New York Times Magazine*, November 4, 2012, SM22.

31 See Katrina Eva Matsa et al., Pew Research Center for Journalism and Media, "Political Polarization and Media Habits" (October 21, 2014), www.journalism.org/2014/10/21/polit ical-polarization-media-habits, accessed August 18, 2019. On the influence of *Breitbart* and new conservative outlets, see Nicole Hemmer, *Messengers of the Right: Conservative Media and the Transformation of American Politics* (Philadelphia: University of Pennsylvania Press, 2016).

32 On the spike in abortion restrictions in 2011, see "States Enact Record Number."

33 On NARAL's fundraising woes, see Sarah Kliff, "Abortion Groups Caught Off Guard," *Politico*, July 30, 2010, www.politico.com/story/2010/07/abortion-groups-caught-off-guard-040413?o=1, accessed August 18, 2019. On the intensity gap and NARAL's response to it, see Sarah Kliff, "Why Young Voters Are Lukewarm on Abortion-Rights," *Newsweek*, April 15, 2010, www.newsweek.com/why-young-voters-are-lukewarm-abortion-rights-70311, accessed August 18, 2019.

34 On the expansion of Planned Parenthood, see Sarah Kliff, "Fight Stokes Planned Parenthood," *Politico*, April 12, 2011, www.politico.com/story/2011/04/fight-stokes-planned-parent hood-052962, accessed August 18, 2019; see also N. C. Aizenman, "Health Care Fuels Abortion Wars," *Washington Post*, March 12, 2011, A3. For Akin's comment, see Robert Mackey, "The Lede: Myth about Rape and Pregnancy Is Not New," *New York Times*, August 20, 2015, https://thelede.blogs.nytimes.com/2012/08/20/myth-about-rape-and-preg nancy-is-not-new, accessed August 18, 2019. For Mourdock's statements, see Annie Groer, "Indiana Senate Hopeful Richard Mourdock Says God 'Intended' Rape Pregnancies," *Washington Post*, October 24, 2012, www.washingtonpost.com/blogs/she-the-people/wp/2012/10/24/indiana-gop-senate-hopeful-richard-mourdock-says-god-intended-rape-pregnancies, accessed August 18, 2019.

35 On the importance of abortion as a 2012 election issue, see Sarah Kliff, "Abortion Gains as Political Issue," *Washington Post*, August 28, 2012, www.washingtonpost.com/politics/abortion-gains-as-political-issue/2012/08/28/7e4dc6fc-edf9-11e1-afd8-097e90f99d05_story.html, accessed August 18, 2012; Timothy Carney, "Democrats Use Abortion to Rally Base, Raise Money," *Washington Examiner*, September 6, 2012, 10. On EMILY's List's founding and influence, see Ellen R. Malcolm and Craig Unger, *When Women Win: EMILY's List and the Rise of Women in Politics* (New York: Harcourt Press, 2016). For examples of the "war on women" arguments, see Beth Baker, "Fighting the War on Women," *Ms. Magazine*,

Spring 2012, 27–31; "The GOP War on Women Continues," *Baltimore Sun*, August 2, 2012, A16; Susan Ferrechio, "Mourdock's Rape Comment Restarts 'War on Women,'" *Washington Examiner*, October 25, 2012, 22. On the fundraising for abortion-rights groups during the 2010 election, see Sarah Kliff, "For Planned Parenthood, Backlash Pays Off," *Washington Post*, February 5, 2012, B1.

36 On the contraceptive mandate and the controversy surrounding it, see Sarah Kliff, "Lawmakers Debate Contraceptive Mandate," *Washington Post*, February 17, 2012, A3; "Health, Faith, and Birth Control," *Los Angeles Times*, August 1, 2012, A16; Kim Geiger and Noam Levey, "The Nation: New Take on Birth Control," *Los Angeles Times*, February 16, 2012, A7.

37 Dave Andrusko, "Bishops Urge House and Senate to Act to Address Religious Liberty Crisis Brought on by Obama Mandate," *National Right to Life News*, September 16, 2012, www.nationalrighttolifenews.org/news/2012/09/bishops-urge-house-and-senate-to-act-to-address-religious-liberty-crisis-brought-on-by-obama-mandate/#.Wcq7OciGM2w, accessed September 26, 2017; see also "U.S. Senate Illinois: Compare, Decide, Vote" (2019), www.nrlc.org/uploads/Senate/IL%20Sen%20Oberweis%20Durbin.pdf, accessed August 18, 2019. On the Manhattan Declaration, see "Manhattan Declaration: A Christian Call to Conscience" (November 20, 2009), www.manhattandeclaration.org, accessed September 20, 2017. For AUL's statement: Americans United for Life, AUL's Freedom of Conscience Project (2009), https://aul.org/2013/03/08/freedom-of-conscience-project, accessed September 26, 2017. On AUL's earlier defense of pharmacists, see Stephanie Simon, "Pharmacists New Players in Abortion Debate," *Los Angeles Times*, March 20, 2004, A18.

38 On the effort of the early antiabortion movement to distance itself from the Catholic Church, see Daniel K. Williams, *Defenders of the Unborn: The Pro-life Movement before Roe v. Wade* (New York: Oxford University Press, 2018), 218–248; Patricia Miller, *Good Catholics: The Battle over Abortion in the Catholic Church* (Berkeley: University of California Press, 2014), 179–183. For an example of advocacy against the contraceptive mandate and what members viewed as abortifacients, see Press Release, "AUL's Legal Team Files 29th Brief Defending Conscience Rights of Americans Opposed to Life-Ending Drugs" (January 11, 2016), https://aul.org/2016/01/11/auls-legal-team-files-29th-brief-defending-conscience-rights-of-americans-opposed-to-life-ending-drugs, accessed November 5, 2018. On the earlier efforts of the pro-life movement to avoid the contraception issue, see James Davison Hunter and Joseph Davis, "Cultural Politics at the Edge of Life," in *The Politics of Abortion and Birth Control in Historical Perspective* ed. Donald T. Critchlow (University Park: Pennsylvania State University Press, 1996), 186–200; Mary Ziegler, *After Roe: The Lost History of the Abortion Debate* (Cambridge, MA: Harvard University Press, 2015), 33–38; Neil J. Young, *We Gather Together: The Religious Right and the Problem of Interfaith Politics* (New York: Oxford University, 2016), 107–110.

39 NARAL Pro-choice America, "Birth Control" (nd, ca. 2010), www.prochoiceamerica.org/issue/birth-control, accessed October 12, 2017. For the Coalition's statement: Erik Eckholm, "Both Sides Eager to Take Birth Control Coverage Issue to Voters," *New York Times*, February 16, 2012, A18.

40 On the early litigation in *Hobby Lobby*, see *Hobby Lobby Stores, Inc. v. Sebelius*, 870 F. Supp. 2d 1278 (W.D. Okla. 2012); *Conestoga Wood Specialties Corporation v. Sebelius*,

917 F.Supp.2d 394 (E.D. Pa. 2012); *Hobby Lobby Stores v. Sebelius*, 723 F.3d 1114 (10th Cir. 2013); *Conestoga Wood Specialties Corporation v. Secretary*, 724 F.3d 377 (3d Cir. 2013). For the text of RFRA: see 42 U.S.C. § 2000 et seq. On the growth of Alliance Defending Freedom, see Amanda Hollis-Brusky and Joshua C. Wilson, "Playing for the Rules: How and Why New Christian Right Public Interest Law Firms Invest in Secular Litigation," *Law and Policy* 39 (2017): 125–126. On ADF's involvement in the challenge to the contraceptive mandate, see Alliance Defending Freedom, "*Conestoga Wood Specialties Corporation v. Burwell*," www.adfmedia.org/News/PRDetail/8451, accessed July 31, 2018.

41 For the Court's decision in *Hobby Lobby*, see *Burwell v. Hobby Lobby Stores, Inc.*, 573 U.S. 682, 691–719 (2014).

42 For a sample of the early litigation in *Zubik* and related cases, see *Geneva College v. Sebelius*, 960 F. Supp. 2d 588 (W.D. Pa. 2013); *Zubik v. Sebelius*, 983 F. Supp. 2d 576 (W.D. Pa. 2013); *Priests for Life v. U.S. Department of Health and Human Services*, 7 F. Supp. 3d 88 (D.D.C. 2013); *Little Sisters for the Poor and Aged, Denver, Colorado v. Burwell*, 794 F.3d 1194 (10th Cir. 2015). For the Court's decision in *Zubik*, see *Zubik v. Burwell*, 136 S. Ct. 1557 (2016). On the use of religious-liberty arguments, see Andrew R. Lewis, *The Rights Turn in Conservative Christian Politics: How Abortion Transformed the Culture Wars* (New York: Cambridge University Press, 2017), 86–119, 145–162; Reva B. Siegel and Douglas NeJaime, "Conscience Wars: Complicity-Based Conscience Claims in Religion and Politics," *Yale Law Journal* 124 (2015): 2540–2545; Laurie Goodstein, "Christian Leaders Unite on Political Issues," *New York Times*, November 20, 2009, www.nytimes.com/2009/11/20/us/politics/20alliance.html?mcubz=3, accessed September 27, 2017.

43 For the Court's decision in *Obergefell*, see *Obergefell v. Hodges*, 135 S. Ct. 2584 (2015). For the decision in *Windsor*, see *United States v. Windsor*, 570 U.S. 744 (2015). For the court's decision in *Goodridge*, see *Goodridge v. Department of Public Health*, 798 N.E.2d 941 (Mass. 2003). On the history of the same-sex marriage struggle, see Michael J. Klarman, *From the Closet to the Altar: Courts, Backlash, and the Struggle for Same-Sex Marriage* (New York: Oxford University Press, 2013); Lillian Faderman, *The Gay Revolution: The Story of the Struggle* (New York: Simon and Schuster, 2015).

44 On Kim Davis' protest, see Sarah Kaplan and James Higdon, "The Defiant Kim Davis, the Kentucky Clerk Who Refuses to Issue Gay Marriage Licenses," *Washington Post*, September 2, 2015, ww.washingtonpost.com/news/morning-mix/wp/2015/09/02/meet-kim-davis-the-ky-clerk-who-defying-the-supreme-court-refuses-to-issue-gay-marriage-licenses, accessed May 3, 2019; Alan Blinder and Richard Pérez-Peña, "Kentucky Clerk Denies Same-Sex Marriage Licenses, Defying Court," *New York Times*, September 1, 2015, www.nytimes.com/2015/09/02/us/same-sex-marriage-kentucky-kim-davis.html, accessed May 3, 2019. For a sample of the court cases on conscience from the period, see *State v. Arlene's Flowers*, 389 P.3d 543 (Wash. 2017); *Craig v. Masterpiece Cakeshop*, 370 P.2d 272 (Colo. 2015); *Elane Photography, LLC v. Willock*, 309 P.3d 53 (N.M. 2013). For Burk's statement, see Joan Desmond, "With Weak Protections for Conscience, 'Obergefell Is Roe on Steroids,'" *National Catholic Register*, June 30, 2015, www.ncregister.com/blog/joan-desmond/with-weak-conscience-protectionsobergefell-is-roe-on-steroids, accessed May 28, 2019.

45 Press Release, "Center for Reproductive Rights, National Women's Law Center, File Freedom of Information Act Request to Investigate HHS Division Devoted to Promoting Health Care Discrimination," January 26, 2018, www.reproductiverights.org/press-room/center-for-reproductive-rights-national-women%E2%80%99s-law-center-file-freedom-of-information-ac, accessed May 3, 2019. For AUL's conscience work, see Press Release, "AUL's Legal Team Files 29th Brief Defending Conscience Rights of Americans Opposed to Life-Ending Drugs," January 11, 2016, https://aul.org/2016/01/11/auls-legal-team-files-29th-brief-defending-conscience-rights-of-americans-opposed-to-life-ending-drugs, accessed May 3, 2019; NeJaime and Siegel, "Conscience Wars," 2202–2679. For NRLC's support of conscience legislation, see "NRLC Letter to Congress on Conscience Protection Act," July 11, 2016, www.nrlc.org/tag/conscience-protection-act, accessed May 3, 2019; "National Right to Life Committee Commends Draft Rules Protecting Rights of Conscience," June 1, 2017, www.nrlc.org/communications/releases/2017/release060117, accessed May 3, 2019. For more on AUL's work on religious liberty, see Peter Samuelson to Richard John Neuhaus (November 8, 2005), RJN, Box 2, Folder 34; "Protecting the Sanctity of Public Life: The Four-Year Strategic Plan of Americans United for Life, 2000–2004" (2000), RJN, Box 2, Folder 34.

46 On the use of reproductive justice arguments by NARAL, Planned Parenthood, and NOW, see Jackie Calmes, "Activists Shun 'Pro-choice' to Expand Message," *New York Times,* July 28, 2014, www.nytimes.com/2014/07/29/us/politics/advocates-shun-pro-choice-to-expand-message.html?_r=1, accessed October 11, 2017 (discussing how the term pro-choice "does not reflect the range of women's health and economic issues now being debated"); Dawn Laguens, "We're Fighting for Access, Not Choice," *Huffington Post,* July 30, 2014, www.huffingtonpost.com/dawn-laguens/were-fighting-for-access_b_5635999.html, accessed October 11, 2017 (noting Planned Parenthood's doubts about the capacity of the "pro-choice" label to fully represent the views of many women); National Organization for Women, "Reproductive Rights and Justice," http://now.org/issues/abortion-rights-reproductive-issues, accessed September 28, 2017.

47 In Our Own Voice: National Black Women's Reproductive Justice Agenda, "About Us," http://blackrj.org/about-us, accessed April 30, 2019. For NOW's statement: National Organization for Women, "Reproductive Justice Is Every Woman's Right" (2019), https://now.org/resource/reproductive-justice-is-every-womans-right, accessed April 30, 2019.

48 On Shout Your Abortion, see Tamar Lewin, "#ShoutYourAbortion Gets Angry Shouts Back," *New York Times,* October 2, 2015, A1; Erik Eckholm, "Silence Order on Abortions Violates Law, Doctor Says," *New York Times,* May 3, 2016, A10; see also "Shout Your Abortion: Abortion Is Normal" (2017), https://shoutyourabortion.com, accessed September 27, 2017. On the Abortion Conversation Project, see Herbert W. Simons, Joan Morreale, and Bruce Gronbeck, *Persuasion in Society* (New York: Taylor and Francis, 2001), 467.

49 On SYA's framing of the issue, see Shout Your Abortion, "Abortion Is Normal" (2019), https://shoutyourabortion.com, accessed March 20, 2019. For more on the response to SYA, see Katie Klabusich, "Why Now More Than Ever, We Need 'Shout Your Abortion,'" https://rewire.news/article/2018/11/30/why-now-more-than-ever-we-need-shout-your-abortion, accessed March 20, 2019. On the backlash to SYA, see Lewin, "#ShoutYour-Abortion Gets Angry Shouts Back."

50 On the abortion restrictions introduced in the period, see "More State Abortion Restrictions Were Enacted in 2011–2013 Than in the Entire Previous Decade," *Guttmacher News In Depth*, January 2014, www.guttmacher.org/article/2014/01/more-state-abortion-restrictions-were-enacted-2011-2013-entire-previous-decade, accessed September 27, 2017; "In Just the Last Four Years, States Have Enacted 231 Restrictions," *Guttmacher News in Depth*, January 2015, www.guttmacher.org/article/2015/01/just-last-four-years-states-have-enacted-231-abortion-restrictions, accessed September 27, 2017; Erik Eckholm, "Abortion-Rights Advocates Preparing for a New Surge of Federal and State Attacks," *New York Times*, November 6, 2014, A16. On the declining abortion rate, see Press Release, Guttmacher Institute, "U.S. Abortion Rate Continues to Decline, Hits Historic Low" (January 17, 2017), www.guttmacher.org/news-release/2017/us-abortion-rate-continues-decline-hits-historic-low, accessed September 27, 2017.

51 For Yoest's statement: *Defending Life 2012: Building a Culture of Life, Exposing and Confronting the Abortion Industry* (Washington, DC: Americans United for Life, 2012), 3.

52 For the model law, see Americans United for Life, "Women's Health Protection Act," in *Legislative and Policy Guide for the 2013 Legislative Year* (Washington, DC: Americans United for Life, 2013), 1–6.

53 On the proposals considered by Texas in 2013, see Matthew Waller, "Texas Legislature: Abortion Continues to Divide 40 Years after Legal Ruling," *San Angelo Standard Times*, January 22, 2013. For the district court's decision enjoining the admitting-privilege requirement, see *Planned Parenthood of Greater Texas Surgical Health Services v. Abbott*, 951 F.Supp. 2d 891 (W.D. Tex. 2013). For the Fifth Circuit's decision reversing the injunction, see *Planned Parenthood of Greater Texas Surgical Health Services v. Abbott*, 734 F.3d 406 (5th Cir. 2013).

54 See Joint Appendix, 183–183, 228–231, 363–370, *Whole Woman's Health v. Hellerstedt*, 136 S. Ct. 2292 (2016).

55 For the 5th Circuit's decision on the merits, see *Planned Parenthood of Greater Texas Surgical Services v. Abbott*, 748 F.3d 583, 593–601 (5th Cir. 2014).

56 For the trial court's analysis of the record evidence, see *Whole Women's Health v. Lakey*, 46 F. Supp. 3d 673, 680–684 (W.D. Tex. 2014).

57 See *Lakey*, 46 F. Supp. at 680–684.

58 See *Cole*, 790 F.3d at 582–583.

59 Amici Curiae Brief of Forty-Four State Legislators in Support of Defendants-Appellants, 15, *Whole Women's Health v. Cole*, 2014 WL 6647162 (C.A.5) (2016) (No. 14–50928) (emphasis in the original).

60 Brief Amicus Curiae of the National Right to Life Committee, 18, *Whole Women's Health v. Cole*, 2014 WL 6647162 (C.A.5) (2016) (No. 14–50928).

61 Brief for Petitioners, 2, *Whole Women's Health v. Cole*, 2014 WL 6647162 (C.A.5) (2016) (No. 14–50928) (citation and quotation omitted). For the ACLU's brief, see Brief Amicus Curiae of the American Civil Liberties Union et al., 4–28, *Whole Women's Health v. Cole*, 2014 WL 6647162 (C.A.5) (2016) (No. 14–50928).

62 On the Texas Policy Evaluation Project and its impact on the Court, see Nina Martin, "How One Abortion Megadonor Forced the Supreme Court's Hand," *Mother Jones*, July 14, 2016, www.motherjones.com/politics/2016/07/abortion-research-buffett, accessed September 27, 2017; Texas Policy Evaluation Project, "Change in Number of Physicians

Providing Abortion Care after HB2," *Texas Policy Evaluation Project Research Brief*, February 29, 2016, https://liberalarts.utexas.edu/txpep/_files/pdf/TxPEP-ResearchBrief-AdmittingPrivileges.pdf, accessed August 18, 2019.

63 On the founding and early work of the Charlotte Lozier Institute and its impact, see Marjorie Dannenfelser, "Chen Case Highlights Coercive and Sex-Selection Abortion," *Washington Examiner*, May 25, 2012, 37; Michelle Andrews, "Health Plans Don't Always Say Whether Abortion Is Covered," *Washington Post*, April 15, 2014, E6; Paige Winfield Cunningham, "New Scholars Join Anti-abortion Research Group," *Washington Examiner*, September 16, 2015, A16. For arguments about deference to Congress, see Brief Amicus Curiae of the National Right to Life Committee, 14–24; Amici Curiae Brief of Forty-Four State Legislators, 12–17.

64 *Whole Woman's Health v. Hellerstedt*, 136 S. Ct. 2292, 2309–2310 (2016). On Scalia's death, see Eva Ruth Moravec, Sari Horvitz, and Jerry Markon, "The Death of Antonin Scalia: Chaos, Confusion and Conflicting Reports," *Washington Post*, February 14, 2016, www.washingtonpost.com/politics/texas-tv-station-scalia-died-of-a-heart-attack/2016/02/14/938e2170-d332-11e5-9823-02b905009f99_story.html, accessed April 30, 2019; Nick Corasaniti, "Scalia's Death Jolts 2016 Presidential Race," *New York Times*, February 13, 2016, www.nytimes.com/live/supreme-court-justice-antonin-scalia-dies-at-79/scalias-death-jolts-presidential-race, accessed April 30, 2019. On the Garland nomination and Congress's response, see Ron Elving, "What Happened with Merrick Garland and Why It Matters Now," *NPR*, June 29, 2018, www.npr.org/2018/06/29/624467256/what-happened-with-merrick-garland-in-2016-and-why-it-matters-now, accessed April 30, 2019.

65 See *Whole Woman's Health*, 2311–2314.

66 Ibid., 2311–2314.

67 See ibid., 2314–2318.

68 On Trump's inflammatory comments, see Janell Roberts, "From Mexican Rapists to Bad Hombres, the Trump Campaign in Two Moments," *Washington Post*, October 20, 2016, www.washingtonpost.com/news/the-fix/wp/2016/10/20/from-mexican-rapists-to-bad-hombres-the-trump-campaign-in-two-moments, accessed September 27, 2017; "Trump's *Access Hollywood* Unmasking and the Searing Power of Video to Shape the Historic Moment," *Los Angeles Times*, October 10, 2016, www.latimes.com/entertainment/movies/la-et-st-trump-video-uproar-20161011-snap-story.html, accessed September 27, 2017; David Farenthold, "Trump Recorded Having Extremely Lewd Conversation about Women in 2005," *Washington Post*, October 8, 2016, www.washingtonpost.com/politics/trump-recorded-having-extremely-lewd-conversation-about-women-in-2005/2016/10/07/3b9ce776-8cb4-11e6-bf8a-3d26847eeed4_story.html, accessed September 27, 2016; John Wagner and Jenna Johnson, "Clinton, Trump Exchange Racially Charged Allegations," *Washington Post*, August 25, 2016, www.washingtonpost.com/politics/ahead-of-speech-targeting-trump-clinton-accuses-him-of-peddling-hate/2016/08/25/fc3f1ade-6a78-11e6-8225-fbb8a6fc65bc_story.html, accessed September 27, 2017. For discussion of Clinton's email servers and subsequent investigation, see Anthony Zurcher, "Hillary Clinton Emails–What Is It All About?" *BBC News*, November 6, 2016, www.bbc.com/news/world-us-canada-31806907, accessed July 25, 2018.

69 For analysis of the 2016 election, see Nate Silver, "The Real Story of 2016," FiveThirtyEight, January 19, 2017, http://fivethirtyeight.com/features/the-real-story-of-2016, accessed

September 27, 2017; "How Donald Trump Won the Election," *The Economist*, November 9, 2016, 21; Alec Tyson and Shiva Maniam, "Behind Trump's Victory: Divisions of Race, Gender, and Education," Pew Research Center, November 9, 2016, www.pewresearch.org/fact-tank/2016/11/09/behind-trumps-victory-divisions-by-race-gender-education, accessed September 27, 2017. On Trump's support among Catholics and evangelicals, see Olga Khazan, "Why Christians Overwhelmingly Backed Trump," *Atlantic*, November 9, 2016, www.theatlantic.com/health/archive/2016/11/why-women-and-christians-backed-trump/507176, accessed May 31, 2018.

70 On Trump's closeness to anti-vaccine activists, see Laura Entis, "Donald Trump Has Long Linked Autism to Vaccines. He Isn't Stopping Now That He's President," *Fortune*, February 16, 2017, http://fortune.com/2017/02/16/donald-trump-autism-vaccines, accessed October 11, 2017; Lena H. Sun, "Trump Energizes the Anti-Vaccine Movement in Texas," *Washington Post*, February 20, 2017, www.washingtonpost.com/national/health-science/trump-energizes-the-anti-vaccine-movement-in-texas/2017/02/20/795bd3ae-ef08-11e6-b4ff-ac2cf509efe5_story.html, accessed October 11, 2017. On the birther debate and Trump's role in it, see Michael Barbaro, "Donald Trump Clung to 'Birther' Lie for Years and Still Isn't Sorry about It," *New York Times*, September 16, 2016, www.nytimes.com/2016/09/17/us/politics/donald-trump-obama-birther.html; Lily Rothman, "This Is How the Whole Birther Thing Actually Started," *Time*, September 16, 2016, http://time.com/4496792/birther-rumor-started; Heidi Beirich and Evelyn Schlatter, "Backlash: Racism and the Presidency of Barack Obama," in *Barack Obama and the Myth of a Post-Racial America* eds. Mark Ledwidge, Kevern Verney, and Inderjeet Parmar (New York: Routledge, 2014), 88–90.

71 On the study completed by Benkler and his colleagues, see Yochai Benkler et al., "Study: Breitbart-Led Conservative Media Ecosystem Altered Broader Media Agenda," *Columbia Journalism Review*, March 3, 2017, www.cjr.org/analysis/breitbart-media-trump-harvard-study.php, accessed March 27, 2017. For more on debate about what constituted "fake news," see Brooke Singman, "'Collusion?' Trump Slams Facebook, 'Fake News' Media for Conspiring against Him," *Fox News*, September 27, 2017, www.foxnews.com/politics/2017/09/27/collusion-trump-slams-facebook-fake-news-media-for-conspiring-against-him.html, accessed September 27, 2017; Greg Krieg, "Donald Trump's Universe of Alternative Facts," *CNN*, February 8, 2017, www.cnn.com/2017/02/08/politics/donald-trump-alternate-universe/index.html, accessed September 20, 2017; Nicholas Fandos, "White House Pushes 'Alternative Facts'; Here Are the Real Ones," *New York Times*, January 22, 2017, www.nytimes.com/2017/01/22/us/politics/president-trump-inauguration-crowd-white-house.html.

72 For Gorsuch's statement: Neil M. Gorsuch, *The Future of Assisted Suicide and Euthanasia* (Princeton, NJ: Princeton University Press, 2006), 157. On the Gorsuch nomination, see Jeanne Mancini, "Neil Gorsuch Will Strengthen the Fight against Abortion Rights," *Time*, March 20, 2017, http://time.com/4705897/neil-gorsuch-anti-abortion, accessed May 31, 2018; "Beyond *Roe v. Wade*: Here's What Gorsuch Means for Abortion," *Bloomberg News*, March 20, 2017, www.bloomberg.com/news/features/2017-03-20/beyond-roe-v-wade-here-s-what-gorsuch-means-for-abortion, accessed May 31, 2018. On the role of the Federalist Society, see Joel Achenbach, "A Look at the List Helping Trump Reshape the

Supreme Court," *Chicago Tribune*, July 8, 2018, www.chicagotribune.com/news/nation
world/politics/ct-trump-supreme-court-list-20180708-story.html, accessed April 30, 2019.

73 For Trump's Title X regulations, see 42 CFR 59. On the impact of the revised regulations,
see Laurie Sobel, Alina Salganicoff, and Brittni Frederiksen, "New Title X Regulations:
Implications for Women and Family Planning Providers," Henry J. Kaiser Family Foundation, March 8, 2019, www.kff.org/womens-health-policy/issue-brief/new-title-x-regulations-
implications-for-women-and-family-planning-providers, accessed May 1, 2019; "Why Abortion Opponents Support Trump's Title X Rule Change" *PBS Newshour*, February 25, 2019,
www.pbs.org/newshour/show/why-abortion-opponents-support-trumps-title-x-rule-change,
accessed May 1, 2019. On the Obria grant, see Kenneth Vogel and Robert Pear, "Trump
Administration Gives Family Planning Grant to Anti-abortion Group," *New York Times*,
March 29, 2019, www.nytimes.com/2019/03/29/us/politics/trump-grant-abortion.html, accessed
May 1, 2019. For the Court's decision in *NIFLA*, see *National Institute of Family and Life
Advocates v. Becerra*, 138 S. Ct. 2361 (2018).

74 *NIFLA*, 138 S. Ct. at 2369–2379.

75 For coverage of Kavanaugh's confirmation, see Jeffrey Toobin, "Should Democrats
Bother Fighting Brett Kavanaugh's Confirmation? History Says Yes," *The New Yorker*,
July 31, 2018, www.newyorker.com/news/daily-comment/should-democrats-bother-fight
ing-brett-kavanaughs-confirmation-history-suggests-yes, accessed July 31, 2018; Karlyn
Bowman, "Brett Kavanaugh and Public Opinion on Supreme Court Nominations,"
Forbes, July 25, 2018, www.forbes.com/sites/bowmanmarsico/2018/07/25/brett-kavanaugh-
and-public-opinion-on-supreme-court-confirmations/#70e5a4786001, accessed May 28,
2019. For a brief overview of the #MeTooMovement, see Jessica Bennett, "The #MeToo
Moment: What's Next?" *New York Times*, January 5, 2018, www.nytimes.com/2018/01/05/
us/the-metoo-moment-whats-next.html, accessed April 19, 2019; The #MeToo Movement,
"About," https://metoomvmt.org/about, accessed April 19, 2019. For Trump's statement on
the reversal of *Roe*: Dan Mangan, "Trump: I'll Appoint Supreme Court Justices to
Overturn *Roe v. Wade* Abortion Case," *CNBC*, October 19, 2016, www.cnbc.com/2016/
10/19/trump-ill-appoint-supreme-court-justices-to-overturn-roe-v-wade-abortion-case.html,
accessed April 30, 2019.

76 Dan Becker, "National Personhood Alliance" (July 16, 2014), www.grtl.org/?q=national-person
hood-alliance, accessed July 31, 2018; see also "Who Is Personhood Alliance?" www.
personhood.org/index.php/press/who-is-national-personhood-alliance, accessed July 31, 2018.
On the failure of personhood efforts in 2014, see Rachana Pradhan and Jennifer Haberkorn,
"Personhood Movement Loses Twice," *Politico*, November 5, 2014, www.politico.com/story/
2014/11/personhood-movement-north-dakota-colorado-112552, accessed July 31, 2018.

77 On the Iowa heartbeat law, see Sasha Ingber, "Iowa Bans Most Abortions as Governor
Signs 'Heartbeat' Bill," *NPR*, May 5, 2018, www.npr.org/sections/thetwo-way/2018/05/05/
608738116/iowa-bans-most-abortions-as-governor-signs-heartbeat-bill, accessed July 31,
2018; Kristine Phillips, "Iowa Governor Signs 'Heartbeat Bill' Banning Abortion after Six
Weeks," *Washington Post*, May 2, 2018, www.washingtonpost.com/news/to-your-health/
wp/2018/05/02/iowa-lawmakers-just-passed-one-of-the-most-restrictive-abortion-bills-in-the-
u-s, accessed July 31, 2018. On the status of other heartbeat bills, see "Heartbeat Bans,"
Rewire Legislative Tracker, May 8, 2018, https://rewire.news/legislative-tracker/law-topic/

heartbeat-bans, accessed July 31, 2018. On Mississippi's fifteen-week ban, see "Mississippi Bans Abortions after Fifteen Weeks; Opponents Swiftly Sue," *New York Times*, March 19, 2018, www.nytimes.com/2018/03/19/us/mississippi-abortion-ban.html, accessed July 31, 2018.

78 Faith2Action, "The Pro-life Heartbeat Bill" (nd, ca. 2019), https://secure6.afo.net/f2a/includes/QnA_support.pdf, accessed March 20, 2019. For more on arguments of this kind, see Janet Folger Porter, Testimony Before the Ohio Senate Health, Human Services and Medicaid Committee, February 19, 2019, file:///C:/Users/Mary/Downloads/SB23Porter.pdf, accessed March 20, 2019. For arguments against the science behind fetal-heartbeat laws, see Adam Rogers, "'Heartbeat' Bills Get the Science of Fetal Heartbeats All Wrong," *Wired*, May 14, 2019, www.wired.com/story/heartbeat-bills-get-the-science-of-fetal-heartbeats-all-wrong; Katie Heaney, "Embryos Don't Have Hearts," *The Cut*, May 24, 2019, www.thecut.com/2019/05/embryos-dont-have-hearts.html, accessed May 31, 2019.

79 On the litigation of the South Dakota waiting-period law, see Robin Marty, "The Next Battle in the Abortion Wars," *Politico*, February 17, 2014, www.politico.com/magazine/story/2014/02/south-dakota-abortion-wars-103596; Lee Strubinger, "Bill Amends Abortion Counseling Bill Held Up in Court," *South Dakota Public Radio*, February 2, 2018, http://listen.sdpb.org/post/bill-amends-abortion-counseling-bill-held-court, accessed July 31, 2018. On the challenge to the law, see Kelley Smith, "New Abortion Law Causes Controversy in South Dakota," *KSFY*, March 8, 2018, www.ksfy.com/content/news/New-abortion-law-causes-controversy-in-South-Dakota-476336143.html, accessed August 19, 2019.

80 Debbie Elliott, "Alabama Lawmakers Move to Ban Abortions in Challenge to *Roe v. Wade*," NPR, May 1, 2019, www.npr.org/2019/05/01/719096129/alabama-lawmakers-move-to-outlaw-abortion-in-challenge-to-roe-v-wade, accessed May 3, 2019. For Kemp's statement: Sarah Mervosh, "Georgia Is Latest State to Pass Heartbeat Bill in Growing Trend," *New York Times*, March 30, 2019, www.nytimes.com/2019/03/30/us/georgia-fetal-heartbeat-abortion-law.html, accessed May 3, 2019. For more on heartbeat bill, see Doug Stanglin, "Ohio Is the Latest State to Pass a 'Heartbeat' Antiabortion Bill," *USA Today*, April 13, 2019, www.usatoday.com/story/news/nation/2019/04/13/fetal-heartbeat-abortion-bills-mount-ohio-passes-legislation/3446560002, accessed May 3, 2019. On the spread of trigger bills and absolute bans, see Amy Morona, "What Are Trigger Laws? Examining States' Preemptive Legislative Bans on Abortion," *PBS*, March 26, 2019, www.pbs.org/weta/washingtonweek/blog-post/what-are-trigger-laws-examining-states-preemptive-legislative-bans-abortion, accessed May 3, 2019; Elliott, "Alabama Lawmakers"; Julia Jacobs, "Failed Texas Bill Would Have Made Death Penalty Possible in Abortion Cases," *New York Times*, April 10, 2019, www.nytimes.com/2019/04/10/us/texas-abortion-death-penalty.html, accessed May 3, 2019. On March for Life and Students for Life's opposition to rape and incest exceptions, see Sarah McCammon, "Anti-abortion-Rights Groups Push GOP to Rethink Rape and Incest Exceptions," NPR, May 22, 2019, www.npr.org/2019/05/22/725634053/anti-abortion-rights-groups-push-gop-to-rethink-rape-and-incest-exceptions, accessed May 28, 2019. For an example of those arguing that women should be punished for abortion, see Georgi Boorman and James Silberman, "3 Negative Consequences from Not Punishing Parents for Obtaining Abortions," *The Federalist*, May 21,

2019, https://thefederalist.com/2019/05/21/3-negative-consequences-not-prosecuting-parents-obtaining-abortions, accessed May 28, 2019.

81 For the claim made by the leader of New York State Right to Life: Emily Jones, "'A Sad and Evil Day': New York Legalizes Abortion up to Baby's Birth Day on Anniversary of *Roe v. Wade*," *CBN News*, January 23, 2019, www1.cbn.com/cbnnews/us/2019/january/a-sad-and-evil-day-new-york-legalizes-abortion-up-to-babys-birth-day-on-anniversary-of-roe-v-wade, accessed May 3, 2019. On Sasse's proposal and debate about it, see Mike DeBonis and Felicia Sonmez, "Senate Blocks Bill on Medical Care for Children Born Alive after an Attempted Abortion," *USA Today*, February 25, 2019, www.washingtonpost.com/politics/senate-blocks-bill-on-medical-care-for-children-born-alive-after-attempted-abortion/2019/02/25/e5d3d4d8-3924-11e9-a06c-3ec8ed509d15_story.html, accessed May 3, 2019; Ben Sasse, "Don't Let Infanticide Be a Partisan Issue. We Can All Protect Born Babies," *USA Today*, February 12, 2019, www.usatoday.com/story/opinion/2019/02/12/ben-sasse-infanticide-abortion-democrats-ralph-northam-column/2836381002, accessed May 3, 2019. For similar state bills, see Renuka Rayasam and Dan Goldberg, "State Republicans Challenge Democrats with 'Born Alive' Bills," *Politico*, April 20, 2019, www.politico.com/story/2019/04/20/republicans-state-born-alive-bills-1365192, accessed May 3, 2019. On the spread of laws protecting abortion-rights, including those patterned on the New York proposal, see Elizabeth Nash, et al., "Radical Attempts to Ban Abortion Dominate State Policy Trends in the First Quarter of 2019," *Guttmacher Institute Policy Analysis*, April 2019, www.guttmacher.org/article/2019/04/radical-attempts-ban-abortion-dominate-state-policy-trends-first-quarter-2019, accessed May 3, 2019. For the Kansas Supreme Court's decision, see *Hodes & Nauser v. Schmidt*, 2019 WL 1868843, 440 P. 3d 461 (Kan. 2019).

82 Brochure, Planned Parenthood, "Medical and Social Health Benefits since Abortion Was Made Legal in the United States" (nd, ca. 2018), www.plannedparenthood.org/uploads/filer_public/eb/38/eb38bdf9-7ebb-4067-8758-13d28afa1d51/pp_med_soc_benefits_abortion_final_1.pdf, accessed May 3, 2019. For the statement on post-abortion regret: Bonnie Willis, "A Woman's View of 'Heartbeat Bill,'" *The Citizen*, April 23, 2019, https://thecitizen.com/2019/04/23/a-womans-view-of-heartbeat-bill, accessed May 3, 2019.

CONCLUSION

1 See William Eskridge Jr. and John Ferejohn, *A Republic of Statutes: The New American Constitution* (New Haven, CT: Yale University Press, 2010), 239–242; William Eskridge Jr., "America's Statutory Constitution," *U. C. Davis Law Review* 41 (2007): 16–17; Cass Sunstein, *One Case at a Time: Judicial Minimalism on the Supreme Court* 2d ed. (Cambridge, MA: Harvard University Press, 2001), 114; Ruth Bader Ginsburg, "Speaking in a Judicial Voice," *New York University Law Review* 67 (1992): 1208; Cass Sunstein, *A Constitution of Many Minds: Why the Founding Document Doesn't Mean What It Meant Before* (Princeton, NJ: Princeton University Press, 2009), 2; Richard A. Posner, *Overcoming Law* (Cambridge: Harvard University Press, 1995), 12, 14, 16, 33; *Planned Parenthood of Southeastern Pennsylvania v. Casey*, 505 U.S. 833, 1000–1002 (1992) (plurality opinion).

2 On the polarization caused by the Court's decision to constitutionalize the conflict, see Elizabeth Mensch and Alan Freeman, *The Politics of Virtue: Is Abortion Debatable?* 2d ed.

(Durham, NC: Duke University Press, 1995), 127; Robin West, "From Choice to Reproductive Justice: De-constitutionalizing Abortion-Rights," *Yale Law Journal* 118 (2009): 1411.

3 Gene Burns, *The Moral Veto: Framing Abortion, Contraception, and Cultural Pluralism in America* (New York: Cambridge University Press, 2005), 225–250; Linda Greenhouse and Reva B. Siegel, "Before (and after) *Roe v. Wade*: New Questions about Backlash" *Yale Law Journal* 28 (2011): 2028–2050; *Before Roe v. Wade: Voices that Shaped the Debate before the Supreme Court Decision* eds. Reva B. Siegel and Linda Greenhouse (New Haven, CT: Yale University Press, 2010); Mary Ziegler, *After Roe: The Lost History of the Abortion Debate* (Cambridge, MA: Harvard University Press, 2015).

4 See Eileen McDonagh, *Breaking the Abortion Deadlock: From Choice to Consent* (New York: Oxford University Press, 1996), 4–10.

Index

CPSIA information can be obtained
at www.ICGtesting.com
Printed in the USA
BVHW031653260722
643052BV00013B/573